Thiébault:
Soldier of Napoleon
Volume 2

GENERAL THIÉBAULT   MADAME THIÉBAULT

Vow of mutual fidelity between
Genl. Thiébault and Fanette Chevrin

Thiébault:
Soldier of Napoleon
Volume 2
A Personal Account of the Revolutionary Wars and Conflicts of the French First Empire

Paul Thiébault

Translated by Arthur John Butler

Thiébault: Soldier of Napoleon Volume 2
A Personal Account of the Revolutionary Wars and Conflicts of the French First Empire
by Paul Thiébault
Translated by Arthur John Butler

First published under the title
The Memoirs of Baron Thiébault Volume 2

Leonaur is an imprint of Oakpast Ltd
Copyright in this form © 2014 Oakpast Ltd

ISBN: 978-1-78282-417-6 (hardcover)
ISBN: 978-1-78282-418-3 (softcover)

http://www.leonaur.com

Publisher's Notes

The views expressed in this book are not necessarily those of the publisher.

Contents

Some Facts about the Battle of Novi	9
Return of Bonaparte	20
Some of my colleagues	30
Life at Paris	48
Quarrel with My Chief	64
Return to France	83
My Marriage	96
Ordered on Active Service	111
Napoleon's Friendliness	168
The Expedition to Portugal	177
My First Sea Voyage	201
An Attack Impending	226
As Good as Dismissed	236
My Work Undone	253
I am Made Governor of Salamanca	263
On the March Again	292
Fall of Rodrigo	325
I Join the Grand Army	338
Back to France for the Last Time	357

—On ne se lassera jamais de lire les récits relatifs à la Révolution et a l'Empire.

CHAPTER 1

Some Facts about the Battle of Novi

While we were effecting our retreat from Naples, important events had been taking place. A Russian army under Suwarrow had invaded North Italy, had captured the citadel of Milan, and entered Turin and Alessandria. On June 17th and the following days Macdonald was beaten on the Trebbia; we were compelled to evacuate Lombardy and almost the whole of Piedmont. Yet Suwarrow's idea of war was that of a wild beast; his sudden rushes, which he doubtless regarded as the swoops of the eagle, often landed him in traps wherein he stuck. It needed all Schérer's incapacity and Macdonald's carelessness to lay them open to the blows of a Suwarrow. Moreau, with a tenth of his numbers, held him in check by well-devised combinations, and by his bold conduct of the clever, complicated strategy which threw some glory over even our reverses. When the Russian bear found himself in presence of an antagonist like Moreau, it was the bear that was beaten.

In Genoa, where I was anxiously watching the struggle of our forces against that formidable Russian army, I collected everyone's narratives and notes; and kept a record of all the feats of arms with all the keener interest that I was unable to share in them. Macdonald lost the Battle of the Trebbia in consequence of fourteen demonstrated mistakes; though when he got back to Paris, where he put up with his friend Beurnonville, he tried to justify himself by spreading a report that Moreau had thrown him over, an audacious assertion which only took in his flatterers.

In spite of the noble blood of which, rightly or wrongly, the Marshal Duke of Tarentum boasted (and which his father certainly did not make more noble by marrying a cook), and of the splendid position which he holds so dear, no one will think of putting up a statue to him as a pendant to that of General Championnet. Having followed closely the parts played by the general in that campaign, and having subsequently studied them with documents and evidence before me, I have never been able to avoid testifying consistently in favour of Moreau, whom since 1813 I have hated, just as I testified in favour of Championnet, whom I loved, and against Macdonald, whom, in spite of his conduct towards his rivals and his carelessness as a commander-in-chief, I have always been disposed to like as a man and as a valiant soldier. I might have hated or loved all alike, and I would have said neither more nor less.

All this while my convalescence did not make so much progress as I had hoped; and a doctor of high reputation, after a careful examination of me, decided that I must return to France and follow a course of treatment which, as he said, was impossible, except with the regular habits of domestic life. Accordingly on June 10 I started in a *felucca* for Nice. Just after passing Savona we fell in with another *felucca*, which went along in company with us. It had General Sarrazin on board, and also a young captain who had been on Bonaparte's staff in Egypt. I have forgotten his name, but he was a clever and enthusiastic young fellow. He was leaving the service to marry, and I took him in my carriage from Nice to Paris.

When we were off the headland of Noli, we saw a very suspicious-looking craft. At that time it was hardly possible to sail in these waters without the risk of meeting a privateer, and my previous experience on my way out prepared me for an adventure of this kind. Our suspicions were quickly confirmed when we saw the strange craft working in between us and the land. We set all sail for the nearest port, and succeeded in getting in just as we were on the point of being caught. But the privateer was not going to relinquish its prey so easily, and hove to outside the port. Being in a hurry, we had to leave the *felucca* and continue our journey by the *Corniche*, while the enemy fired some shots after us, which luckily all missed.

At Nice we were warned of a new danger. Provence was infested by bands, which, just as elsewhere in France, under the pretext of political and religious aims, and under the names of 'Companions of the Faith,' 'Companions of Jesus,' and the like, thought it a work of honour to rob the coaches, attack post-chaises, and commit murder alike on the high road and in private houses. The road from Nice to Aix and beyond, being the way by which many people known or supposed to have money were returning to France, was dangerous to the last degree. Consequently people only left Nice as a rule between ten o'clock and mid-day, and in caravans. This dawdling method did not suit us at all.

Hearing that the brigands were having all persons in any way conspicuous watched at Nice, I had my carriage loaded, and ordered my horses for the hour when everyone was starting; then, just when the spies were likely to be about, I suddenly invented an excuse of orders that might force me to return to Genoa, and feigning to be in a very bad temper, I countermanded the horses, but without taking anything out of the carriage. In the evening I went to the play, as if I had nothing to do; and on leaving the theatre, going to the posting-station, when everyone was asleep, I took out myself the three horses I required. On reaching my inn, I had them put to, and at half-past eleven, to everyone's surprise, the gates of Nice were opened for me. I paid the postilions well, and travelled as fast as possible along the road, which, as no one expected me, was quite clear.

Everything went as well as possible till Saint-Maximin; but at the entrance to that village one of my springs broke, causing a delay of three hours. While waiting, I was overtaken and passed by two coaches full of officers, which I should have been glad to follow. At last the horses were put to again, and when I was in, the postilion, before cracking his whip for the start, turned round and said, "Aix road?"

"No; Toulon road."

In truth, if there was a single brigand left in the district, he would be on the look-out for me along the direct road, now that they had notice of my coming; and to throw them off the scent, I had to make up my mind to go a long way round.

Sleeping that night at Toulon, I went on the next day to Marseilles. There I met, with hardly a rag on, the brothers Lallemand, now officers of high rank. They had been in one of the two coaches which had gone by me at Saint-Maximin. A league further on they and all their companions had been completely stripped of their goods. They knew no one in the place, and I had to hand them the money they required to get some clothes and continue their journey, while congratulating myself on the circumstances which had made me change my route and escape Legitimist zeal.

The road from Marseilles to Aix being not much safer, I did what I had done at Nice—went to the play, fetched my horses as I went home, started at midnight, and went to Aix full speed. From thence my journey was merely travelling. At the Hermitage, where I halted for breakfast, I had my carriage loaded with some of the excellent wine they had served me. I slept at Lyons, and nowhere else till Paris.

When I had returned to Paris at the end of 1797, the brilliant campaigns of the Army of Italy seemed written on all men's faces, no less than spoken of by all men's mouths. No soldier from Italy could pass without all eyes being turned to him. The two years that had elapsed since then had left no trace of the elation of those days. I had had the feeling of this when I crossed our frontier. Every town had seemed more stern; while as for Paris, ovation seemed to have given place to inquisition. People vied in asking you about the loss of Naples, of the Roman States, of Tuscany, the Marches, all the Cisalpine Republic, and the effacement of so much renown by the disgrace of our late defeats. If we kept the Rhine from Holland to Basle, the boundary which nature has bestowed on France, which we lost only by treachery, and which cowardice alone would fail to take the opportunity of recovering, on the other hand there remained to us out of the whole of Italy only a wretched strip of land ending at Genoa. Masséna alone was holding his ground in Switzerland and defying all the efforts of the Coalition; and thus in the midst of the anxiety justified by a state of things that became daily more threatening, our last hopes were fixed on him.

If we did not in that terrible year 1799 lose Italy for good and all, it was thanks to the blunders of Suwarrow, who though victor at the Trebbia did not at once crush the remains of the Army of Naples, but allowed it to effect a junction with that of Moreau; did not seize Genoa, but permitted us to organise our defensive on the *Corniche*, as threatening a position as an army could occupy; and let us have this respite, as the coalesced forces had done, in order that he might amuse himself with fortresses which his preponderant force entitled him to neglect. But just at the critical moment when Moreau, by the most scientific strategy, was taking advantage of this barbaric application of the laws of war to regain his own footing, the Directory, under the impression that it was as easy to bespeak a victory as to arrange for a festivity in the Champ de Mars, or a performance at the opera, had sent its commanders-in-chief the order to win.

It was done so formally that Joubert, whose age, no less than the fact that he was making his first start in chief command, condemned him to passive obedience, went on August 15, with a force nearly one-third recruits and almost no cavalry, and offered battle at Novi to an army under Suwarrow, consisting, when Kray's force had joined it, of

75,000 veteran troops inspirited by their victories. Joubert, as is well known, was killed at the very beginning of the battle, when only his skirmishers were engaged. It is also well known how obstinately our army was attacked, how furiously it defended itself, how heavily the Russians lost, and what a fearful impression their losses produced on the Austrians and on Suwarrow himself, who even in his reminiscences of Ismailoff could find no comparison appropriate to so destructive a struggle. But what are less known, or known wrong, are the circumstances relating to the death of Joubert. These are worth preserving, and I am certain of the facts, though they have been related by historians and represented in illustrations with a wealth of melodramatic phrases and detail quite arbitrarily invented.

Joubert was not killed when advancing with one of his attacking columns, nor yet when dashing forward at the head of his grenadiers, nor did he point out the enemy to them, and cry, "Keep on marching, soldiers." He was doing his duty no less well, but in a less theatrical fashion. If I pause to set some facts right, which, strictly speaking, are not within the scope of these *Memoirs*, it is not only because they have an historical value, but because they offer another opportunity of pointing out to honest historians the errors into which contemporary notices and engravings—nay, even official documents and all written statements, put about as the interest or passion of the moment dictated—may lead people. Historical truth will never be established upon papers.

General Joubert, who had just, most unwillingly, resumed command of that unlucky Army of Italy, had practically two chiefs of staff: one, General Suchet, for office work, and another, General Préval, for fighting purposes. The first fulfilled all the written duties of the post; but the other never left the commander-in-chief, slept in his room, and merely had a portfolio carried by an orderly.

Now it befell that on the day of that disastrous Battle of Novi, some shots having been heard, Préval, whom the commander-in-chief employed in reconnoitring no less than in drawing up orders, or transmitting them and seeing that they were earned out, and who was always the first to mount and the last to dismount, wished to go and see what they were. Riding all along the line of our advanced posts, he discovered a mound commanding the enemy's position. From the number and depth of the columns which his field-glass enabled him to see, he judged that their movements were the prelude to a great battle; and having a native instinct as well as a love for war, he thought it important that the commander-in-chief should judge for himself of the formation of the masses which the enemy was getting ready to set in movement. Accordingly he galloped at the full speed of his horse to tell Joubert.

The battle had already begun, and our skirmishers, being driven in, were climbing the mound while the enemy concentrated his fire upon it. Just then Joubert, recognising the importance of the position, came up, guided by Préval. He had hardly levelled his field-glass when a bullet struck him full in the heart, and he expired. It was a strange destiny which made him find his death in a command which he had so often refused, and only accepted, it might be said, by main force, and which made his most devoted subordinate the involuntary cause of his death.

Ordering the general's body to be covered and taken away, and his death to be kept as secret as possible, Préval, with a few officers, at once went in among the skirmishers, in order to send them forward again and prevent them from finding out the loss that had befallen the army. After this he hastened to send news to General Pérignon, commanding the left, who was some distance away, then to Moreau, commanding the centre, and Saint-Cyr, commanding the right. No doubt the commander-in-chief devolved by the unhesitating agreement of all on Moreau; but he could not leave the centre, where indeed he did wonders.

Thus the Battle of Novi was practically fought without the French army having any commander-in-chief, and without the possibility of a single thought and will being there to maintain the necessary harmony and combination in the day's operations; without any means of utilising forces which at one point had become useless, at any other; and without anything to prevent our army from appearing as three corps acting each on its own account, or to enable us to meet a general battle with anything but isolated engagements. Thus our two wings were beaten, though one may believe they would have held out if the forces which had become useless at the centre, where our victory was complete, could have been got to them in time.

The Battle of Novi was lost. I need not say anything about the blunders which decided the issue of it; especially the incredible stupidity of a commander on the left, who got all his guns, to the number of some twenty, into the bottom of a ravine, instead of taking them along the high ground, with the result that in order to stop the whole lot without a hope of saving them, and get them disastrously taken, it was only necessary for a single Austrian sharpshooter to kill the horses of the leading gun. But what language has no words to characterize as it deserves is the fact that from the moment when the left was routed, Generals Grouchy, Pérignon, and Colli should have imagined that the whole army was lost. Pérignon had feebly commanded the left, with the still feebler assistance of Grouchy; and the three generals, reckoning that to avoid ill-treatment it is always best to be the earliest prisoners, and that you run fewer risks by being taken in a village than in the open field, in the day than in the night, three together than one alone, in the course of the battle than in the last desperate struggle, agreed to remain in the village of Pasturana.

It was a point which, as they had omitted to put it in a state of defence, the left had had to abandon; so letting their troops retire, and hiding themselves in the recess formed by the two projecting wings of an inn, they waited there to surrender to the first Austrian general or officer who might turn up. Now the captain of a light company, having noticed them there at a time when retreat was still open to them, and thinking he ought to sacrifice himself to give them a chance, blocked the main street of the village with his men. This, heroic resistance formed no part of the three generals' plan, and they sent an order to the captain to put a handkerchief on the point of his sword. It was a needless disgrace. At that moment came up a swarm of Austrian hussars, who exterminated the company and took the officer prisoner. Proceeding on their way, the foremost of them, on arriving at the recess of the inn and suddenly catching sight of the generals with one or two officers, did them the honour to take them for an ambuscade, and treated them to a few sabre-cuts. General Pérignon got his head laid open, and Grouchy the same, and a scar into the bargain—to this day the best ornament he has to his marshal's baton. From Novi he wrote to his sister:

> I have three dangerous wounds: they will not have to trephine me; Pérignon will be saved.

Amid the bustle all this would have remained unknown, for the accomplices would never have told of each other; but besides the captain who told the story when he got his exchange and returned to France, it had been witnessed by a lieutenant of the 26th, named Deney, afterwards secretary to General Delmas. In his indignation he reported the matter to Moreau, who advised him to hold his tongue. However, General Delmas heard of it through him; and when his story was confirmed on the return of the captain, Delmas thought himself no longer bound to silence, and let the truth come out. Other persons knew of the incident in other ways, among whom I may mention Marshal Moncey, Duke of Conegliano. But the facts speak for themselves. Three divisional generals were captured together: therefore none of them can have been at his post, which no man has a right to leave during a battle. They were far away from their troops: therefore they must have abandoned them. Lastly, they were captured without a single circumstance, I will not say to justify, but to explain the capture of one of them. Anyhow, Heaven took their chastisement upon itself; and not to recur to the sabre-cuts, which if better applied might have saved France from greater disasters,[1] they misjudged the consequences of the battle, and were the only French generals who adorned Suwarrow's triumphal car.

Meanwhile Moreau, at the head of his troops, thrice beat back the Russian columns from his centre. Suwarrow led them in person to the last attack, and retired, roaring like an angry lion, only when the greater part of his best regiments had been destroyed. Nothing could be more splendid than Moreau's conduct; nothing more characteristic than his coolness. Falling with the second horse that had been shot under him, he picked himself up, puffing at his cigar no slower and no faster. But it was decreed that in this battle the centre alone should sustain the honour of the French arms. It is with pain that I have to mention a fact which in infamy far outdoes the conduct of the three generals; for they, by surrendering, only gave up three men to the enemy, and all one can regret is that France had not lost them sooner.

The right, under Saint-Cyr, consisted of the old Army of Naples reduced to two divisions. General Watrin, commanding one of these, was occupying the base of the hill at the top of which was Saint-Cyr with the reserve. Seeing some Austrian corps forming for an attack in his front, Watrin thought he had better not wait for them, but march briskly upon them and attack them while they were forming. Not wishing, however, to encroach on the rights of his chief, he went himself to Saint-Cyr, spoke of his plan, and asked for orders. The only answer he got was, "Do as you like." Now with an unemotional, laconic, icy man like Saint-Cyr, especially at a moment when a chief ought to do everything to kindle the ardour of his subordinates, words like

---

1. [The part which Grouchy played, or rather did not play, at Waterloo is well known.] *The Battle of Wavre and Grouchy's Retreat* by W. Hyde Kelly is also published by Leonaur.

these could only signify approbation, that is, an order, for to approve an attack is to order it. Préval, who was present, and had been for the last half-hour examining with General Saint-Cyr the enormous force of cavalry which the enemy was massing in front of the position, could not refrain from exclaiming, "But, general, he will be smashed!"

"Yes," replied Saint-Cyr, with a calmness which horrifies one only to think of, "but it will do no harm to let these generals of the Naples army have a lesson or two." And in fact Watrin was hardly well on the plain when he was attacked, broken, overwhelmed, and furiously pursued by General de Lusignan, who, at the head of a large body of cavalry, penetrated as far as Saint-Cyr's reserve, being by them repulsed and himself seriously wounded.

Let us just consider this incident, which, unhappily, is explained by only too many more in the life of that great soldier.[2] Saint-Cyr was so placed as to be able to judge of both the possibility and the opportuneness of the movement; Watrin was not. By coming to ask for orders, the latter covered his own responsibility by that of his chief, and it was a sacred duty for Saint-Cyr, who had just calculated the fatal issue of the movement, to forbid him to stir. At a moment when Trance was sustaining so unequal a conflict, it was treason to her knowingly to allow a division to be destroyed—and for what purpose? In order that when the battle was going badly he, Saint-Cyr, might have, as happened indeed for a moment, the credit of restoring it.

While fully recognising Saint-Cyr's extraordinary ability, one has to admit! that he always played only for his own hand. Having no regard for any interests save his own, he was always a dangerous comrade; and any sign of devotion to his country or other generous sentiment that might appear in him could be only the result of cold calculation. Nor could the sequel of that battle justify his "Do as you please;" for though he had the immediate advantage of driving off Watrin's pursuers, he soon had to abandon a position which but for the disaster to the sacrificed division he might perhaps have retained,—a supposition rendered probable by the fact that with the troops remaining to him he executed a superb retreat in the face of superior force.

This ardour to sacrifice a rival in order to bring out one's own merits is, alas! very common. Without much racking of my memory, I can call up various generals keeping their troops motionless for

---

2. Thiébault's judgement of Saint-Cyr is remarkably confirmed by a no less significant scene recorded by General Marbot: *Mémoires*, vol. iii., ED. [Compare the estimate of him in Marshal Castellane's *Journal*, under March 20, 1830.]

the pleasure of seeing an envied competitor get beaten. There is Ney, crowded up with artillery, and refusing to let Soult have a few pieces after the loss of all his batteries at Oporto. There are Dorsenne and Marmont, never missing a chance of damaging each other. There is Soult, failing to go to Santarem, in order to prevent Masséna from conquering Portugal, out of which he himself had been so disgracefully driven. Indeed, it was owing to an incident of this kind that we were able to keep Genoa when it was at the mercy of the enemy. Suwarrow and Melas discussed whether the place should be occupied in the name of the Emperor of Russia or in that of the Emperor of Austria. It had to be referred to those sovereigns, who were no more willing than their generals to give way on the point. While diplomacy was discussing, the chance was lost; and so the eternal honour of the blockade of Genoa, which made it possible for the First Consul to win at Marengo, was added to Masséna's glory.

An event like the Battle of Novi was bound to produce a great sensation in France and, above all, in Paris; and we all deplored the subservience of Joubert to the Directory in the teeth of his own convictions and the opinions of other illustrious chiefs. The Directory, however, instead of regretting, renewed the same business in regard to Masséna, accusing him of remaining inactive in Switzerland.[3] They even went so far as to have him attacked in newspaper articles, with the object of preparing public opinion for his disgrace. He bided his time, however, and when his plans were matured, a fortnight sufficed him to beat and annihilate three armies and three army corps composed of different troops; to secure the occupation of Switzerland, after one of the best of Austrian commanders-in-chief had lost his life on the field, and the northern bear had been sent home to roar in his den, and die there of rage at having been beaten.

These victories were absolutely essential for the preservation of France from immediate invasion; yet this campaign, with its glorious deliverance, could not muzzle Masséna's slanderers; and while hostile Europe was everywhere proclaiming his greatness,[4] those at Paris were shameless enough to get up a newspaper debate with the view of proving that if he had acted sooner he would have gained greater advantages. Learning that those impertinences emanated from a suf-

---

3. [See Marbot, *Mémoires*, vol. iii. How very near Masséna came to being superseded is related in the same work, vol. i.]
4. [A false rumour of his death at Genoa made people cheerful in England for a whole week soon after this.]

ficiently high quarter to deserve a more serious reception than mere contempt, I wrote to refute them. Not being able to procure the insertion of what I had written in the paper which had been the aggressor, I rewrote it, had it printed under the title *The Victories of Masséna*, and distributed it widely. I concluded by prophesying the speedy triumph of our arms, rendered possible by the victories in Switzerland.

Now that the fear of invasion was dispelled, in my desire to see the prophecies of my pamphlet fulfilled, I was possessed as by a monomania by the idea of the reconquest of Italy. I dreamt all night and thought all day of the means of effacing the disgrace of 1799 from our annals. Several plans occurred to my mind; but one appeared to me most convincing and most decisive. To give more precision to my thought, I wrote it down and had a fair copy made by a sister who was then acting as my copyist. Then I showed it to my father, who thought it of more importance than I had myself done, and advised me to take it to the Minister for War and to the President of the Directory. This I decided to do.

CHAPTER 2

Return of Bonaparte

On October 14 something took me to the Palais Royal. I had hardly entered when I saw a gradually increasing group form at the further end. Presently men and women began running at their full speed. I walked towards the group, which now broke up into a number of smaller knots, fresh persons continually joining them and going off again with signs of great excitement as soon as they had caught a word or two. I tried to question some of these as they hurried past me. No one would stop, but one man as he ran, panted out the words: "General Bonaparte has just landed at Fréjus." [1] After a moment's stupefaction I also went out.

The general commotion in Paris left no doubt as to the truth of the news. The regimental bands belonging to the garrison of the city were already promenading the streets as a sign of the public cheerfulness, swarms of people and soldiers following them. At night illuminations were hastily got up in every quarter, and in all the theatres the return was announced by shouts of "Long live the Republic!" "Long live Bonaparte!" It was not the return of a general; it was the return of a head in the garb of a general; of a head of whom we seemed to stand in need alike for the army, for our policy, for the government, the last especially. Only the ghost of a government remained in France. Breached by all parties, the Directory was at the mercy of the first assault. It was not without talents, character, and patriotism; but what could five men of no fortune, of no family, with no future and no common principles dress them up and lodge them how you might do against military leaders renowned in so many fields? Were

1. [The actual landing took place on the 9th, according to Bourrienne.] *Memoirs of Napoleon Bonaparte* in 3 volumes by Louis Antoine Fauvelet de Bourrienne is also published by Leonaur.

the conquerors of kings to deem themselves fitly represented by a Moulin, a creature so insignificant that his uniform had been no bar to his admission? Moulin giving orders to Kléber, Saint-Cyr, Moreau, Masséna, Bonaparte, was merely comic.

As for Bonaparte himself, all our disasters had taken place since he had been in Egypt; and thus he had been the object of regrets and wishes which no other general of the Republic could efface. If, thanks to Masséna, victory seemed ready to return to our lines, it was in Bonaparte alone that any security was seen for its permanence. By the morning of the 16th, the smallest house in the Rue Chantereine, which was at once by acclamation named Rue de la Victoire, held the man whose destiny, henceforth irrevocable, was about to offer the most terrible example of human vicissitudes.

Yet in the midst of the popular joy some notes of blame were heard. Bonaparte was accused of having left his army, in the first place, because the expedition to Egypt could not now have a fortunate issue; and, secondly, because he saw that the army must at last succumb. On the first count he was charged with cowardice; on the second with desertion in presence of the enemy. And in truth, from a purely military point of view, there was no excuse for Bonaparte, and Sieyès was quite right when, referring to an intentional piece of disrespect on his part, he spoke of "the little fellow's insolence towards a member of an authority who ought to have had him shot." He had indeed set an example of conduct which he himself would in later days have punished with death, and it only added to his guilt that he had ventured to bring with him officers who had no business to leave Egypt without the orders of their government, and who, as they had returned in this way, could henceforth be considered only as his creatures or his accomplices.

The violation of the quarantine laws was an equally grave crime, and the two charges together were sufficient motive for Bernadotte's proposal to bring General Bonaparte before a court-martial. But they were afraid of driving him into immediate rebellion, and it was unquestionably this which made Gohier, the President of the Directory, give him the fraternal embrace. You could not take strong measures against a man whose journey from Fréjus to Paris had been one triumph, and whom the very guard of the Directors greeted with cries of "Long live Bonaparte!" Yet it was evident that with him patriotism was only the cloak for ambition; nor could it be disguised that his very return had been equivalent to hoisting the standard; of revolt.

Dexterity, good luck, and the audacity essential to success saved him; but speculate as he might on the admiration of some, the weakness of others, the need of order and repose, the misfortunes of the time and all that was rotten in the state of affairs, he cannot have avoided the conviction that for him there was no choice save between complete success and an unpardonable crime, between a throne and the gallows. So the charge of cowardice is somewhat absurd, since in order to return to France he needed the energy and courage of a party-leader.

I had studied him and followed his career both in the Home Army and during his immortal campaigns with too much attention to be under any mistake as to the consequences of his course, or on the drift of the phrase he had used before his departure for Egypt: "The pear is not yet ripe." So I had no doubt that he had been brought back not by patriotism but by ambition; and yet I yielded to the general enthusiasm, enjoying in anticipation the victories guaranteed by the great soldier's return. I gave way all the more freely to my joy because I had not calculated that for the execution of his schemes for destroying freedom he would choose first the moment when France needed him most, when all military operations were postponed by the time of year, and when all were in the intoxication of his return. In spite of all the symptoms I did not suspect that we were close upon the crisis announced by his sudden presence.

On the 18th I presented myself at General Bonaparte's door. He was out, and I left my name. On the 21st I went again, and found a good many there. He made a step towards me as I approached, greeted me very kindly, and received good-naturedly the congratulations which I addressed to France on his return; then, as I made way for some one else, he said, "I hope to see you again." On the 26th (4th *Brumaire*), I took advantage of this kind of invitation. It was half-past ten when I entered the drawing-room. Bonaparte was standing up, deep in conversation with a man whom I did not know, who was walking up and down with him at the further end of the room. I went to the fireplace; and when Mme Bonaparte came in, I chatted with her. In about half an hour he took leave of his companion, and came towards us, saying, in a friendly way, "Good morning, Thiébault;" then rang for breakfast and, turning to me, added, "You will breakfast with us?" Hardly were we seated, the three of us only, when he began to talk to me about the two last campaigns. Dwelling on that of Naples, he said, "I know you behaved well there." Soon afterwards, without mentioning Championnet's name, but as his way was, personifying the general part played by the army in his turn of phrase, he said, "You were the only one who did anything good while I was away."

Something he said made me think of speaking to him of my plan for a new campaign in Italy; but the opportunity vanished owing to the sudden way in which he all at once contrasted with what we were saying about the devotion of the troops and the zeal of the commanders that which had gone on and was going on at home. He attacked the government with a violence which confounded me. Here are a few phrases which my memory recalls:

> A nation is always what you have the wit to make it. . . . The triumph of faction, parties, divisions, is the fault of those in authority only. . . . No people is bad under a good government, just as no troops are bad under good generals. But what can you expect of fellows who know neither their country nor its needs, who understand neither the age nor the men of it, and who meet only with resistance where they should find support?

Then he went off in a volley of attacks on the Directory:

> I left peace, and I come back to war. The influence of victory has been replaced by shameful defeats. Italy had been won; now it is invaded, and France is threatened. I left millions, and everywhere there is poverty. These men are bringing France down to the level of their own blundering. They are degrading her, and she is beginning to repudiate them.

Napoleon used to say:

> If you want to dine well, dine with Cambacérès; if you want to dine badly, dine with Le Brun; if you want to dine quick, dine with me.

And indeed his dinners often did not last more than half an hour, while the breakfast of which I speak lasted much less. In spite of this, and flattered as I may have felt by my presence at this little repast, when fortune smiled on me to no profit, it seemed to me long before it was over. From the time that he began this kind of anathema against the Directory I had preserved strict silence, and tried to make my countenance as mute as my mouth; but every moment the situation became more awkward, and it was with a real feeling of relief that I saw the time come when I might give my arm to Mme Bonaparte to return to the drawing-room. There we found General Sérurier, then in Paris as a prisoner on parole, which was a fresh piece of luck to me. Bonaparte, who had not seen him since his return, at once began talking about General Schérer's campaign, handling him worse than the enemy had done. He said only a word about the affair at the bridge of Polo, which General Sérurier could excuse, and hastened to explain.

He passed lightly over the Battle of the Adda, which had been no less unfortunate than creditable to Sérurier; and then coming back to the Directory showing that he had a definite line in his mind he went off into fresh reproaches and expressions of disgust at the idea of the selection of generals depending on intrigues, ignorance, and the authority of a few lawyers. This word "lawyer," which he used in such a way as to express the last degree of contempt, seemed to please him; he brought it in several times, and when Sérurier complained of the Directory, Bonaparte said:

> Well, and what can generals expect of this government of lawyers? For lieutenants to care about their work they want a chief capable of appreciating them, diverting them, backing them up.

From the tone in which the word "lieutenants" was spoken, I thought I was listening to Caesar; the ground seemed uneasy beneath me, and I took my leave. I had parted from General Bonaparte by the fireplace, leaving him intentionally in the middle of a sentence. Hardly had I shut the door of the room when he reopened it, and disposing of me as though I belonged to him, flung his order at me in the kindliest manner: "Go and give your address to Berthier." I answered by a bow.

The position of those who had escaped from Alessandria, and above all that of him whom Bernadotte called "the deserter," had all along seemed to me a false one; and the more clearly I saw their game, the more I suspected them. I had made an exception for a great man, my former commander-in-chief in the Home Army and in that of Italy; but there was nothing of the kind to my eyes in Berthier's favour, and I did not see, or did not care to see, what I could have to do with that general. I remembered the odious dishonesty of his conduct towards Masséna at Rome, and saw no more reason to call on him than on any general unemployed. However, I went as usual to consult my father, and told him all that had happened at breakfast. We had no longer any doubt as to the early execution of a seditious plan. I certainly did not care much for the Directors: I knew none of them personally, and their actions were no recommendation. I could have no esteem for the ambitious Sieyès or his satellite Ducos, nor for the honest but incapable Gohier and his satellite Moulin; least of all for Barras "the rotten," as they called him in those days.

Still the Directors were part of the Constitution to which I had taken an oath; and I held to my oaths, and always had a horror for the part of conspirator. We agreed, therefore, that I had better say nothing about what I had heard and noticed, but not call on Bonaparte again; and that as I had given my address to the Minister for War and the military governor, I had no occasion to give it to anyone else, least of all to General Berthier.

To save appearances, I went out little during the following days. I was unwell also, and from November 6 to 9 (15th to 18th *Brumaire*) I did not leave my room. I learnt from the newspapers how Bonaparte had given Moreau a splendid Damascus sword set with diamonds, and how the Houses had given a banquet to Generals Moreau and Bonaparte—at which, by the way, the latter ate nothing but eggs—in the Church of Saint-Sulpice, now the Temple of Victory. My friends had other things to do than to come and bring me the news. Thus on the morning of the 19th *Brumaire*, not having yet received my paper, I knew just nothing of what had happened on the previous day. Just then the Chevalier de Satur was announced. The *chevalier* was an old member of the Light Horse or Lunéville Gendarmes.

He was a tall man of over sixty, once very handsome, and remarkable in many ways; a good Latin scholar, a good mathematician, a man of wit, character and capacity, and moreover a great chess-player, which often brought us together. He was a great friend of ours, and, being full of the events of the previous day and night, he had hastened to tell me as follows. Four Directors had resigned. The Council of the Five Hundred had been transferred to Saint-Cloud, and General Bonaparte, appointed commandant of the Paris division, was in charge of the business of transferring it. He informed me, moreover, that that very morning Bonaparte had just started for Saint-Cloud, preceded by numerous bodies of troops, and accompanied by a crowd of generals and staff-officers on horseback.

If this news contained nothing to surprise me, it was none the less of a kind to give me plenty to think about, and also to indicate duties to be performed. I put on my uniform and ordered my carriage. M. de

Satur accompanied me to the door, and said—I have never forgotten the words, as they were not without effect on my fortunes—

"You are about to witness memorable events. As for General Bonaparte, by tonight he will be lower than Cromwell, or greater than Epaminondas."

In spite of what he had told me as to the Directors, I went to the Luxembourg, to see for myself what had happened, and in any case to fulfil a duty. Only one side of the great folding-doors was open; and just as I had alighted and was about to pass through, a sentry belonging to the 80th of the Line stopped me, entrance to the Luxembourg being forbidden. I asked for the officer of the guard; he came, and I questioned him. "By whose orders am I prevented from entering?"

"By General Moreau's."

"General Moreau's?"

"Yes, he commands here."

"Can I speak to him?"

"No, general."

I went off to the War Office and asked for the minister, Dubois-Crancé.

"He is out."

"Is it known where he is?"

"No, general."

So I set off for Saint-Cloud, as the only place where I could decide upon my future conduct. As I alighted at the gate of the park I saw an officer coming from the palace, and asked him what was going on. "Nothing as yet," he answered. "The rooms where the Council is to sit are not yet ready, and they are waiting." I thought it a good opportunity to breakfast.

Seeing nobody up the grand staircase, I left the gallery on the left and entered a suite of rooms. In the third of them I found the generals and staff-officers who had formed Bonaparte's retinue. I went up to some of them whom I knew best, but do what I would nothing passed beyond a few words spoken almost in a whisper. People looked at each other, but did not speak; no one seemed to dare to ask, everyone was afraid to answer. This was no fit arena for the brave men who filled it. Some minutes passed in a situation more calculated to increase my ill-temper than to disperse it.

At length a door opened on the right of the room, opposite the second window, and General Bonaparte appeared. He said, "Someone go and fetch Major X———." An *aide-de-camp* went off at once and soon returned with the major. Word was taken to Bonaparte, who reappeared, and, addressing the field-officer in the harshest manner, asked him by whose orders he had shifted such and such a post. The officer named the person who had given him the order, observing that it was not the first order he had had from him. The answer was perfectly proper, and, coming from a field-officer, deserved consideration. This, however, did not prevent Bonaparte from continuing in a tone of the sharpest anger: "There are no orders here but mine; arrest this man and put him in prison." Four or five of the hangers-on who were present, carrying zeal to the point of violence, threw themselves on the major and dragged him away.

I was disgusted, as no doubt were others, but they knew how to hold their tongues. I had not much self-control in those days, and was less discreet. "So it was to witness that sort of thing that we came here," I exclaimed. Then seeing that no one opened his mouth, while a cloud came over some faces, and some of those near me looked like edging away, I lost my head entirely, and, in spite of the example of silence set by many of my seniors, I added, "This sort of thing does not suit me, and I am going back to Paris."

César Berthier had just entered the room, and heard me. He threw himself in my way, saying, "General Thiébault, what are you about?"

"Very nice of you to ask," I said; "did not I speak loud enough?" So I went out in spite of him, and an hour or so later I was back at my father's. I had laid up for the time to come an endless series of tribulations and injustices, in place of the favours, the promotion of all kinds, and the brilliant future which fortune had for a moment placed within my reach.

Next morning we heard pretty early of all that had taken place at Saint-Cloud; of the threatening way in which the sitting of the Five Hundred had opened, and the manner in which General Bonaparte had made his way in and how he had been received by that House; of his state of fright, evidenced by the incoherence of his words;[2] of the help given by the officers, without which he must have perished; of how General Gardanne, about whose action Lucien was inexplicably silent, had to carry him off in his arms, to prevent his being murdered by the deputies, most of whom had daggers; and lastly of the charge with the bayonet which the grenadiers under Murat executed in the

---

2. On leaving the hall of the Five Hundred, Bonaparte met Sieyès, and said, "General, they have outlawed me." "So much the better," replied Sieyès, laughing at the rank conferred on him; "they are outside the law now themselves."

Chamber to the sound of the drums, forcing the deputies to decamp through doors and windows.

We also learnt how Lucien, by his presence of mind and steadiness, made Sieyès' plan capable of being carried out, not only by stimulating the troops, but by collecting some fifty deputies and forming them into a council, which, without being too precise about figures, people called "the Council of the Thirty." [3] During the night he had boldly carried them on till they substituted consular for directorial government. When we knew that General Bonaparte was appointed one of the three Consuls, my father's first words were, "Well, what are you going to do with your plan of campaign?"

"And with myself?" I replied, smiling. He looked grave, but I went on: "I serve my country, whoever may be at the head of it, without dirtying my hands with conspiracies. Thus, as General Bonaparte is invested with authority, I shall forward my work to him in a few days; and to know how I stand with him, I shall attend his first audience."

My father would have liked me to ask for a private audience. "But if it was not granted? Besides, what should I look like, not daring to see the new master in the presence of witnesses? I should seem to be apologising for my behaviour, trying to redeem it by a sort of appeal for mercy." My only resource now being an attitude, it must be a dignified one. The greatest favour that the First Consul could have shown me would have been to reproach me; and to this I should have to reply by excuses,—that is, to own myself in fault. No; it was playing too high to run the risk of a pardon in the case of Bonaparte, and it was difficult enough for me to show him the face of a man who had been able to resist his blandishments. Consequently, I contented myself with sending him my plan on Nov. 16; and on the following *Décadi*, the day fixed for the first Consular audience, I presented myself at the Luxembourg with the steadiness and confidence of a man who has not faltered in his duty.

The reception-room was on the ground-floor, and not very large. Though it had not struck eight when I arrived, there were plenty of people; and when on the stroke the First Consul appeared, a circle was suddenly formed. I placed myself in the front rank, so that he could not pass appearing not to see me. As we went round the circle to his left hand, the First Consul, who always looked four or five ahead, caught sight of me. I had my eyes fixed on him, watching for the impression that the sight of me might make, so that no movement of

---

3. [Des Trente.]

his countenance escaped me. I could have no doubt; his face, which had been gracious enough till I came into view, clouded over. It was a long way from this face to that of General Bonaparte saying, "Go and give Berthier your address." However, though he remained grave, his expression seemed to soften, and he stared at me rather with the air of one surprised to see me there.

Although that extraordinary man exercised a magnetic influence over me such as no other power could ever attain to, I was not upset by this reception. He stopped in front of me, and taking a step backwards said in a dry tone, "You seem to know the roads into Italy very well." It might have been an opening for a compliment; but I confined myself to replying, "General Consul, I thought it my duty to lay before you the work that I had the honour to send you; and it was this that emboldened me to do so." He made no answer, looked hard at me again, finished taking a pinch of snuff, and passed on. The scene, though short, was enough to fix all eyes on me. I might have got something worse; yet I never set foot in the Luxembourg again, thereby making a gratuitous mistake.

Thus my behaviour at Saint-Cloud, aggravated by that at Paris, shut me out from all favours, though my plan of campaign might have made them doubly sure. This is not the place to publish a document of the kind; [4] but I may say that in many respects it anticipated that so brilliantly carried into effect at Marengo. I do not know whether it was to this I owed, not the goodwill of the First Consul—I had lost that for ever—but his favourable opinion. As I learnt from those about him, he never failed to see that some use could be made of me; but he never forgave me for not having followed him when he most needed adherents, and of this, those about him whom I had offended took advantage. My chiefs, knowing I was in disgrace, did not care to dwell upon my zeal or my successes; the result being, not that my services were dispensed with, as in the case of so many others, but that I had to dispense with the profits of them.

---

4. It is reproduced in the second volume of his *Journal des opérations du blocus de Gênes*, edition of 1847, with another account of these events. Ed

Chapter 3
Some of my colleagues

Switzerland no longer offered to Masséna a field of action worthy of his power. Austria and her allies had the upper hand only on the Rhine and in Italy, and these now became the centres of two commands, one of which fell to Moreau, the other to Masséna, but with this difference, that while the former found not only an army in fine condition and superior to that of the enemy, as well as a country abounding in resources, the latter found only poor worn-out wretches devoured by misery and disease, the shreds of what was still called the Army of Italy, distributed among positions which they could not leave; positions too so dangerous that even with a victorious army it would have been criminal in a commander-in-chief to occupy them, were it only for a week, in presence even of a beaten force.

Before taking command of the Army of Italy, Masséna had to come to Paris to obtain reinforcements, money, provisions, clothing; he was urgent in his demands, and he was met with liberal promises. Nothing was refused him, the object being to decide him to start without delay for Genoa; but it did not go beyond words, and, when once he had been got off, no more trouble was taken to provide him with the succour that had been guaranteed. All efforts, almost all resources, were devoted to pressing forward the organisation of the army of reserve which was to enter Italy under Bonaparte, who at a moment when he saw glory to be won was not the man to leave to others the opportunity of winning it, nor to furnish them with the means of doing so.

As soon as I heard of Masséna's arrival in Paris I called upon him. I had no need to make any request. "You belong to my military household," had been his first word; "join me at Genoa as quickly as possible." I was still in poorish health, ;and should have been glad to delay my return to the army, but nothing could stay my departure as soon as it was a case of rejoining Masséna.

Just before setting out I went to take leave of General Berthier, who was now Minister for War. "How do you travel?" said he.

"In my own carriage."

"Then you will be able to take charge of 100,000 *francs*, urgently needed for the hospitals of the army."

"Certainly; but you know how unsafe the roads are."

"Very good; sit down and write out an order for the escorts which you think you will want."

I did so; he signed it, and gave me a draft on the treasury for the 100,000 *francs*. As I left the office I caught sight of Major Coutard, whom I had liked and esteemed ever since the Naples campaign. At once it occurred to me to take him with me. He was not the man to break his parole, nor was I capable of suggesting such a thing; but in Paris he might have to wait years before getting his exchange, and there would be an end of his career, while if he came with me I might manage to exchange him against the first Austrian officer of his rank whom we might make prisoner. He agreed, and we started the next day but one.

With a view to arriving sooner, I decided to go from Lyons to Avignon in what was called a post-boat; and though the Rhone was enormously high, I accomplished the journey. However, there was a violent wind, and when night came on the boatman declared we must stop till daylight. I refused, but as they were tired we had to go ashore to an inn, where we found General Oudinot[1] on his way to join Masséna as chief of the staff. He advised me to do like him and pass the night there, but I was determined to get on at any price, and at eleven I started again, say what anyone would. I went near to paying dearly for my imprudence, for in the middle of the night the wretched boat, built of ill-fitted planks and destined to be broken up at Avignon, was spun right round by the wind. The boatmen shrieked aloud, but fortunately it was only a puff.

Towards nine in the morning the boatmen told us that we were getting near the bridge of Saint-Esprit, and asked us if we wished to land, warning us that later it would be impossible. I had often heard talk of that bridge, and of the alarming rapidity with which one passed under the arches, and I was not going to miss the experience, especially when the weather, the height of the water, and the violence of

---

1. *Memoirs of Marshal Oudinot* by Eugénie de Coucy & Gaston Stiegler is also published by Leonaur.

the current rendered it so complete. In order that we might not miss anything, Coutard and I took our place on the box-seat of my carriage. The bridge soon rose before our eyes; I wished to fix my gaze on the arch which we had to go through, but no more bridge was to be seen, and when I turned my head I saw that we were a quarter of a mile beyond it.

As soon as we could stop we went ashore and went back on foot to look at the bridge. We were lucky enough to see another boat go through, and got a full idea of the inconceivable speed with which we had just made the same passage. So dangerous is it that a boat which gets under a wrong arch or misses by ever so little the middle of the current is totally lost.[2] At Avignon, just as I was finishing my dinner, a messenger came to ask for a shirt for General Oudinot. I sent at once what was wanted, after which I called on the general, who told me that his boatmen had run against the bank in landing, that his carriage had rolled into the Rhone, and that he had tumbled in himself, so that not having a dry thread on him he had had to apply to me. Thus my imprudence had cost me only a moment's danger, while his wisdom had not saved him from accident, whereby he lost a box containing a pretty large sum in gold.

In due time I reached Nice. The commander-in-chief had just left, but the paymaster-general and his subordinate were still there, and I handed the money over to them. They were in extreme need of it, for the plague was in the hospitals and even in the town. Its ravages were such that during the four days that I passed at Nice, 1500 persons died; whether the 100,000 *francs* made things any better I do not know.

Of the two ways of getting from Nice to Genoa, that by land involved an intolerable number of halts. At the same time the sea-voyage was risky, owing to the enemy's cruisers, from which there was not much of escape even for a *felucca*. But we got hold of a Maltese *speronare*, and this, being painted the colour of the sea, lying almost flush with the water, having no sails but moving entirely by oars, combined with the advantage of being invisible more than three quarters of a mile away that of travelling with incredible speed. As, however, there was only room for one passenger in addition to the master and eight rowers, Coutard continued his journey by land. Before starting I had my little craft fresh tallowed all over; and though the night was fairly

---

2. [Readers of General Marbot's *Mémoires* will remember that a few weeks before this he had a very narrow escape under the same bridge, and .was wrecked before he reached Avignon.]

bright, I passed with impunity through the whole English fleet, and arrived safely at Genoa. I was then to learn a great lesson from the military point of view; indeed I may say that, such as I have been, I owed all to the teaching and the example of Duhesme and Masséna, and that the siege of Genoa was going to be my best school.

On landing I went straight to the commander-in-chief, and presented all the letters that had come for him to Nice, or had been sent from that town. He seemed glad to see me; but as for the correspondence, all he did was to open two dispatches from the Minister for War, and barely glance at them. Then, giving me back all the letters, together with an enormous heap of others, he observed:

> Take all these and keep them: you will have to see to all my military correspondence. At seven tomorrow morning you will report to me on the contents of them, and I will give you my orders as to the replies. You are lodged in my house, so that you can get to work at once, and you can have all the secretaries you want.

An hour later I was at work, and by the next day a *précis* had been made of a hundred and thirty-four letters, the answers had been sent off, and the general's correspondence was up to date.

Knowing Masséna's quickness, I arranged the work so as to meet the requirements of extreme speed. I classified all the letters, and laid them before him in groups arranged in paper wrappers, ruled in a double column. On one side was a summary of my reports, each occupying four or five lines only, the other being reserved for his decisions. Important passages were underlined in red ink. When all was ready, I went and read my reports to the commander-in-chief, with a promptitude suited to his quickness. As a rule his decision was uttered simultaneously with my last words, sometimes even before them. It came like a flash of lightning, and yet was as precise and complete as could be desired.

Sometimes when I had vainly sought to solve a point, I was amazed at the way he took it as it were on the volley, and quite bewildered by his accuracy and sagacity. In order not to waste the time of which he was so chary, I soon contrived to write down the decision in pencil even while I was reading the next report; but though it had only the effect of making me read a little slower, I was soon obliged to give up even that. It got to such a point that at Milan, for example, when there were never less than sixty to eighty reports in a day, the general's work with me did not take ten minutes. Except where some verification was needed, or unforeseen circumstances turned up, every day's business was finished the next day.

Another thing that was of great use to me was the responsibility that Masséna laid on me. At first he used to keep the letters to sign in the morning, so as to read them over when his head was rested; but very soon he only ran through the more important, and at last he would neither keep them nor read them. One day at Milan I begged him to attend to two letters, which I did not wish to take the initiative even of drawing up. He replied, in the presence of two members of the Cisalpine Government, "I know you will end by getting me hung, but I have taken my line." I may be allowed to add that of the thousands of letters which he thus signed with his eyes shut, not one was ever found fault with.

Beside myself, Masséna had three adjutants-general on his staff. The first was General Reille, who had the luck, shared by no other of Masséna's officers, to be in favour with both him and Napoleon. He became the emperor's *aide-de-camp*, was made count, had a large endowment in addition to an ever-increasing fortune, and commanded armies. What was more curious was, that the fact of having been so well treated by one who treated his earliest patron so badly, did not estrange this latter from him; and after Napoleon's final fall, he married Masséna's daughter. Though Masséna died under the Restoration in a disgrace which itself was a scandal, Reille was no less well thought of by Louis XVIII and Charles X, from whom he received honours of all kinds, and at the moment of the July affair [3] he was on the point of being created a marshal of France.

The others were Campana, a distinguished officer, who soon left the military career to become prefect at Turin or Alessandria, and Gautier, a man who was all gentleness in private life and iron in presence of the enemy. He had every gift to qualify him for speedy accession to high command, yet the reputation gained by a score of brilliant feats and eminent services was all of no avail; and in spite of the high regard of his chiefs, the admiration of his comrades, the unspeakable confidence and respect of his subordinates, he was only a major-general when he fell at Wagram. To say this is to condemn those who treated him unjustly, and notably Marshal Davout. It was owing to sheer bad luck that I remained a major-general for eight years; but

---

3. [When the elder branch of the Bourbons was expelled and Louis Philippe became king.]

when I saw poor Gautier for the last time at Bayonne in December 1808, he being then still major-general while I was lieutenant-general, I was deeply grieved. When he congratulated me on my promotion, I said, "I ought not to have had it before you, but you ought to have had it long ago;" thereby only repeating what General Villatte had said to me when, after I had left him at Tours, where as a major he had been military governor under my orders, I came upon him again as lieutenant-general in Poland.

I am not going to write here the history of the blockade of Genoa, to which I have devoted a special work.[4] We reached Genoa in January, and hostilities did not recommence till April. Soon after my arrival Mariette, the lady whose acquaintance I had made on my first visit to Marseilles, landed at Genoa, together with the gambling-house keeper with whom she lived. They at once opened a house of the same kind, the expense of which was defrayed by the visits of officers of all ranks. Burthe, for whom a green cloth was an irresistible loadstone, got what is called a terrible scouring there, but the person whom I saw lose the heaviest sums was General Oudinot. I remember one occasion on which I saw him in much less than half an hour four times give the key of his desk to his senior *aide-de-camp*, saying, "Go and fetch me a *rouleau* of 100 *louis*," and no sooner had the unfortunate *louis* arrived than they went to swell the pile of gold in front of the banker. I hated play, but as all my seniors and all my comrades went to these gatherings, I used to go with them, and for want of better amusement watched the phases of inconstant fortune.

Among the most regular players I soon noticed Wast, the paymaster.[5] He never sat down, but played two or three times, and then left the room, coming back for a few moments, but soon withdrawing entirely. As all the other players had the habit of looking out for and disputing for the possession of any vacant chairs, Wast, who played standing, made such a contrast to them that I had the curiosity to speak to him about it. Under a seal of secrecy, which I have kept till now, he gave me the following explanation, which seems worth quoting.

---

4. The author's *Journal of the Operations of the Siege of Genoa*, which appeared in 1801, went through several editions, was translated into English (London, 1819), and was finally recast and, so to say, rewritten by himself. The last edition appeared in 1847, after the author's death. Ed.

5. Wast had been sent to Tuscany. When he came back, Préval made the following verses, which drove him frantic: "*Wast a terminé son séjour Dans la Toscane épouvantée. Que nous aunonce son retour? Que la Toscane est dévastée!*" This may be paralleled by the well-known epigram upon Rapinat in Switzerland.

The whims of Fortune are not wholly a matter of uncertainty, but you must follow them, and never defy her. Now the method which I have adopted and found wonderfully successful, and which I will in confidence enable you to verify if it amuses you, is as follows: I bring five *louis* every time with me; I follow the play for a while without taking any part, but try to judge the winning colour. When it seems to me to be settled, I risk one *louis*; if it wins, I go double: if I win again, I withdraw my stake, leaving three *louis*, and if I win the third *coup*, which makes me six *louis* to the good, I regard my luck as exhausted for the evening, and leave off playing.

If, on the other hand, I lose my first, second, or third trial, I leave the game for a short time, so as to put an interval between my loss and a fresh attempt. I do the same when I lose a second, a third, or a fourth stake, but as soon as I lose the fifth I retire for good and all. If after a few unlucky shots I succeed in getting back my five *louis*, I do not risk another. Thus, whether my five *louis* have been lost or doubled, I leave off playing, so that, as you see, I require five unlucky *coups* or series in order to lose, while one is sufficient to make me win. In any case I never get excited, and I keep clear of that plunging, of all those doubles or quits which make the fortune of a gambling-house.

Wishing to judge for myself the chances of this method, I followed it for eighteen days, not with *louis* but with *piastres*. Twice I came off neither winner nor loser, three times I lost, finally I had won fifty *piastres* when the blockade put an end to these meetings. One evening, the banker having looked hard at Wast and myself several times, I wanted to know what he thought of our mode of playing, he said;

> If everyone adopted it, the banker's occupation would be gone. Without confining oneself to the system adopted by M. Wast, it is only the people who sit down that make us rich, and our fortune comes especially from those who will persist in applying fixed and sequent calculations to that which admits of neither calculation, fixity, nor sequence.

Meanwhile a far more serious game and one not less difficult to play was being prepared for us; and in spite of all the energy which Masséna threw into his combinations for success, all the chances of success were slipping from us. We were awaiting a convoy of provisions, and the English fleet assembled off Genoa allowed us no further hope of its arrival. We were expecting further reinforcements; but when General Melas had carried the heights of San Giacomo, thrown General Suchet back towards La Pietra, and separated the centre of the army from the right, our three corps were isolated, and no concerted action was possible. Genoa had to depend exclusively on the troops forming the right wing, who to the number of 10,500 guarded the city and its outposts; while 3,500 were in position before Savona, and 5,000 were concentrated round Finale. Against these 19,000 men Melas detached 60,000 from his entire force of 135,000.

Such was the situation of which Masséna in his patriotism had accepted the formidable responsibility. How, when blockaded in Genoa, he held the Austrian force in check for fifty-eight days and in ninety engagements; how he gained such influence over the inhabitants that he prevented all danger of revolt from them, and persuaded them to undergo the horrors of the siege with us and no less heroically than we; how the blockade to seaward by the English fleet forbade all revictualling until the inhabitants in numbers died of famine, while the combatants were rationed on a few ounces of horseflesh and the same of bread, the latter a filthy mixture of the consistency of putty,—all this is well known. The result of this heroism is also well known; without the loss of time and men that it caused to the Austrians, the victory of Marengo would have been impossible. When Bonaparte, who was to draw such gigantic advantage from that victory, next met Masséna, his first words ought to have been nothing but, "Let us go and thank the gods together." But Bonaparte had too much interest in sacrificing a man like Masséna, to be likely to forgive him for such a service rendered.

All the phases of that great military drama have already been noted in *my Journal of the Blockade*, and I need not repeat them here; but there are a few details which please me to recall. I may begin with one relating to the *Journal*. On April 21, when I had finished my work with the commander-in-chief, he said:

Thiébault, my correspondence has come down to a very few letters, so you must have time to spare. I wish you would write an account of our blockade, which is sure to be memorable.

"General," I answered, "that work has been begun ever since the 5th, and I was only waiting till I had got a little more forward with it to tell you about it and to ask your leave to show it to you." He was touched by this evidence of zeal, and said that I was at liberty to come whenever he was in his bath and read him what I had written, and also that I might apply to him for any information I wanted. So I used to read the work to him when he took his bath, which he did three times a week, and completed the revision of it at Milan.

My intimacy with the general soon enabled me to get Coutard exchanged. As a prisoner on parole he was devoured with impatience at seeing his comrades fighting and not being allowed to bear arms with them. Nor was this the worst feature in his position. If Genoa were to fall, Coutard would be captured, as he could not fail to be, amid an army on active service, and far from the domestic hearth which he was pledged in honour not to leave. Luckily, when we retook Monte Faccio on April 7, among the 1500 prisoners whom we captured was Baron d'Aspre, a lieutenant-colonel of Austrian hussars, of a rank, that is, pretty nearly equivalent to Coutard's. He was, however, a man of more importance than his rank implied, so that Masséna was not very willing to let him go cheaply, and only with great difficulty granted the favour I asked. Ultimately, however, the exchange was effected, and Coutard could appear once more in the field and distinguish himself, giving me an opportunity of getting him not only presented, but, on Colonel Wouillemont's promotion to general, put in command of his old corps, the 73rd of the Line.

Another anecdote of captured prisoners shall be recorded, as it may offer a useful hint to officers on campaign. On April 10 we were marching on Varazze. In one of our charges we had just secured several prisoners, among them a young Austrian officer. On being brought to me, he said, "General, the day is over for me, while for you it is just beginning, and may be long. Allow me to offer you some provisions, which are of no further use to me, and may be necessary for you." And he handed me a lemon and a cake of chocolate. Really one needs nothing more to save one from hunger and thirst through a whole day; I tested it so well that day that I resolved never again to mount my horse without a lemon and a piece of chocolate in my pocket, and in war-time I have often found them of great service.

If I gained Coutard, I lost Dath, who was taken prisoner before long in carrying a dispatch from the commander-in-chief to General Soult,—a duty on which five officers in succession were sent, without being able to get to him. Commanders in those days had often to make their own inspiration stand in the place of orders which did not come to hand. Among the superior officers who were killed or wounded, I may mention Colonel Villaret, whose death was a grief to us all; Gautier, whose life was only saved by a miracle; and Mouton, the future Marshal and Count of Lobau, who owed his recovery only to the care taken of him. His wound reminds me of an incident worth recording. On April 30 I had just taken a verbal order to him to recapture Fort Quezzi with the two first battalions of his regiment—the 3rd. "That is a beast of an order you bring me," said he. I said that it was an order like any other, and would give him the chance of earning further distinction. "No," he retorted; "it is a beast of an order." Calling his servant, he took off a new coat that he had on and took an old one, gave the servant his purse and watches, and went off, a prey to gloomy forebodings. A quarter of an hour later he was brought back mortally wounded, as it was thought, by a bullet that had gone through his left arm and his body.

In the mouth of an officer who was notoriously brave, and subsequently gave numerous proofs of his quality, one might be sure that an answer of this kind was not called forth by ill-humour or lack of spirit, but by some strange presentiment, such as is by no means unknown. I need only quote the case of La Salle at Wagram. He was a man to whom a battle was a treat, a charge positive enjoyment, yet, when he mounted his horse on that day, he had the conviction that he would be killed in the course of it. Being unable to overcome his gloomy mood or to conceal his foreboding, he would have none of his officers near him; and in this frame of mind, unintelligible to his *aides-de-camp*, but revealed by an intimate friend, he received the expected bullet in his forehead.

By the middle of May the report went about as a certain fact that the First Consul was coming with the army of reserve, and was manoeuvring with a view of cutting off the enemy's line of retreat. On the 26th Major Franceschi, General Soult's *aide-de-camp*, who had been sent to the commander-in-chief by the First Consul a month ago, returned, after making his way through every sort of danger, and announced that he had left General Bonaparte coming down from the Great St. Bernard, and that the army of reserve, as soon as it reached Ivrea, would come on to Genoa by forced marches, and raise the blockade on the 30th.

However, May 31 and June 1 passed without bringing us any aid, the officers brought forward strategic reasons to explain the delay in our deliverance, and looked for favourable sides to the most alarming indications; but the soldiers could no longer suppress their discouragement, gave way to disorder, and deserted in numbers. Despair and rage were depicted on all countenances; inhabitants as well as garrison seemed to be at the end of their strength. The ravages of famine and sickness grew every day more terrible; covered waggons went about the town to carry off the corpses which were laid naked at the corners of the streets. No further attempts could be made in a military way, for the soldiers and most of the officers were incapable of enduring the fatigue of a combat or even of a simple march. Sentries had to sit down at their posts, and often were taken ill on the way there. Negotiations for the evacuation began on June 1.

In these negotiations Masséna showed himself what he was, a commander incapable of a mistake, and a clever manager of men. During the blockade his hair had grown quite white, but he had lost nothing of his mental power. He understood excellently how to make use of the sullen jealousy of the allied diplomatists. At the right moment he flattered the pride of the English at the expense of the Austrian self-conceit, and was able so well to put on the appearance of being at his ease, was so fertile in happy flashes, that he succeeded in obtaining leave to take away even the five privateers that were in Genoa. A story is connected with one of these which it amuses me to relate.

There was a *tartane* which, in the opinion of M. Morin, Masséna's excellent political secretary, was well adapted for the purpose of a privateer, and had been fitted by him before the blockade for this object. Unluckily he put it under the command of one Bavastro,[6] a man who would have been extremely well suited to such an office had his honesty been on a par with his courage. All that I know is that, besides the shares of the crew and commander, the produce of the rich prizes on which we reckoned was to have been divided in twenty-four parts, the bonds for which were held, twelve by the commander-in-chief, who gave the letters of marque, six by Morin, six by me.

However, these hopes vanished like so many others. Bavastro saw vessels on their way; instead of chasing them, he only made poor prizes, and that only to be able to say he had made them. The dividend of millions which he had promised us was reduced to our share in the indemnities which we had to pay. The result was less tragic though more expensive than that of my former attempt at Pescara, and at least I gained from it two ships' biscuits a day during the last month of the blockade, which came out of the stores of the vessel. I was thus saved from the alternative of eating bread which made the dogs sick, or paying 36 *francs* a pound for good bread.

---

6. [He was Masséna's cousin, and the two had as boys gone to sea together.]

When we had finally reached the end of that glorious death-struggle and got a treaty which allowed us our honour and our freedom, I set sail for Nice in the same vessel, taking the opportunity of carrying off from the arsenal of Genoa twelve handsome bronze 12-pounders, which were placed in the hold under mattresses and packages. Masséna had embarked at daybreak on the 5th for Antibes, and his officers were free to depart in their turn. We were exhausted with hunger and fatigue, as may be supposed our vessel was not provisioned, and I had ordered Bavastro to take us with all speed to Nice, where we were in a hurry to arrive in order to eat something. When we were off Albenga, an English frigate came sailing down upon us, and fired a shot as a signal to stop. Bavastro was for heaving to; I objected, being indignant at the bare idea of anyone wanting to hinder our progress.

So we sailed on; but the frigate gained on us, and when she was within range fired a shot, which went through one of our sails. As might was right, we stopped; the frigate, with all sail set, soon caught us up, and sent a boat on board of us with a young officer to know who we were and what we had on board, and also to look at our papers. Seeing that he spoke French very well, I said, "Upon my word, sir, it's cruelty to stop famishing people like this." I spoke in an emphatic tone of ill-temper, hoping to influence the young officer, who seemed a gallant fellow, and thus prevent his making a thorough examination of our vessel, since the twelve guns were something more than contraband.

Learning who I was, he was extremely polite, and, after disturbing only a few packages, took his leave. Hardly, however, was he on board his vessel when another shot was fired, and we had again to heave to. I was fairly savage; but at last the young officer came on board us once more, and told us that his captain, being touched with our condition, and glad to testify his admiration of the men who had defended Genoa, begged me to accept some victuals. Accordingly he handed me two huge bags of biscuit, three hams, two baskets containing a dozen of wine each, and, by a refinement of kindness, a basket of fresh salad with all the requisites for dressing it. I shook hands with the young man, and asked the names of his frigate, his captain, and himself. I wrote them down, but have, I am sorry to say, lost them. Then thanking him once more for his share in this new kind of duty, I bade him take our compliments to the captain, and gave a *louis* to each of the two sailors who had brought the provisions on board; and so we parted.

We entered the port of Nice at eight next morning, overjoyed at once more seeing France, and all eagerness to tread her soil. We were trying who could land first, when a sanitary official, accompanied by four soldiers, came up and told us that, as we had been in communication with an enemy's ship, we were liable to quarantine. I hardly know how the man escaped being thrown overboard; he was assaulted on all sides, his men lowered their bayonets, and twenty sabres—I should be sorry to say that mine was not one—were drawn. The soldiers were overpowered, and presently not a soul remained on board.

Some of my comrades and I had just finished such a breakfast as we had not made for months, and as we had washed it down as it deserved,[7] we were extremely merry, when an officer came in and informed me that a complaint having been laid by the head of the health department, an order had just been given for my arrest, on the ground that my rank and the authority I held over the officers who had sailed with me made me responsible for all. This was past a joke, and I hastened to General Oudinot, who by good luck was at Nice. "The devil!" he said; "this is serious."

"Did General Bonaparte let himself be quarantined at Fréjus?" I returned.

"He did not land with drawn sword. Besides, a precedent like that is no justification; and in order that there may be no mistake about it the First Consul has just been revising the sanitary laws and ordering their strict execution. Do not stay at Nice, but go and join Masséna at Antibes."

An hour later I was relating my adventure, or misadventure, to Masséna. "All right," he said, "stay with me: we will be off at four to-morrow morning, and the sound of the guns will put all that straight." And I never heard anything more about the matter.

Masséna had retained all his rights under the treaty of evacuation, and he was not the man to remain inactive, especially when a division might be of assistance to the army of reserve. He resolved to call together all that remained available of the Army of Italy, some 10,000 men, and re-open the campaign with them. He now let me continue my journey from Nice by land with all the belongings of the staff, while he himself, having a wound in the leg, went on board a *felucca* with Reille and Oudinot. Keeping close inshore, and sending a fast

---

7. Some officers, on landing at Nice, remained at table for seven hours on end, eating everything that they could get. I need not say that the sudden change from hunger to repletion caused several fresh death.

boat on in front to see that the coast was clear, he reached Finale without being caught. There he stayed and devoted some days to re-organising what remained of the troops of the right and centre; and there we overtook him.

When I entered Finale, a combat had just been going on between an English brig and the garrison of the little port, one trying to take and the other to defend two *feluccas* loaded with grain, lately arrived from Nice; and the brig had been beaten off. The affair had just been reported to the commander-in-chief when I presented myself. I asked if someone should not see to the unloading of the two vessels, but was told that it was late, and they would not be unloaded till the morning. Next morning I was sleeping soundly when two of my servants came into my room, crying out, "Here are the English!" The drums beat at the same time, and I thought they were landing: so I jumped out of bed, telling one of my servants to saddle me a horse, and the other to bring my clothes. The poor lad, who was not eighteen, and had by this time lost his head, brought me a sword instead of boots and a hat instead of breeches. However, I got dressed before long, and started for the commander-in-chief's.

As I crossed the Piazza della Pietra, where I lodged, which looked on the sea, I saw an English ship of the line, followed by a frigate, a corvette, and the brig that had been beaten off the day before. They were coming in close column with all sails set towards the quay, which formed the south side of the *piazza*, and off which the two *feluccas* were moored. Not only did they approach so near that the ship's bowsprit projected over the quay, but they seemed to be handled by magic. Not a man was to be seen on deck or in the rigging, the reason being to escape our musketry, which had done much execution the day before among the brig's crew. Eight in front of the *piazza* the ship of the line let fly a formidable broadside of round and grape, the frigate, corvette, and brig taking up the fire as they ranged alongside. Having passed the *piazza*, all four went about, and grazing it again on the other tack poured in their larboard broadsides, and sailed off.

I never saw a manoeuvre executed with more accuracy, audacity, and majesty. The ship's first fire had smashed the two *feluccas*, and the sea to a great distance was covered with wreckage and grain, amid which floated the corpse of a sailor who had been asleep and unable to escape. The other broadsides had damaged the *piazza* considerably and killed some of our men, who could take no revenge, having nothing to fire at but empty decks or portholes.

One of our non-commissioned officers met his death as by predestination. He was on duty at the headquarters, and, reclining in a roomy armchair in front of a window in the brilliant sunshine, was watching the evolutions of the four vessels, when a case of grape which had not had room to scatter took him in the breast. My own escape was due to the wild panic of my servants, who had saved me by waking me. My house at the upper end of the *piazza* was one of the worst knocked about, and my room worst of all, as I learnt by hearing that people were flocking from all sides to look at it. The space between the windows had been driven in; several round-shot, coming in by the windows, had gone right through the house; while one shot and two grapeshot had rebounded off the wall on to a bed, and others were lying about. Asleep or awake, I should have been done for by one of them. The thickness of the dust in the room was extraordinary. A shirt, a hat, and an overcoat that were lying on the chairs were all the same colour.

A circumstance of some importance is connected with Masséna's stay at Finale. As soon as he got there, General Suchet called on him, and did all he could to obtain the order to anticipate the movement planned by the commander-in-chief, and start at once with all the troops, in order to lose no time in supporting the First Consul's operations. Nothing could seem better or more plausible from a military point of view; but things are not always what they seem, as both Suchet and Masséna proved on this occasion. Suchet was displaying a fine zeal for the service in trying to elicit the order to quicken by thirty-six hours an offensive movement which might even be decisive; but at bottom all he wanted was to have the sole merit of it. It was a clever dodge to put himself at the head of the army instead of the commander-in-chief.

Suchet was reproducing at Finale the part played by Soult at Genoa, when, knowing that it was the only point from the defence of which any glory was to be gained, he did all he could to prevent Masséna from fixing his headquarters there, on the score that the commander-in-chief's place was with the whole of his army, and not with a wing which might be cut off. But Masséna was too sagacious to fail to see the hidden reason, and too sharp to show his hand. Moreover, Suchet's recent performances as commander of an army in a position to which he had but lately obtained, had not been exceedingly brilliant, and it was by no means clear that anything would be gained by starting thirty-six hours sooner under him than by waiting the same time till

Masséna was ready. Moreover, it was absolutely necessary to allow the troops returning from the Var, and still more those from Genoa, a little time to rest and get into condition.

Accordingly, not wishing to say to his lieutenant, "I quite see your game, and am not going to play up to it," Masséna assumed an air of justifiable wrath, in order to get out of the difficulty under the guise of petulance; complaining that none of the promises on the faith of which he had accepted the command of the Army of Italy had been kept, and that he had been deceived, indeed deserted, sacrificed. Finally, to put an end to Suchet's importunity, he launched this parting shaft at the First Consul, "I have done quite enough for that little——."

But, in spite of appearances, how did each act? While Masséna was organising his march with the utmost rapidity and preparing in all haste for the co-operation at which he had just been grumbling, Suchet sent an order to Adjutant-General Préval, his chief of staff, bidding him start at once with a few hundred men and let the First Consul know that aid was coming, and that, if there had been any delay, it had been due to Masséna's reluctance to act.

Préval set off in pursuance of this order, but found in front of him the twenty squadrons which the enemy were keeping in these parts to watch the reassembled force from Genoa and Suchet's troops, and which, if they had not been thus kept immobile, would have been more than enough to prevent the movement which won the Battle of Marengo. Seeing that they continually retreated before his 500 horse, Préval suspected a trick, and did not proceed without scouting as far as possible to his front and on his flanks. As he advanced thus, he met Soult's *aide-de-camp*, Colonel Franceschi, from whom he heard of the victory of Marengo and its magical results.

Any announcement of aid now seemed useless, and not seeing the use of going on merely to report Suchet's march to the First Consul, Préval halted, merely sending back word to Suchet of the battle, the consequent armistice, and the treaty that followed, whereby fifteen fortresses were surrendered and the whole right bank of the Adige evacuated by Melas as the result of twelve hours' fighting.

The defence of Genoa had already become a subject of almost legendary admiration, being regarded as the one thing which had made the First Consul's victories possible. Everyone was repeating the answer made to Berthier by the quartermaster-general of the Austrian Army. When the treaty of Alessandria was being signed, Berthier, by way of making himself known to the officers present on the other side, said, "It must be a consolation to have been beaten only by a fine army under the greatest general in the world." The Austrian officer replied briskly, "The Battle of Marengo was not lost here, but before Genoa;" and this famous answer, which passed from mouth to mouth, confirmed the opinion already current that the defenders of Genoa were the saviours of the country.

Since April 30 I had held the rank of general of brigade. I have only referred incidentally in these *Memoirs* to that brilliant day on which three important positions were recaptured, including Fort Quezzi, in the attack on which Colonel Mouton was wounded, as I have already related. Deprived of their chief, the troops had retreated, and Masséna, who was personally superintending the operations, had told me to take half a battalion and go straight for the fort at the double, while General Miollis would attack on the right, and Adjutant Hector on the left. I had the roughest work, but, thanks to the wonderful energy of my half-battalion, Masséna was able to come up with the last reserves, and joining me on the ground which I held, aid me in definitely routing the troops guarding the approaches and carrying the fort by assault. I had needed the utmost energy to keep my half-battalion together under the deadly fire which enveloped us, and the commander-in-chief had appointed me general of brigade on the field; a favour of which I was fortunate enough to secure the completion on the same day by obtaining for Coutard and Wouillemont steps no less worthily earned.

In consequence of the treaty, our prospect of a laborious military march was exchanged for that of a triumphal progress. We proceeded thus to Milan; and when I went to Masséna, the morning after our arrival, he was about to call on the First Consul, whither I accompanied him. It might have been thought that the defender of Genoa, indirectly the victor of Marengo, when going to one who as commander of the army had reaped all the glory of the event, and as head of the State was reaping all the fruit, would have come proud of his conduct and strong in the justice that was his due. Yet it was far from being so.

A few words which had slipped from an indiscreet circle had given a hint of possible unpleasantness. Some ventured to doubt if Masséna would retain his command; some knew on the best authority that, at the very time when he was doing everything to sustain a hopeless struggle, the succession to his post had been promised to General Desaix. Even a successor of such merit could not have blinded anyone to the disgrace of the fact; and when the force of circumstances prevailed over jealous hostility, it was only with regret at the impossibility of acting otherwise that the course which could not be helped was taken. Even this was only for a time, and we soon saw the great Masséna replaced by one of the most insignificant of our generals.

Naturally no one but Berthier was present at the interview between the First Consul and Masséna. The other officers who accompanied the latter remained with those on duty. Murat, Junot, and Duroc were there. This meeting between men who had just taken part in two such great feats of arms was bound to lead to an exchange of remarks. We took the lead in offering congratulations and asking questions; but we ran up against the reserve which was an attitude of caution around Bonaparte, and became the official attitude around Napoleon. The embarrassment and uneasiness between the staff of the First Consul and Berthier and that of Masséna looked like continuing, when some one or other started a change of topic.

This diversion, the only thing I remember about my appearance in the First Consul's quarters at Milan, was a trial of strength between Murat and a major of artillery. Murat as a general was no longer in a position to engage in a rough-and-tumble with anyone; so the two champions took their seats on either side of a small table, rested their right elbows on it, each clasping the other's hand with interlaced fingers, and trying to force back the other's arms. These efforts remained without result, but the pressure of the fingers on the hand of either adversary had been such that the blood had come under each finger.

This diversion lasted for only a comparatively short time, while the interview between the First Consul and Masséna was very long; our only resource was patience, but at last the general reappeared. All eyes turned towards him; his face expressed at once agitation and content, but our suspense was presently ended by these words, "Gentlemen, the First Consul is returning to Paris, and I command the army."

The First Consul started for Paris, I think, next day; and I at once resumed the same duties with the commander-in-chief as I had performed at Genoa. One of the first matters to which I attended was the exchange of Dath, who, as I have said, was taken prisoner at Genoa. Nothing could exceed the kind manner in which General Melas acceded to the request which I addressed to him.

Chapter 4

Life at Paris

The time was at hand when the First Consul and his *vizier* Berthier considered, apparently, that Masséna's recent claim to glory would be sufficiently forgotten, and after three months' command in time of peace he was superseded, just when people were predicting the renewal of hostilities, and superseded, of all people in the world, by General Brune, who, in spite of his campaign in Holland, the credit of which belonged to Vandamme rather than to him, was far from having the qualifications of a real commander. His short Italian campaign after the supersession of Masséna being outside of my personal recollection, there is no object in pointing out its mistakes in this place. I need only mention the fact that he marched three corps of his army on a single road, so that the centre and left divisions started and came in so late that the days were spent in moving and the nights in deploying. Our poor soldiers, who punish their commanders' mistakes by pleasantries and avenge the needless waste of their own blood by jokes, called this way of advancing, marching *à la Brune*.[1] Phrases like this are none the less final judgements for taking the outward form of puns.

Brune—who, for want of a will of his own, lost himself, wasted all his time in feeling his way about, was under the influence of a few favoured generals, and always agreed with the last person who spoke to him was none the less a stout revolutionary and a man of honour, wholly devoted to his country and to everything connected with his duty. Unluckily this is not the same thing as having merits whether as a man or as a commander; at the head of an army he was wanting in both capacity and vigour, and when he was made marshal it was of him that people were able to say that a crutch would have suited

---

1. [In the dusk.]

him better than the baton, too short as that was for his stature and too heavy for his arm.

Thus, in spite of the advantage that we gained by holding all the fortresses of Italy, and so being in rear as well as in front of the enemy, one cannot say what would have happened to that army if it had fought for long so feebly commanded. But Moreau won the Battle of Hohenlinden, and the peace that was signed a month later at Lunéville made it possible to regret neither Masséna's forced inaction nor Brune's employment.

It was about six in the morning when Masséna received the dispatch announcing his supersession. He at once came to my room with the deplorable news, and announced that he should start for Paris that evening. He also expressed a desire to take with him a copy of the *Journal of the Blockade of Genoa*. Luckily I had just revised a copy. I took it to him half an hour afterwards, and we did our last piece of work together, leaving not a single letter to be answered; the dispatches that came in during the day were left unopened for General Brune. When everything was settled, I said, "I have a last favour to ask you, general; namely, that you would kindly sign this permission for me to go to Paris."

"You do not stay with Brune?"

"No, general."

"Do you start at the same time as I do?"

"Give me leave to remain a little longer at Milan."

At ten in the evening he had left the army, next day he had left Italy, while I had left the palace in which he had been residing.

I remained full of regret. I was losing a chief who had honoured me with his confidence and intimacy, whose board and lodgings I had shared, who had heaped kindness upon me, whom I liked as much as I respected him. To complete what I have said about Masséna, I will tell the following story. An old officer of the Royal Italian Regiment, who had as captain commanded the company in which Masséna had started as a private, came to Milan and called upon his old subordinate, now become commander-in-chief. As soon as he was announced the general hurried to meet him and took him into his own study. He kept him to dinner, invited all the generals who were at the headquarters to meet him, and introduced him to them in these words:

> Gentlemen, you see my old captain, the first officer under whom I ever had the honour to serve, and whose kindness I shall always remember.

When dinner was announced, he took his old captain by the hand, led him to the table, set him on his right, and during the whole meal showed him so much attention that the poor old fellow could not restrain his tears.

All those with whom I had been in daily relations had now departed; I had practically abdicated an authority which made my position so conspicuous; I had again become a stranger to the movements of that great machine called the army, so many of whose strings had vibrated under my hand; I saw a chief, who was physically a giant of six feet high and mentally a dwarf of a few inches, figuring as understudy in a part which he did not seem to me to suit; in short, after a life every day of which had been claimed by important duties, I had fallen into complete inaction. A longer stay at Milan became impossible. Resolved as I was not to serve immediately at least with Masséna's successor, I could no longer form part of his headquarter staff. I had leave of absence to use it and to go away; not to use it meant to be sent as soon as it expired to one of the divisions of the army.

If I went to France, I thought I should retain more control of my future than if I were employed in a division even with the rank of general of brigade. Besides, I had not yet had my rank confirmed, and General Brune might dispute it, nor could he recognise it without laying me under an obligation, and this, for Masséna's sake, I could not allow. A letter from my father was a fresh motive for hastening my resignation; and finally, a last attempt on General Brune's part to retain me, put me under the alternative of either remaining with him or fixing a day for my departure.

As soon as my intention of going was known, it seemed as if the word had gone round to load me with commissions. My carriage was piled with parcels, among them several sums of money, including one of 600 *louis*—all in gold. I may say I was also the bearer of a necklace consisting of three rows of fine pearls, valued at 30,000 *francs*, which General Vignolle gave me for Mme Murat. Let me say that I gave no receipt for these valuables, as I did not wish to incur a ruinous responsibility for the sake of obliging my friends. I had to go through Piedmont, where the roads were so far from safe that not a week passed without the news of some carriage having been stopped by brigands, which made me none the less anxious about carrying such goods in trust. Moreover, among the other articles of value which it was my destiny to take back to France, was General Poinsot's wife, the general having asked me to see her as far as Lyons. As he was in command at

Alessandria, I was forced to go by that town, which accordingly was my first sleeping-place.

General Poinsot was a man of extraordinary bravery, and a very good fellow too; but otherwise ordinary both in style and in manners. He was far from being stupid, and thus did not fail to justify his name.[2] Several things that he said struck me at the time, but I only remember one. On my expressing my surprise that he should separate from his wife without necessity, this was his answer:

> When I get my marching orders for active service, I buy a property, the cost to be defrayed by the campaign. As soon as the conquest is made, I get a command somewhere, and when things are pretty quiet again send for my wife. Then, when I have got together the sum necessary to pay off the debt contracted on the security of the war, Mme Poinsot goes herself to effect the payment, clear the new property, and sometimes enlarge it.

Nothing could be clearer.

Next morning I started at daybreak with the lady, *my aide-de-camp* Richebourg, my valet, and Jacques Dewint, who was my devoted servant till 1814. We had an escort of twenty-four cavalry, under the command of a sergeant. This suited me well enough; for while securing Mme Poinsot's safety, they also guaranteed that of the articles entrusted to me. They were to accompany us to Novalese; but they delayed our progress, so that when night came on we were still a good league from Turin, and I was sound asleep. We were roused by a shout. Richebourg and Jacques were on the defensive, and replying by a pistol-shot to two shots that had been fired at us. My first thought was for Mme Murat's necklace, which was in a case by my side.

In a moment I took it out and fastened it round my neck; then I took my pistols, and, as the carriage had stopped, I was about to jump out when the sergeant, who had, as he should not have done, fallen behind, galloped up with his men. The tables were turned, and our assailants fled. Luckily nothing was wounded but one of our horses, so we were able to proceed at once, and the only inconvenience of the adventure was that I had to go and report it to the general commanding at Turin. Next day we crossed the Mont Cenis, and went without stopping to Lyons. There I left Mme Poinsot, and travelled on at full speed day and night towards Paris. Ten in the evening was striking as I passed

---

2. [*Point sot*—a sufficiently obvious jest.]

the Barrière de l'Enfer, and at a quarter past I alighted at my father's.

Many things had to be talked over. My father had seen Masséna on his arrival in Paris, and, learning from the general's first words how anxious he was to see my *Journal of the Blockade* published, had offered to get it printed. Fifty copies were awaiting me, sent by the general. Next morning I was awoke by Mme Murat's secretary asking if I was the bearer of her pearl necklace. Two hours later I placed it in her hands, saying, "You will not have the first wearing of it;" which necessitated the story of how I had had to put it round my own neck.

I breakfasted with Murat and his wife. Nothing could have been more simple than he, or more unaffected than the future Queen of Naples. In a position seeming all the higher for its distance from that in which they had begun, both at the age which is most becoming,— she beautiful as an angel, he magnificent in figure, strength, face, and covered with laurels reaped in Italy, Germany, and Egypt,—what could they lack to their happiness, their prospects, their peace of mind? All the more did I appreciate their perfect good-nature. After our excellent breakfast, served on fine porcelain, there was brought in a pot of the coarsest earthenware, containing a kind of jam. "It is a treat from my own country," said Murat; "my mother made it and sent it me." I liked the feeling that prompted the, words, and the jam tasted all the better for it; but it was clear that it would not be eaten in his honour much longer, and that before long no more traces would remain of this taste of childhood than now remained of the envy he had felt of my position at the camp of Marly.

On leaving Murat I called on Masséna. He was full of regard for my father and of thanks for the trouble he had taken in bringing out the *Journal of the Blockade*. "What about the First Consul?" I asked.

The general said:

> As for him, this is what happened. The day when the work was to appear, I received a note asking for a copy, and forbidding me to dispose of any others until I had had an interview. Next day I went to the Tuileries. When the First Consul saw me he came up, and said, 'I have read the *Journal of the Blockade of Genoa*; it is a good piece of work, and I am satisfied with it, and everybody ought to be.'

I had carefully avoided inserting any reference to the plan for an Italian campaign which I had submitted to the First Consul,[3] and

---

3. As we have said, it will be found in the edition published in 1847. Ed.

which, by a coincidence of which I am proud, he had just carried out. This prudent reticence may have shielded me from the consular thunders; but that was all I could expect, and my *Journal* only aggravated my former sins. It was a fresh offence to have proclaimed to the world the glory of Masséna just when a flagrant piece of injustice had been committed towards him. Accordingly I resolved not to run the risk of a refusal by taking any personal or direct steps to obtain the confirmation of my rank as major-general. I had not touched on the subject with Murat, and naturally had said nothing to Masséna. As I could not wait on either the Minister for War or the First Consul without asking to be confirmed, I kept away from both of them, merely continuing to use the title of my rank.

I received many compliments on my book, including one from Prince Henry of Prussia, speaking in high terms of Masséna, to whom I showed it. I allowed no copies to be made;[4] but General Pamphile Lacroix, who heard it read, wrote it out from memory. By this means it reached the highest circles, where it caused much displeasure. Among those who, being unable to criticise or correct these statements of the book, avenged themselves by taking it in bad part, was General Soult. Yet I had eulogised him, if anything, to excess; as I remarked one day to Masséna when walking with him in his park at Rueil: "What else," I said, "ought I to have done in order to avoid incurring his dislike?"

"What ought you to have done?" returned Masséna, in his usual sharp way; "you ought not to have mentioned me in your work."

I saw but few people at this time, chiefly old friends of my father—Dr. Bacher, M. Joly, M. and Mme Bitaubé—or of my own—Rivierre de l'Isle, Lenoir, Gassicourt—these and other young men who with fine manners combined a wit at once kindly and fertile in brilliant flashes. Charming men they were, such as in truth I do not meet nowadays. The type seems to have been lost since Frenchmen have abdicated their national character, and taken to posing as teachers before they have gone to school, while keeping so little control over their own heads that they think themselves capable of controlling the world.

Through these kind friends I gradually came to know others. Rivierre introduced me to M. Clavier, the famous Greek scholar, and his wife, afterwards the mother-in-law of poor Paul Louis Courier; also to Mme Winch, a lively and graceful Creole. I forget at whose house I met Fabien; but the meeting suddenly revived all my old love of fencing, and I agreed with Fabien that he should come and fence

---

4. It is now published in the above-mentioned edition of the *Journal*. Ed.

with me every morning from eight to eleven. He could not be classed with Saint-Georges, who had put himself beyond all comparison; but he was none the less a very remarkable fencer, and it was both profitable and pleasant to match oneself against him, though during the first weeks I was nowhere. Gradually I managed to defend myself; and though always his inferior, I succeeded in touching him pretty often. Ultimately, on his recommendation, I took to going in the evenings, when my father did not want me, to a fencing school in the Rue Richelieu, where I beat the master and all the amateurs, and took rank in the first class.

One evening as I was fencing there about eight o'clock, in full fencing costume, a loud report was heard. "Hallo!" cried someone, "there are the guns announcing the peace." But I knew the sound of guns too well to recognise it this time; and as some tumult was heard, and the explosion could not have taken place far away, I went out, mask in hand, and as I was.

As I reached the gate in the Rue Richelieu the First Consul's carriage on his way to the opera stopped a little to my left, and General Bonaparte, coming to the window, said to one of the officers of his escort, "Go and order the whole Consular guard to turn out." To another he said, "Go and tell Mme Bonaparte to join me at the opera." And the carriage went on.

Everyone was moving towards the Rue Saint-Honoré. I changed my clothes, and followed the crowd, which bore me along towards the upper end of the Rue Saint-Nicaise. There people were pointing out a waggon wrecked, doors driven in, windows broken; but no one could say anything certain as to the cause of the disaster. Each was still interpreting it in life own fashion, though people were beginning to suspect that it was a case of an attempt on the life of the First Consul. Getting tired of being shoved, squeezed, and elbowed, I had worked my way nearly to the Rue Saint-Honoré, when the cry was heard, "Another explosion!" There was a general rush, people were upset and trampled upon in all directions, terrible shrieks resounded, and more people were injured in this disturbance, brought about simply by a trick of which the thieves took advantage, than had been hurt by the infernal machine, for it is needless to say it is of that that I am speaking.

Having been so placed as to be able to gather sooner than almost anyone some certain details as to this diabolical crime, I hastened to carry the news of it to my father, and there were two of us to preserve an exact remembrance of it. Some time after I received a medal struck on the occasion; but I saw nothing written on it save a scrap from a romance. Thus history receives its consecration.

One day my father found himself dining at Dr. Bacher's in company with Junot, then *aide-de-camp* to the First Consul and Governor of Paris. On Junot's learning who my father was, "Why, hang it all," said he; "is your son here, and has never been to see me?"

"General," replied my father, "he has often regretted it; but he is entitled to a confirmation of rank which he has not had, and he cannot bear to solicit favours. Accordingly he had decided not to show himself anywhere, lest the motive of his visit might be mistaken."

"That is nonsense," replied Junot; "tell him to come to breakfast with me tomorrow."

I went in response to this invitation, and Junot received me most kindly. He had not long been married to Mlle Laure Permon, and he presented me to his wife. It is impossible to imagine anything prettier, more lively, more amiable, or more striking than was that young lady. She was charming, and has always remained in my mind as I saw her then, the most graceful being that ever appeared.

I had hardly come in when Talma was announced. I was delighted to have the chance of seeing that great artist otherwise than in character, and of estimating the actor as a man. The result of the test was by no means unfavourable. I saw a man of simple character, but with confidence in his own worth, educated and capable, without swagger, keeping in his own place, but dignifying that; a man who would have ennobled his profession if it had been of a nature to be ennobled, and who at least placed himself in the front rank of possible exceptions. To pass from the man himself to his talent, I should say, while feeble so long as he chose to follow the lines marked out by Lekain, Talma rose in proportion as he got farther from them; while Larive, for instance, could successfully follow none but roads already marked. Larive redeemed what he lacked in genius by less roughness than his master, and by a more dignified style. He had learnt well what had been taught him, and was able to teach it to others; and our tragic stage will, no doubt, have more Larives.

But Talma, the child, so to say, of himself, having displayed no true talent till the day when he had forgotten his teachers, could not bequeath to his successors his own originality. The course which Lekain opened, Talma closed; genius has no pupils. In default of this merit he had at least that of arousing the enthusiasm of the world during thirty years, and of having substituted costumes of some probability for the ridiculous get-up of old days, so that we no longer see Roman emperors in powder, Greeks in silk stockings and pumps, or gods in knee-breeches.

When we left the table, Junot took me aside and said, "Well, are you sulking?"

"No, indeed; but I cannot call upon anyone except people from whom I have nothing to get."

"Those that don't ask, don't want. However good your cause may be, you have got to plead it. How do you stand?"

I explained.

"Come now, be at the First Consul's tomorrow at nine, and wait for me if you are there first."

"Thanks; but please tell me which staircase I must go up by?"

"Do you mean to say you have not set foot in the Tuileries?"

"Not yet."

"In that case," he said, with a smile, "you must go up by the staircase in the Pavilion de l'Horloge, and tell the doorkeepers from me to let you go into the room where the First Consul receives my reports."

As will be seen, no one could be kinder.

Next morning I was at the Tuileries at five minutes to nine. My explanation to the usher was brief, and I was shown in. At nine came General Mortier, commanding the first military district. A minute later, Junot had joined us, and he had hardly done so when the First Consul appeared. After a glance which took in all the room, and only rested on me as on something unexpected, he went up to Mortier, and all the while he listened to him continued to stride about, taking pinch after pinch of snuff. Meanwhile I stood motionless near one corner of the great room, and Junot stayed by the fireplace.

After receiving a few papers, also some explanations or reports, to which he replied only by motions of the head or by monosyllables which I did not catch, the First Consul halted rather near me and exclaimed, "More attacks on coaches? more robberies of public money? And cannot anyone think of any way to stop these crimes?" And when Mortier—agreeably to the saying, "*A big mortar has a short range*" (he is six feet high)—made no reply, the First Consul resumed his walk, continuing in a loud voice, with short intervals after every clause and emphasis on every word:

The tops of the coaches must be made into a kind of little

forts. Parapets must be formed with thick narrow mattresses, loopholes made in them, and as many soldiers, all good shots, as there is room for, placed behind them. Come, general, see that these orders are carried out quickly.

When Mortier retired, Junot approached the First Consul, who, after listening a moment to him and making no answer, came abruptly to me and said, "You are General Thiébault?"

At first, not seeing his meaning, I could hardly repress a half-smile, for it seemed odd that he should appear to ask if I was what I came to request him to make me: but it called for the answer which I was eager to give, "To be so, General Consul, I require your confirmation."

"You may count on it." Now was the moment to express my gratitude, my profound loyalty, and my respect. "So you are at Paris?"

"On leave, but ready to start for Italy again."

"That we shall see. Good morning, General Thiébault."

In this brief but complete colloquy I was put, thanks to Junot, to no great expense in the way of eloquence and pleading. Also the First Consul said not a word about Genoa or my *Journal*; but by his opening affirmation rather than interrogation, "You are General Thiébault," avoided any need on my part for saying how I was so, or rather through whom I was so, which I only understood when turning over the details of the interview in my memory.

Before three days had elapsed from this audience, I received official advice that my rank was confirmed, and that from the date of the 10th *Floréal*, Year VIII (April 30, 1800); that is, from the day on which I had earned the step by the recapture of Fort Quezzi at Genoa. I at once called on General Masséna, not to speak of the audience I had had, but to thank him anew. From him I went to Junot, and finally to the Minister for War, with the double object of thanking him for the promptitude with which the matter had been settled and of knowing whether, when my leave expired, I was to carry out the order which it contained to return to Milan, or whether fresh orders would be necessary. Berthier replied: "I do not know what are the First Consul's intentions with regard to you, but you must wait till he is pleased to make them known."

"Could you not, general, do me the favour of representing to him how anxious I am to justify his recent kindness, and to find myself again as soon as possible on the scene of his immortal campaign beyond the Alps?"

"I will speak to him about it." He did speak to him, but when I saw him again he told me that the First Consul had answered nothing but: "General Thiébault may be easy; I will attend to him when the time comes." It seemed to me that nothing was less calculated to put me at my ease. The agreement of the reply with that which the First Consul had made to me directly, "We shall see that," when I asked him if I had to start again for Italy, gave me a glimpse of a decided intention to send me somewhere else.

Not long after this I was asked to dine at the Tuileries; naturally I could not refuse, and made a point of appearing as contented as possible. Among the guests were the Russian General Sprechporten and the Marquis Lucchesini. After dinner, when we returned into the drawing-room, which afterwards became the throne-room, the First Consul, in his red coat with gold embroidery, was wearing for the first time hung to a cross-belt a sword which he had had set with the finest diamonds belonging to France, the Sancy on the pommel and the Regent on the guard: in short, he was exactly as he is represented in the picture that he had painted at that time and gave to the Second Consul.

Noticing how attentively people were looking at this sword, he said, taking it out of the belt, "You see, gentlemen, the sword of the Head of the French government: it contains diamonds to the value of 14 million *francs*." When Lucchesini came forward to get a nearer view of it, Bonaparte put it in his hands, from his hands it passed to mine, from mine to those of General Sprechporten and other people present. I do not know how the momentary possession of that ornament felt to them, but I had, after the first surprise was over, the sensation of holding in my hands the symbol of a new spirit, the glorification of a military force as figured in the inconceivable wealth lavished on a sword.

Talking about General Sprechporten, I forget with whom and about what I was chatting when he came and joined in our conversation, and in reference to some date took the liberty of saying, "Yes, that was the time when the French invaded the kingdom of Naples." He was alluding to Championnet's campaign, and it was an extreme shock to hear the word in the mouth of a Kalmuck.

"General," I rejoined, "I beg your pardon, but it is only hordes that invade; the armies of civilised nations conquer."

"Ah! yes, conquer," he replied. The same general expressed himself more fortunately in another place: being unable to check a gesture at the moment when Masséna was introduced to him at the War Office, he had the happy thought of putting his gesture right by these words:

> You cannot fail, general, to understand my surprise; it is but natural on one's first meeting with the first man since Charles XII who has had the honour to beat the armies of Russia.

One night about this time Rivierre carried me off to the opera ball. It was an important business for him, for me a curiosity. Nobody expected me there or attracted me, while he was running I do not know how many amorous intrigues at once. As soon as he appeared various masks set upon him, competing for the first place. In fact, he was so charming, sparkling with wit, always laughing, at once elegant and athletic in build, that it was natural that a number of women should wish to take possession of him. "I have some very amusing things to tell you," cried one. "I've got some that will please you finely," cried another. He did not know which to listen to, and as they all dragged him right and left he kept saying, with a laugh, "Pray fight for the possession of me; I will be the prize of victory."

Called upon to answer for myself, I soon lost sight of him. The first mask who attacked me said that when one managed the affairs of one's country so well one ought to think of one's own, but that I treated my fortune as I did my old friends. Except for the last reproach, that might be true; anyhow there was no wit and no point about it, and nothing to puzzle me seriously. The scene changed, however, when I was engaged with a second mask; it was impossible to employ the jargon of masked balls more prettily, more smartly, or more maliciously. There was a rolling fire of it, but what upset me was that there was no business, no interest, no private thought of mine of which that confounded little mask did not speak to me, and in the wittiest and maddest fashion. I thought of every device to guess who was the charming fairy that I had to answer,—all was useless; I only got baffled in the most extraordinary way.

Just when she might have been boasting of having managed the most successful mystification, she was accosted by another mask and went off. However, if I was rid of her she was not rid of me. I did not lose sight of her, but followed her till I reached the door of exit. She got into her carriage with her companion; and although I was very hot, and it was snowing, and I had no time to fetch my overcoat, I was determined to follow my fortune-teller. Luckily she lived in the

Rue Neuve des Bons Enfants, so I soon got there, and just in time for her confusion, when, having taken off her mask, she found me at the door, and had to take my hand to alight from her carriage. One of the ladies was Mme Clavier, the charming wife of the Greek scholar; the other her friend Mme Winch, both of them acquainted with Rivierre, through whom the one who had talked to me, Mme Clavier, had got such accurate information of all that concerned me.

Besides opera balls, I have many other memories of festivities connected with that period. Our victories at home and abroad, the definitive abandonment of the coalition by Russia, the pacification of La Vendée and the peace on the Continent, the end of anarchy and the return to order, all formed as it were a new era, while the power of Bonaparte seemed to restore universal confidence. The moment had therefore come for recalling Paris to pleasure and luxury, and to this end General Berthier, Minister for War, gave a party consisting of a dramatic performance and a grand ball. It was the first thing of the kind at which the First Consul and his family had been present; and invitations had been sent out in immense numbers, to show the general adhesion to and enthusiasm for the new government and its head. Astonishment, curiosity, the novelty of the thing, made everyone accept; the concourse was beyond calculation.

Had there not been so many thousands of witnesses, one would fear to be accused of hoaxing when one says that carriages emerging from the Pont Royal at nine did not reach the War Office till four in the morning; that one person living in the Rue du Bac was three hours advancing and backing before he could get out of his front gate and take his place in the line; and that in that same terrible street all the pies, cold meat, cake, bread, even saveloys, that were to be found in the Faubourg Saint-Germain, were eaten, by masters and servants alike, during the long and repeated halts. One poor lady, who had left her baby and come as a matter of duty, stayed an hour at the ball, and could not get her carriage till she had waited in the first room for three hours, crying so that everybody pitied her.

It was arranged that I should escort a certain Mme Texier to this ball; her friend Michele Lagreca, who had left Naples with our army, being the third. The fourth place was taken by Trénis, the most wonderful society dancer that has ever lived. He was the man who, wishing to express the full grace and softness of the dance, averred that it was "like oil flowing over roses." Someone said to him: "Monsieur Trénis, I saw you dancing yesterday."

He replied quite simply, "Had you a good place for seeing?" Yet, in spite of these specimens of affectation and coxcombry, Trénis was none the less a very good fellow, a charming man, well-mannered and witty, deservedly liked, and sought for, even fought for, all round. Poor fellow! he ended his days a lunatic at Bicêtre, in abject poverty.

After some delay by the block in the streets, during which Trénis kept us diverted with his conversation and anecdotes, we succeeded in gaining admission by the help of a friendly officer of *gendarmerie*, into the line of official carriages, and arrived just as the play was over, and the First Consul was passing from the room that had served as theatre into the ballroom. I was in his path, and he gave me one of the most unpleasant looks I ever had from him. Till then great simplicity in dress had been usual, and this was quite to my taste.

I did not like and never have liked luxury, and had gone to this ball in a new uniform, but without embroidery. Now Bonaparte, while retaining the simplest style of dress himself, wished to make an impression by the magnificence of those around him, and of all who belonged to his government. Thus his *aides-de-camp*, his ministers, and nearly all his generals were covered with gold and embroidery even to excess, making loyalty and policy an excuse for vanity.

Amid all this state, my costume, I must own, was a trifle modest; and owing to the contrast, I even seemed to advertise a kind of contempt for the ideas which the First Consul adopted, and for the deference which he required. The day at Saint-Cloud must have persuaded him of this; and from the date of this ball he showed towards me a little more of the ill-humour which in a Corsican was bound to last for ever. I thought next day that it would have been better if our carriage had remained in the string, or if we had not met the obliging *gendarme*.

My old commander, the Count of Valence, was one of the first to be struck off the list of those "who had gone abroad," and I heard that he had returned to France and was in Paris. I called on him, and was much touched with the pleasure he seemed to feel at seeing me again. He invited me to dinner the next day, and introduced me to his aunt the Duchess of Montesson, with whom he was staying. One evening there was a large party at her house, including Count Metternich and Mme de Staël. I had been saying a few words to Mme de Montesson, and as I moved away Mme de Staël, who was sitting near, and whom I had never seen before, said, "Who is that general?"

Mme de Montesson replied, "That is General Thiébault," to which

Mme de Staël, who had heard imperfectly, and saw me with more than indulgent eyes, returned, "Of course I see that he is handsome (*beau*), but I ask what is his name."

Thereupon a laugh went round the ladies; and as they looked at me, I could not pretend not to see that I was the object of their fits of contagious laughter. Indeed I was so puzzled that I asked the reason of them; and thus I was able to make sure that in consequence of this little misunderstanding the nickname of "General *Très-beau*" should not—as someone tried to insinuate it did—stick to me. It was not true, especially in the superlative, and would have hugely annoyed me.

Among the frequenters of Mme de Montesson's drawing-room I one day heard the name of the Duke of Guines. It could, not fail to recall the brilliant duke, mentioned in the early part of these *Memoirs*, who acted as my godfather, being at that time ambassador from France at the Prussian court. I could not believe that the little, lean, puny old man whom I saw, banished as it were to the recess of a window in that sumptuous room, was identical with the most vigorous of our colonels, the most showy of our ambassadors,—the man who, having taken offence at something or other, had dared to appear before Frederick the Great in a morning-coat and a round hat, with a riding-whip, in his hand. I begged M. de Valence to tell me what the relation was between this M. de Guines and the ambassador. "What relation? Only that of identity."

On my exclaiming in surprise, M. de Valence questioned me, and learnt that I knew the duke in right of being his godson: whereupon he took my hand, and, leading me up to him, said, "Duke, let me present to you one for whom you are answerable before God."

I never saw anything like the change that came over the duke's, face. "*I* am answerable, Count?" said he, in a tone of positive dismay, hardly venturing to look at me in my general's uniform. The count, having explained who I was and added some kindly words, left us, and I did my best to put the old gentleman at his ease, but could not succeed in doing so. When I told him how glad my father would be to hear of him, and no less anxious than I was myself to pay his respects, he merely repeated that he would come to see us, and bade me give his compliments to my father. I left him, much saddened by the sight of the wreck of a man once so brilliant.

When I imparted my feelings to the Count of Valence, he owned that only a fragment survived of the man whom I had known. He added:

> Time and misfortunes have helped to break him down. He is very badly off; lives in rooms that are something less than plain, and is waited on only by a single woman, who takes him every morning to Mass and sometimes to friends' houses, whence she brings him home like a child.

Two days afterwards my father and I left our names at his house, and before long we heard of his death.

I had stayed in Paris longer than I had thought possible, when people began to talk of the formation of a corps of observation in the Gironde. It was assembling between the Garonne and the Bidassoa, under the command of General Leclerc, brother-in-law to the First Consul. Soon afterwards we heard of the concentration of a corps at Poitiers, and simultaneously that a squadron, under Admiral Bruix, was collecting at Rochefort. Public opinion pointed to Portugal as the object of these preparations. At the same time I received orders to go to Poitiers and take command of the troops who were arriving there, and of whom a statement was sent me. I further had instructions to the effect that I was at once to see to the provision of all that might be deficient in clothing, equipment, and arms, or in men and horses, for all battalions, squadrons, and batteries, in order to bring them into a condition for active service.

Chapter 5

Quarrel with My Chief

As I posted to Poitiers, I subjected myself to a sort of examination, to get an idea of the judgement likely to be formed of me by the *vox populi*, which in the case of soldiers is, unquestionably, the *vox Dei*. I considered that general officers came in contact with the men in four principal ways: first, as concerns material needs of the troops; secondly, in regard to order and discipline; thirdly, in manoeuvres; fourthly, in direct command on the march and in presence of the enemy.

Under the first of these heads, I felt confident of evincing enough interest in and care for my troops to ensure their speedy gratitude and attachment. So far as the second went, I would not gratuitously insult them by supposing that they would not appreciate the necessity for order, punctuality, and discipline; and as I meant to make a point of being just, I hoped for success here also. But as regarded the third point, that of manoeuvres, I might have more cause for anxiety, having never had occasion to direct any of those complicated evolutions, so useful for keeping troops on the drill-ground, or as a distraction in the leisure of peace or in garrison life, but of no use in war.

I have, in the course of twenty campaigns, been engaged in two hundred or more combats, and the manoeuvres I have seen performed in presence of the enemy may be reduced to very few: flank marches, formation from line into column and column into line, two or three changes of front, once only—on the eve of the Battle of Austerlitz—a march by regimental squares, and a few other momentary formations of the same nature; marches in line, one or two movements in *échelon*, once a movement in *échelon* in squares. All these simple manoeuvres I had always regarded as indispensable, and they were familiar to me. But, as I was going on active service, the elegances of drill-ground evolutions did not seem essential in presence of the enemy, and I felt at ease.

In regard to marching, choice of position for attack or defence, or the management of an action, I had seen too much of these to he much afraid; and, besides, they were my constant subject of study. Indeed, when I was travelling, or even taking a walk, I never saw any natural feature without considering how I would attack or defend it, with any kind or number of troops, and at any hour of the day or night. Thus I felt myself sufficiently prepared to meet my troops from all these points of view; and as I had sufficient power of talking to be able to impress them, I saw no reason for aught but confidence.

Soon after reaching Poitiers, I received a letter from Admiral Bruix, commanding the fleet at Rochefort, in which he asked for information as to a part of the corps which I had under me. The correspondence soon grew brisk, and he mentioned that, in one of his letters to the First Consul, he had congratulated himself on having to deal with me. Very soon came an order to place at his disposal any troops that he might require, and some of them began at once to move towards Rochefort. I was wondering more and more what the result of this displacement would be to me, when I received, on May 5, an order, issued directly from Malmaison, bidding me embark for a destination which I should only learn when 250 miles at sea. It was a confidential mission, and I was assured the expedition would not be very distant.

Just at this time my *aide-de-camp* had made friends with a M. Dupaty, a young man who had an enthusiasm for military service and for me. He sent me word that if I would take him, and would do my best to get him a commission, he would come with me as a volunteer, and do the duties of orderly officer. "But," I answered, "does he know the rumours current about the expedition?"

"He says that he could put up with a conquest of Brazil; that he would not like Egypt at all; but that he would be delighted with a landing in Portugal, where he would be the foremost in making advances to the Portuguese ladies."

At this point he came in himself, and repeated the proposal with so much gaiety and so much resolution that I told him he would be welcome, and that I would do all in my power to open a career to him in which he seemed likely to distinguish himself.

In pursuance of my orders, I had sent all the rest of my troops, some to Bordeaux, some to Rochefort, whither I myself went to take command of those who were to sail in Admiral Bruix' fleet. An orderly met me there, and took me to the lodging that the admiral had secured for me. I called on him at once, and was most kindly received.

He spoke of the troops I had sent, and of their fine condition; of the staff-officers attached to the expedition, and of General d'Houdetot, who commanded under him; of the fleet, of his most distinguished captains, of the *Foudroyant*,[1] on board of which I was to be; of his hope to be under sail in eight or ten days, in spite of the English cruiser, which, however, caused him no small anxiety. All this was said with remarkable energy, not by a sailor such as we generally fancy them—sturdy, sunburnt, forbidding—of the type of General Duperré, but by a little, thin, pale, puny man, almost hairless, who made me think of a plucked parrot, or of a corpse that had forgotten to cease living.

As I was about to take leave of him, he said: "General, I reckoned on your doing me the honour to dine with me; and I have asked an *aide-de-camp* of the First Consul, General Savary, to meet you." I was delighted to see once more my old comrade of the Armies of the Rhine and of Rome. The captain of the *Foudroyant* was also there. After a merry dinner we went with the admiral to the theatre. We were chatting in his box after the first piece, when a quarrel broke out in the pit between a naval officer and a group of local persons. All the other naval officers in the boxes rushed to the aid of their comrade. The admiral, who, with the liveliness of a midshipman, was very near jumping down from his box, dashed off with all of us, I being followed by all the military officers. Swords were already drawn, and we arrived just in time to stop a very unseemly scuffle.

Four days after my arrival an 80-gun ship was launched. It was a beautiful day, and the crowd was immense. When the stays had been cut, the ladies trembled for the carpenter whose duty it was to knock away the last shore. Their fears were needless. The huge hull remained an instant motionless, then slid slowly on the well-soaped ways, and, suddenly gaining speed, shot like lightning across the Charente, and stuck—more than fifteen feet of her—in the mud of the opposite bank. Cheers arose, no doubt because she had not capsized; but she cut a doleful figure, stuck in the mud as though cast away. A hundred yoke of oxen were attached to the stern, and in this way she was pulled out, and went off to Oléron to be fitted.

Savary went home with me, and we were chatting—I forget in what connection—about my works. He spoke of what he was kind enough to call my capability, and of the enthusiasm which I naturally possessed, and which the First Consul was so well fitted to stimulate.

---

1. [Not to be confused with the *Foudroyant* captured from the French in 1758, which did good service throughout the war against her former owners.]

"There is no man of your kind about him," he added. "You would share usefully in our duties; but besides that, you might be collecting materials for the history of that great man, which are every day perishing irretrievably."

"What prevents you from collecting them yourself?" I said.

"You would do it better than I, and, besides, I am always running about. But on what terms are you with the First Consul?" I told him the business of the 18th *Brumaire*, and reminded him of the line I had taken at Rome against Berthier. He thought these bad antecedents, but still did not give up his first idea, and left me under the impression that he would try to get me attached to the First Consul. That is all I have ever known. If he did take any steps, they remained without result, as they were bound to do. There are some chances, of which one never again picks up the thread if one has once dropped it. And yet it depended on this alone that the *Memorial of St. Helena* did not begin with the century.

A few days after this, orders were given to take all the baggage on board. My *aides-de-camp* saw to the transport, and I passed all day and most of the night writing. Towards four in the morning I fell asleep, and did not wake till nine, when I heard that the embarkation was put off. I went to Savary's, and found him sitting by the fire and reading, very thoughtfully, a letter from the First Consul—four pages long, and all in his own writing, if that word may be used to express letters all distorted, words all abbreviated, and lines all aslant. I sat down at Savary's bidding on the other side of the fireplace. For himself, after finishing the letter, reading it over again with equal attention, making some notes, unintelligible to anyone but himself, and casting his eyes once more over two passages, he stretched out the hand in which he held it, and dropped it into the fire. "What are you doing?" I exclaimed.

"What my orders prescribe. Letters written by the First Consul himself are wholly confidential; and as the contents must not be known by any other person than those to whom they are addressed, they have to be destroyed as soon as read."

"Truly," I said, "the idea of not preserving such historic relics for one's children, existing or to come, quite upsets me. Besides, you give orders and act according to the tenor of these letters; and as the First Consul surely does not write himself," I added with a smile, "for the pleasure of writing, and the object of the letter is clearly important, how would you put yourself right in the event of an omission on his part, or a mistake made by you owing to an ambiguity?"

"I do not trouble myself about all that," said Savary. "As for my responsibility, so long as I leave no doubt as to my boundless devotion, that is all I care about; while, as to any children that I may have, the example of that devotion is the only thing I am anxious about leaving them."

I was struck with the remark, which I have often recalled. Without it Savary's life will be impossible to understand; with it, that life becomes wholly consistent.

To change the subject, he asked about my own doings. I admitted that I did not like the orders to embark. I was irked by being put in a position superior to General d'Houdetot, my senior by twenty years, while my father's age and the situation of my family tied me to the mainland. "Nothing but duty would make one go to sea," said Savary, "if one is not a naval officer. As to d'Houdetot, the admiral has never been fair to him, and I can understand that, though he has only praise for your conduct, the position cannot be pleasant to him. Well, write to the First Consul, saying nothing to make him think you do not want to sail, but confining yourself to stating as simply and briefly as possible how you stand with regard to d'Houdetot. My messenger goes in two hours, and will take your letter."

In a week Savary and the admiral, who had also written, had answers. General d'Houdetot resumed command of the expeditionary force, and I rejoined the headquarters of the corps of observation in the Gironde, commonly called "The Army of Portugal." I called, with Savary, on the admiral, who had already sent me my orders, but was none the less; annoyed at my departure.

"When do you leave us?" said he.

"At midnight."

However, he insisted that I should dine with him, but our dinner was grave.

At the port I was attacked by the masters of two vessels offering to take me to Bordeaux. The one I chose, as the fastest, had not a good record. She had capsized in the previous year, drowning all on board but one man, on the very passage I was about to make. Nowadays I should select the other; one holds tighter to life the nearer it is to taking flight. We spun along, laid over till sailors and passengers had to lie flat on their stomachs; but, thanks to the breeze, leaving Royan at four in the morning, we were in Bordeaux as it struck two in the afternoon.

I passed a quarter of an hour with General Leclerc before his departure for Bayonne. Leclerc, who was brother to Davout's wife, was also brother-in-law of the First Consul by his marriage with Pauline Bonaparte. His manner had more of self-sufficiency than of dignity. It cannot be denied that he was a clever man, nor, at the same time, that he was far inferior to the position he held and the opinion that he had of himself. A proof of this is that having, except for the colour of his hair, a certain resemblance in face, figure, thinness, and general cut, to the Bonaparte of that period, he had got the idea that to render the identity quite complete he needed only to copy his postures, manner, and gestures.

Thus he held himself and walked like his famous brother-in-law, put his hands behind his back like him, and talked in brief and jerky sentences. He tried to imitate his looks, his smiles, the movements of his lips, with the result of substituting grimaces for that incomparable play of feature which often decided a man's fate before a word had been uttered. He had his boots and clothes cut in the same style, even to the grey overcoat and the monumental hat, which he put on his head in such a fashion that the whole of the First Consul—except the man himself—was accurately reproduced in the "blond Bonaparte," as he was called.

As I have said, my interview with him was but momentary. Nearly all the troops were already at Bayonne, and he himself was starting to lead the first division. All that happened was that I was put in command of the two last regiments, and told to bring them on to join the headquarters at Rodrigo.

Besides my *aide-de-camp* Richebourg, and Dupaty, abovementioned, I had three travelling companions. One was Texier, the husband of the lady whose name has already occurred. He was the son of a rich merchant of Bordeaux, but had quarrelled with his family. The others were Delost, a kind of ill-built Hercules, who, in consequence of several duels, had already had to pass some time in Spain, where he had become a leading spirit among a band of smugglers, and Delpech, the son of a nobleman of Périgord. His father had forbidden him to go abroad, and also to take service on the staff of the Count of Valence; so he had become contractor-in-chief to the Army of the North. He was a man of calm demeanour and elegant appearance, but of extraordinary energy and activity of mind.

In April 1795, as *aide-de-camp* to Pichegru, he had given vigorous assistance in suppressing the revolts of the *faubourgs*. Once, in reply to some insulting remark, he sent a challenge to Sébastiani, who has since become more celebrated than illustrious. His seconds were Junot and Kerbourg; but his reputation as a swordsman decided the valiant Sebastian! to substitute the most humble apology for arrogant insult, and even to offer a written reparation, which Delpech disdained. A person who continued Marat's *Ami du Peuple* attacked him in one of his numbers. Delpech went to see him, but got only threats and renewed insults. He then got together the fifty soundest pensioners to be found at the Invalides, made them drunk, armed some of them with hunting whips, divided them into two bands, went to the journalist's office, had him thrashed within an inch of his life, and his presses thrown out of window. He escaped all pursuit, and even succeeded in putting them on a false scent as to the perpetrator of the chastisement.

Anyone who crossed the Landes at the time of which I am speaking cannot have forgotten their sands, into which the carriage wheels used to sink up to the naves. The recollection is all the more lasting because this lifeless, desert, monotonous region, which produces nothing but pines, and has no crop but turpentine, is suddenly succeeded by a picturesque and fertile country, to the west of which, where the Nive and Adour meet, stands the capital of the most lively, gayest, and most active of peoples, not less remarkable for the beauty of the inhabitants than for the gayness of their costumes.

When we left Bayonne on June 7, 1801, the younger members of our party were determined to try panniers, as the saddles are called that have seats attached on either side of them, so as to enable every horse to carry two persons. Naturally it is necessary to balance the weight of the persons, an arrangement which, reckoning them as meat by the pound, paired Richebourg with Dupaty, Texier with Delost. Delpech and I were content with a horse saddled in the usual way apiece. In this way we went I do not know how many leagues at a smart trot without being able to outstrip the two Basques from whom we hired our horses, and who went with us to bring them back. They appeared to feel neither fatigue nor shortness of breath, in spite of the speed and length of the journey, and the proverb *"to go like a Basque"* seemed to us more than justified.

We liked the panniers much; it is a pleasant way of travelling side by side with a person to whom one can talk at one's ease. Nothing seems to me better to show the turn of these people's minds, their need of intercourse, and, I may add, their confidence in each other; for if by a trick such as Richebourg played on Dupaty one of the two occupants of the pannier jumps suddenly from his seat, the other necessarily goes head over heels.

Towards the end of the day, when we left Bayonne, intending to join our carriages at Saint Jean de Luz and my brigade at Irun, it began to rain. We had been otherwise delayed, and the bad condition of the road impeded our progress still more. On approaching the Bidassoa, which we did not reach till ten in the evening, we even had to alight to relieve our carriage-horses, and we were put out by all these delays when some custom-house officers came up to us. One of them, with the air of barring a passage which no one thought of forcing, put his left fist against my breast. I cannot exactly say how it happened, but his paw had hardly come in contact with my body when a cut of a cane across his face overturned him in the mud. Cries of "To arms!" at once resounded, and thirty men with their muskets at once surrounded us. Our first reply was to burst out laughing, which disconcerted them to begin with; but as an end had to be made of the affair, I asked for the officer in command, who came forward.

I knew that he and his men had been bribed to allow contraband goods to the value of a million and a half to pass out of France into Spain. I threatened to inform against him, and further demanded that our carriages should be searched, and that the name of the official who had behaved insolently to me should be given up to me. I made no use of the name, but, in order to anticipate any consequences of my threats, the officer lodged a complaint on his side, addressed to the Minister for War, which meant that it came into the hands of my friend Lomet. He threw it in the fire, but persuaded my father to write and advise me to behave with more moderation. In this way I contracted a debt towards these officials, payment of which had necessarily to be postponed till my return to France.

Reaching San Sebastian, where we stayed twenty-four hours, we went on to Tolosa, at the junction of the roads to Navarre and Castile; from this point I did not again leave my troops. At Vitoria I reviewed them in the square where the bull-fights are held. At Miranda we crossed the Ebro. We passed the night at Burgos, and so on to Valladolid, where my quarters were in the house of a canon of Santiago, a wealthy man living in very handsome style. He was extremely polite and good-natured, and insisted on our dining with him. The first day we were alone, but on the following day all the most distinguished people of Valladolid were asked to meet us, notably the Grand Inquisitor, with whom I had much interesting conversation.

After dinner I touched upon the subject of the Inquisition, speaking, as may be supposed, not in the tone of one who was attacking, but as one seeking information. I admitted, all the same, that that morning we had visited and been not unmoved by the judgement-hall and one of the dungeons of the Inquisition. I spared him, however, the strong language which that visit had elicited from us, and said nothing about the pranks of Dupaty, who had sat down on the judges' bench, and put on one of their four-cornered caps, afterwards assuming a doleful demeanour as he took his place on the seat of the victims.

My Grand Inquisitor kept up his part; he was a clever man, and being forced by his cloth to justify the hateful institution of which he was an official, he showed much tact in appealing against what he called the falsehoods retailed on that subject. Talking about the authors who had said most in condemnation of the Inquisition, I was able, almost naturally, to bring in the question, "Do you know the *Compère Mathieu?*" [2]

He started, but I had put so much good humour into my tone and my look that he recovered himself, and answered, "I have heard of the work, but never had the chance of reading it."

Emboldened by his phrase "the chance," I rejoined, "I must make full allowance for your superior talent and your lofty position to venture to add that the passage seems to me, nevertheless, well worth your knowing; if you like to come as far as my room, I will put the volume containing it in your hands, and you can look over it." He hesitated, but not wishing to give me a right to say that he either lacked self-control or was dull, he followed me. In my room I took the edition of the book which I had with me, opened it at the page where the passage begins, and withdrew. After time enough to have read it through the Grand Inquisitor reappeared in the drawing-room. To pursue the subject further would have been in excess of the limits of propriety, so we had no more asides on the subject, and he seemed to appreciate my delicacy. After all, I lost nothing by it so far as regarded the pleasure of having made a Grand Inquisitor read that formidable chapter.

On the road to Nava del Rey, the day being very hot, our party, travelling in carriages, had fallen considerably in rear of the column, when an alarm of brigands was raised. We were warned of an impending attack by the "great band "as it was called, but I refused to go

---

2. [A somewhat famous attack on Christianity written by the Abbé Dulaurens, and published in 1765. It was written in so vigorous and pungent a style that it was at first ascribed to Voltaire.]

back, thinking it unlikely that brigands would venture upon a road on which the tracks of a strong column were still visible. Instead of this, I adopted the plan of compelling every person whom we saw to join our caravan. Casual passers-by, peasants on their way home from gathering wood, even a priest on his mule, were pressed into the service, until we reached the number of sixty persons, which, with our horses and carriages, looked almost like a column on the march.

On reaching Nava I sent for the *corregidor*, to inquire about the band, and why no steps were taken to destroy it. I learnt that it consisted of 300 men, and had already fought several engagements. Although some hundred men belonging to it were now awaiting their trial in the prison of Nava, it had been lately recruited, and had just beaten two detachments of the king's troops. It had levied several thousand *reals* in that province, and was the terror of the countryside. Just now it was hanging about Nava, in the hope of breaking into the prison and freeing its comrades. "And what means," said I, "have you for frustrating the scheme?"

"Not much," he replied; "but I have made up my mind, and am all ready with what I have. And I have told the chief that if he attacks, I shall begin by hamstringing all the prisoners."[3]

Here is another characteristic touch of the Spanish of that period. One of my battalions reached a village—I forget what—just as one of the principal houses had happened to catch fire. The inhabitants, on their knees before the church door and about the streets, were seeking to extinguish the fire by prayer. The officer commanding the battalion called a halt, and detached one hundred men without their arms to get the fire under, compelling the inhabitants to help. In this way he saved the village, and the inhabitants, in course of time, understood the service that had been done them.

A deputation, headed by the parson and the *corregidor*, came in due form to thank the officer; in spite of which, three unlucky soldiers of the battalion, who had been left behind when it moved on, were murdered on leaving the village next morning, though they had given no cause for complaint. More than a hundred others shared the same fate in the course of that campaign, though there was no question of a revolution in Spain. We were the king's allies against Portugal, and were to have fought under the orders of the Prince of the Peace, of

---

3. M. Delpech reminds me of this characteristic anecdote, which I had forgotten, and also that the word used, which made us laugh a good deal, was *descortezar*. [If so, the *corregidor's* threat was to *flay* his prisoners!]

whose army we formed the right wing,[4] nor did my force ever maintain stricter discipline.

Salamanca, which I reached on June 26, might have been expected to offer more interest than that of a night's rest; but the headquarters were at Ciudad Rodrigo, and I was in a hurry to get there, and see how I should be treated by a chief who, as an army-leader, was not indeed very formidable, but could be decidedly so for subordinates whom he did not like. I had reason to be fully satisfied with his reception of me. After a few words on my journey and on the state of the troops whom I brought with me, he added that he had three infantry divisions, commanded by generals of my rank, but all my seniors, and offered me the advance-guard, consisting of three infantry regiments, one of *chasseurs*, and six guns. Its right rested on Fort Concepcion, its left on the Sierra de Francia. The headquarters were to be at Gallegos, a village near the centre of the line. The Portuguese army, numerous, though not of much value, was not to be lost sight of, and I was to keep the general posted up with all the information I could gain about it.

I took the opportunity of calling upon various officers, including Mesny, the paymaster of the army, whose acquaintance I had made at Épinal in 1792, when we used to practise music together; and the excellent La Salle, whom I never met without fresh pleasure. Next morning, just when I was about leaving Rodrigo, I learnt that General Gouvion Saint-Cyr was in the place, though holding no avowed position of authority, nor discharging any recognised duties. What could the presence of a general of his calibre, in apparent inactivity, in a sort of incognito, mean? I was not long in doubt; he was an adviser to decide upon operations in the event of war. Nothing could be better calculated to sustain the confidence of the troops; but what was the price set upon this obliging conduct, this sacrifice beforehand of glory which could be due only to the adviser, and would be reaped by: the advised? A war alone could have answered that question, and, as it happened, we did not fire a single round; but it is known that the mere good intentions were rewarded by an embassy. Anyhow, though on the point of leaving Rodrigo, I went to pay my respects to Saint-Cyr. He talked only of Italy and Rome, and avoided everything connected with the subjects of which he might most naturally have spoken, with

---

4. [This is not strictly correct, for the treaty of Badajoz had been signed some weeks before, and the war between Spain and Portugal was at an end. Godoy by no means desired French "help" at this time.]

General Leclerc, or our army, or Spain and the Portuguese.

I inspected the troops at Gallegos the day after my arrival and, visited Fort Concepcion, which, having been recently constructed and restored, looked more like a sugar-plum box than a military work. I was not satisfied with the situation of the regiment on my left, encamped at the foot of the Francia Hill, and the officer in command of it said that his position was deplorable, but that it had been selected by the commander-in-chief himself, and he did not see how to change it without orders from him. However, as on reconnoitring the hill I found an admirable position above its lower spurs, preferring the risk of a reprimand to that of totally losing the regiment, I at once established it on the higher ground. Then, in order to have a clear notion of the strength and position of the Portuguese Army in front of us, such as, if necessary, to justify to the commander-in-chief my shifting of the regiment, and hearing that more than a league intervened between their advanced posts and their camp, I crossed the line of outposts with 125 cavalry at an ordinary trot, stopping at the villages to get intelligence.

In this way I went some seven miles between the enemy's outposts and his main army, and returned to Gallegos by way of Fort Concepcion without having received a shot or exchanged a sword-cut. The Portuguese Army was all in movement behind me, and I decided to pass the night with all my troops under arms, the guns harnessed and the cavalry ready to mount. But it was doing our enemy too much honour; that extraordinary reconnoissance had frightened rather than emboldened them. They did not forget it, though, for when I was at Lisbon in December 1807, the Marquis of Alorna, the youngest general in that army, and the only one worth anything, spoke to me about it. He added, "We ought to have taken you prisoner."

"That is true," I answered, laughing. "It was not a fair match, for I was playing thirty-one years against fifteen hundred"—the sum of their generals' united ages. However, if I got off well as regarded the Portuguese Army, it was not so as regarded Leclerc, who was not best pleased with the lesson I had given him in full view of the troops. He said nothing about that, but got his compensation by disapproving my trip through the Portuguese Army. Yet, from a military point of view, I was right enough.

Our stay at Gallegos was not entertaining in itself, but we had plenty of cigars, and smoked like chimneys. My companions were amiable and amusing—Richebourg the inexhaustible; Dupaty in a state of permanent enthusiasm and exaggeration; another *aide-de-camp*, Fréhot, a dull man, but a good butt; and Texier, who, though eccentric at times, was a good-natured fellow and sang admirably. Without these distractions our tranquillity would have been lethargy. As we were awaiting the end of it, I received an order from General Leclerc to come to Rodrigo, and preside over a court of revision,, to consider the case of a soldier condemned to death by a court-martial, a kind of duty that has always been repugnant to me. When I arrived, the commander-in-chief took me aside, and enlarged on the need of giving the army an example—that is, on the necessity for confirming the sentence. All that I could say was, that if the condemned had deserved his sentence it would be confirmed. However, in spite of the efforts of one member of the court, the man was acquitted. The result of the verdict was a lively scene between the commander-in-chief and myself, which sent me back to Gallegos in a bad temper, to keep the festival of July 14.

I thought I had done with this trying kind of work, but I was wrong. Soon afterwards another man, belonging to the military train, was condemned to death. He appealed, and I was again sent for to preside over the court of revision. It was composed more carefully than the former one, and Leclerc gave each of the members a talking-to, while with me he went so far as to give his recommendations the character of threats. Thinking that so much trouble could not be taken for a good motive, I examined the case with especial care, and did all I could to find a good man to defend the prisoner. This was difficult, and I was in a perplexity, when some one suggested, as a suitable man for the purpose, a young fellow called Meulan, sergeant in the 5th Dragoons, commanded by Louis Bonaparte.

I sent for him at once, but when I told him of the duty which I wished to entrust to him, instead of the thanks I expected, he expressed his inability to respond to the selection I had so kindly made. Called upon to explain, he pointed out that his application for the rank of sub-lieutenant was just then under consideration, and that he was afraid to risk it by offending the brother-in-law of the First Consul and of his own colonel. A few words from me as to a man's duty towards himself, even towards his family and his name, when he is lucky enough to have an honourable name, made him waver a little. "And," I continued, "when the life of a man is at stake, you make everything turn on a matter of personal interest. I have only one further question to ask you if this man is innocent, and perishes for want of such a defence as you might make for him, will you be able to forgive yourself?"

"General," said the young man vehemently, "I withdraw the answer I made. I undertake the man's defence, and will defend him to the best of my power." He made an able defence, and the man, who was no more guilty than the other had been, was acquitted. The sub-lieutenant's commission was luckily on the way, and came a few days later.

In 18—, having occasion to speak to the Count of Meulan, quartermaster-general, I called upon him. When our business was finished, he asked me if I did not recognise him, adding, "You gave me a lesson, though, which I have never forgotten." And reminding me of this story, which, like so many others, I had forgotten, he told me that he was the hero of it.

However, if Meulan could look back upon his conduct in this matter untroubled by any associations, it was not so with me. To leave no doubt of his anger, General Leclerc at once suppressed the advance-guard, and sent me to command a brigade in the 1st Division under General Monnet, one of the dullest men I ever knew. Nor was that all. Happening to review the division a few days later, he had a man of my brigade arrested on some wretched pretext—I forget what—summoned a court-martial at once, composed of officers whom he could trust, and without my being able to offer any opposition, had the poor fellow condemned and shot then and there. After this it was all over between General Leclerc and me; and as I tried no more to disguise my indignation than he his anger, I made an enemy, who was all the more implacable for having been able to revenge himself on me only by committing a crime.

On August 10 the headquarters and the 1st Division moved back to Salamanca. Here, except for one field-day a week, we were totally idle. La Salle, however, kept us alive by all kinds of occupations, and by his incomparable fun. Every two or three days he used to make the commander-in-chief go out shooting; and every day he practised music with me for two or three hours, which enabled him to say to Leclerc one day at dinner:

> I have had a singular destiny in your army, general. I have given you a taste for shooting; I have restored General Thiébault's taste for music; and there is nothing left for me to do but to awaken in General Monnet a taste for intelligence!

La Salle contrived to put infinite grace into things of the least graceful kind. I mean that, with his charming manners, he was a drinker, a libertine, a gambler, a rowdy practical joker.[5] At Salamanca he started a club called "The Thirsty Souls," no member of which was ever allowed to own that he was not dry. I forget how many lunatics belonged to it, but what is certain is that in less than a month they had drunk all the foreign wine in Salamanca, Once, when he had been giving me the score of empty bottles, I said, "Do you want to kill yourself?"

"My dear friend," he replied, "a hussar who is not dead by the time he is thirty is a dirty sneak. I am making my arrangements not to pass that limit."

A captain of engineers at Salamanca had a very pretty mistress. That demon La Salle, who wrote a tender letter every day to his own wife, made love to this lady somewhat more violently than her recognised adorer could approve. A challenge followed and a duel with sabres, a weapon with which La Salle, being both strong and lissom, was the most dangerous man in existence. The only chance of escape for the captain lay in the generosity of his opponent. Of this there was no question, but there was also no question but that he would use it to play some mad freak, Estimating at once the disparity of force, he abstained altogether from attacking and confined himself to parrying, but did that with such vigour that the poor engineer's wrist broke down. Whenever the poor man took a moment's rest Master La Salle would skip round him amid a thousand jokes, monkey-tricks and grimaces, give him a spank behind with the flat of his sword, and go off in a burst of laughter. Ten times was this trick repeated, and, furious as the poor officer was, he was quite exhausted. When it was evident that he could stand no more, La Salle put an end to the contest, saying:

> If you had known me better, you would have attached less importance to the incident that has vexed you; and if I had known you better, I should have abstained from poaching on your preserves. Accept this declaration and let us end this unequal contest, which has only served to show still plainer what a man of honour you are.

From Salamanca I made an excursion with Richebourg and Dupaty to Madrid, where I saw several bull-fights, and met, among other

---

5. [Compare General Marbot's account of La Salle, *Mémoires*, vol. ii., chap. 24.]

people, the canon who had entertained us so hospitably at Valladolid. On our return to Salamanca we found a changed state of things. The headquarters, the cavalry division, the second infantry division, which had come from Rodrigo in my absence, and other portions of the force had gone to Valladolid, so that the place was occupied only by the 1st Division, of which I commanded the 1st brigade. While General Leclerc had been at Salamanca, I had met the bishop of that see, by name Tavira; a good prelate and distinguished man of letters, called, for his worth, his wisdom, and his apostolic qualities, "the Fénelon of Spain." He had always noticed me to some extent, but after my return from Madrid his kindness became more marked, and I used to dine alone with him twice a week.

One day as we were looking from the balcony of his magnificent palace, and I was feeling rather more than usual disgust at the sight of the wretched houses which lay between it and the no less magnificent cathedral, I asked him how it was they had not already been cleared away so as to let the two buildings be seen, he said:

> My dear general, you revive one of my griefs. When I first came to the town, I had the idea of getting rid of those frightful dwellings. I laboured at the plan for ten years; I had recourse to the influence of such inhabitants as desired to see them demolished, even to the authority of the king, who had no objection. I even offered to pay part of the compensation out of my private fortune, but the chapter to whom they belong put insurmountable obstacles in the way of my efforts, and after a struggle, as prolonged as it was useless, I had to give up on this point as on so many others.

I apologised for having directed his thoughts to a painful memory; and we were both of us far from realising that I was destined to carry his dream into effect, and that in 1811 I should create the open space at Salamanca which he, the bishop of the town—and a powerful bishop too—had failed to get made.

The inaction of Salamanca, annoying to the officers, was unendurable to the men. As long as there was a prospect of war they only troubled themselves about Spain enough to make jokes upon it; but when that prospect vanished, and they saw their stay in those melancholy regions prolonged, homesickness seized them, and the mortality among the recruits became alarming. Every other day I went to the hospitals and spent hours in trying to keep up the poor boys' spirits, telling some that we were soon going back to France, and joking with others,—I was glad to think not entirely without success.

However, these distresses did not prevent some madcaps from amusing themselves—Richebourg, Dupaty, and Texier among them. I had sometimes to stop their nonsense, even after I had laughed at it. There was some fresh folly every day. One evening, coming in at nightfall, we passed a bone-house, above which, in a little niche, was a skull in the rays of a lamp. Richebourg took it down, and bought a candle-end, which he lighted and put inside the skull. At the door of our hotel he stuck his own hat upon it, put it on his head, covering that with his cloak, and rang the bell. The maid who opened the door fainted away. I gave him a lecture, but it was no good.

Next day I did not go to the theatre. My idiots went, armed with very long telescopes, which they levelled at all the ladies, provoking an uproar which interrupted the performance twenty times. Hulin was military governor of Salamanca. The following morning in his report he complained of the three nuisances, and I had to put them under arrest for three days. They were not very dull, for in the house where we lived there were three very pretty girls, and almost every evening was passed in laughing and dancing with them. Dupaty, one of the two or three best dancers of his time, tried all he could to learn the *bolero*, but never succeeded. It requires a movement of the hips and shoulders which can only be acquired in the supple days of childhood.

General Lamarque, who commanded our 3rd Division, being summoned by Leclerc to take part in the expedition to San Domingo, I was ordered to take his place, the headquarters being at Toro.[6] I have no recollections of the place beyond that it was very dull and the weather was bad. But I had hardly been there ten days when orders came to return to France. The army was in a state not merely of joy but of ecstasy, as I have said no country was ever more hateful to our troops. One might have said that they had a presentiment of the 400,000 men with whom we were to enter that country between 1808 and 1813, but for the loss of whom we should have remained masters of the world.

At Valladolid I hoped to have seen my canon again, but he was absent when I passed through that town. On the road through Castile I bought two handsome setters. One of the latter cost me three hun-

---

6. Lamarque wrote pitying me for having to live in such a dull place, where there was no society: "You will not be surprised, however, if you consider *que les femmes de Toro sont des vaches.*" In spite of the pun, there were some charming women there.

dred *pesetas*; from his incredible speed he was called Pegasus. He was said to have cleared a canal twenty feet wide. He had hardly been delivered to me when the vendor wanted me to give him back and take back my money. He was a kind of pride of the neighbourhood, and there was general lamentation at his departure. I might as well have left him, for in the following October at Tours the dog showed symptoms of rabies and had to be destroyed. Besides the dogs I took away a very curious animal, evidently the offspring of a dog-fox and a bitch; we had seen it at Rodrigo, and while I was at Salamanca Delost, hearing me express a wish to take the curious creature back to Paris, had gone to get it without letting me know. When I talked of repayment, he said he had got it very cheap; perhaps he had got it for nothing, if, as I am much afraid, he had stolen it.

On arriving at Vitoria, where the reminiscences of my first stay in the Peninsula come to an end, I found that I was lodged in the house of the Marquis of Monte Hermoso; I was very kindly received, and on the following day thirty people were invited to dinner to meet me. Among them was a Spanish general, who was not devoid of talent or of intelligence in his profession. Inevitably we spoke of war and of our distinguished military men; it was natural to place the First Consul outside of all comparison, but the general asked me to tell him whether the prior rank as a commander ought to be given to Moreau or Masséna. After pointing out their character, their style of ability, and their education, calling attention to their principal feats of arms, and making it clear that mountain warfare was more especially Masséna's line, war on level ground Moreau's, I said:

> Let us suppose that these two commanders unexpectedly found themselves face to face with similar forces and appliances in broken ground equally suited to both sides. In such a situation Moreau would undoubtedly have the advantage at first; but as it is impossible not to make some mistakes in the course of a great battle, and as it is no less unquestionable that Masséna with his eagle eye would estimate all his enemy's mistakes and take advantage of them with the swiftness of lightning, he would end by snatching the victory even if it seemed desperate.
> Whence I conclude that Moreau is our first soldier, Masséna our first warrior; or, in other words, that Moreau is the first of our army leaders, Masséna the first of our fighting generals. But I equally draw the inference, that, up to a certain point, Moreau,

as a man of thought and recent experience, will be able to grow old with impunity, while Masséna, as a man of inspiration and impulse, will not be able; which brings me to the corollary that, so long as Masséna is in the full vigour of his age, he will have an advantage over Moreau dependent upon natural powers, which advantage Moreau will resume in proportion as calculation and reasoning make up for that which can only result from activity, manly vigour, and warm blood.

This opinion struck my hearer so much that I remembered it myself, though at that time I had no suspicion that it would be confirmed in the Peninsula. Masséna ceased to be a fighting man after the Polish campaign and the haemorrhages which he then had; from that time he was no longer himself. He was wasted, altered in feature, and without strength, when he was sent into Portugal to tarnish by his own deed, and at the cost of the remainder of his life, a fame which was envied because he had won it for himself. In those days he was only a man who had outlived himself, unequal and incomplete. In the march from Almeida to Santarem, in the long halt on the Tagus, I will say that his tenacity alone was left, but not a single inspiration. He found that all his authority was gone, and was defied by men who not long before would have rushed to carry out the least of his orders. As for Moreau, in the disgraceful position to which justice was done by a French cannon-ball, he was still capable in 1813, as adjutant-general to Alexander, of devising an excellent plan of campaign; he was cool enough to give the advice which brought about our disasters:

> Retreat whenever you have Napoleon in front of you; attack whenever you have only his generals to fight.

Never losing his clear-headedness even in the midst of treason, he caused the soil of France to be sullied by the hordes who snatched from us the frontiers given us by nature and by victory.

CHAPTER 6

Return to France

If, with the exception of a few hours spent at Vitoria, my journey across Spain was monotonous and melancholy to the last degree, the journey from the Bidassoa to Paris was neither one nor the other. I had a debt to settle with the French custom-house officers on the Bidassoa; we had a grudge against each other, they for the cut which one of their men had received from my stick, I for their impertinence in denouncing me. If I had let my *aide-de-camp* and the thirty troopers of my escort have their way, there would have been a violent scene, but I was determined, with adversaries of this kind, to keep clear of any violent correction until they provoked it; and in order not to treat them with more importance than they deserved, I resolved to begin by having some fun with them.

Consequently, as I was marching with the last brigade of my division, I had all my property, and that of my *aides-de-camp* and my servants, packed in the baggage-waggons of the second brigade, so that all our things, including the contraband cloth bought at Segovia, entered France twenty-four hours before I did. When I reached the Bidassoa, therefore, I had not even so much as a hand-bag with me, though nothing revealed the fact. First my waggon, then my carriage, both closely shut, went in front of me, and I trotted after them as if they contained the most valuable articles.

After crossing the Bidassoa, I saw all my friends of the custom-house under arms and in full fig, drawn up in line in front of their house. When I came abreast of them, the officers and a dozen men came forward; but I went on some hundred paces, chatting with Richebourg and affecting not to see them, or to notice that they wanted to speak to me till I had got them sufficiently out of breath. When I had given the word to halt, they examined the carriage, and were much surprised to find it empty. Then I gave them the keys of the two padlocks on the waggon, and they threw themselves upon it as if they were taking it by storm. More than ten of them climbed up on the three sides which would be left free when the cover was lifted, and when that was done all craned their heads forward, eager to make the first discovery.

Never was zeal more rewarded; the waggon contained only our ten dogs and the fox-dog, which had been shut up there for more than two hours, and, wild to regain their liberty, leaped at the faces of the officials, who were nearly all thrown to the ground. Falling in a heap with the dogs, the poor wretches got up as they best could, some bruised by their fall, others more or less scratched, all with their embroidered coats muddy and torn. When they were on their legs again, I inquired gravely, "Is your examination over? "On their answering that it was, much to the disgust of my escort, whom I had some trouble to hold back, I confined my revenge to this intervention of our dogs.

At Bayonne I fell in with M. Desportes, first secretary to the Madrid Embassy, who was following his chief, Lucien Bonaparte, to Paris. As he had no carriage I offered him a place in mine, and he told me a heap of anecdotes about Spanish affairs, the court of Charles IV, and the events in which I had almost blindly been taking part. We went at one stretch from Bayonne to Barbezieux, where we stayed at the comfortable inn of one Gaudaubert, who worthily maintained the credit of the pies of Barbezieux. Our stay there was therefore pleasant enough, but our issue from the town provided less agreeable entertainment. In those days the roads in France had got into a very bad state; and in order to raise the necessary funds for their repair, toll-bars had been established at every posting-stage, an abominable method, which cost more than it earned, and gave rise to all kinds of swindles. Soldiers provided with passes were free of toll.

Now the toll-keeper on the Angouleme road at Barbezieux, named Mouchère, was one of the most ill-bred among them. He would often hide himself, and if a peasant, not seeing him about, hurried through on the chance of escaping the toll, the terrible toll-keeper would run after him, arrest him, and make him pay the penalty. When I handed him my pass in reply to his demand for payment, he looked angrily at me, exclaiming, "Oh! yes, they rob me every day, but d——d if I will be robbed today." Then he fell to spelling my pass out word by word, including the notes. I asked him to get it done a little quicker. "Oh, I'm in no hurry," he answered, and began again at the beginning.

A saint could not have stood it; the cold was bitter, and the carriage-windows were standing open. I thought of the 450 miles we still had before us, and, losing patience, I snatched my pass out of his hand, telling him that I would pay the toll, and that he would have to pay for his insolence. "You may pay the toll or not," he said: "I am going to shut the bar to begin with;" and he did so. I had already jumped out of the carriage, my sword being in the belt; and when he saw me going towards the bar with the intention of opening, this powerful, thick-set man, calling his son, who came running up to help him, leapt upon me like a maniac, and seizing the collar of my waistcoat, for my overcoat was open, tore it all the way down. I could hardly say what I felt, but I will confine myself to facts, and merely add that when the son, a big fellow of twenty or twenty-five, came up to me, he found the point of my sword against his breast, while I had made the father let go by cutting through three bones in his wrist-joint.

One of my assailants was thus disabled, and the other was retreating when M. Desportes alighted and persuaded me to go with him and end the business before the *sub-prefect,* whom he knew. We went off, followed by the two Mouchères and escorted by a curious crowd. The facts were stated on both sides, and Gaudaubert, who had heard of the affair and come in, was of great service to us in quoting all sorts of incidents to Mouchère's disadvantage. Finally the *sub-prefect,* after warning us that he had no power to stay judicial proceedings, sent two *gendarmes* to open the bar for us.

We were hardly through it when M. Desportes said:

> You were perhaps surprised that I remained a passive witness of your fight with those two jokers, and doubtless I need not say that if you had been in danger you would not have waited long for my help. But when you had struck your blow, I thought of the consequences of the incident, and considered that if, not being a soldier, I had taken part in the struggle, you would not have escaped the assizes; while as no civilian was mixed in the affair, you can easily get it brought before a court-martial.

Nevertheless the adventure did not leave us free from anxiety. On the one hand, I was summoned to the assizes; and on the other, Mouchère very nearly died. M. Joly, my father's early friend, my friend and counsellor in difficult circumstances, was a member of the Paris Court of Appeal, and a much-respected magistrate. He advised an interview with the Minister of Justice, Abrial, whom I had known at Naples, and took me to him. Our discussion was long and serious, though there was a moment of merriment when I said that "I would have sabred the Supreme Being if he had laid his hands on me." M. Joly insisted on the facts that I was a soldier on active service, travelling on duty, that no civilian was implicated in the affair, and that I had been assaulted; and succeeded in getting me sent before the military tribunals.

The court-martial sitting at Périgueux was therefore put in possession of the affair; and as by good luck the president of it was my friend General Gardanne, and Mouchère moreover got no more than his deserts, all that was left for him was, he felt, to get some money out of me. Just then Salafon came through Barbezieux. He was good enough to stay and wind up the unpleasant business, and warmly supported by Gaudaubert, whose zeal I had stimulated by an order for two pies a month, he settled the whole thing for five hundred *francs*. This was about the amount of Mouchère's doctor's bill; and he had lost his place and was maimed into the bargain. As for me, between "tips," pies, expenses, and compensation, I got off for forty *napoleons* and a waistcoat.

Every time that I had returned to France during the last nine years, even amid the intoxication of victory and the turmoil of public rejoicings, I had found the country uneasy, suffering from the stoppage to foreign trade and the death of nearly all her industries. Bordeaux above all had fallen from its prosperity, being reduced to rooting up the vines and using the land for other crops. As for Paris, deprived of the masses of foreigners, and of the movement of business necessary to maintain life, it was dreary. Money was plentiful, but unproductive for want of confidence and circulation. Now, thanks to the power and genius with which France was governed by the First Consul, a genuine expansion had taken the place of these continual and increasing losses. As soon as peace was signed with England, Bordeaux began again to export its wines, and unloaded its cellars; while land which had been selling at one year's purchase recovered a high value. Paris became once more the meeting-place of a crowd of distinguished strangers, who brought the gold of Europe flowing in, when my return to it took place amid the influence of this sense of fortune and prosperity.

Passing on to the year 1802, one of the most important events which it brings to mind was the Concordat. I need not inquire into the necessity nor the opportuneness of this return to Catholic worship; but what is certain is that at that time the enemies of the First

Consul and of the Republic rejoiced at it, while their friends and the army as a whole were in consternation. As for the First Consul, if he had any doubts left of his power, this gave him a proof of its immensity, for what other than he but would have made shipwreck over such an attempt. To show how colossal his power already was, the clergy were able in that ceremony to insult and defy with impunity in the face of the world all the generals of France. Will it be believed that when invited to go to Notre Dame, nearly all the generals who were in Paris went there; following the example, not of Moreau, who did not set foot in the place, but of Masséna, of Ney, of Lefebvre, and so many more?

Places had been prepared in Notre Dame for everyone except the generals, so that some sixty of them, blocked in the passage leading up the nave, knew neither where to go nor what to do. To their right they saw about sixty priests, seated at their ease, and looking almost with a grin at these officers, the honour and glory of their country. The murmurs that arose, not unmixed with strong language, may be imagined. A steward of the ceremonies came up, and, impertinent even in his difficulty, mumbled that he did not know what was to be done, seeing that there was no room anywhere. "You go and be d——d," answered Masséna; then seizing the chair of the nearest priest and shaking it, he made him turn out and took the place. The example was at once followed, with the result of somewhat roughly substituting officers for priests. They ought not, in the circumstances, to have been left to find places for themselves; and the exasperation caused by so gratuitous a blunder only added to an almost universal disapprobation. General Delmas, who would break a window without troubling himself about who was going to pay for it, ventured to say one day to the First Consul:

> The only thing you can do now is to give us rosaries instead of our sword-knots. As for France, she must console herself as best she can for the loss of the million of men whom she will in vain have sacrificed to be rid of the rubbish you are reviving.[7]

The army corps to which I belonged had been broken up on January 16, 1802; but we were still on full pay, and I was in enjoyment of it when on March 22 I received orders to serve in the 22nd Division, the

---

7. [Mme d'Abrantès and Lanfrey, who both quote this remark, give it somewhat differently, and there are other variants. But the point is the same. Delmas was a nobleman who had accepted the Republic. He was banished for a time.]

headquarters of which were at Tours. It was commanded by General Liébert, under whom I had not been very fortunate in 1795, when he was chief of Pichegru's headquarter staff. He gave me my choice of residence between Le Mans and Tours. I was inclined to select the former, but Richebourg, who belonged to Touraine and happened to be at Tours at the moment, made use of his influence over me to make me change my mind. General Liébert was also kind enough to exert pressure on the same side.

I reached Tours on June 2, and, according to the established etiquette, had to pay three visits on the first day to the divisional general, to the archbishop, and to the prefect. I had made some inquiries as to the two last, and thus the archbishop, Mgr de Boisgelin, the prelate who had preached on the occasion of the ceremony in Notre Dame, and who had only just been appointed indeed, he had not been installed when I saw him was surprised when I talked to him not about the honourable part he had played in the States-General and the Constituent Assembly, not about the share he had taken in the Concordat, but about the good works which he had left in yet earlier days in Provence: a school at Lambesc, a bridge at Lavaur where he had been bishop, and a canal. He seemed touched, and the flattering remarks I had occasion to make earned me his marked and consistent good-will, shown with the tact and delicacy natural to him.

What I had heard of General Pommereul, the prefect, in respect of his literary and scientific works, his service, the missions which he had discharged, and his general capacity, was far inferior to what I found in him. When he got hold of a subject, he could set it out with equal arrangement, clearness, and depth; and these advantages were supplemented by a noble bearing, and a countenance showing not less character than sagacity.

To pass from these two remarkable men to General Liébert is to go down. Once a sergeant of artillery, he seemed, so far as style and manners went, to be one still. His merit was not such as to justify his ever having been chief of the staff to a great army; but no one could have shown more zeal for his duties, and, as for his personal qualities, no one could be kinder or more obliging. I was able to convince myself that Donzelot's political cowardice could account for seven-eighths of the severity practised towards me, in 1793 and 1794, in the name of General Liébert. We remained good friends till his death.

The Sunday after my arrival I went to walk on the public promenade. Formerly shaded by secular trees, it was now adorned only by saplings of three or four years' growth; and what was remembered most indignantly was that the Vandals of 1793 had cut down the old trees in August, when the sap was up, so that the navy, for which they were intended, could make no use of them, and the wood, being of no further value, even for burning, had been left to rot where it lay.

One morning Adjutant-General de Flavigny was announced. He was a man of very good family, of great gallantry, and far from devoid of ability; but mad, not with the madness which gets people shut up, but with that which ultimately prevents their employment. In 1796, after one of the great battles, I forget which, fought by the Army of Italy, he had been ordered to escort a column of prisoners to the rear. Feeling this a humiliating office, in a laudable spirit he took advantage of a report that he had to send to General Bonaparte, to write as follows:

While you continue to cover yourself with glory, Flavigny is getting covered with dust.

About the same time a revolt had broken out in Piedmont, and Flavigny had been sent to repress it. In a few days he had beaten, killed, dispersed, or captured all the insurgents. He then assembled all his prisoners in an open space; and when they were all expecting to be shot, he formed them in a circle, and addressed them in French to this effect:

Wretches, you have dared to revolt against the armies of the Republic; assassination has been your method, and the death of the greater part of you has been the beginning of the vengeance, which, for its completion, demands your punishment. Yes, you have all deserved death, and I ought to have you shot this minute. Yet I stay the arm of justice, I yield to pity, and I grant you life. Go, those of you who have fathers, and console your fathers; those who have wives and children, go and embrace children and wives; as for those who have neither—

Here Flavigny, at the end of his eloquence, after repeating several times, "who have neither," added, in delight at the inspiration: "Well, those who have neither may go and be jolly well jiggered." The poor creatures, half-dead with fear, and not understanding a word, stood there bewildered; so he fell upon them with a whip, but just then someone signed to them to fly, and they bolted in all directions. The scene was witnessed by many, and soon widely known. Flavigny's discourse was repeated everywhere, including the final jest, so that, instead of the service he had done being considered, no one did anything but laugh at him.

After ceasing to be employed, he came and lived at Tours on his half-pay, and his visit to me was for the purpose of gaining my support towards his further employment on active service, and of communicating to me the letter he proposed to send the First Consul. Here it is:

General Consul,
You have filled the whole world with your glory, and Flavigny sits and spits in the fire.
   Greeting and respect.
            Flavigny.

This letter was the crowning achievement. It bore its answer in it, and I had not the courage to give poor Flavigny much hope.

The festival of July 14 was kept at Tours; I think for the last time in France. I only remember that there was a procession, that General Liébert made a speech, that a proclamation of the First Consul was read, and that, to make the thing complete, it was very hot. Indeed this was the hottest year I ever remember. Hares were found dead in the fields, and partridge-eggs roasted. One Sunday the heat put all the instruments out of tune, so that I had to stop the band playing.

Throughout the Revolution, July 14 and the horrible August 10 kept their old names, in spite of the Republican Calendar; but for one's own safety, one did not venture to pronounce or write those names without adding "old style." At this last July 14 the other thing remarkable, besides the heat, was that General Liébert's boy of four took part in it, hand in hand with an old soldier of the Touraine regiment, aged a hundred and four, so that there was just a century between the two.

This old man was named Turrel. He was born at Dijon in September 1697, entered the Touraine regiment in 1712, served under every government from Louis XIV to the emperor. He had been at the battles of Lawfeld, Raucoux, and Fontenoy. When he completed his seventy-five years' service in 1787, he was presented to Louis XVI by the Count of Mirabeau. A tray was brought in with a bottle of Malaga and four glasses. The first was filled and presented to the king, who drank it; Turrel had the second, Monsieur the third, the Count of Artois the fourth. Many great persons, including the Duke of Richelieu, had him to dine. Now he was living on a pension, six hundred *francs* from the king and princes, and three hundred from the ladies of France, which, on a report from me to the First Consul, was raised to one thousand five hundred. He was often asked to dinner by the chief military authorities, but we warned each other to see that he did not eat too much. He was married to his fourth or fifth wife, and made her mind him. He had never had more than one daughter, and never regretted not having a son.

An easygoing old fellow, he had retained his good spirits, and liked nothing better than to sing his little song at dessert. Nor was he at all devoid of shrewdness. A lady said to him one day at my house, "Turrel, God must surely love you well, to give you so long a life. I am sure you often pray to Him and thank Him."

"Madam," he replied with the slyest smile, "I have never been in the habit of boring my friends."

At a hundred and seven he expired, never having been wounded nor infirm in any way.

To return to July 14, 1802, it was to be a great date in my life. At the country-house of a common friend I had met a young lady, daughter of a former landowner in San Domingo, who had at one time enjoyed one of the finest fortunes in France. Her name was Elizabeth Chenais, and she was considered one of the cleverest and most accomplished persons in Tours' society. I had met her more than once, and been charmed by her beauty and by her wit, when, on the evening of that 14th of July, as I was strolling about the fair which was then open, I met a friend who was going to call on the Chenais family, and wished to introduce me. M. Chenais, the father, was born at Nantes, and originally destined for the Church; but nine duels, which he fought in one morning with officers of the garrison, fully showed that his vocation did not lie there, and he went off to seek his fortune in the Antilles. When the insurrection broke out in 1792 among the negroes of San Domingo, he lost much of his wealth, but he had a good deal invested in France. Much of this was lost in the unlucky purchase and sale of an estate, and he was now living at Tours in reduced circumstances.

I returned home after my visit, recognising that I had met my fate. Other meetings in friends' houses increased our intimacy with each other, and before very long we were engaged to be married, though a year elapsed before we actually were so.

On August 3, a dispatch was brought to General Liébert, from the Minister for War, informing him that Toussaint-Louverture, whom

General Leclerc had sent to France, had just landed at Brest, and was to be taken by post to the Castle of Joux, the generals commanding along the road being responsible for him while within the limits of their districts. General Liébert, when communicating the order to me, told me that I was answerable as far as Blois, to which point I was to have Toussaint-Louverture accompanied by my *aide-de-camp* Richebourg, who would there be relieved by an *aide-de-camp* of General Verdier, and take a receipt for the prisoner. I did not wish to lose this unique opportunity of seeing a man, in his own way extraordinary, a kind of specimen of the highest degree of capacity in a negro,—a man no doubt to inspire horror, in that he did not stick at any means, even the most cruel, and piled up disasters which he might have diminished.

Still, he had been able, after creating a vast state, to win and preserve the sovereignty of it, which perhaps it would have been better to have allowed him to keep. His boasting also interested me, and I wished to see the man who had not been afraid to write to the First Consul: "The first of black men to the first of white." So I ordered that, at whatever hour of night or day he might arrive, I was to be told, and he was to be detained until I had seen him. In the evening of August 18 I heard that he had passed through Saumur at five o'clock, and at two o'clock on the following morning I was aroused by the words: "Toussaint-Louverture is at the post station." I had a horse already saddled, and galloped off to the negro commander.

Reaching the door of his carriage, which I found open, I said:

> I wish to see you, to learn if you had any complaints to make as to the manner of your journey or the respect that ought to be shown you.

He replied in his negro accent:

> I have no complaint, I only wish to reach Paris very quickly; the sooner to see the First Consul, to whom I have important communications to make. He will understand that it is his interest to send me back quickly to San Domingo. Still, I have plenty to see and to learn in France, where I shall visit, especially, the powder-mills, the arm-factories, arsenals, and foundries.

While he was talking I was looking at that frightful countenance, the lower part of which, projecting like a monkey's muzzle, was covered with the white tufts of his beard. His mouth, with its thick and pendulous lips surrounded by equally pendulous black skin, contained only a few stumps of teeth, and projected beyond the flattest nose ever seen, above which, however, were two eyes blazing like carbuncles. However, what struck me even more than this hideous caricature was to find him in a temperature which, even at night, did not fall much below 70, wrapped up in three overcoats, and to learn that not only did he never take off his wraps, but did not allow a window to be opened in a carriage which had become a regular travelling oven. Richebourg, who, on the road to Blois, had to use a whole bottle of toilet vinegar to disguise the powerful flavour, repeated incessantly that he ought to accustom himself to the air of France, and that nothing was more wholesome than the open air.

"Poor devil!" thought I, as I left the old man who had achieved little short of renown. "I had rather that another than I should reveal your destiny to you. Happily, you will not suffer long, for the first north wind that blows into the loopholes of the fort of Joux will be the breath of death for you."

Meanwhile more important events were claiming our attention. The peace with England—a peace which that Power had never intended to make more than a truce—had been abruptly replaced by hostilities without any preliminary declaration, the result of which was, that we quickly lost nearly all the vessels which, in reliance upon treaties, we had at sea. Yet our irreconcilable enemies had gained by that peace something more advantageous for them than the most fortunate campaign could have been. It practically made us lose the whole of Moreau's army, for which the yellow fever at San Domingo so pitilessly accounted, and the loss became the subject of terrible reflections and of remarks often repeated, which, if credit were to be given them, would be no less terrible for the First Consul.

No one could any longer mistake his ambitious projects. "Without being able to explain in what way he would realise them, it was not supposed that he would be content with the consulate for life, which he had got substituted for the five years' term. Everything was being arranged for putting a throne in place of the consular chair, and replacing by a crown the general's hat, or the cap of the republican First Magistrate. We foresaw in Bonaparte the man who was one day to say, "I mean my dynasty to be, before ten years are out, the most ancient in Europe." But, in order to realise those plans for slaying liberty which cost France and mankind so dear in the carrying out, he had alarming obstacles to overcome.

With the old Army of Italy he could not dream of doing it, and in his limitless foresight he had buried that at the foot of the pyramids. Moreau, the rival to whom his renown was an insult, and who in such a cause could not have failed to be backed by a host of generals, would have been invincible, if the army which he had so gloriously commanded had still trodden the soil of the country. But the yellow fever had accounted for it, and, as a special favour, Moreau had been banished before the empire took the place of the consulate. Among the men most capable of judging, there was at that time none who was not convinced that the necessity for getting rid of that last army was the predominant motive in the expedition to San Domingo. Thus the peace with England, short as it was, had been sufficient for Bonaparte's good fortune to profit, in the most astounding way, by the ruin of a commander and the disappearance of an army that blocked his road to power.[8]

To return to England. The rupture that she had provoked was keenly felt, especially in our wine-growing districts. The government proclaimed her bad faith, and all the authorities responded to its voice. All the bishops and archbishops in France united their anathemas to the general indignation. At the same time, as is well known, the First Consul created the Army of Boulogne, attacked and rapidly conquered Hanover, and to complete the reprisals issued, on May 22, 1803, a decree to the effect that all Englishmen [9] liable to enrolment in the militia, and aged between eighteen and sixty, or holding a commission from His Britannic Majesty, who were at that time in France, should immediately be constituted prisoners of war, to answer for those citizens of the Republic who should have been taken prisoners by His Majesty's ships previous to the declaration of war.

Things soon, however, returned to their ordinary course; balls and parties went on at Tours without interruption. In the course of the summer I had occasion to go on duty to Paris, where I breakfasted with Junot, then commanding the first military division. He asked what I was doing at Tours.

What I will do wherever I am employed—my duty to the best of my ability.

---

8. [It is worth while reading what Lanfrey, vol. ii. says on this point. He does not admit a conscious design on Bonaparte's part, but holds him none the less guilty.]
9. [This included Englishwomen, as "France" included Italy. Tourists, ambassadors, men of letters, were swept up indiscriminately. War had to all intents and purposes been declared a week before.]

He was good enough to assure me that he believed it, and offered me the subdivision of Versailles and Chartres, which was at his disposal. This was an offer of a very pleasant residence, and, though it involved a separation of some months from my future bride, I accepted. She approved, though not without a tear; but hope kept up our spirits. So I left Touraine, that garden of France, where the air has a softness that I never felt elsewhere, and where the philosophy of the inhabitants is limited to enjoying life.

CHAPTER 7

My Marriage

It was not long before I recognised the advantages of my residence at Versailles, under the direction of a chief so brilliant as General Junot. Besides, I had six times as many troops to command as I had had at Tours. In addition to several infantry regiments, the 3rd Hussars in garrison at Chartres, and three dragoon regiments at Versailles, I had under my orders the 3rd Cuirassiers, occupying Saint-Germain; a regiment commanded by a colonel who had been made adjutant-general in Italy almost at the same time as myself, though for some reason or other we had not sought each other's acquaintance at that time. This was Colonel Préval, one of the handsomest as well as the most fortunate colonels in our army; but what is more, one of the best educated and most capable officers, and one of the most intrepid soldiers that France ever possessed.

The 3rd Cuirassiers, which I inspected soon after my arrival, was a picked corps in respect of appearance, discipline, instruction, spirit, and selection of men—a model corps in every sense of the term. The inspection first enabled me thoroughly to know and estimate an officer who had in a measure sacrificed himself in order to solve the problems connected with a command of that kind. In 1800 Préval had preferred the command of the regiment to the rank of major-general, which was twice offered him. I mention this, not only because it did him great honour, but because it is characteristic of the spirit of the soldiers of that time. The best officers then regarded their company, their battalion, their regiment, as a man regards the spire of the village where he was born. They served for the honour of doing good service, without any thought of ambition or greed.

Nansouty and others had similarly refused promotion; Préval would not quit the head of his regiment till he was thoroughly acquainted with all the detail of it, which he afterwards put together in his work on *New Regulations for Service and Drill*. Also he took a pride in turning an obscure and shabby regiment into the finest *cuirassier* regiment in the service. He became in this way one of the first officers of French cavalry, though he suffered in some respects for the sacrifice and made himself enemies.

Having ridden to Saint-Germain, I returned to Versailles in the same manner, accompanied by Préval and several of his officers, whom I asked to dinner. In this way began my intimacy with Préval, which, though it did not become very close till after the Restoration, made me fully recognise his distinction alike as a man of the world, a man of education and wit, and a soldier.

On my arrival at Versailles, I was entrusted with the reorganisation of the three dragoon regiments, upon the system according to which regiments of that arm ought to be equally well adapted for fighting on horseback or on foot. Accordingly we were expected first to prove to them, regarded as cavalry, that nothing in the world could resist a mounted troop, well composed, well commanded, well instructed, employing with ability and vigour at the right moment the power resulting from speed and impact; while on the other hand, regarded as infantry, they had to learn that the best cavalry in the world must be annihilated by infantry which remains steady and makes the best use of its fire and its bayonets; the result being, when once they had learnt their lesson, to inspire them with a profound dread of infantry when they were mounted, and of cavalry when they were on foot. Had not they been Frenchmen, we should at great expense have been forming corps which by reason of this preliminary intimidation had been as useless on foot as on horseback.

As I was at breakfast one morning, there came in a fresh little old gentleman, who said in a deliberate tone, "General, will you kindly receive a visit from the father of General Berthier, the Minister for War?" I assured him that I should have made a point of calling first, had I known that he was at Versailles—I might have added, had I known that he was in existence—and begged him to do me the honour of breakfasting with me. He would only take a cup of coffee; and it occurred to me to propose accompanying him to the War Office, which he said he had built himself, and in which he had lived and his children had been born.

He was delighted, and we set off together. Had he been proposing to sell me the place, he could not have shown me more thoroughly over it, or given me the history of the whole edifice more fully from cellar to garret. At length we reached the attics. "Here," said he, "were my quarters." Stopping before a small and more than modest apartment with a recess, "And here," he added proudly, "Alexander was born." If it had been the king of Macedonia, he could not have retailed a longer string of recollections than he did. I thought this was the gem of all that he had to show me, and that my task was ended, and had already congratulated him on his back-sinews, which I said seemed in this building to regain the vigour they must have possessed in the days of its construction, when he told me that the most curious sight of all were the roofs.

Straightway he went through a skylight, and towing me after him, as he ran and climbed like a cat, he marched me from ridge to ridge, from valley to valley, at the risk of breaking my neck twenty times over. Indeed, he made me tremble for himself, and in this connection for myself afresh; for if he had tumbled off the top of the building, General Berthier might have held me in part responsible for his father's death. Not that it would have anticipated the old gentleman's natural decease by a great deal, for we were now in November, and he died in the following May.

Having in Richebourg an *aide-de-camp* on whom I could depend, I was able to go frequently to Paris. There were few days on which I did not see General Junot. One day when I had breakfasted with him, I did not return to Versailles till after the play. I found a note which an orderly had brought, dated 5 p.m., and bidding me breakfast again with him without fail on the morrow. I guessed that some serious and pressing matter was on foot; and indeed that breakfast did not resemble those to which I had been accustomed there. Merry anecdotes were replaced by recollections of the wars. Mme Junot, who generally, with the indescribable charm of her wit and imagination, bore the chief part in these gatherings, hardly took any share in the conversation, and seemed something more than grave.

On leaving table, Junot and I went into his study; and he at once told me that the First Consul was giving him charge of an expedition to which great importance was attached:

> It is not Europe, it is an expedition by sea; but it will not last long. I am counting on you as second in command of the troops; and if you accept, I will bring you back in six months a lieutenant-general.

I said:

> General," I am devoted to you, and there is nothing I would not take under your orders. For anyone else and without the prospects you hold out to me, I should merely obey, for I shall be grieved by my father's grief at my going, and have a marriage on hand which I would not exchange for my life; but as I am going with you, I ask only two questions: whither? and when?

Taking my hand, he said, "You must go to Saintes, where the troops are arriving today"—it was December 23—"and start in two days, so as to take my place till I come. You will have your orders tomorrow."

"One word more, please: do you keep the command of Paris?"

"No; Murat replaces me."

"Will you be able to keep the Versailles command for me?"

"I will speak to him about it; I hope so."

I was at Tours by mid-day on the 26th.

I have forgotten to mention that, two hours before leaving Paris, I received my nomination to the Legion of Honour; as legionary, that is. Everyone began with that rank, the only one given at the first institution of the order. At Tours I took the oath, and it is curious, remembering how it was only a few months before the establishment of the empire, to recall the terms of that oath. They must have made Bonaparte laugh as Napoleon was to laugh later on:

> This day appeared ——, who has sworn before us on his honour to devote himself to the service of the Republic, and to the maintenance of the existing laws; to resist by every means that justice, reason, and law authorize, any attempt to re-establish the feudal system or to reproduce the titles and qualities which pertained to it.—(Thus it ran).

Reaching Saintes early on December 28, I found all the troops, with the exception of the grenadiers, in a state of mutiny. The pretext, I was told, was that their pay was six months in arrear; but the real reason was their aversion to a voyage, of which soldiers had ceased to have any idea. On inquiry, I found reason to believe that they would decamp the very next night; and as the paymaster was not expected for three or four days, something had to be done. I called on the *prefect*, and asked him to advance the money. He replied, "I cannot be a party to any misapplication of funds; the orders are too strict."

"Well," I said, "as *prefect*, decline to comply with the written requisition I shall send you; but kindly give me your personal help. Now between ourselves, what funds has your treasurer?"

"None; all the money was sent off yesterday."

"Do you mean that in all this town every cashbox is empty?"

"The highway board has 300,000 *francs* for urgent works now going on; but I must remind you that to divert special funds, even for a moment, is a capital offence."

I thanked him and went away.

On reaching my quarters, I drew up my requisition to the *prefect*, saying that, in case of his refusal, I should force the cashbox of the highway board, and requesting his presence at that operation. This I sent in duplicate by Richebourg, who brought me back the *prefect's* refusal in duplicate. I then issued an order of the day, announcing that I should review the troops at ten next morning, and that they would receive an instalment of their pay in the course of that day. Then, followed by a company of grenadiers, I went with the officers and the commissary to the cashier in charge of the funds of the highway board. He had had notice from the prefect, and, when I demanded the sum I required, he refused it. Twelve grenadiers went through the form of forcing the strong-box, and the sum required for each corps was handed to each quartermaster or paymaster, a statement being drawn up by the commissary and signed by every officer present. The payments were made, and the review took place.

I made the twelve men who were reported as ringleaders fall out, and sent them off under arrest, after which the troops marched past, and order was re-established. I drew up a report of the whole affair, which I sent to Junot, and to the Ministers for War, Home Affairs, and Finance; but as no one either could disapprove, or might approve, I had no answer except from Junot. He praised my conduct, but said that his destination was changed, and that he was going to Arras, to take command of 12,000 grenadiers forming the reserve of the Army of England, being replaced in command of the troops at Saintes by General Lagrange.

I was bitterly disappointed and wrote both to Junot and to Murat, reminding the former that I had only gone to Saintes to be with him, and telling the latter of my desire to serve under him. Both wrote at the same time and in the most friendly way to say that my wishes were granted. I was once more saved from a voyage for which I had no taste. Twenty-one days, however, elapsed before I got my orders of recall. The prefect and his wife showed me every kindness, and tried to make me forget my annoyances. My orders were to wait for General Lagrange and hand over the command to him; but of this I took no notice, seeing that the senior colonel could take my place admirably, and actually did so; and posted off to Tours. The prefect gave me, as a parting present, two bottles of brandy of 1696.

I had not meant to stay at Tours more than a few days, but the days passed so quickly that they seemed to be days only by the calendar. "No one," said my intended, "will carry Versailles away in your absence, and whenever you get there you are sure to find it where you left it." And in truth nothing seemed to make my presence there necessary, my orders were in no way urgent, and I might even have stayed at Saintes during all the time which I spent at Tours. But none of these good reasons which I gave myself in my own excuse prevented, not indeed Versailles from changing its place, but, as will be seen, my place from being changed.

Just when yielding to necessity I had got permission to depart, General Liébert came and asked me to take a letter to Moreau, a confidential letter, which was to be given only to the person for whom it was intended. I promised to do as he wished, and did not think it any special favour, for I knew the old friendship that existed between these two ex-sergeants of artillery, and I had as little reason to think that there could be anything serious between them, as to suppose that there was anything dangerous in Moreau's position or in the part he was playing. Thus reaching Paris on the evening of February 17, I executed General Liébert's commission on the following morning.

I had never served under Moreau, I had never spoken to him; I had, in fact, merely had a glimpse of him with the Army of the North in 1794, at Genoa in 1799, in Paris on the 18th *Brumaire*. I had sent him as an eminent military man a copy of my works and had received polite letters from him, but there our dealings ended, and if he remembered my name it was as much as he could do. My bringing the letter in question should therefore only have led on his part to a few friendly words in return for the phrases in which I had expressed my happiness at having this opportunity of paying my respects to him.

What, then, was my surprise when having read General Liébert's letter without inquiring whence I came, if I was employed or how, looking upon me no doubt only as a friend of General Liébert, perhaps having heard of my misadventure at Saint-Cloud, and the powerful enemies which the blockade of Genoa had gained for me, and judging therefrom that I was not likely to be friendly to the existing order of things, he began with the utmost vehemence to express his opinion against the government and the First Consul! I was again in presence of a scene similar to that which General Bonaparte had exhibited to me three days before he struck his blow, but with the difference that Bonaparte had expressed his thoughts in the form of indignation and wrath, while Moreau, in harmony with his character, employed contempt and disdain. To quote some of his phrases:

> Liébert is still at Tours—When you have children and no money you must serve at any price, though you have to serve as stepping-stone to the most ambitious soldier that ever lived—this is the end of all our labours, all these hopes, all that glory; that's what so many brave men, whole armies, have been sacrificed—for authority isn't enough for that insatiable appetite, it will be wanting the purple and the hereditary principle to hand down the fruits of usurpation—and it is we who are to surrender to these encroachments, this slaughter of liberty, we who are to be cowards enough to let them come to pass.

He was walking up and down his study, quickening his pace more and more, when he began this discourse. I had followed him for some minutes; presently I had stopped without his halting in his walk. At last he could not help perceiving from the indifference of my face and from my silence that I did not share his exasperation, and that if I delayed my departure it was because there was no third person present to make it possible. So after coming up to me he stopped, ending up with wishes for France, to which I answered in polite phrases; then I took leave of him, resolved not to see him again.[1]

To tell the truth, I was amazed both at General Moreau's frame of mind and at his boldness in confiding it to me. No doubt I understood that one of the two greatest generals in France after Bonaparte, and the only one who could have any aspirations towards power—for Masséna had never thought of laying claim to it—would not be likely to forgive him who had attained to it. The enmity was inevitable ;as the result of the nature of things, of human infirmity, of the power of self-interest. Even if Moreau was apathetic enough to let his hatred remain inactive, he was urged on by his wife, still more by his mother-in-law, till he never missed an occasion of finding fault with the inten-

---

1. [It may be noted that if General Thiébault is correct in his dates, the order for Moreau's arrest had, when this interview took place, been signed three days ago. If the general was aware of the state of affairs, his exasperation was justifiable.]

tions and conduct of the man to whose laws he had to submit after having preceded him by so many years in the path of military glory.

On the 18th *Brumaire*, it is true, Moreau had joined Bonaparte and even undertaken to become the gaoler of the Directors, while the Directory was in its death-struggle. But it may be said that he was dragged on by events which he had no means of opposing. He presently accepted the command of the Army of the Rhine, but no sooner was he at the head of his old troops and on the scene of his victories than he took up a hostile attitude. General Fririon, who was present, gave me the following anecdote in writing.

Soon after making himself Consul, General Bonaparte had a fancy to go and inspect the armies on the Rhine and see the generals commanding them. But much as he might wish, he did not venture to carry it out nor even make any announcement on the subject without giving notice to Moreau. Accordingly he sent under some pretext his *aide-de-camp*, Duroc, one of the most conciliatory and moderate of men. Duroc went to Basle and found Moreau at breakfast with some of his officers. After exchanging some commonplace phrases, Duroc recurred to the Army of the Rhine, the fame of its generals, the high distinction of its commander, and the great interest which the First Consul would take in visiting them on the very scene of their triumphs.

"Colonel Duroc," replied Moreau, emerging from his habitual calm, "does Bonaparte take us for Philistines? Tell him that if I were going to Italy I should be delighted for him to come and see me and give me advice, but I know Germany better than he does, and you can tell him, my dear Duroc,—that if he comes, I shall leave the command to him." Duroc saw directly that there was nothing to be got there, so he declared that he must have expressed himself badly if he had let it be supposed that the First Consul had any intention of coming, and he said nothing more except as to a vague desire which the First Consul might have had of finding an opportunity for giving Moreau a renewed assurance of his attachment.

Still it was a long way from this to playing a criminal part, a long way from rivalry or sarcasm to revolt; but from what he had now said to me, and from the tone and manner in which it was said, there was but a step to revolt, and that step it seemed to me that he had made up his mind to take. On getting home I told my father of the interview, and he was no less uneasy than I had been. Neither of us understood the degree of fury required to make this man, on the first occasion of my speaking to him, reveal so fully to me the secret of so hostile a frame of mind. What was my duty if not immediately to report the interview to Murat, under whose command I was? My horror of anything like tale-bearing prevented the idea from even occurring to me. Nevertheless, when Moreau was arrested and brought to trial a few days after Pichegru, I was very uneasy both as to the contents of the letter which I had brought in which my name might occur, and as to what Moreau's answer might contain regarding me.

My poor father even passed a night with me in packing up many of my papers and putting them in a place of security. In fact, our anxiety lasted till after the trial; that is, until Moreau was banished and Pichegru dead. Pichegru's death was imputed to Napoleon, who was content to refute the charge with the phrase, "You do not dirty your hands with a coin that is out of circulation." Pichegru would pass no longer; he was not worth a crime, but with any pluck he was bound to evade the scaffold.[2]

On leaving Moreau, I went to call on Murat. "But, my dear Thiébault," he said, after the exchange of a few friendly words, "what has become of you for the last three weeks?"

"Was I wrong in thinking that there was no urgent reason to bring me back?"

"Certainly you were. Some meetings have been taking place in the forest of the Trou d'Enfer. The First Consul heard of them, and asked me who was the general in command at Versailles, so as to send him orders and instructions without delay. I named you, but I was forced to add that you were not yet back from Saintes; and in the present serious state of affairs someone had to be appointed to take your place, and he was to go, and did go, to Versailles in two hours' time. I kept Orleans for you, and I have added Chartres to it, so that you might retain some portion of your old command. In this way, with the exception of Versailles, you will still have the most important part of the division."

There was a kindness in the regret he was good enough to express, and in the arrangement he had made, for which I could not but thank him; and I left him as much consoled as I could be for the loss of the finest command which a general of brigade could have had in time of peace; for the exchange of a command that was in every way delightful, might lead to anything, for one of the least pleasant in France,

---

2. [This defence of Napoleon seems to overlook the facts that he was a Corsican, and that, among those against whom he had a grudge, Pichegru was not the only person who died by a convenient suicide.]

which could lead to nothing. It was with all the keener annoyance that I had to recognise that I was the sole cause of it, and if a loss was ever deserved, that surely was.

On being informed by Murat of the change, I asked for orders, and expressed a desire to reside at Chartres. "At Chartres!" he exclaimed; "why, there is no comparison between that town and Orleans in point of importance." But as I pressed it, he said, "Well, you shall go to Chartres." And on February 20, 1804, my orders were sent accordingly. However, one day when I was dining with him, he told me to reconsider my choice. I preferred Chartres simply because my future wife detested Orleans, and of all the cities of France it is the most tiresome, by reason of its inhabitants. But the weight of considerations in its favour outweighed a mere antipathy, and ten days later I received my orders for Orleans, and took up my quarters there accordingly.

As I have mentioned, the First Consul had decreed that, by way of reprisals for the perfidious aggression of England, all the English in France should be regarded as prisoners of war. They were settled in several places, and Orleans became the residence of some sixty of them, the most notable being Lord Elgin and General Count O'Connell, uncle of the man who is now upsetting England.

The former, who had been English Ambassador at Constantinople, and had gained a certain reputation for the harm which, as a good Englishman, he had done us, was a man of rather over forty,[3] not very tall, rather strong, and of distinguished merit and manners. Apart from the relations which his position compelled him to bear with me, and in which I tried to save appearances, three circumstances combined to establish a regular intimacy between us. First of all, he shared the first floor of the Hôtel du Loiret with me, and we often passed our evenings in each other's company. Further, he was just then building a fine house on his Scotch estates, and I had a fancy at that time for laying out gardens and country-places. He was as keen to show me his plans as I was to see them; and whatever his preference for the plans which had been drawn after the ideas and suggestions of eminent architects in London, Vienna, Constantinople, and Paris, I persuaded him to make such important changes that it became necessary to revise the plans: a duty which, at his request, I entrusted, on one of my expeditions to Paris, to an able draughtsman there.

---

3. [Not quite thirty-eight, as a matter of fact. His reputation rests more on the abstraction of the Parthenon sculptures than on any particular success in injuring France.]

Lastly, just at this moment when my marriage was approaching, Lord Elgin's affection for his wife was another cause which drew me to him. When he had been forced to leave Paris, Lady Elgin was near her confinement, and his grief at leaving her was such that he could never speak of it without tears in his eyes. When her time drew near, I felt so sorry for him that I advised him to write to the First Consul for leave to spend at least the time of her confinement with her, and I supported his request to Murat and to the Minister for War. We could, however, obtain no concession; and while he was in that state of despair, I felt it to be a scandalous piece of gratuitous cruelty. He used to have news of her by special messenger every morning and evening for the first ten days after the event.

Though I can never think of Lord Elgin without paying a deserved tribute to his merits, he was far inferior to Count O'Connell, whose career was not less worthy of admiration than himself of respect. Born in Ireland about 1745, he had entered the French service as a sub-lieutenant in the Royal Swedish regiment in 1760. In 1771 he was in the Mauritius with the force assembled there by Choiseul to act against the Indian possessions of England. Afterwards he served at the sieges of Port Mahon and Gibraltar, when he rose to the rank of colonel. He was at Cadiz, about to take command of an expedition by sea, when he was summoned to Neuf-Brisach to reorganise the Anhalt regiment, which had been ruined by lack of discipline; and having accomplished this duty, was placed on the committee appointed in 1788 to revise our military regulations.

After the third sitting the other members decided to leave the whole task in his hands, reserving only the right of discussing the scheme of the chapters. They found nothing to alter in the way he had drawn it up, and thus it is to Count O'Connell that France owes the Regulations of 1788, the basis and model of everything that has been done, or will in future be done, in the way of military legislation. An addition of 6,000 *francs* to his pension and the rank of major-general were the reward for his service.

In 1792 he decided to go abroad, and presented himself to the Duke of Broglie at Coblenz. Being told that all the posts were filled up, he served the campaign of 1793 with the Bercheny as a simple trooper. When the princes deserted the army and went to Russia, O'Connell returned to England, where he married a refugee French lady, a widow with two daughters. Meanwhile the hopes of the royalist party waned more and more; and by 1801 the power of the First

Consul had become gigantic, and the might of France irresistible. Mme O'Connell had interests in France; and as the law no longer forbade their return, they went back in 1802. The younger daughter before long married M. d'Etchegoyen, who afterwards became one of Napoleon's hundred chamberlains, and whose elder brother some years after married her sister.[4]

On learning that the author of the Regulations of 1788 was in France, the First Consul wished to attach him to his government, and sent most honourable offers to him with that view; but O'Connell replied, "I am too old to desert a cause which I have served all my life." The functionary who had called on him came again with no more success, and then a third time. This time he warned the count that no further advances would be made, adding:

> Make your own terms, and they will be complied with. It is not proposed that you should go on active service; it only rests with you to be the head of the First Consul's Cabinet. If you persist in your refusal, consider how much offence it may give, and do not disguise from yourself that it is calculated to call forth severe measures against you.

If the count's mind had not been made up, it would have been after this threat. Methods of that kind could have no effect on a man of his stamp. As for the First Consul, he ordered him to be arrested and taken to the Temple, a step to which the count submitted with inflexible resignation. By the efforts of a devoted friend, Senator Fargues, his detention in the Temple was commuted to residence at Orleans as prisoner of war, and in this way Count O'Connell came to be among the prisoners for whom I was responsible.

When I received his first visit, the facts I have related were not known to me; but his handsome venerable face, his white hair, and the calm dignity to which his lofty stature gave full effect, together with his natural, noble bearing, and the confidence one felt in the least word of his simple yet powerful converse, showed me that I was dealing with a man above the common; and it was with ever-increasing cordiality that I showed him how much I was drawn to vie with his old friends in zeal for him.

It was not long before I had an opportunity of proving this. One morning I received orders to send off all the English at Orleans, for

---

4. [An account of O'Connell, differing in certain details from Thiébault's, will be found in the *Dictionary of National Biography*.]

the Fort of Bitche, within twenty-four hours. For the sixty families or individuals concerned, this was a calamity which it was not in my nature to help feeling. But the orders were imperative, and you did not palter much with the First Consul or those who ministered to his will. However, while carrying out this cruel transfer, I ventured to take it on myself to except O'Connell and Lord Elgin, though I was far from mistaking the consequences of such a bold step. It occurred to me to write to Murat, saying that Lord Elgin and Count O'Connell, being at Orleans under special orders, I had thought that they would have been mentioned by name, if they were included in the general order which I had earned out; and delaying the departure of my letter for a day, I made both write at once to their friends, so that they might take advantage of the twenty-four hours' start to back me up, or rather pave the way for me; and in this way we obtained leave for them to remain at Orleans.

On Wednesday, May 2, I received an address, all ready drawn up, the object of which was to present a humble petition to the First Consul to allow himself to be named emperor. It had to be read at once to all the military officials and all the troops at Orleans, and, when backed by the greatest possible number of signatures, to be sent back by messenger so as to reach Paris on the Saturday evening. The covering letter further ordered me, with the major, to be at Saint-Cloud by eleven on the Sunday following, in order to take part in the ceremony of acceding to the desire expressed in the address. This was duly executed, but in order to arrive at the hour named we had to travel by special post; that is to say, incur an expense the compensation for which, it would seem, was to be found in the honour shown us, and in the happiness we must feel at the accomplishment of what I may say in passing neither of us had the least wish for. Nor indeed was our desire to be granted, save to the misfortune of him who had directed it and of those who were obliged, willy-nilly, to express it.

On May 19—the morrow, that is, of the day on which the decree of the Senate conferred on him the imperial dignity—the emperor re-created the order of marshals, under the title of Marshals of the Empire. Eighteen were named, fourteen for military service and four who belonged to the Senate, and were, it appeared, not to be actively employed in future. Kellermann was an exception, though he only held commands connected with the organisation of troops or the so-called reserve armies.

In this re-establishing the marshals Napoleon was afraid of his own work. He feared lest great services, enough to carry men to so lofty a position, should set up a power which might become dangerous. To preserve himself from this, he thought it best to lower the credit of the institution by his selections, and these were so made that favour prevailed entirely over justice. He also took advantage of this opportunity to show that, if he could make a great personage of a man without any recognisable claim, he could with the same ease annihilate anyone, whatever his claims might be, who might give him offence, who did not offer sufficient security of devotion to his person, or who simply was not fortunate enough to please him. Many of his selections were scandalous instead of encouraging, and tarnished the lustre which but for them would have been possessed by the great dignity of the marshalate. I well remember the tone, half of wrath, half of contempt, with which Masséna, in reply to my congratulations, uttered the scoff, "There are fourteen of us!"

Not long after Napoleon's accession to the imperial throne, Eugène Beauharnais came to Orleans on his way to preside over the electoral college of the department at Blois. Coming to the Hotel du Loiret and asking for a private room, he was shown by the landlord, who did not like to make him go higher than the first floor, into my dining-room. He at once came to apologise, and I went to keep him company while he breakfasted. It shows what a bad actor I was, that while I could without too much effort use the words "Emperor," and even "His Majesty the Emperor," when speaking of Bonaparte, I could not bring myself to use "Empress" and "Majesty" of Joséphine, who, in spite of her husband's transformation and her own share in his honours, was for me still Mme Bonaparte. I could only ask after her by saying to Eugène, "How is your mother?"

This awkwardness, to call it no more, made him smile, and then I was again awkward enough to laugh too. I have often recalled this bit of clumsiness, and I have found plenty of people besides myself who would have done the like. One had got accustomed to look upon Bonaparte as greater than anything that had hitherto been considered greatness; but how could it be the same with regard to his wife, who, raised as she was by many rare qualities and adorned by an infinity of graces, remained, nevertheless, for me as for so many others, merely Joséphine, the mistress of Barras, who had been made Mme Bonaparte in return for the command of the Army of Italy? However, I gradually fell in with the style of the period, and very soon there were no imperial qualities that I should not have found in Joséphine.

On May 21 I had to administer the oath of fidelity to the officers and local officials, and on June 12 I was ordered to Saint-Cloud to be present at the ceremony of taking the oath by the emperor. When I had made the journey to Paris, I was told it would not take place. On the 20th I was informed that a certain number of generals and colonels would be admitted to the ceremony, and I was invited to join those who had been summoned to it by His Imperial Highness the Lord High Constable.

Finally, on June 25, I was informed that I had expressed a desire that a solemn *Te Deum* should be sung in the church of the Invalides, to return thanks for the happy accession of Napoleon Bonaparte to the throne of the French Empire; but that, in order to assist in giving that august ceremony (which took place at 8 p.m. on August 15) all the splendour it admitted of, I was to be docked of five days' pay. It will be seen that in this travail, which was to bring to the birth an emperor all ready made, no expense was spared, whether of parade, writings, documents, or money, so long as it was other people's; and in this way was brought about the great deliverance which was to end in the most terrible subjection of France to her most implacable enemies.

In the course of the summer I was married to Mlle Élisabeth Chenais, to whom I shall in future refer by the name of Zozotte, a Creole abbreviation of her Christian name by which she was known to her intimate friends. General Liébert and the *prefect*, M. de Pommereul, were my witnesses on the occasion. My cross, or star, as we then called it, of Commandant of the Legion of Honour, to which grade I had recently been raised, being the first of its kind seen at Tours, was a great centre of attraction.

After four days of entertaining and being entertained, we left Tours for Orleans.

CHAPTER 8

Ordered on Active Service

On October 21 my wife and I went to Paris for the emperor's coronation. We were late, and had great difficulty in finding a lodging, but after much search I secured an attic at the price of fifteen *francs* a day. I need not describe the vast bustle, amid all conceivable magnificence, which marked the next three months. After the bald simplicity of the Committee of Public Safety, the puny parade of the Directory, and the prelude of the Consulate, it was the outburst of a return to all the prodigality of ostentation. Others besides me will recall that luxury, which indeed was maintained, if it did not increase, as long as the Empire lasted.

In the course of the gathering, ceremonies, and festivities, no less sumptuous than imposing, Berthier, now Prince of Neuchâtel, conceived the idea, or received the suggestion, of a party to be given for the emperor by all the generals and admirals in Paris; and César Berthier was entrusted with the duty of putting the idea about and getting it adopted. Nothing was easier who would have ventured to discuss it? So the agreement was unanimous. A committee was appointed, consisting of eight lieutenant-generals including one vice-admiral, and ten major-generals or generals of brigade, of whom I was one. After settling preliminaries, the committee were deputed to inform the emperor of their wish to celebrate the great and happy event in the person of the princes and great dignitaries of France, and to beg His Majesty, with the empress and the prince and princesses of the imperial family, to honour the ball with his presence.

On the following Sunday the committee met at the Tuileries, and, as soon as the persons who had come for the audience after the Mass were gone, General Dumuy, the senior general of division, asked the chamberlain on duty to inform the emperor that a deputation from the generals and admirals awaited His Majesty's orders.

The chamberlain went off to discharge his errand, and we were already gloating over the friendly reception with which we were about to meet, and the agreeable and profitable recollection of each of us which the reason for this audience would leave, when he reappeared and struck us dumb with the word:

> His Majesty orders me to tell you that, as the generals do not form a corporation, no deputation from them can be recognised."

A painter who should have undertaken to render the scene could have had no better or more varied models, for every age and every character had its representative grimace. Naturally we began by reproaching the speaker for using the word which had brought this rebuff upon us. Someone thought that, having paid our compliment, we might stop there and economize the expenses, which ultimately came to three thousand *francs* for each lieutenant-general and one thousand five hundred for a major-general; twice that for committeemen. However, it was finally agreed that General Dumuy and Admiral Ganteaume should attend the reception that evening and give the invitation as they best could. This was done, and it was graciously accepted.

The ball was held in the Dramatic Hall in the Rue Chantereine. It lasted till daylight, and supper was served continuously after one o'clock. As a member of the committee, I could not go with my wife, but I had bidden her to be there punctually at eight. At that hour I went to meet her at the door, but having waited for some time, and being called away by my duties, I was obliged to leave her to her own resources. Somewhat angry and anxious, I was soon on my way back to the entrance, when I saw Zozotte on the front seat of a first-row box, reserved for the court and the high dignitaries. I hastened to her, and, on my expressing my astonishment at seeing her there, she burst out laughing and said, "You see, there are powers more potent than yours."

The fact was that, not finding me at the carriage entrance, and not knowing what to do, she caught sight of Marshal Masséna as he arrived, went straight up to him, and said, "Marshal, you see the wife of one of your most devoted officers, who will be puzzled what to do with herself if you do not take her for a moment under your protection." On learning who she was, the marshal most gallantly offered his arm, and, taking her to the corridor of the first tier, had the box opened in which I found her, placed her there, and chatted with her for some minutes.

The marshals' ball, which was the necessary consequence of the generals', was like the crowning piece of all these splendours, but it cost each marshal twenty thousand *francs*. Zozotte had a great success. People followed her and asked who she was. I doubt if at that gathering any other woman received so many compliments no less unanimous than flattering. General Suchet, passing near me as I was walking with her on my arm, stopped and whispered, "Who is that with you?" On my reply, he exclaimed audibly, "The deuce!"—making us both laugh. She was waltzing with my friend Rivierre, and there was a block just as they were opposite the imperial throne.

They had hardly stopped, when Zozotte's eyes turned to the empress, and that kind Joséphine, an infallible judge of everything like perfection, bent towards her, saying, in the caressing tone so natural to her, "It is impossible to be prettier or to waltz more gracefully." Zozotte, taken aback, yet delighted, could only answer by a deep courtesy and a charming blush.

"Well, my friend," said Rivierre, when he told me of this success, "you know I am no friend of those people; but was I not right when I told you that in your position you were wrong not to take Mme Thiébault to court?"

The marshals' ball was somewhat spoilt for me by a squabble that I had with César Berthier. He had had the politeness at the generals' ball to cause some ladies of his acquaintance to eat the supper intended for eight ladies whom I had gone to fetch. His behaviour had annoyed me more than the thing itself, which only involved a quarter of an hour's delay, but I had not been able to suppress my irritation; and when César met us again at the marshals' ball, he said something, I forget upon what subject, which I thought out of place. As bad luck would have it, I was chatting with Masséna and Lannes, and, as the presence of these witnesses increased both his bad manners and my bad temper, I answered no less drily than ironically. César was going to reply. "Go about your business," said I; whereupon he added, "I will fetch my brother."

Lannes exploded with laughter, while Masséna said, "You are going to have all the family on your back"—and, in fact, I was quits with General César, but I should not have got off so cheaply with his elder brother the marshal, and I had to retreat.

The ball given by the Minister of Marine was very fine; few localities were better fitted for a party. As is well known, it was the old palace of the Royal Warehouse, full of early recollections for me. M. Decrès also did the honours of his ball admirably; few men had more wit or finer manners. It was he who said of Talleyrand, with reference to his fortune, "How should you expect the man not to be rich when he has sold all those who have bought him? "Many others of his sayings were quoted; I remember one of them. After the First Consul appointed his ministers, he had allowed them handsome salaries on the understanding that they made a good show; but he had at the same time ordered Fouché to have some spies in the household of every one of them. Soon after this Decrès gave a grand dinner to his colleagues, where they were waited on by many footmen in rich liveries. "The deuce!" said Fouché—"you have got a household quite like a great lord of old times; it must cost you a great deal!"

"Not so very much," answered Decrès, "seeing that it is your business to pay the wages."

This Duke Decrès was a very bad horseman, and the saying was, that when he rode the only thing he hurt was his stomach!

The last reminiscence that I shall give of this period of the coronation relates to the substitution for the old colours and standards of what were afterwards called the "eagles," because of the eagles on the top of the poles. The Champ de Mars, which is the scene of all political and military displays, had been chosen for this ceremony. On the emperor's arrival, a general roll of the drums was heard, after which the troops broke into sections, and were marched past to give up their old colours and to receive from the emperor's own hand the eagles intended for them. More than one tear was shed at that moment to the regulation shouts of "Long live the Emperor!" However, the exchange was carried out as arranged, and at the end of the ceremony the Champ de Mars was gay with the most brilliant eagles. These eagles promptly received from the soldiers the name of "cuckoos," which stuck to them in the dialect of the barrack-room.

Until then nothing had weakened the solemn effect of the distribution, but either by a purpose hard to conceive, or by an oversight which would be still more astonishing, no one had remembered to tell the men who had brought the eagles and received the colours in exchange what they were to do with those colours; so that when the emperor was gone and the stands were empty, finding it tiresome to be loaded with the colours, all the more as it began to rain, they could think of nothing better than to throw them down,—that is, in the mud. There they were trampled under foot just as the regiments were passing on their way back to their quarters.

Indignant at the insult to what they had been honouring and defending for thirteen years, the regiments began to grumble. Presently oaths and imprecations burst out, while some grenadiers even wanted to fly to their old colours and resume possession of them. My carriage not having yet gone on, I hurried to find the commander of the Military School. Failing him, I met one of his adjutants, and told him to fetch all the men that could be found of those who were keeping the ground; then, having ordered them to raise up the colours, I had them carried into one of the rooms of the Military School. This done, my first idea was to go at once and report the incident to Murat; but reflection soon decided me to hold my tongue.

Either one thing or the other; either they had really forgotten to give any orders on the subject, or else they had taken this opportunity to advertise contempt for those old witnesses to the glory of the Republic, while providing a means of punishing, if necessary, those on whom responsibility for the insult might have been laid. Now, in the first case, my report would have implied a reproach; in the second, it would have been a piece of awkwardness, and, under either supposition, it would have put me in the wrong. Moreover, it had nothing to do with my duty; lastly, and above all, I was quite convinced that no one of the details of that profanation had been the result of chance.

January was drawing to an end, and with it the time that I could remain away from my command, and moreover, from the condition of my purse, I judged that we had had amusement enough. My wife had made acquaintance with many of my friends; we had dined more than once with M. and Mme Maret, the future Duke and Duchess of Bassano, whose acquaintance we had made at the house of his brother, the prefect at Orleans. Mme Maret was a splendid woman, who in private life was no less amiable and kindly than unpretending. One evening, on going to a reception at the Orleans prefecture, we had found her hemming napkins for her sister-in-law, and our arrival had not prevented her from going on with her occupation without a thought of either apologising for it or even alluding to it.

In public she knew how to replace good nature by dignity, and made the noblest and most graceful duchess that could be imagined. We also dined with Cambacérès. His table could not fail to be appreciated as it deserved by "Mlle Chenais," who, without having her whole appetite concentrated like her father upon the pleasure of eating, was none the less his worthy daughter in this respect. Lastly, as she wished to receive the Pope's blessing, we went one day to the Capuchins' Church in the Chaussée d'Antin when his Holiness officiated. Thus petted by all our friends, having been present at all the festivities, congratulated by the empress, blessed by the Pope, Zozotte had nothing left to desire when we took our way back to Orleans, where, as she said, if one only considered the inhabitants, one would have been forced to admit that except for sugar the word refinement would have been unknown.

On the morning of June 14 our first child was born, and received the name of Edward. Our doctor, unfortunately, was only a specialist, and, though successful in his own line, had not the faculty of foreseeing results. For sixty-two days Zozotte was extremely ill, and just when she was beginning to improve I received orders to go to Chartres to inspect the 3rd Hussars. Military orders are despotic, and I had to go, though determined to get my business over as soon as possible. Still, though I worked night and day, eleven days were required to verify everything and to draw up my report.

Returning home on August 30, in the evening, I ran up into the drawing-room—a spacious and airy apartment—in which, before my departure, the bed of the mother and the cradle of the child had been placed. A sad picture offered itself to my view. The infant lay on the knees of a strange nurse, while his poor mother, rising with difficulty at the sight of me, burst into tears, and for all answer to my cry, "What is the matter?" pointed to her child, livid and motionless. Her own illness had affected the child's health and brought on some malignant inflammation, which had progressed too far to render the aid of a fresh nurse of any avail. The poor infant only lived two days longer. Zozotte remained for some time prostrated and almost lethargic, and I had to put aside my own grief to console her. Such was the state of things when, not many hours after the death of our child, a messenger passing by Orleans brought me the order to set out, within six hours, for Landau in Bavaria, there to take command of the 1st Brigade of Saint-Hilaire's division, forming part of the 1st Army Corps under the command of Marshal Soult.

I felt as if a thunderbolt had fallen on me. I vainly tried to soothe Zozotte and to persuade her that this order would not have to be literally executed. It was the last blow for her; she was seized with a violent hysterical fit. I sent an express messenger to Mme Chenais, who arrived on the evening of the next day, when, in order that my wife should not be left alone, our regular medical man, Dr. Latour, had a room prepared for her in his house, whither she was taken before my departure.

I was carried from Orleans to Paris without recovering my full consciousness. On my arrival I had barely strength to go to bed and I had not strength to get up. Gassicourt and Rivierre, who were expecting me, hastened to my side, while Richebourg and my servant Jacques went to buy the postchaise which I required, and loaded it. On the following day I received a letter from Dr. Latour, as we had agreed, in which I learnt that my wife was going on as well as could be expected. I replied at once, writing also to my poor wife, and to the prefect, M. Maret, to ask him to see to the placing of a stone on the child's grave. Then I continued my melancholy journey.

As my readers will have surmised, the meaning of the order which had compelled me to start at such short notice was that a new campaign was on foot. England had just financed a third coalition, the most necessary of all to her. Her object was to cause the breakup of the camp at Boulogne and render useless the flotilla at which people made believe to laugh, but which required only a little smart manoeuvring and a good breeze to enable it to throw upon the coast of England 150,000 men, under a chief who increased their strength tenfold. This coalition re-opened hostilities with Austria and Russia, which had been interrupted for two and a half years.

Yet what hope could those two Powers have of beating an army which Napoleon had for the last two years been training for the war, which was amply provided, and had been stimulated to the highest pitch of enthusiasm? Thus, nothing could be more shameless than the way in which Francis and Alexander took their pay, trafficking in this way—I will not say in the honour of their arms, compromised as that already was, but in the blood of their soldiers.

Taking advantage of the fact that Napoleon, being occupied with his plan of invading England, did not seem to be in a position allowing him for two months to come to appear in Germany with a sufficient force, the Coalition had in arms to meet him 417,000 men, ready for active service, besides another 100,000 in the depots and recently raised. To this formidable array he could only oppose 247,000 men; but on August 30, the very day when he had received news at Boulogne of the armament on foot, abandoning his vast flotilla, the stores he had ready, and all his plans, he had settled the organisation of the Grand Army, and twenty-eight days later that army, the greater part of which crossed the Rhine between Strasburg and Spires, was marching under his command to meet the enemy. Murat was second in command. The force consisted of six cavalry divisions and two divisions of dismounted dragoons, ten battalions of the Imperial Guard under Bessières, ten of grenadiers under Oudinot, and seven army corps commanded by Bernadotte, Marmont, Davout, Soult, Lannes, Ney, and Augereau, to which an eighth under Mortier was afterwards added. The Bavarians under Wrede formed a ninth corps.

Austria, having succeeded in disguising her preparations, was the first to act. Mack, at the head of 80,000 men, had already crossed Bavaria, and was posted on the Iller, with his right at Ulm and his left at Memmingen, a position whence he could threaten us, and where he expected to be joined by a second Austrian and two Russian armies in time to be able to offer a successful opposition to any enterprise of ours.

The emperor's only chance lay in rapid and unerring movement. His task was to anticipate the junction of the allied armies in full force by attacking and destroying the first army that stood in his way before the other corps had come up. With this object, instead of marching directly upon Mack's army, he advanced by the left bank of the Danube, past Ulm, on which Mack's right rested, and made his entire force converge upon Donauwerth. Capturing this town, but only passing through it, he crossed the Danube, and by this unexpected stroke, no less clever than bold, found himself in Mack's rear. That general, who already had been unlucky at seeing through Napoleon's designs, was unlucky once again. He might have tried either to open the way to Munich, and so preserve his line of communications, or to fall back on Tyrol, whence his reinforcements were to come. Instead of this he packed himself into Ulm, in the hope of being joined by the three armies that he was expecting, in time to get Napoleon between two fires.

But the battle at Wertingen, in which Murat distinguished himself, settled the reinforcements from Tyrol. Key attacked the bridge of Günzburg (where the good Colonel Lacuée was killed) and drove back the Austrian corps that held it; the 4th Corps took Memmingen; the Archduke Ferdinand cut his way through and took refuge in Bohemia, where, thanks to Murat, his troops arrived in a fragmentary state. This series of reverses made Mack's position so critical that, like Wurmser at Mantua, or Melas at Alexandria, he had to capitulate; like the former, laying down his arms. Thus a single operation and a few slight actions sufficed to destroy, with hardly any loss, an army which it ought to have cost us a third of our entire force merely to beat, and only delayed our progress for eight days. Within a month from our crossing the Rhine Napoleon was in Munich. More than thirty actions, fought, so to say, in our stride, resulted in as many victories, and, among other results, had the effect of destroying the Russian reputation for invincibility which, in spite of the defeats of Korsakoff and Suwarrow, the boasts of their allies had assigned them.

My division took only a secondary part in this campaign, and my reminiscences of it are connected more with marching than with fighting. Such as they are, however, they have a place in my *Memoirs*. My orders, received on September 2, were to the effect that I was to report myself at Germersheim by the 12th. If my mind had not been full of more serious matters, touching me more nearly, I should have felt more keenly the annoyance of being placed under the orders of Marshal Soult, who for the last five years had been making no secret of feelings towards me, which his character, aided by the difference between his position and mine, might easily render disastrous to me.

I hoped that the first interview would at least pass without a dispute; but I was mistaken. Indeed, the marshal seemed to throw a touch of spite into the abrupt information that he had placed me in Saint-Hilaire's division, and that, as General Morand commanded the first brigade, I should have the second, General Varé remaining in reserve. "My lord," I said—as the etiquette then ran—"I am a friend of Morand's, but I am also his senior, and I ought to command the first brigade!"

"A commander-in-chief," he replied, "can place his generals as he likes"—confusing, as regarded himself, between the commander of an army and of an army corps, and, as regarded the fact, between employment and rank. However, I merely pointed out that this could not extend to matters of organisation, which were governed by superior regulations; and to settle the question I added that, if General Saint-Hilaire were to be absent, it would be my right to replace him provisionally, which was not compatible with the command of the second brigade.

"Very well," said the marshal, with a touch of temper; "I shall form an advance-guard for Morand." This left him with only one regiment, instead of two or three, but kept him at the head of the column. In this way Saint-Hilaire's division, the first of the army corps, was thus composed: the 10th Light Infantry, under Morand, as advance-guard;

a first brigade, made up of the 14th and 36th, under me; and a second, made up of the 57th and 105th, under Varé.

From the fact of my original order having been to set out in six hours, and the date fixed for my arrival, I had thought that I should only be just in time for the crossing of the Rhine, Ten whole days passed in complete inaction, during which all that I could do was to make acquaintance with my new "military family." I will introduce them. To begin with my chief, General Saint-Hilaire, I could only deem myself happy to serve under him. He was an excellent man, of charming manners, and made friends with me at once. He soon confided to me that I was in his division by the emperor's special appointment, which gave me an opportunity of saying that the more I appreciated the good fortune of being in his division, the happier I was to owe it to goodwill in such high quarters. I also explained to him my relations with Marshal Soult, which he was good enough to bear well in mind.

I was glad to see Morand again, as a reminder of Roman days—I might almost say as a friend of those days. He did not seem to bear me much of a grudge for the loss of his brigade, though, indeed, I have always felt sure that the marshal, who favoured him without concealment, had told him that he should, none the less, be general of division at the end of the campaign, and have the first promotion. We lived on good terms and met nearly every day. I even had to thank him for an excellent *aide-de-camp*, a devoted officer named Parguez. Morand was well educated, a man with some flexibility in his ideas, and as much capacity as his small head would hold. To sum him up, he was admirable as a major, quite above the average as a colonel, distinguished as a general of brigade, and up to his work as a general of division, though overparted with the command of an army corps. As an infantry officer he was specially remarkable, and in that capacity one of the men who had seen most service and done best. He was one of those whose elevation to the Chamber of Peers could be viewed without offence, when so many others were rather pitchforked into it by favour than borne into it by their deserts.

General Varé calls for no remark. Of Colonel Mazas, commanding the 14th, I retain a recollection founded on well-deserved esteem and regard. The commander of the 36th, Colonel Houdar de Lamotte, was as energetic before the enemy as Mazas, and a man of talent as well; of perfect manners, and fine appearance and reputation, he was engaged to Mlle Baraguey d'Hilliers, who married General Foy, and would have had a fine career had he not been killed at Jena.

To go outside my own division, from this campaign I date my lively and lifelong friendship with General Margaron, who commanded the cavalry of the 4th corps. We had fought together before Solre-le-Château, in 1793, when he was captain in the Ardennes Hussars and I in the 24th Light Infantry. Lastly, I wish to record here the name of General Jordy, whose acquaintance I made at Landau. I do not mention him, I may truly say, as an example of manners, or cleverness, or even high capacity, for he had none of the qualities which make a genius or a man of the world. But, born with a passion for war and an instinct for it, he was one of the rare heroes who are the boast of their chiefs and the honour of the armies to which they belong.

His too short career was illustrated by a score of feats, notably the attack on the island of Noirmoutier, which he continued to direct with his left thigh and his skull fractured. Indeed he had, in despair, been obliged to leave the active army eight years before this time, though he had served two campaigns since losing the use of his left leg, as well as the sight of an eye by the same shot which had broken his skull. Then, however, his zeal could no longer hold out against eighteen wounds, some of which kept re-opening. He was at first recompensed by the command of Strasburg, with pay as on active service; but on the classification of the fortresses he had to leave Strasburg and take command at Landau.

I have mentioned General Jordy as an example of the reputations which, though based on numerous deeds of heroism, confirmed by orders of the day, by letters from the Directory, by promotion on the field of battle, and by national rewards, have none the less fallen into profound oblivion. His name, and the names of others, with which our armies so deservedly rang, are no longer known to the present generation. It does not take long for contemporary pygmies to hide the giants of times past; the old horizon of renown is every day covered by thicker mists, and only a few colossal figures remain uneffaced.

On September 26 there was a general movement. We broke up our cantonments, crossed the Rhine at Spires, and entered upon the campaign. I have given the general facts of it. As concerns the part played by the troops with whom I was, we proceeded by way of Heilbronn, Hall, Ellwangen, and Nordlingen. We crossed the Danube at Donauwerth, merely passing through. Thence Saint-Hilaire had orders to march on Augsburg, where I went to see the hall in which Melanchthon presented the articles of his schism to Charles V. Next day, being

October 7, we started for Landsberg, a march of over twenty miles. We had gone fourteen or so, and Saint-Hilaire, Morand, and I were riding together at the head of my brigade, chatting as we went, when Philippe de Ségur,[1] the emperor's orderly officer, overtook us and handed to Saint-Hilaire a letter which, to my great surprise, he read out aloud. Here it is, *verbatim*:

> General Saint-Hilaire,
> Sir,—I send you this letter to tell you that the enemy is occupying Landsberg. I think that you will give me a good account of him, and therewith I pray God to have you in His holy keeping.—Nap.

"Come, gentlemen," said the general at once, "let us hurry on, so as to get there today, and justify the emperor's confidence." The men, learning the contents of the letter, quickened their pace, singing and shouting "Long live the Emperor!"

We had been getting along in this fine style for a quarter of an hour, when an *aide-de-camp* from Murat, galloping as fast as his horse could go over the ploughed land, appeared on our right, and beckoned to us. As soon as he was near enough to be recognised and heard, he shouted us to halt. On doing so, we learnt that the prince was engaged with a much superior force of the enemy, and ordered us to join him with all speed.

"Impossible!" answered Saint-Hilaire; "look at the emperor's orders, sir."

"The issue is at Ulm, not at Landsberg," replied the officer; "what will become of you, too, if the prince is overwhelmed, and General Mack gets out?"

These reasons, strong enough in themselves, being backed by the roar of cannon in the direction of Mindelheim, he urged that not a moment should be lost. "Oh, gentlemen," said Saint-Hilaire to us, "what is to be done?"

His eyes seemed to rest on me as he ended his exclamation, and I said, "March on the sound of the guns, general." The quotation of this maxim appeared to decide him.

"Well then, gentlemen," he said, "regiments, right wheel; advance in columns." The word of command was passed along, and we were soon on our way to Murat in five infantry columns, his *aide-de-camp* going forward to let him know.

---

1. *Aide-de-Camp to Napoleon* by Philippe-Paul de Ségur is also published by Leonaur.

We had been marching in this way for another quarter of an hour when a cry of "Halt!" brought us to a standstill. Murat's *aide-de-camp* had disappeared, the fire was slackening, and Saint-Hilaire, having no longer anything to keep him to the point, had changed his mind. Calling us together, he explained that we were disobeying the emperor's orders, his written orders even, that we were perhaps spoiling some superb operation, that we were losing the opportunity of distinguishing ourselves and of playing a part of our own, and all in pursuance of orders from one who had no right to order us. "Therefore, gentlemen, we are going to march on Landsberg. Columns, left wheel."

Thus, after wasting three-quarters of an hour in time, and three-quarters of a league in laborious marching, and not disguising our ill-humour, we resumed, over ploughed ground, the direction of a road which we had rightly left. We had struck it, and were following it once more, when Murat's guns were again heard, so much nearer to us now that we could distinguish the musketry. The soldiers—infallible judges—formed their opinion of the military blunder, and of the fault in not keeping a promise which in the circumstances should have been sacred. A murmur arose, and poor General Saint-Hilaire was all the more distressed by an increase in the firing. He came back to us, swearing at his position, which left him only a choice of disobediences, and compelled him to act in the dark, with the risk of putting his foot into it, whatever he did, "But, general," said Morand, "it is ten to one that the force which was at Landsberg has combined with that which the prince is fighting."

So the division changed its direction for the third time in less than an hour, and wheeled to the right again. The result of all these false movements was that we came up just as Murat's vigorous attacks had succeeded in repulsing both a corps coming up from Tyrol, and that from Landsberg as well. By arriving in time we should have helped, not only to beat them, but to surround them. Naturally we were not well received, nor was Murat's "Good-morning" in the least gracious to anyone save me, which exception I set down to the advice I had given in the hearing of his *aide-de-camp*. Nor did anyone trouble himself about us. We had some difficulty in finding shelter; and as for my men, they had to bivouac, and it was a very cold night.

Next day, the 9th, we started in the morning for Landsberg. Rain no less copious than icy had been falling continuously since daybreak; the roads were horrible, and we only reached Landsberg at night, wet and chilled to our bones, to discover that by orders from headquarters all the furniture and equipages had gone back to Augsburg, so that I had no second horse, no servant, not even a dry shirt or pair of boots. To crown my troubles, I could not get off my right boot, on the side, that is, upon which the rain had driven, without slitting it from top to bottom. Bidding my landlord buy me a pair of boots during the night, I went to bed dead-tired.

When the morning dawn woke me, I called for the boots which were to have been bought; none could be got at any price. If my landlord had not been a tomtit with a foot hardly as big as a woman's, I would have made a compulsory purchase of his; but it was no good to think of that. I had the town scoured for an old pair, at any rate; but it was lost trouble. Meanwhile the division was marching out. There was nothing for it but to put on, with infinite labour, my remaining sound boot, and fasten the other round my leg with a bit of rope. Thus shod, with my clothes still wet, and snow falling thickly, I jumped on my horse and followed the rearguard only just in time, for as I went out at one end of the market-place of Landsberg I saw the Austrian hussars entering at the other.

The road from Landsberg to Memmingen goes through vast pine-forests, and we could admire the picturesque effects of the snow at our leisure, as it never stopped all day. We passed the night at Mindelheim, and drew near Memmingen on the 11th, as night was drawing on. The troops were ordered to bivouac, and Saint-Hilaire went forward to find quarters, leaving his chief of staff to get the various corps into their proper lines, and an *aide-de-camp* to bring Morand and myself to a house where we should find fire, bed, and supper. Morand went off at once; but it was against my principles to leave my men till they had piled arms, so I had the direction of the house pointed out to me as well as the darkness allowed, and on this somewhat vague indication I dismissed the *aide-de-camp*, glad enough not to have to wait.

In half an hour I set out to rejoin General Saint-Hilaire, but the night had grown so dark that while trying to follow the direction pointed out, I got stuck in the mud, and found a brook in front of me of which I knew neither the breadth nor the depth, and which formed a swamp that I had much trouble to get out of. Was there any ford or bridge? No dwelling appeared, no light, no inhabitant. I could distinguish nothing but the wood, of which I had been told, forming a black edging to the other side of the brook. Richebourg, assisted by one of my orderlies, looked for a way across, and looked in vain.

At length, after having wandered about for some time in the snow and the mud, we heard a man and succeeded in catching him up. It was a dragoon going back to his regiment, which was cantoned a good league away. We followed him, hungry, dead-beat, frozen, and no longer thinking of anything but shelter, which when we reached the cantonment seemed to be offered by a house of fair size. Richebourg and I dismounted, and going in, found a room full of straw, lighted by a wretched hanging lamp, and warmed by a cast-iron stove almost red-hot. Not even the stifling heat and the awful odour could stop us. The floor was covered with dragoons lying under and upon the straw; we flung ourselves among the snorers. By dint of treading on the feet of some and hands of others till they yelled, I managed to find just room enough to hold me between two of them, and fell asleep, convinced though I was that it would require a miracle to prevent the stove setting fire to the straw and broiling us like bacon.

At daybreak the "boots and saddles" roused half a squadron out of this stinking den, together with Richebourg and myself. But Richebourg, who no less than I had been soaked like a sponge for the last forty hours, having wished to profit by the heat of the stove to dry his clothes, had been rewarded for this bit of luxury by finding one of his coat-tails entirely burnt, a disaster which his face and his rage would have made comic had our situation been less wretched. We remounted, he with one coat-tail, I with one boot, but at any rate we had a guide who took us to the country-house, where they had waited dinner a whole hour for us the evening before. To complete our ill-luck we got there just as the general was mounting—that is, when breakfast was over; and as they had left nothing but some bread and cheese, we ate that on horseback, washing it down with wine drunk straight from the neck of the bottle.

That day passed in negotiations resulting in the capitulation of Memmingen, but if the capture of the place did not cost us a single man, the fury of plunder did cost a few. At the moment when our cavalry forced the outposts to fall back in a hurry, the horses of a cart, which was going towards the town, had been killed close up to the gates, the drivers had fled, and the cart had been abandoned. Our soldiers had somehow discovered that among the load of the cart was a case of jewellery and another of watches, after which it was impossible to hold them back. Neither the most imperative orders nor the lire of round shot, grape and musketry, directed at all who approached the cart, could check them. More than forty were killed, but the two cases were broken open and emptied; which was what these madmen called making war on their own account.

This brings me to a painful reminiscence. The task of taking Memmingen accomplished, Soult's orders were to march to Biberach in order to blockade Ulm more closely on that side. The capitulation was signed in the evening, and the marshal left Legrand's division, I think, to occupy the place until the captured garrison and artillery had been started off for France, and set out with the rest of his troops for Biberach. But he had completely overlooked two precautions: first, to establish an order of marching for the troops of all arms, including the artillery; and secondly, to have the road reconnoitred.

Now it happened that for a distance of about five miles the road was formed by a deep hollow way; the artillery were among the first to get into this, while it should on all accounts have brought up the rear of the column; it was followed by the infantry and the cavalry mixed up together. The road soon became abominable, night came on; many of the guns and tumbrils got stuck in the mud or broken, while everything that came after them was compelled to stop. It was thought that this halt would only be momentary, and in order to gain as much ground as possible the troops were locked up closer and closer till no one could stir. Still for some time they remained patient, but as it grew quite dark and an icy rain began to fall heavily and promised to last all night, thousands of men up to their ankles in mud getting wetter and wetter and unable to shelter themselves, to sit down, to light a fire, to advance or to retreat, began to swear and grumble, and ended by the most fearful imprecations against the generals who could do nothing, staff officers who were quite innocent, and the marshal who was alone responsible for the situation.

In order to find out the reason for the stoppage and, if possible, to remedy it, the generals had ordered their *aides-de-camp* to reach the head of the column and report what was going on; but not one of them could advance even a few hundred paces, and those who ventured came near to be murdered. One general officer tried to make his way through and got into very great danger, so that he had to give it up and leave the troops to stick in the hole by themselves. My brigade fortunately reaching the hollow way just when the confusion began, I was able to halt it in time and extend it in front of a village which came just before the entrance of this horrible road. For the rest of the troops, however, it was a lamentable night, and it dealt a fatal blow to the confidence and discipline of the soldiers. When the officers were mixed up with their men, scenes of really atrocious mutiny and brutality occurred which could not be checked. Such a want of foresight would have been a blot upon the career of a corporal, and cuts a still worse figure in the military life of a marshal of France.

Daylight unravelled the abominable tangle, but instead of getting to Biberach in the early morning it was towards evening when we arrived. By a piece of good luck on which we had no right to count, this made no difference; but if Mack, who was at his last gasp, had taken advantage of that night to break out of Ulm by the valley of the Iller, he would have caught us in a state of confusion which would have made resistance impossible. We were still in the period when fortune in alliance with genius marked our enterprises by victories only. It was a time of illusion and spell, when everything succeeded beyond all that could have been foreseen, and blunders were committed with impunity—a lucky time, but not lasting for ever.

All we had to do at Biberach was to wait three days, until Mack and his army had finally passed under the yoke. So far as concerned myself, when I reached that cantonment I had not had a meal nor gone to bed for four days, passing days and nights in alternations of snow and rain. My stockings had never been dry, nor had I untied the cord which fastened my boot. I think it was the hardest week of my whole life; but now I was in a comfortable Swabian peasant's house, and in a village where razors, food, and a bed were to be had. As for my boot, heaven provided me. An orderly happening to leave Augsburg to join General Saint-Hilaire, my servant Jacques had the sense to give him a pair of boots, one containing a shirt and stock, the other a pair of stockings and some handkerchiefs. As bad luck would have it, the string that tied the boots together broke, and the boot with the shirt in it was lost; but on the other hand, as good luck would have it, the lost boot was the left one, so that the one which reached me made a pair with the one I had left.

Ulm surrendered, its fortifications were levelled, and we concentrated once more on Augsburg, whence we started for Munich and Vienna, the general movement beginning on the 18th. I said that the night following our departure from Memmingen dealt a serious blow at discipline, and it was not long before we had a proof of this. The troops, who up till now had by their good behaviour shown themselves worthy to have formed part of the camp of Boulogne, took to pillaging, and even, in pursuance of their maxim, "*The enemy is like a sheaf of corn: the more you beat him the more he yields,*" got into the way of thrashing the peasants to make them give up their money.

One can hardly believe the pitch to which they carried the tactics of plunder. When searching a house, they made the master of it go with them, watched his most furtive glances, and broke into every place on which his eye had rested. Without wishing to blame other corps, I may say that my own brigade was one of those in which the best order was kept.

On the march I used to place in rear of each regiment a squad of non-commissioned officers commanded by a firm and efficient officer, who allowed no one to lag behind, and to this end searched every house or farm near which we passed, while I myself, as well as my *aides-de-camp*—one of them was always at one end of the column when I was at the other—kept continually moving to and fro, to keep an eye on everything. I had trained my colonels to this system, and at length got them to back me up. I halted frequently, and no man might fall out unless accompanied by a corporal, and leaving his musket with his next man. On the bivouac, lastly, not only did no one go to fetch rations, wood, or water, save with a detachment, but I surrounded the brigade with a ring of sentries, which neither my own men nor those of other corps were allowed to pass, while I remained on the front of the lines all night.

I recall one incident. Some soldiers from another division came one evening to get some of my men to go marauding with them. I had heard of the scheme, and accordingly was on the spot when they came; and as my line of sentries had some difficulty in stopping them, I had to interfere. I thought I had done with them; but an hour later, as it was getting dusk, they returned in larger numbers, having been cunning enough to break up into small groups, and make their appearance simultaneously at several points. They ran past my line of sentries, and were about to get among my men, when I made the picket stand to arms and fire with ball at the foremost. The lesson produced two good results; for the fellows went off as hard as they could run and did not reappear, while my men became more manageable and their officers firmer.

"What!" said the good-natured Saint-Hilaire, when I reported to him, "you dared to fire on the emperor's soldiers?"

"I do not recognise soldiers without discipline," I replied; "the laws which condemn pillage are the same for the emperor's soldiers as for anyone else. Besides, on the day when discipline ceases in my brigade, I shall cease to command it. I may observe too," I added, laughing, "that, killed or wounded, no one was hit." Still, I should have acted in the same way, whether or not they had been; and General Saint-Hilaire's phrase expresses better than any words of mine the degree of independence which certain troops had reached. Thanks to the kind of varnish which their title of "the emperor's soldiers" put on, they acquired, with weak commanders, a sort of inviolability of which they took advantage to commit excesses of a grim kind.

The amount of thrashing I did in that campaign is incredible, and it must be admitted that I did not go at it with a slack hand, for I broke two canes. The incident that cost me the second is one that depicts our French soldier admirably, and in a sense does him honour. I had let my brigade go forward, I think, while I stopped to breakfast; several other corps had passed me, and I was trotting on to rejoin it, when I heard fearful shrieks coming from a solitary house a few yards to the left of the road. I dismounted at once and ran to the house. I found it full of soldiers, rummaging in all the cupboards, even in the drawers, to see, as one of them had the impudence to say, that there were no Austrians hidden there; others had got very tight hold of the wife and daughter of the house. Using my cane freely, I made them bolt out of door and window. Then I was told that the cellar was full of soldiers, and the wine flowing in streams. I rushed down the stairs, but no sooner was I in the cellar, than all the rascals blew out their lights and bolted, while I broke my cane over somebody's back, and drew my sword to make a better job of it.

Meanwhile the last had made off, shutting the door behind him, and in perfect darkness I stumbled over tubs and against barrels, only getting out by dint of bawling till I was at last heard. I searched the house and courtyard to see that all the looters were gone, and saw the last of them climbing over a wooden fence that surrounded the garden. They shouted any number of threats and fooleries at me, one of them having the audacity to say that I should die by no hand but his; so advising the people to shut their doors and shutters and open to no one, I remounted.

On resuming my road, I saw that it made a long circuit round a hillock, on the other side of which was some level ground, which seemed to offer a short cut. I urged my horse that way, but he had gone only a few steps when his hoofs sunk in; he tried to back, I spurred him; then he leaped forward, and gave a great many bounds as though paddling through water; at last he was right in the mud, and, as it were, floating on his stomach. I was in one of those abominable swamps, frequent enough in Germany, which there is nothing on the surface to show, while they often cover a wide space, and in some cases are bottomless. I soon saw that I could look for no support save from my horse; but he sank imperceptibly, and the least effort that he made to get out involved him further.

Richebourg and my orderly were in despair, not knowing how to help me, and we were getting very uneasy when the same soldiers whom I had just been whacking and who had sworn to kill me, but who at bottom knew quite well that I had done my duty, and in this case, at all events, made no mistake as to theirs, having reached the point where the road looked down from the hill, saw the danger I was in. With a spontaneous movement they scrambled down the steep side, threw down their knapsacks and arms, ran to the wooden fence round the house from which I had just driven them, broke it up and returned each with his load of planks to the edge of the quagmire. Making a floating floor on this, they succeeded in reaching and saving me; and not content with their first exploit, they pushed their planks all round my horse, and then, by the help of cords, levers, and girths, they lifted him and dragged him by his head and tail out of the horrible mud, and brought him back to me. "Come," I said, patting one of them on the shoulder, "there is a bit of devil about you sometimes, but you are good fellows all the same. Here," I added, pulling out two *napoleons*, "take this to drink the emperor's health with."

"We have drunk that quite often enough," said one of them, and they went off laughing, but nothing would they take.

When I did not lodge in the same place with General Saint-Hilaire, he had the next best country-house to that which he occupied himself reserved for me. One evening, however, getting in later than usual, well after nightfall, and having a mile and a half to go from the bivouac to my allotted quarters, being moreover very tired and not at all hungry, and having to start again before daybreak, I took possession of a deserted house by the roadside. As it had been previously occupied in succession by any number of officers or men, the stove of the principal room was still burning, and the room was therefore warm. As it was also full of straw, without further examination I lay down between the stove and a man who had not moved on our arrival.

At daybreak I got up, shook my cloak, and was just about to go, when my eyes fell on my neighbour. It struck me that the sounder he slept the less I ought to leave him in a place which, after the troops were gone, might not be very safe. I called him, but got no answer. I seized his arm; it was stiff and cold. I touched him with my foot; he rolled over on his face and remained so. As may be supposed, no one took the trouble to identify him; and in this way men disappeared in our armies by hundreds of thousands, without anyone thinking to give their families any proof of their decease, while we were obliged to draw up a formal statement of the death of every horse. A strict account was kept of horses, but it was no one's business to account for a man.

At midnight we received the pay due to us. The paymaster, while counting out my money, said that he had to stop one day's pay.

"Why this stoppage, pray?"

"For a monument at Boulogne."

"What monument?"

"A monument which the marshal is having put up to the glory of the emperor."

"And have I to pay for it?"

"It is being done by subscriptions from all the generals, officers, and men of the 4th Army Corps, fixed at one day's pay per month."

Unable to escape, I submitted to the stoppage; but I thought that Marshal Soult, who was making us pay the piper, would have been the greatest man in the world if glory could have been raked in as easily as money, or if he had proved as terrible to those he had to fight as to those he fleeced.

When I alighted at Wels, my billet bore the words, "At the abbey." Hearing that the marshal was to sleep at Wels, I asked where his quarters were, and was told, "At the abbey."

"And Salligny?" (the chief of the headquarter staff).

"At the abbey."

"And General Saint-Hilaire?"

"At the abbey." In short, everyone's address was the abbey. Thinking that we should be very uncomfortable there, I tried to get another lodging, but in vain. Resigning myself, and not in a very good temper, I went there, and found an immense palace, lighted up like a town. I handed my billet, and at once a servant in livery showed me into a handsome set of rooms, admirably furnished, every room warmed, and lighted with wax candles. In one of them a table was laid with six places; and at the hour I fixed, dinner was served to perfection, with two servants to wait. Everything went on as by magic, and without my seeing anyone to thank.

It was the same thing at breakfast, and I could only wish that their friends might be as well entertained by the monks as their enemies were; for indeed, though in their own country, the Austrians did not always receive the best treatment. On one occasion, in passing through a forest where a battle had taken place two days previously, I chanced to enter a hovel full of wounded Austrians, who had been left there all those two days without food and fire in the bitter cold. I had to send for the regimental surgeon of the 36th, and bid him do what he could for them, waiting with a guard till I could send food and the first necessaries for dressing their wounds from the next village I came to, and find means to remove them to the nearest town.

While the 4th Corps was accomplishing the passage of the Inn at Mühldorf, I had gone in company with General Saint-Hilaire to visit Marshal Soult. Stretched at full length on a table, supported on his crossed arms, and with several maps spread out beneath him, he was shifting from one to the other, while he read over and over again some instructions that he had just received from the emperor. He hardly appeared to notice our entrance. Thrice, at long intervals, Saint-Hilaire repeated the question he wished; to ask him; and when we got the answer at last, we had been there a good half-hour, and the marshal had neither moved nor looked round. No doubt he had afforded us the spectacle of close attention and great perseverance, but also that of great slowness of perception; and Saint-Hilaire and I were finally convinced that, if few men were capable of more persevering efforts than Marshal Soult, at the same time no one had less keen penetration, less sagacity, fewer of those rapid and brilliant inspirations which go to make up a distinguished soldier. The marshal's career has confirmed the judgement we then formed of him.

It is always delightful to beat an enemy, but it is intoxicating after 250 miles of victories to enter his capital—above all, when that is the capital of the modern Caesars. I myself only passed one night at Vienna, and that in the house of a magnate who owned one of the first vintages of Hungary. My host, a chamberlain to the Emperor of Austria, had left Vienna some time before our arrival, but he had left a steward, who was as much edified by our temperance as we were satisfied by the way in which he did the honours of his master's rooms, kitchen, and cellar.

The law of a soldier's life is, after a mansion, a hovel—after plenty, want. I got up in a palace at Vienna, and I went to bed at Stockerau in the most wretched hole, after the worst possible dinner, in contrast to my splendid breakfast. More than that, we left Austria proper, and it was strange what an effect our entry into Moravia produced on us.

That part of the Austrian monarchy differs little from its neighbours—soil, climate, buildings are alike. The inhabitants, burnt out and sacked by the Russians, received us as liberators—better, that is, than we had been received in friendly countries. It even happened to our soldiers to help the natives to repair the ravages committed by their allies, and to the emperor to make his escort halt and work at putting out a fire. The people, moreover, seemed as gentle as their language, which sounded all the softer to us after German. Yet that soft-sounding name of Moravia became matter for a sinister play on words, and many of us could not resist a presentiment that, in their case, the country was to give death in exchange for life.[2] No doubt, put in this way, it looks a mere childish pun; but there are certain moments in war, as well as certain periods in life, when to play on words may correspond with a frame of mind, and this frame of mind was a genuine uneasiness.

Richebourg, a brave man, of intelligence far above the average, felt something like horror at entering Moravia, where destiny had marked his grave. Colonel Mazas was so struck by the verbal jingle that he was incessantly repeating it, and a good many officers, who had been fighting and risking their lives on many fields for the last ten years, thought, for the first time in their lives, of making a will. Like many others, I fell a prey to this uneasiness, which I had never felt before.

We had recrossed the Danube on November 17, at daybreak, paying our compliments to the chivalrous impulse to which Murat had yielded when, being informed on approaching Vienna that the bridge over the Danube was made of wood and was going to be burnt, he hastened off to it without going through the town, crossing it in the teeth of the sentries who were guarding it, reached the left bank, went boldly up to General Auersperg, who commanded the rear-guard of the allied army, and got him into conversation.[3]

Meanwhile, several men joined him, and he ventured to resist the intended burning of the bridge. In this way, he allowed time for some troops to come up and save it; an immense service, for if the bridge had been destroyed, we should, in order to reconstruct it, have had to cross the river in boats, an operation always risky in face of a large army and on a river like the Danube. In any case it would have involved a delay of twelve or fifteen days, which might have changed

---

2. [*Mort à vie.*]
3. [As a matter of fact, Murat and Lannes saved the bridge by telling a deliberate lie, to the effect that an armistice had been concluded, a stratagem which even in the French Army was thought rather sharp practice. See General Marbot's *Mémoires*, vol. i.]

the fortune of this Hundred Days' War. So it was called, though only sixty-two elapsed from our passage of the Danube at Donauwerth, when hostilities really began, to the morrow of Austerlitz.

Napoleon's position, after recrossing the Danube, was in truth complicated. In order to be prepared, or at least able to be prepared to act, if necessary, against the King of Prussia, the Archduke Charles, the two emperors, and the Archduke Ferdinand, or to mass his forces against a divided enemy, he left the corps of Augereau and Ney in observation on the Upper Danube, within reach of the reserves at Strasburg and Mainz, to act in concert with our Army of the North, and hold the Prussians and Swedes. The Bavarians were to keep the Archduke Charles in check; Reille with the Wurtembergers, and Lauriston with the Badeners, commanded at Linz and Braunau, to secure our communications; Marmont occupied Vienna; while the rest of the army, that is, the corps under Bernadotte, Davout, Soult, Lannes, and Mortier, the Imperial Guard, the grenadier reserve, and four cavalry divisions, marched under Napoleon's direct command to Brünn.

This fortress was stuffed with stores and ammunition, and it was thought that the allies would not leave it to us without trying the chance of a battle. But on our approach they withdrew, and continued their retreat as far as Olmütz. There they concentrated in a formidable position, making Napoleon think that they would remain there for some time; the more so that part of their troops were tired, and had already lost heavily, and they were expecting the Grand Duke Constantine with the Guards' corps.

At this juncture the emperor was informed that the Archduke Charles must have passed Göritz. At once he sent Mortier's corps and half of Davout's back to Vienna, combining them there with Marmont's corps, in order to guard the capital, occupy Gratz, and be able to assemble 40,000 men there with a view of checking the Archduke's march and, after being joined by Masséna, of crushing him. As a final precaution, he kept in touch with Vienna by placing Friant's division of Davout's corps and one division of dragoons at Nikolsburg. As a result of this disposition, he was able to reinforce himself at all points, and be prepared to beat the enemy's different corps one after the other. But the uncertainty of the allies' operations, and the disorder that prevailed in their management, were in these circumstances as good as a stratagem in the way that they baffled Napoleon's previsions.

While he believed that the allies were thinking only of completing their concentration, and fortifying themselves at Olmütz, they had reached that town on November 23, and, expecting to be joined on the 25th by Constantine with the final reinforcements, suddenly resolved to advance again, and move on the 25th. In consequence of this grotesque change of plan, the orders in execution of the new arrangement were issued on the 24th. Two days' rations, however, were to be distributed to the troops during the course of the 24th, and as these ran short the start had to be put off till the 26th.

But on that day it turned out that the generals had not yet comprehended the orders and instructions which they had received on the 24th, and it was only on the 27th that the army of the two emperors was again on the march. Their unexpected movement was to bring about the shock; and just as he had reason to expect a long rest, Napoleon suddenly found himself on the eve of a great and decisive battle.

This battle, which was to be the chastisement of a most faithless aggression, and which, as the result of a series of gigantic conceptions, was to crown by the most brilliant of victories such a campaign as no army will ever again enter upon, has been often enough described. I will therefore only speak about it so far as is necessary to my story.

The hostile force which was advancing to give battle amounted to 104,000 [4] men, including 16,000 cavalry. I give these figures from what I was told at Brünn, where I lay wounded after the departure of the army, by General Weirother, who was appointed Governor of Moravia at the peace, and who, at the time of the battle, was quartermaster-general of the allied army, of which Kutusoff was commander-in-chief.

At the moment when these 104,000 men got into movement, and marched upon us in a body, our troops were thus distributed. Four regiments of light cavalry at Wischau, where, I do not know how or why, 104 infantry were captured; at Austerlitz and in the neighbouring villages the 4th Corps under Marshal Soult, which came up by way of the Convent of Raigern; at Bosenitz, Holübitz, and Welspitz, the 5th Corps under Lannes; at Schlapanitz the 1st Corps under Bernadotte; on the road from Brünn to Wischau the cavalry of the Line, under the immediate command of Murat; at Brünn the grenadier reserve, the Imperial Guard, and the emperor.

On the morning of the 28th the enemy appeared before Wischau. Our four regiments of light cavalry, attacked in front and outflanked by the three cavalry divisions of Prince Bagration's advance-guard and

---

4. [The number of the allies is usually given now at about 80,000, of whom 16,000 were Austrians. The French seem to have been slightly more numerous.]

by General Kienmayer's advance-guard, fell back. In spite of several charges which delayed them, they effected their retreat in good order by the Brünn road, till they were in rear of Rausnitz, which we evacuated in the course of the evening, and the enemy occupied at once. All the troops passed the night under arms, and from the heights of Austerlitz, where the 4th Corps bivouacked, we counted seven lines of the enemy's bivouacs, ruled to an immense length across the heights in front of Wischau. In rear of those lines of fire, at Prosnitz, the entire reserve formed the guard of the two emperors, while in front of them Bagration and Kienmayer were in position between us and Rausnitz.

While everything was thus getting ready for a terrible shock, flags of truce were passing more actively than ever. On that very 28th General Gyulai and Count Stadion arrived at Brünn to negotiate, but Napoleon, having just put an end to an armistice which had been extorted from Murat on November 15 and was only a trap, sent the plenipotentiaries in haste back to Vienna under the pretext of resuming the conferences begun at Mölk. On the evening of the same day they were followed by Count Haugwitz, the Prussian Minister for Foreign Affairs; but the emperor, pointing out that he might be in danger amid the hurly-burly of a great battle, advised him also to go to Vienna. I may say that the negotiations continued until the cannon began to roar and were interrupted only by it; for on the next day, and again on that following, Savary was sent to Alexander, while on the morrow of the Battle of Austerlitz Prince Lichtenstein began the negotiations which led up to the peace.

There was, indeed, talk of an interview between the two sovereigns; the Emperor Alexander had expressed a desire for it, but those about him were opposed to it. As for Napoleon, on hearing that Alexander's *aide-de-camp*, Prince Dolgorouki, was at the outposts, he went there from a motive which people were far from guessing. The arrogance of the Russian, the extravagance of the claims which he was bidden to maintain, seemed of such a kind that Dolgorouki was pretty sharply sent back. Two things were striking in these interviews—one the contempt for the Austrians which the Russian officers from the imperial headquarters very unjustly proclaimed, attributing to them all the reverses of the campaign; the other the ignorance under which the same officers lay with regard to what had passed.

They believed that they had nowhere been beaten, were convinced that we had more than shared their losses, and were certain a hundred times over not only of beating us but of annihilating us. Alexander

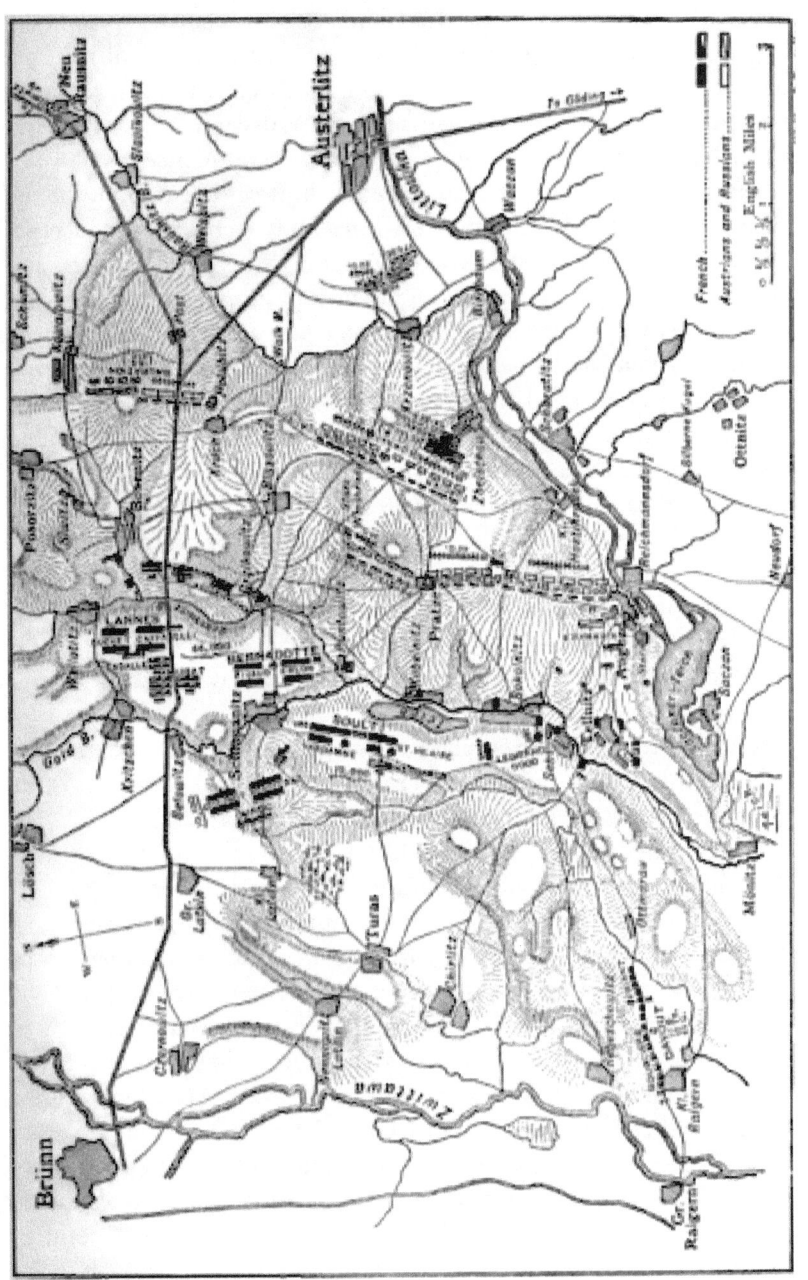

himself carried this mistaken confidence to the highest point, and it certainly had its influence upon the disaster towards which he and his army were marching. I have always been convinced that Napoleon, in determining to see Dolgorouki, had wished to judge of this fact for himself, and that not only thus did he fully convince himself from their bragging of the incompetence of the Russian commanders, but that he also succeeded in adding to their fatal confidence.

No sooner had Count Haugwitz left him on the evening of the 28th, than Napoleon mounted his horse and went off to the posthouse in rear of Welspitz, where Murat had his headquarters, and where he and Soult were just then discussing our position with regard to the disparity of forces. Lannes having just come in, they put the position so vigorously before him that not only did they persuade him of the urgent need for a retreat, but they persuaded him also to take advantage of the freedom of speech which he had maintained towards Napoleon, and write to let him know the opinion of all three. Lannes never lacked courage to express his convictions; no man in the world was braver, and equally no man was franker or more straightforward. He at once took the pen, and was finishing his letter when the emperor entered. "Well, gentlemen, we are pretty comfortable here," were his first words.

"We do not think so," answered Lannes, "and I was writing to your Majesty to that effect."

Without replying, the emperor took up the letter and read it. When he had finished, he continued: "What! Lannes advises retreat? It is the first time that has ever happened. And you, Marshal Soult?"

Soult replied with an evasion, "In whatever way your Majesty employs the 4th Corps, it will account for twice its number."

Indignant at what he called a bit of humbug, Lannes rejoined angrily, "I have not been here a quarter of an hour, and I know nothing about our position but what these gentlemen have told me. My opinion was founded and formed on their statements, just as it was at their instance that I was writing to you; so that Marshal Soult's answer is that of a dirty sneak, and such as I was far from expecting. I regard it as an insult, and I will have satisfaction for it."

Soult tried to explain away a motive and a method too worthy of himself for any mistake about them to be possible; but it was at no time an easy matter to mislead Marshal Lannes about any point of conduct or honourable dealing, and he continued to treat Soult in the most insulting fashion. As for the emperor, he walked up and down for some moments without troubling himself about the quarrel, or even seeming to be aware of it. Suddenly he stopped short, and after saying, "I, too, think a retreat necessary," abruptly opened the door of the room, through which Major Subervie, Lannes' senior *aide-de-camp*, had heard all that I have just related, and ordered him to send and fetch Marshal Berthier. He was in the act of dismounting, having just come from Brünn, and came in instantly. Murat, Soult, and Lannes withdrew at once; the emperor dictated an order for what was an evolution rather than a retreat, in pursuance of which Lannes' corps fell back on the "Santon" [5] a little before daybreak on the 29th, and Soult's in inverse order; so that Saint-Hilaire's division was behind Kobelnitz, Vandamme's behind Puntowitz, Legrand's behind Sokolnitz.

The two corps executed this movement in squares, chequer-wise, reminding Morand of the marches in Egypt amid immovable swarms of Mamelouks. For my own part I was no less struck by the novelty than by the magnificence of the spectacle. Nothing could be finer or more imposing than those thirty moving masses, which after two hours' march were extended over a distance of five miles, while their arms sparkled in the sun. As for the troops composing them, proud of the leisurely way in which they were executing this retrograde movement in broad daylight, they seemed in that formation to be challenging the lines and columns of the enemy's cavalry, which covered the whole horizon but did not venture to attack us.[6]

While the two army corps were thus retiring, our cavalry and artillery filled the gaps; and on the completion of the movement the cavalry of the Line took up a position behind Grzikowitz, which was occupied by one of Bernadotte's divisions, the other remaining at Schlapanitz; Friant's division at Nikolsburg was ordered to advance with all speed to Raigern; while the grenadier reserve and the Imperial Guard left Brünn and encamped round the emperor's bivouac, which was on a hillock in rear of the village of Kritschen. In this position, ready to fall back or to advance, but more inclined to the former, unless the enemy made the mistake on which he reckoned, the emperor resolved to await events.

---

5. [This name was given by the men who had been in Egypt to a hill having a chapel on the top, with a spire suggesting a minaret. Now called "Napoleon's Hugel."]

6. In the emperor's fifth note in General Stutterheim's *Relation*, he says, "Marshal Soult's corps evacuated Austerlitz at 3 in the morning, and by 7 was in position behind Puntowitz and Schlapanitz." There are two mistakes here. We did not leave Austerlitz till it was full daylight, and the 4th Corps never had a single man behind Schlapanitz.

Prince Dolgorouki, who had shown himself so arrogant in his interview with the emperor, wishing to justify in the field the part he had played in diplomacy, snapped up everything which seemed at all conspicuous; at least, in General Kutusoff's official report, he was credited with the only feat of arms in connection with this movement. He it was who on the 28th succeeded, with a battalion of *jägers* and another of musketeers, in overcoming 104 infantry who had been left in Wischau—though in that desperate position they had during some hours stopped Prince Bagration's first division. He again it was who, on the evening of the same day, with two battalions of Arkhangelgorod musketeers, supported by all the Russian advance-guard, triumphantly entered the little town of Rausnitz, which we certainly had no idea of holding, and only defended for a moment in order to make the prince pay for what we should anyhow have evacuated for nothing. This advance brought Bagration's advance-guard to Kovalowitz; the 4th and 5th columns in front of Austerlitz nearly to Blasowitz; the 1st, 2nd, and 3rd columns took up a position on the heights of Pratzen; General Kutusoff's headquarters being at Hodiegitz, and on December 1 at Krzenowitz, where the emperor's quarters ;also were.

In possession of the heights from Posorzitz to the lake of Satschan, and holding a position of an extent proportioned to their strength; having 25,000 men more than we on the ground, with the possibility of having 35,000, the allies, who till then had marched with the caution consequent on their ignorance of our strength and positions, on reaching our outposts could do nothing better than attack us. This was so much the case that, if they had on the 30th offered battle with an unbroken front, Napoleon would have fallen back to meet his reinforcements, to find ground better suited to his plans and less to the enemy's. But upon the 28th the Russians especially were convinced that we dared not face them.

This opinion was based on the fact that, instead of opposing them on the march, we had evacuated all the points which they had either attacked or threatened; had, as they put it, fled from Wischau, Rausnitz, and Austerlitz, and that at night; had retreated eight miles without halting, and, instead of threatening one of their wings, had concentrated our forces. These signs of hesitation and apprehension, this appearance of backing down, seemed to them a final proof that our nerve was shaken and for themselves a sure presage of victory.

I need not here enlarge upon the three courses which were open to them for attacking us. The first possible plan consisted in turning our right, and taking us in reverse by the wooded heights to the north of the "Santon"; this would threaten our proper line of operations, divide us from the Bavarians, threaten our rear, and cut us off from Ney's and Augereau's corps. This plan, alarming for us, was rejected on futile grounds. The Russians threw contempt on the second,—namely, an attack on our centre, which could only lead to an ordinary battle and victory. They dreamt of something better; aspiring to annihilate us at one blow, they expected to attain that end by adopting the third plan. This was that of attacking on our right, by forcing the gaps of Sokolnitz and Telnitz—a plan of which the result could only be either useless or disastrous.

If the allies won, instead of separating, splitting up, and cutting off the whole body of troops with the emperor, they would practically concentrate them, leaving their operations perfectly free for retreat; while, if beaten, it was they who would be cut up and cut off. And, in their infatuation, instead of falling upon Napoleon before he was prepared, they had not been afraid to waste three days within striking distance of him, to manoeuvre in full view, not even doing us the honour of keeping it secret, and to refrain from calling up the 10,000 men under General Essen, which would have brought their superiority up to 35,000 men. They intended this corps to combine with that under the Archduke Ferdinand and beat the Bavarians before we could join them, and take us in rear, cutting us off from possible reinforcements. In this way they imagined that they could bring our 80,000 men to action with the 134,000 which they had, including the archduke's force, and that we should be done for; and, dismissing the idea of breaking up the mass of our army, they abandoned themselves with enthusiasm to the idea of surrounding and taking the whole body of troops round the emperor.

Possibly, if this plan had been adopted against a general of the calibre of him who conceived it and carried it out, it might have had a chance of success; but it was just what intoxicated the allies with pride that gave Napoleon the means of destroying them.

The "Santon," forming the pivot of our left, bristled with earthworks and artillery; the allies kept away from it, so as to neutralise our chief means of defence. Our centre was guarded by some difficult approaches; it was our right only that rested on nothing and offered no obstacle capable of stopping a powerful force. Moreover, the idea that they would find themselves on the road to Vienna immediately after getting past Sokolnitz and Telnitz elated the allies; while the necessity of fighting on a line six miles in extent did not check them any more than did the risk in concentrating two-fifths of their troops on one extremity of that line, and to this end denuding the high ground which ought to have been the centre of their position. They saw no importance in the fact that on the field of battle everything becomes a question of space and time; and forgetting, apparently, that they were at hand-grips with the greatest captain of the age, they failed to see that his actions, even when they seemed least considered, were perforce connected with the most profound calculations.

None of these considerations, I say, modified the elation of the allies. They wasted November 29 and 30, and part of December 1, in substituting fresh instructions and explanations for those issued in the first instance, and in this way allowed Davout time to reach Raigern with 4,000 men of Friant's division and, I think, a division of dragoons. Finally, at 3 p.m. on December 1, after passing the morning in reconnoissances and outpost firing, and having let the soldiers have their soup, they began to execute the movement which as it seemed was to achieve our destruction, and which resulted, as it was bound to do, in that of the allies.

Thus at Austerlitz, as at Ulna, the emperor's prevision was entirely fulfilled. Here he deceived the enemy by packing himself into a trap, as he did there by weakening himself at the most important point.[7] He also wished for no ordinary victory; and just as at Ulm he had annihilated the Austrian Grand Army, so now he did not wish to come to blows with the Russians without crushing them. With this view, being the weaker, he would, if the allies had not by a gross blunder compensated for the difference, have refused battle; but he was happy to accept it when he saw them falling head over ears into the trap that he had set for them.

Towards evening an order of the day announced the forthcoming battle to the army. One phrase especially roused the troops; that, namely, in which the emperor proclaimed that, if they justified his expectations, he should confine himself to directing the movements; but, in the contrary event, he should expose himself where danger was greatest. No sooner had the order been read to all the corps than the emperor passed *incognito* and without escort along the front of several regiments. He was at once recognised, and was the object of the greatest enthusiasm. Just as he was in front of the 28th a soldier

---

7. [It will be observed that in each case the enemy was induced actually to commit the mistake which Napoleon appeared to commit in the other.]

cried, "We promise you that you will only have to fight with your eyes tomorrow!"

Halting in front of Ferny's brigade, composed of the 46th and 57th, he asked the men if their supply of cartridges were complete. "No," answered one; "but the Russians taught us in the Grisons that only bayonets were needed for them. We will show you tomorrow!"

Between one army excited to this point and another composed of fanatics, the battle of the next day was bound to be decisive and merciless. But the next day was December 2, the anniversary of the coronation. This coincidence, joined with the conviction of success, put the troops into such a state of enthusiasm that they wished to give some sign of general rejoicing as an announcement to the emperor of the celebration they were preparing for him; in which they also wanted to let the enemy share, as he had just allowed us to witness those last manoeuvres executed under our very noses, as if to terrify us. Hardly had night fallen[8] when, by a spontaneous impulse hardly credible, nearly 80,000 men, distributed among a dozen bivouacs, suddenly armed themselves with long poles bearing bundles of lighted straw. They kept renewing them for half an hour, carrying them about and waving them, as they danced a *farandole* and shouted "Long live the Emperor!"

Out of the 80,000, 25,000 to 30,000 were to transform this festival field into a field of slaughter; but it is the way of our soldiers to mingle the gayest with the most terrible images. At the first shouts, and still more at the way in which they were redoubled on all sides, our surprise made us turn out; and, as the Imperial Guard was shouting louder than the rest, Morand and I leapt on our horses and galloped to the emperor's bivouac. What were my astonishment and delight to find there General Junot, whom I believed to be still ambassador at Lisbon. He had galloped from Lisbon to Bayonne, there had jumped into a carriage, and had continued his race without losing a minute all the way to Austerlitz. Excited by his successful journey, he related every sort of crazy performance—laughing like a madman, for example, when he told us how a Spanish postilion, who was galloping with him through a regular hurricane wet to the skin, said, at sight of the white *pelisse* with all its embroideries and orders, which he wore as Colonel of Hussars, as wet as his own clothes, "Sir, this is not ambassador's weather."

---

8. [Marbot says it was close upon midnight, and that the idea was given by Napoleon's escort, as he went the rounds, lighting some torches to show the way.]

On returning to Kobelnitz, about 11 o'clock, I found the order to have my brigade under arms at 3 a.m., to lead it in front of the village, and there join the rest of the division. It was a ridiculous order, for the sun did not rise till nearly 8 o'clock, and no risk would have been run by letting the men have another three hours' rest; but in the harness one obeys and does not argue, though one may think none the less. Richebourg and I thought it was not worth while going to bed for three hours, so we passed the rest of that night—for poor Richebourg the last on this side eternity—in playing chess.

Meanwhile the emperor was receiving hourly reports of the continued movement on the part of the whole left of the allied army, so far as could be judged from the noise of the artillery waggons, each report being a source of fresh joy to him. At 3 o'clock nothing more was heard. It was the hour of rest preceding the shock, but it was also the moment when our divisions were silently assembling in the bright and bitterly cold night. In order to mislead the enemy, they made up the fires which they were leaving.

The emperor was on horseback well before daylight. Before 8 o'clock he had gathered round him Murat, Bernadotte, Lannes, Soult, Bessières, Oudinot, and Berthier. Though the moment was so important, and the incident so little to the point, I may mention that after the scene in the post-house Lannes had sent a challenge to Soult, and had received no reply. Finding him there, he said, "I thought you had got a sword, and I have been waiting for you."

Soult merely answered, "We have got more important matters to attend to today."

"You are a poor creature!" retorted Lannes.

As the sun was rising word was brought to the emperor that the last of the Russian troops, who had passed the night on the Pratzen plateau, were leaving it and moving towards Telnitz. "How long will your troops take to crown the Pratzen plateau?" thereupon asked Napoleon of Soult. On the answer that twenty minutes at most would be enough, the emperor, wishing to turn to advantage a fog which covered the valleys and concealed our troops, added, "Very good; we will wait another quarter of an hour." That time having expired, and everyone having received his final orders and instructions, he gave the signal to start. Each man hastened to his post; he himself started, exclaiming, "Let us finish this war with a thunderclap"; and to the cry of "Long live the Emperor!" repeated by the troops, we finally separated, each to do all that lay in his power towards making effective the thunderclap announced by him who then held the thunderbolt.

When traversing the Pratzen heights on November 21,—that is, at the moment when the allies were retiring on Olmütz, and there was reason to think that the time of year and the need of waiting for new troops and resting those whom they had would decide them to suspend warlike operations at least for some weeks to come,—the emperor had said to the officers of his suite, "Take a good look at those heights; you will be fighting here in less than two months." On the same reconnoissance, when going through the villages of Grzikowitz, Puntowitz, Kobelnitz, Sokolnitz, Telnitz, and Mönitz, he had also said:

> If I wished to stop the enemy from passing, it is here that I should post myself; but I should only have an ordinary battle. If, on the other hand, I refuse my right, withdrawing it towards Brünn, and the Russians leave the heights, if there were 300,000 of them, they would be caught *in flagranti delicto* and hopelessly lost.

On the morning of December 1, when he saw the Pratzen heights covered with Russians, his words were, "The enemy will have to stay a long time if he waits till I go and turn him out of that;" but returning to his bivouac about midnight on the same day, and getting confirmation of the news that a great part of the enemy had already left these heights, was in force before Telnitz, and was continuing to mass troops on that point, he cried, "That army is ours tomorrow!"

On the very morning of the battle, still equally ready to retreat or to fight, he delayed the attack for a quarter of an hour because Soult told him that it would take twenty minutes to crown the heights; nor did he give the signal until an *aide-de-camp* came and told him (a little prematurely) that the heights were abandoned. Half an hour later, to use his own expression, "*The Russians were no longer fighting for victory, but only for their lives.*"

These are memorable sayings, as showing that on November 21, that is, when the emperor crossed the ground for the first time, his unerring glance showed him all that might be done with it. On that day he devised the means of getting the Russians to attack him in that position and annihilating them. The poor idea which their performances gave him of the commanders of the allied army further confirmed him in the hope of getting them to make the mistakes he wanted, and winning, against an army more numerous than his own and as brave, a victory neither costly nor indecisive. The Battle of Austerlitz, with its vast results, one may add with its details, was in his head from the day when he passed Brünn. He pushed on to Wischau, but he only occupied the little town with four regiments of light cavalry, intended to serve as a bait. Rausnitz and Austerlitz, occupied by army corps, were to be evacuated at the first appearance of the enemy, to intoxicate him with the show of success. All the rest of his conduct, the pretended retreat, the haste to send all the plenipotentiaries to Vienna as though they would not be safe even in rear of his army, his personal interview with Alexander's *aide-de-camp*, broken only after several pieces of impertinence by one of those outbursts which look more like temper than prudence, was intended to raise the spirits of the Russian commander by a showing of wishing for peace without fighting.

As for the positions which he occupied, the "Santon," a pretty steep hillock a little in front of our left, was fortified in order to check any desire on the part of the Russians to march on our left; our centre, being solidly held with all our forces converging upon it, could only be reached by forcing some narrow roads with considerable loss. There remained our right, which had indeed no support, but could not be attacked and still less turned except by making an immense circuit, in which the attacking force would have to spread itself over several leagues, abandon all the heights, and endanger the road to Olmütz, its true line of operations.

Yet the emperor's aim and his hope was to draw that army against that right. He had Sokolnitz and Telnitz occupied only by the 3rd, together with two battalions, a Corsican and an Italian, from Legrand's division, a few guns, and Margaron's light cavalry brigade; and it was only after the firing had begun, towards nine in the morning, that he had them reinforced by 4,000 men of Friant's division. They were admirable troops, and twice retook the village of Telnitz; but all they had to do was necessarily confined to compelling the enemy to employ against them as many corps as possible and to deceive him completely as to the aim that the emperor had in view. Their defeat, it will be seen, was essential, and the success of the allies at that point was the corollary to Napoleon's stratagem, and so effective that, out of the 75,000 men whom he had, to meet 104,000 he did not need to bring more than 50,000 into action.

What has gone before explains the whole battle, and I need only indicate the chief phases of it. The rising sun of December 2, 1805, the sun of Austerlitz, was saluted by the attack upon Telnitz and Sokolnitz, where our troops did wonders against the first three Russian columns. It lighted up the retrograde movement of Legrand and Friant, who, unable to withstand the masses of their assailants, retired, but in such a way as to draw the Russians as far as possible from the point where the fortune of battle was to be decided. The same sun shone upon Saint-Hilaire's and Vandamme's divisions as they marched to the attack, climbing the Pratzen heights disposed as follows: Morand's advance-guard to attack the plateau which commands the southern part of those heights, Varé's brigade and the whole of Vandamme's division to attack the eastern part, and my brigade to carry the village.

The Russians, being attacked when they were themselves attacking: and thinking that we were determined not to engage, threatened at their centre while they were only acting against the insignificant extremity of one of our wings, losing the heights which were the key of all their positions, or, rather, having abandoned them to send nearly half their army astray in a direction where presently it would find no enemy to fight, and would be cut off from the rest of the army, perceived at length that they were in a serious situation and made the greatest efforts to retake the Pratzen heights. Four combats, maintained or renewed with desperation for more than three hours, took place at this point, but they could not repair their mistake in having ventured in presence of Napoleon to unguard positions the retention of which meant victory, and they paid for their temerity by a frightful rout.

During these combats the fire had been taken up all along the line, while more than 400 guns had in succession mingled their thunder with the musketry of 150,000 men. On our extreme left, in advance of the "Santon," Marshal Lannes had sustained a brilliant conflict with Bagration's corps; he had driven him out of Posorzitz and forced him back upon Holübitz; to his right, our cavalry, commanded by Murat, had taken several of the enemy's batteries, but, in spite of that advantage, contended with only varying success against the immense cavalry of the allies until General Kellermann decided the victory by a fortunate and destructive ambuscade.

The first division of the 5th Corps had fought for possession of Blasowitz with the Grand Duke Constantine's reserve, overthrowing it in several successive shocks and capturing its colours and guns. Vandamme's division, reinforced by Varé's brigade, beat all the troops in the fourth column of the allied army, less the four regiments detached against us, and had got as far as Augezd. Finally, Saint-Hilaire's division had succeeded an driving away the enemy's corps opposed to them on the southern Pratzen heights, and had pursued them as far as in front of Sokolnitz.

At all these points, then, victory had declared for us; the right of the allied army effected its retreat on Austerlitz, where their centre and even the Imperial Russian Guard arrived in great disorder. Marshal Lannes, who next to Masséna was of all the generals the one who possessed the soldier's eye in the highest degree, together with the flashes of genius which are called inspiration and the promptitude which blends the execution with the thought, seizing the possibilities of the situation, immediately marched on the right flank with his first division, and, reinforced by Bernadotte's first division, reached the Pratzen heights in his turn, whither all the cavalry, the Imperial Guard, and the grenadier reserve, who never had occasion to fire a shot, also proceeded.

Lannes' movement deserves record all the more because he executed it entirely on his own initiative. The emperor meant to make honourable mention of it, but thought, unluckily, that he could attain. this end by putting in his thirtieth bulletin, "Marshal Lannes marched by regiments in *échelon* as though on the parade-ground." Lannes was offended, because in the report of a battle like that of Austerlitz no personal mention was made of him save in connection with an evolution, and, in spite of the summary that "the left under Marshal Lannes charged three times and always victoriously," he left the army straightway and returned to Paris. On hearing of his departure and the ground of it, the emperor sent Murat after him in all haste to soothe him and bring him back; but when Murat reached Vienna, Lannes had already left it; indeed, he had only stopped long enough to write to the emperor, asking that if he had justified his confidence on the field of Austerlitz the emperor would kindly remember it with reference to his senior *aide-de-camp*, Major Subervie, who had remained at Brünn wounded. Three days after that officer received his commission as colonel, and the emperor, when informing Lannes of this, added, "I count on you none the less if the present armistice does not lead to peace."

The troops above-mentioned reached the Pratzen plateau just as Vandamme's and Saint-Hilaire's divisions had left them, in pursuit of the Russians towards Telnitz and Sokolnitz. The three columns which in the morning had made an analogous movement in order to surround us found themselves attacked by us and forced back to these, their last positions. They lost all their guns, remnants only of them getting away, and these, being cut off from the Olmütz road, were compelled to retreat in the direction of Hungary. Even these remnants would have been lost but for the show of magnanimity which Napoleon managed to get taken for policy and generosity, though others saw nothing in it but pride and vanity if his object really was only to have it said that he had spared Alexander 15,000 men.

All this generosity, vain-glory, or trickery made some people very angry. At the head of these was General Vandamme, who exclaimed on hearing of it, "To spare them today is to have them in Paris six years hence." Eight years hence they were there. That day ought to have incapacitated the Russians from playing any military part in Europe for several years to come; yet, great as their losses were, they did not prevent the emperor from being, when little more than two years had elapsed, again at close quarters with Russia, then in alliance with Prussia. The latter had their Ulm at Jena, but, unhappily, on the plains of Poland Napoleon found no Mack, no Kutusoff, neither the trap of Ulm nor the hills of Austerlitz, neither the enthusiastic soldiers of the first Grand Army, nor the Russians of 1805; and the eagle of vast swoop flapped at Eylau with one wing only, and only rose once more at Friedland to fall again heavily, for good and all.

To return to the Battle of Austerlitz. About 3 p.m. I was wounded, beyond the *château* of Sokolnitz, and the battle was over for me; nor was it long before it was so for everyone. The firing only lasted another half-hour, and its only object was, on the enemy's side, to render the retreat of his three first corps less disastrous, and on ours to do all the damage possible. Masses of men were taken in the course of this half-hour, and 3,000 or 4,000 were drowned in attempting to cross the lake of Satschan, the ice upon which was broken by the fire of twenty-four guns belonging to the Imperial Guard. An immense quantity of artillery was captured, being left undefended, and the heap of trophies was greater than in any battle of modern times.

As to the part which I personally took in the Battle of Austerlitz, I may lay exclusive claim to four military achievements. When at daybreak Marshal Soult gave the word to advance, Morand was ordered by General Saint-Hilaire to mount the Pratzen plateau and take up a position there, Varé was to follow General Vandamme's movement and take orders from him, and I was to drive the enemy out of the village of Pratzen and then to rejoin our advance-guard on the plateau,, towards which Saint-Hilaire proceeded simultaneously with Morand.

As he had told me that only the enemy's pickets were likely to be in the village, in order to gain time, to save part of my troops the trouble of going out of their way, and to proportion forces to requirements, I had confined myself to leaving the attack in the hands of Colonel Mazas and his 1st battalion; however, as extra precaution, I followed him with my three other battalions in line of battalions, and it was just as well I did so.

Whatever General Kutusoff may say in his narrative, not only had the two battalions appointed to occupy the village as the advance-guard of the fourth column had time to get there, but they had also had time to pass through the village and lie down flat, so that we might come upon them before we saw them. They sprang up just when Mazas, marching in line, found himself checked by the very wide ravine before the village, and poured such a murderous fire almost point-blank into him that in their surprise and alarm the whole 1st battalion of the 14th broke and fled. How an officer with his experience of war could have fallen into such an ambush for want of sending forward some scouts to reconnoitre the ravine and find out the Russians, I do not know.

But there was no time to waste on reprimands, so I rode forward, calling to Mazas to rally his battalion. Then, having dismounted and ordered the 36th to march on the village and force their way in, I set off, crying, "Long live the Emperor!" and charging at the head of the 2nd battalion of the 14th, which deployed as it ran, I flung myself into the ravine where my horse could not have got down, attacked the Russians with the bayonet, and routed them, avenging on them the losses of the 1st battalion.

Our left being cleared, I followed Morand's movement. He was already being attacked by a force out of all proportion to his own, for with only the 10th Light Infantry he was facing the whole of Kamenski's brigade, which outflanked him to right and left, so that he was in danger of being taken in reverse. Just then Saint-Hilaire hurried up to ask for one of my battalions, and went forward with the 1st of the 14th. Moving at the double, they formed up on the right of the 10th, and restored the balance of the fight.

I came up almost as soon as they, and was about to join Morand and finish with Kamenski's brigade, which we estimated at 4,000 to 5,000 men, when I perceived four regiments in close order marching towards us from the direction of Krzenowitz; that is, on our left flank and in rear of Morand's line. On seeing them, I halted the three battalions I had with me, and, being at once rejoined by Saint-Hilaire, we examined the approaching masses through our field-glasses, but could see nothing to show that they were the enemy. Soon, however, we heard their bands, and presently an officer from them, having come within shouting distance, called out, "Do not fire; we are Bavarians."

"Hallo!" said General Saint-Hilaire; "what were we going to do?"

"General," I answered, with a sharpness I could not repress, "these Bavarians look to me very suspicious, and the officer, who did not venture to come close up to us, looks still more so."

"Would you run the risk of firing on the emperor's allies?" he asked.

"And how do you suppose that allies of the emperor would be marching on us?"

He tried hard to make me see how fatal such a mistake would be. I replied that a surprise would be disastrous, adding that I was going to make my arrangements as if they were the enemy, and then go and have a look at them myself. In fact, we could not make out either Bavarian uniforms or their commander, and we had heard in the night that a Bavarian corps had already joined. I ordered the 36th to deploy with all speed, resting on Morand's regiment so as to form the pivot about which I might manoeuvre, and placed the 2nd battalion of the 14th in column on the left of my line, so as to have a mass which I could oppose, if necessary, to those which were advancing towards us, and a force with which I could, without disturbing my line, meet any cavalry or other corps that might try to surround us.

Morand was using three of the guns belonging to the division, so I placed the three others between the two battalions of the 36th; but just then Major Fontenay brought us six 12-pounders by order of the emperor, who judged how serious our position was getting. These I placed, three and three, on each wing of the 36th; and, with my line thus bristling at three points, I masked my guns with squads of infantry and galloped off at full speed to reconnoitre the newcomers. Morand, who thought quite as seriously as I of the four regiments, had taken the same step, and we met half-way between them and my line. Just as he came up to me an officer belonging to those regiments was joined by one whom I saw come from Kamenski's brigade. They talked together for a minute, and then each went quickly back to whence he came. If I had had any doubts before, this incident would have put an end to them, and I left Morand, saying, "Do not trouble yourself any more about them; I will see to them."

Returning to my line, I amended my arrangements. I bade Major Fontenay (a cousin of Gassicourt's) load all the guns with round and grape, and to his remark that this would ruin them I added, "It will be all right if they last ten minutes." I had them laid for a distance of thirty or forty yards, and had ten cases of grape and ten round-shot laid by each. I repeated to the men the injunction to take good aim before firing, and to aim at the men's belts and the centre of the sections, so as to waste no shots. Having thus utilised every moment, I let the formidable masses approach to the appointed distance, and then my nine guns, abruptly unmasked, and my whole line poured in one of the most destructive fires ever seen.

Without inquiring whether their commander hoped up to the last moment to surprise us, there is no doubt that these regiments thought they were approaching a line without artillery till they found themselves at the muzzles of nine pieces of large calibre, served with incredible smartness, and equally well .aimed, loaded, as I have said, with round and grape. Their fire vied with that of my line, which was the best infantry in the world for standing firm, aiming straight and knocking over the enemy with perfect coolness. My satisfaction may be imagined when I saw every round tear large square holes through these regiments till they retired a flying mass from the attack on my three battalions. I had not lost a single man, and if I had had a brigade of cavalry at my disposal not one of my assailants would have escaped. The regiments were commanded by General Kollowrath, the inventor of the artifice above mentioned, and he was marching with them in person in pursuance of orders just given him by the Emperor Alexander, who was in front of Krzenowitz, exposing himself to real danger in his desire to drive us from the heights.

I have always been very proud of the part I played in checking that attempt. By anticipating a shock which we were in no condition to resist, I saved my own brigade and the advance guard under Morand; and in this way we were enabled to hold our ground on the Pratzen plateau, the loss of which would have been no less fatal than its retention was decisive. It was, indeed, immediately after this that, in conjunction with Morand, we drove Kamenski's brigade smartly back, and captured two batteries, all ready harnessed, instead of, as we might have done, losing all ours.

On reaching the highest point of the Pratzen plateau, we commanded a wide horizon. Far away to our left we could see Lannes' troops firing at those of Prince Bagration; between him and us, but still five miles off, Bernadotte's first division were engaged with the Grand Duke Constantine's reserve; while between [9] these two groups of combatants Oudinot was opposed to the greater part of the allies' fourth column—that is, all of them who had not been opposed to us. In our rear, or within supporting distance of us, not a Frenchman was to be seen. The emperor's narrative says that Le Vasseur's brigade formed our reserve; but, if so, none of us knew anything of it. If General Le Vasseur had been informed of it he did nothing to let us know, and certainly if General Saint-Hilaire had had any idea of it he would not have waited till now to be reinforced by it; rather he would have called it up at the double.

It seems, however, that it was between us and Kobelnitz, but, being concealed by the undulating ground, no one noticed it. Moreover, we had no news either of the imperial headquarters nor of Marshal Soult, and it was with a certain anxiety that we became convinced of our isolation. We held the heights, but we had not done with having to defend them.

Once out of range of our guns, the remains of the regiments we had repulsed had been promptly re-formed; and when Kamenski's brigade, reinforced by two regiments, had restored the balance of the fight with us, it was joined by those regiments. It had resumed the offensive with desperation, and, in spite of our former success, our position could not fail to be still highly critical. We saw marching on our front a hostile force four or five times stronger than ourselves, while on our right as far as Turas, that is, three-quarters surrounding us, were fifty-five Russian battalions with three or four thousand cavalry.

Morand and I never met in after-days without recalling that position, he used to say:

> I have seen plenty of fighting, I was lucky enough since the time of the Army of Egypt to be present at all the great battles fought by the emperor; but I never saw anything like our position there.

Indeed, what could become of his three battalions and my three, thus attacked and surrounded, seeing no one to support them, bound to get weaker owing to their losses, in face of troops who were incessantly being reinforced? The enemy had hurled himself upon us from all sides, and, though we struggled desperately for the ground, we were

---

9. [This must refer to apparent position, for Oudinot's place in the French line was between Bernadotte's and Soult's divisions.]

forced in turn to give way. Indeed, it was only by yielding to the more violent shocks that we kept some sort of dressing among our troops and saved our guns, the loss inflicted by them no longer checking an enemy who seemed maddened by our resistance. At last, after a terrible tussle lasting more than twenty minutes, we had managed to get a breathing space, and a brisk fire almost at point-blank range had again taken the place of the bayonet, when General Saint-Hilaire called Morand and myself to him and said, "This is becoming unbearable, and I propose, gentlemen, that we should take up some position to our rear which we can defend."

Hardly had he uttered the last word when Colonel Pouzet of the 10th,[10] behind which we were standing, having heard the proposal, was in the middle of us with one spring of his horse. Taking upon himself to advise without being asked, and not leaving Morand and me time to open our mouths, he burst out, "Retire, general? If we take one pace to the rear, we are done for. There is only one way to get out of this with honour, and that is, to put our heads down and go at everything in front of us; and, above all, not leave the enemy time to count us." This was admirably accurate and honourable at once.

"Bravo, Colonel Pouzet!" I exclaimed; "this is one of the finest moments of your life." We ran back to our regiments and redoubled our efforts; and, thanks to the magnificent attitude of our men, without yielding a foot of ground, we repulsed repeated charges delivered with fury and with the frightful howls usual to the Russians. Thanks to this prodigious tenacity, at the end of half an hour,—in which we had lost Colonel Mazas, my poor Richebourg, shot through the windpipe, our orderly officer, and many more brave men; while more were wounded, including General Saint-Hilaire [11] and Colonel Houdar de Lamotte, while I had two horses killed under me,—our turn came at length to execute a decisive charge, breaking the enemy's line, capturing three batteries (from one of which I unharnessed a little grey horse and rode him), and becoming for good and all masters of that part of the Pratzen plateau. The 14th and 36th had two-thirds of their officers killed or wounded; while of the 236 grenadiers of the 36th, seventeen only remained with the colours in the evening.

---

10. This intrepid officer had been in the Imperial Guard. He was a major-general when he fell at Wagram [*sic*, but it was Essling], where General Saint-Hilaire also perished. [For Pouzet's death, see Marbot's *Mémoires*, vol. ii.]

11. *Chronicles of the First Empire* by Émile Marco St. Hilaire & Hippolyte Bellangé is also published by Leonaur.

This is the place to record a creditable action. I have said that at the moment of that terrible struggle we were without news from the headquarters. Just as we had checked our men's tendency to fall back, Colonel de Girardin, *aide-de-camp* to Marshal Berthier, the adjutant-general, rode up. His duty would no doubt have been fulfilled if, having formed a clear idea of our position, he had gone back and reported it. But it was a fearful moment, and with a devoted courage which, as the last living witness of the fact, I feel bound to record, he remained with Morand and me; and riding incessantly to and fro from end to end of our lines, brushing the men's knapsacks, as one may say, he gave powerful aid in supporting and cheering them on, and only quitted us when we had resumed the offensive, leaving us with a high opinion of him.

But how can I speak of our brave men without equally calling attention to the valiant way in which the Russians fought? In those terrible shocks whole battalions of them were killed without one man leaving his rank, and their corpses lay in the lines in which the battalions had stood. Up till the last hour of that battle we took no prisoners, except those who contrived to constitute themselves such. It is true we had been warned that the Russians, even when too severely wounded to be able to march, would take up their arms again after their enemy had gone forward, reload them, and put their conquerors between two fires. Now, in a struggle of such obstinacy, when we always had to do with three or four times our own number, it would not do to run any risk; one could stick at nothing, and thus not a single living enemy remained to our rear.

This melancholy reminiscence has often come back to me, but I cannot think that I am accusing myself in noting it down. Just as at Naples I burnt the whole Capua suburb and put the inhabitants to the sword, even so on those Pratzen heights I gave orders to take no prisoners and to leave no one in our rear. I had this order carried out because the safety of my troops demanded it, because victory was a matter of life or death for France, because necessity, and consequently duty, demanded it. But whenever it was possible to dispense with such a cruel performance of orders, our soldiers were ready enough to offer generous treatment to those Russians whose bravery they admired, as the following anecdote may show. Just as the battle was at its end, 1500 to 1800 Russians were surrounded on all sides, with the lake of Satschan behind them.

They had just seen 3,000 or 4,000 of their own people perish beneath the ice on the lake, and to the fire that was poured on them they made no reply, save by a fire of the most sustained kind. A bayonet-charge would have cost too many lives and was unnecessary, so the artillery was brought up, and every round caused frightful ravages among the poor fellows. It was painful to be driven to such an extremity against men who were dying in this heroic fashion, but their obstinacy left us no choice. They held out a moment longer, but they soon began to waver, and almost instantly threw down: their arms. At that moment our soldiers flung themselves in front of the guns, crying out, "Cease firing—they surrender!"

To resume my narrative. Our next object was to drive back the troops who were retreating before us towards Telnitz. We reached the hill-side which overhangs the *château* of Sokolnitz towards the east. This *château* was still occupied by the Russians with the advanced guard of one of the corps which had marched on Turas, and were crowning the hill opposite to that which we had reached. The division had been fighting without respite since the morning, and, as I was commanding it in the absence of General Saint-Hilaire, who had left us to get his wound dressed, as I had no orders and could not by myself cross the Sokolnitz valley, I took up a position with the 10th Light Infantry on the right of my brigade, and Le Vasseur's brigade, which at last to our astonishment had joined us, on the left, and then I gave the troops the rest they needed.

We had been there a quarter of an hour when General Saint-Hilaire came back, bringing the order to carry the *château* and pursue the Russians. While Vandamme was forcing the village of Augezd, and Morand and Le Vasseur resumed their march to turn the *château* on either side, I received orders to attack it in front. The Russians who were on the flanks of the *château* made little resistance, but those who guarded the house and its outbuildings made a desperate defence. Avenues, stables, barns—everything served them for shelter, and everywhere they fought till the last extremity. A great massacre took place there. All had to be vanquished, man by man. I saw some all alone defending themselves as they might have done in the middle of their battalions; I saw some shot through and through and ready to drop, loading as calmly as at drill; so we suffered heavily, and the capture of that house, which forms the third action that I can claim on that day, proved to me the truth of the saying that it is easier to kill six Russian soldiers than to conquer one.

Finally, having left the *chateau* behind me, as I was reforming my sections on the march in order to get back into line with Morand and Le Vasseur, and reach the Russians' last fighting-line simultaneously with them, I saw to my right 120 men taking long shots at a battery which was playing upon the outlets from the *château*. This sort of shooting could only be ridiculous, and I put a stop to it. There was a sub-lieutenant there; I told him to form his men in squads, and then looked round for a captain or major to order him to march with these squads upon the battery, which was on a hillock between the objective points of my brigade and that of Morand's troops. I could not see a captain—officers were getting scarce—and as my columns were in movement, and the fire of the guns might do them a good deal of damage, while the battery was so near that three or four minutes would be enough to take it, I resolved to carry it myself, and trotted off with my little force.

Although mounted on a small Russian artillery horse, I went of necessity faster than my men, so that, having got within fifty paces of the guns, I was fifteen paces ahead of them. I was turning half round with the view of calling to them to quicken their pace, when the last round which those guns were destined to fire went off, knocking over a score of my men. The sub-lieutenant of whom I have spoken, one of the finest young men I remember, was killed, and I was wounded by a grapeshot which, after smashing my right shoulder, bruised my breast-bone in two places and went through my collar-bone. At a longer distance it is a hundred to one that I should have been thrown from my horse, but the force of the blow was such that it took all its effect in penetration, and only shook me internally.

I thought I was struck by lightning. My first word was, "I am a dead man!" the next, "Avenge me" the third, "I shall never fight again!" "the fourth, "Well, I've had my money's worth!" Such was the succession of thoughts which passed through my mind at that shot. I could still see as though unconsciously my men carrying the battery and slaughtering all the gunners, then the Russian troops who were supporting it broken and pursued as my columns came up, and then everything disappeared for me. I remained for a long time dazed on my horse. Recovering from this condition, I dismounted, but my right arm did not follow the movement of my body; it hung swaying over the right side of my horse, and I had some trouble to get hold of it with my left hand and bring it over to my body.

The ambulance was at Schlapanitz, and I tried to reach it on foot; but after going a few hundred yards, shot still falling around, my strength gave way. Attempts were made to get a cart at the *château*, but the only thing that could be found was a limber; but on a vehicle of that kind, at each frightful jolt, as I crossed the deep furrows of the Moravian fields, I could feel my bones rubbing and crackling, tearing through the skin as the splintered ends rode one over the other. So they made a kind of stretcher with poles, planks, and anything that was handy, and laid me on it. Seeing some poor Russians straying about close by, I sent for them and made them carry me; but some grenadiers of my brigade, several of them wounded themselves, caught sight of the Russian bearers and drove them away, in spite of all I could say, declaring that it was their business to carry their general.

Just then Marshal Berthier came by and witnessed the scene. It passed into an anecdote, such as people are eager for in these cases, and, though I was the person concerned, it got into the *Moniteur*. In the emperor's narrative it appears in a modified form as a sentiment of the grenadiers generally: "The honour of our wounded generals belongs to us"—but the fact is as I give it. I was already reckoned among the slain, and, as people are glad enough to make it up with them, the circumstance was regarded, perhaps, as a ground for showing me goodwill. So indeed it struck me when I begged Berthier to tell the emperor that I had always served him to the best of my power, that on this great day I thought I had done useful service, and that I commended my children to him.

It was not from Berthier, however, that the emperor heard of my wound, but from General Bertrand, from whom I have the following fact. At the words, "General Thiébault is wounded, sir," the emperor asked if I was severely wounded. "Mortally, sir."

After a moment's silence the emperor replied, "No man could die at a finer opportunity." Such was the funeral oration which he thought he was uttering over my grave. The thirtieth bulletin announced my wound; the thirty-sixth, dated from Schönbrunn, stated, rather prematurely in my case, that the wounded generals were all on the high road to recovery.

I was 700 miles away from those dear to me; I had lost in Richebourg the best friend I had in the army, and the only one who could have morally alleviated my grievous position. I did not expect to recover from my wound. Still, I would not give in to the weakness which I felt was getting hold of me, and to drive away these doleful thoughts I sang till my voice failed, and then I whistled.

An officer of the 36th, who had thought it right to stay with me till

I found my servant, was so surprised that he said, "Why, general, what kind of stuff are you made of?" However, it was one of my chances of salvation, weak as they were; I felt that if I let myself break down I was lost. A wounded infantry officer was being carried near me. He was wailing like a child, and at first I made a great effort to endure his groans, but soon anger got the upper hand, and, bidding him go to the deuce, I made his bearers take him further away.

The surgeon-major of the 4th, Joseph Bonaparte's regiment, saw me, came up, and put me through a first dressing, which, in spite of the blood I was losing, consisted in making two great gashes at the spring of the shoulder, above and below the point of entrance of the bullet. Linen was needed, and Mother La Joie, who had for years been the *vivandière* of the 36th and was thought a great deal of in the regiment, came forward with some. I asked for a glass of brandy, which she at once poured out, and I handed her a *louis*. She burst into tears and gave it me back. I told my father of this; and my friend Rivierre, when he had a picture painted of the incident, based on the account in the *Moniteur*, had the good *vivandière* put into it.

At length I saw a man running towards me at full speed; it was my faithful and devoted valet—that same Jacques Dewint who, as the Duke of Abrantès said, served me as no general officer was ever served. A good fellow, no less than a plucky one, hearing that I was wounded, he had been scouring the battlefield to find me. Nothing could have so much comforted me; and to him I was indebted for a speedy arrival at Schlapanitz, and the diminution, so far as might be, of the horrors of the journey.

I was placed in the best bed in the best room of the best house in the village, and my wound was regularly dressed, Next day I had to be moved to Brünn, but so weak was I that this seemed difficult. However, a low and roomy carriage was discovered which, I think, had not been out for a hundred years, numerous mattresses were placed in it, and, with infinite precautions on the part of Jacques and the surgeon, who was attached to me from this time till my arrival in Paris, they contrived to get me as far as Brünn. My transference from the carriage to the room where the problem of life or death was to be solved for me was even a more difficult business. Quarters had been taken for me in a deserted house, so that I had not the attention which one never expects in vain from German kindness. For company, therefore, save for a few visitors, I was reduced to the surgeon, and he was not much with me except at night, being busy all day in the hospitals; but my faithful Jacques was a real providence for me by his devoted care.

Next morning, in order to judge of my condition, and make ready for my first big dressing, there met in my room M. Percy, surgeon-general to the French Army, and the first military surgeon in the world, M. Yvan; the emperor's private surgeon, M. Larrey, chief surgeon in the Imperial Guard, the surgeon-major of the 8th Hussars, and my own surgeon. One could not have more luminaries round one, but it did not appear as if they were destined to illuminate a long future for me. Independently of the fact that seven fractures are always serious, especially in the region of the chest, it seemed inevitable, in the general opinion, that, in the course of nine inches which the projectile had taken from its entry in the shoulder to its exit by the sternum, some artery must have been wounded; in which case, when the wound cleared, as it would do about the third day, haemorrhage must come on and death follow immediately. So they considered that I had not more than thirty-six hours to live; and, while dressing me to the best of their power, they confined themselves to holding out hopes calculated to keep up a few hours' illusion, but to which no one really gave credence.

At daybreak on December 6 the surgeon of the 8th Hussars came in with the air of a man who had not liked to go past my door without finding out what kind of a night I had had. This, together with the way in which, to my answer "Much as usual," he returned "Ah! that's well"—a surprise which he could not conceal, combined with a slightly puzzled air, and observations or turns of phrase, none of which escaped my watchfulness—struck me so much that, when M. Percy and his colleagues arrived for the dressing, I joked with him about it. He replied in his kindly and no less persuasive tone, smiling, doubtless in order to make the more show of security:

> You have escaped the greater danger of your condition. We feared that some artery was injured; this fear is now set at rest, and it was in order to learn the true state of the case that I wished to hear news of you as early as possible. Now I reckon on your recovery, all the more so because your moral courage is so remarkable.

In truth, weak as I was, I made a point of getting up every day and walking to my sofa supported by Jacques and my surgeon, so afraid was I of the weakening effects of lying in bed.

My progress towards recovery, however, underwent many drawbacks, and for some time the ultimate issue was uncertain. I had been fighting death for twelve or fourteen days, when I received a letter from my wife dated on the evening of December 2. She said that she had been in her mother's room at three o'clock that afternoon, working near the window and talking over her griefs and sorrows, when a flame like the flash of a gun passed before her eyes. She had cried out at once, and taken refuge by her mother's side. She added;

> The horror which I felt of the Cher at the moment when I was losing my poor brother comes back to my mind. I am not superstitious, but after such cruel misfortunes, and after a fact of that kind, all apprehensions are horrible. I shall not get over the shock it caused me until I have had news from you later than that day.

To understand this passage, I should mention that in the previous September her young brother, who had just joined the 24th Mounted Chasseurs, had been drowned in fording the Dora near Turin. Zozotte was then living at Tours, and on that day had gone to stay with a friend at Saint-Avertin. The two were walking beside the Cher, when Zozotte started as if in fright, covered her eyes with her handkerchief, and only answered her friend's urgent inquiries with the words, "Let us go in; the sight of the water makes me shudder." Now this repugnance at the sight of water had come on just at the moment when Amédée was drowned, and her letter which I received at Brünn, dated on the day of the Battle of Austerlitz, showed an analogous coincidence of presentiment; it surprised me, therefore, in spite of the curious instances of prescience and second sight which I witnessed both before and afterwards.

Meanwhile the news reached her, unluckily, through the *Moniteur* before she heard it from myself, and she became seriously ill. Everyone at Tours showed the utmost kindness; even the postmaster never went to bed till he had sent all the letters addressed to her. She also had news of me through the *Moniteur*, which even announced, prematurely, that I was out of danger. Her first thought had been to come and nurse me, but, luckily, her father required my consent before letting her go, and my doctors were dead against it. M. Percy said, "There are sometimes cases when the last chance of saving a person who is ill is to keep his dearest friends at a distance;" and, indeed, if I had seen her in the course of the first weeks, the emotion must have killed me. When I began to mend, there was not sufficient reason for her to make the journey at the worst time of year.

On December 14, 1805, I completed my thirty-sixth year. When I awoke, Jacques wished me many happy returns, saying, "I shall wish you the same, general, twenty-five years hence, and then I shall remind you of this time." He kept his word, poor man, on December 14, 1830, bringing his two sons with him; but he did not long survive the occasion. It seems long ago to me now, though in 1805 I thought I should never reach it.

The same day, feeling less oppressed than I had done, after my family letters, I dictated another to General Saint-Hilaire. It went by one of the emperor's messengers, and he answered it next day, giving me a fine testimonial to my conduct, and assuring me that the emperor would take it all into account. From all sides, both by writing and by word of mouth, I was told that I was made general of division, and a letter from one about the emperor congratulated me on it "as a positive fact." It will be seen in the sequel, owing to what influence it came about that this announcement was not confirmed, even by my nomination as grand officer, which would have been a poor substitute for a division.

At the end of his order of the day to the army of Austerlitz, Napoleon had said,:

> Soldiers, when all that is necessary for the happiness and welfare of our country is achieved, I will take you back to France, and you shall be the object of my tenderest solicitude. My people will greet you with transports of joy. It will be enough for you to say, 'I was at Austerlitz,' to bring the answer, 'There is a hero!'

These pompous words and the promise of tender solicitude raised higher hopes than were realised. It is the old story of all that is prompted by the enthusiasm of today, and has to be modified by the morrow. Personal claims were exaggerated, deferred, forgotten, or modified as predilections or antipathies dictated; while what related to the method of celebrating the glorious event was subject to new considerations. The Madeleine was transformed by decree into a "temple of renown," in which every marshal present at the battle was to have a statue, every division a *bas-relief*, on which every general officer was to appear in sculpture; while special distinctions were reserved for wounded generals. Each officer, non-commissioned officer, and soldier was to see his name engraved on tablets of brass. As we know, the plan was never carried out, and, instead of a vast monument, Austerlitz has its plain stone slab on the Arch of Triumph.

One hall in the Napoleon Museum was to be devoted to a collection of all the curiosities brought from Vienna. This was never done, and Gerard's picture is the only memorial of the battle that I know of; but the bridge of the King's Garden received the name of Austerlitz, while the square separating it from the garden was called after Valhubert, the only general who died of wounds received there; and the space in front of it took the name of Colonel Mazas, of the 14th—the first regiment of my brigade—who fell in the battle. But the column in the Place Vendôme, cast from the guns captured at Austerlitz, will always be the chief monument to recall to our descendants the part which their ancestors played in that battle.

To close this series of reminiscences and reflections suggested by the Battle of Austerlitz, and to sum up what I have related of it in a few comparisons, it may be said that on the side of Kutusoff and his understudies it was the result of ignorance, incapacity, indecision, and presumption; while on that of Napoleon it was the fruit of rapid inspiration and profound calculation. Kutusoff—for on the field of battle Alexander and Francis were only his lieutenants—ventured to march against the emperor without having either the number or distribution of his forces, nor yet the opportunities afforded by his adversary's position; while Napoleon had, so to say, traced out the road by which his enemy was to arrive at the destination that he foresaw.

But what assigns to destiny a share in Kutusoff's inaptitude and to luck a share in the other's genius, is that General Buxhoewden, who commanded the three columns that executed the fatal turning movement which formed the basis of Kutusoff's plan, remained for a good hour with retreat open to him; that is, escaped from the consequences of that disastrous idea, and yet he continued the movement imperturbably when it could have no further object or excuse, and only understood his position when it was past retrieving. Yet further, at a moment when no retreat was possible save at one point, the Mönitz defile between the lakes of Satschan and Vessel, he pushed on his first column towards another point above, and could not fail to be surrounded and destroyed. As we see, there were mistakes and bad luck on one side, genius and good luck on the other; valour in all three armies—indescribable enthusiasm among our troops. It took all this to make the Battle of Austerlitz.

Yet does it follow that only the enemy can be accused of mistakes, and that because they were committed with impunity, for the present at least, none can be laid to the charge of Napoleon? On the contrary, five can be pointed out, and they are extraordinary enough to be worth calling attention to. To begin with, when we were on the Pratzen heights he did not have us supported either by Le Vasseur's brigade or by any battalion of the reserve; an imprudence all the more serious, since it is impossible to say how it came about that we were not twice broken and driven off the plateau. He ought never to have laid himself open to such a check at that point, seeing that if it had taken place the enemy's three columns which were marching to their own destruction would have found themselves again in touch with the troops, who would have regained possession of the plateau, and nothing could have hindered their junction and the consequent improvement of their position. This was what Alexander was aiming at in his efforts to take the heights from us; and, if it had occurred, the emperor's whole plan would have been frustrated, and he would have been forced to retreat.

It will not do to excuse Napoleon by saying that our situation was unknown to him. No doubt he had been misled by the *aide-de-camp* who came and told him at half-past eight that the enemy's last corps had left the Pratzen heights, when the whole of Kamenski's brigade, the Fanagorski and Riajski regiments, and the fourth column which was to follow the movement of the first three, were still there. But our tremendous fire could not fail to enlighten him by revealing how hard a struggle we were maintaining; and, besides, was he under any mistake when he sent us those six 12-pounders? They brought us up before long to a rate of a gun for every 200 men—a proportion which is excusable when one is short of troops, but ought never to be allowed for any other reason, considering the impossibility of saving so much material in the event of a retreat. If only for that reason, Napoleon should have supported us with a reserve.

If he did not do so, I have always been convinced that it was in order to be able to say, "By the might of my genius"—we had not yet got to the star—"I had in that battle no need either of the second division of the 1st Corps, nor of my grenadier reserve, nor of my guard." It was this bit of swagger which prevented him from taking 15,000 more prisoners; for, while he was drawing the three columns against his right, in order to cut them off, he ought to have guarded the Mönitz defile, the only line of retreat open to the fragments of them. If at that moment he had hurried up his reserves on to the Pratzen plateau, he could have made them take our place in the attack on Sokolnitz, and then have sent us at the double with Vandamme's division, and Varé's and Le Vasseur's brigades, to the Mönitz defile, which unquestionably would have delivered into his hands the fugitives of these three columns to the very last man.

Nor did he support us with any cavalry; yet, if the enemy at one of our two worst moments had attacked us with a cavalry brigade, we should have been unable to reply, while, if we had had a brigade within reach, we should have made thousands of prisoners.

Again, ought he to have left so large an interval between our division and Vandamme's without placing troops between them to support whichever required it? He left them to take their chance of a reverse, and in Saint-Hilaire's case, especially, how little more was wanted for that reverse to happen! No doubt Napoleon was justified by the event; he split up his attacks, did not reinforce them at the right moment, and yet each of his attacks succeeded and became a victory. But after profoundly studying and considering the subject, and talking it over with many competent officers, we have retained the conviction that in the triumph of genius luck must be credited with its share.

Lastly, ought not Napoleon to have taken advantage of his victory to incapacitate his enemies, by an unrelenting pursuit, for reappearing on a field of battle for many years to come? He was so well aware of this that, on returning from his conference with the Emperor of Austria, he said, "That man has made me commit a blunder; I might have followed up my victory and captured the whole Austrian and Russian army. Well, rather fewer tears will be shed." [12]

Here I had meant to end, but I cannot leave the subject till I have exhausted it. Of the various narratives, General Kutusoff's is a mere irrelevance; Major Stutterheim's is the work of an honourable man, though it has inevitable mistakes as to our movements. Napoleon did him the honour to annotate it; but in many points of detail he has not even noticed the errors any more than in the narrative he himself dictated. This was written, revised, and modified at various periods in his study, and is not free from the omissions or inaccuracies which a commander-in-chief, who has only a general view, cannot avoid. So far as concerns myself, I have endeavoured to supply the gaps.

As for Marshal Soult, who now talks with pride about the Battle of Austerlitz, I will give the measure of him, if only to let the reader

---

12. [It will be observed that Thiébault seems to know nothing of the current belief that the Russian plan had been communicated to Napoleon before the battle.]

know the value of the biographies which reckon that memorable battle to his fame. In spite of the critical position in which Saint-Hilaire's troops were for the space of three hours, Marshal Soult never appeared either to direct them in case of need, to encourage them by his presence, or to judge if it was necessary to reinforce them. Still, I had a doubt remaining as to whether the marshal had not fulfilled his duty as commander of an army corps; not with General Legrand, who with six battalions had nothing to do but draw the enemy's leading columns astray, and who, as the emperor himself remarks, remained almost outside the battle; nor with General Le Vasseur, whose brigade had hardly any fighting, especially in the morning; but with General Vandamme, who, with his own division and Varé's brigade, had kept up such a brilliant fight on the Pratzen heights.

I could not indeed disguise from myself that General Vandamme was not the sort of man to welcome the presence of a mentor, who would practically have commanded his troops; but I could not see my way to allowing that in the Battle of Austerlitz Marshal Soult had fulfilled none of the functions of a soldier or shared the danger of any of the men of his corps. I was told, indeed, that that morning he had complained of inflammation of the eyes, and had put on a green silk shade just when the battle began—not the movement, because he had nothing on his eyes when he started us a little before sunrise.

Indeed the sun of December 2, in Moravia, is not very dazzling, whatever legendary splendour it may have borrowed from our victory; and, besides, in such circumstances one might defer precautions of this kind for a few hours, though even a green silk eye-shade need not prevent a man of spirit from doing his duty in battle. Thus I did not find the green silk sufficient ground to assume anything so serious, and this determined me to inquire of Lieutenant-General Vincent, at that time *aide-de-camp* to General Vandamme, whom he never left throughout the day.

He formally declares that on December 2, at daybreak, Marshal Soult came to Vandamme's division and set it in movement, as he had just done with Saint-Hilaire's, and that the division saw no more of him till two in the afternoon, when all it heavy fighting was over and it was entering Augezd. The reserves, the Imperial Guard, Marshal Lannes with one division, our cavalry, and the emperor himself were then on the Pratzen heights, and the battle was coining to an end. Then Marshal Soult only appeared to convey the order to cut off the Russians' retreat by the shore of the Satschan lake, as he gave

Saint-Hilaire, then returning from the field-hospital, the order to attack Sokolnitz.

Thus it is clear that Marshal Soult took no personal part in the Battle of Austerlitz, unless one can consider the transmission of a few orders at points where fighting was no longer going on as the part of the commander of an army corps. I own it is difficult to believe, and it took a long time and much inquiry to make me do so. But I wished to verify the suspicions which Saint-Hilaire, Morand, and I had conceived when we did not once see the marshal, whose business was to have been constantly going from one to another of his divisions, to stop with them, to back up the generals. I can still hear the exclamations which ten times over burst from each of us: "What! no news of the marshal? And is he not going to turn up himself?"

There is no way out of it; and yet Marshal Soult, who no more fought the enemy that day than he fought Lannes, reckons Austerlitz among his titles to fame. The fame belongs by right not to him but to his army. The emperor made no mistake, and when he gave him a title he did not call him I will not say Duke of Austerlitz—Lannes would not have stood that—but after any town or village recalling the name of a victory.

CHAPTER 9

Napoleon's Friendliness

By January 25 I was able to start for Vienna, where I had to stay for a week; and at noon on February 4 I arrived at Linz. Marshal Soult was there, but no one of Saint-Hilaire's division, and I determined to dine and go on without seeing anyone. An *aide-de-camp* of the marshal's, however, announced that he was coming to call on me, so, rather than be under any obligation, I called on him. He received me kindly enough, but I had a right to complain of the way I had been treated in his reports, as a consequence of which my junior had been promoted over my head, and I asked him for an explanation. He seemed embarrassed, and said that no one had done more justice to me than he had. I only said that I did not see what I could have done more than I had done. He said, "General Thiébault, you are quite mistaken if you think I did not specially mention you in my report; and if you ever become acquainted with it, you will be flattered by the way in which it treats you."

"My lord," I said, "you have had a grudge against me for the last six years, on account of my narrative of the blockade of Genoa."

He owned that he had been displeased with it, because I had not made him play a part worthy of him. I should have liked to go into details, but he postponed a discussion likely to tire me, and only said, "We will talk of all that at Paris." He never spoke to me again of it.

My wife and I both reached Paris on February 26. There is no need to describe the joy of our meeting or the kindness of our friends. I was invited everywhere, and Napoleon himself showed some interest and goodwill toward me. I never appeared at the Tuileries without his having a word for me, were it only to ask how my arm was going on. One evening, after a ballet performed in the Hall of the Marshals by dancers from the Opera, in presence of the imperial family, some of the company had gone out on the south terrace of the palace, and I among them. The emperor came up, and, catching sight of me, took me by the left arm and brought me in again, saying, "Do not stay there; night air is no good for wounds." All my friends urged me to take advantage of the opportunity, in the absence of Soult and Berthier, to extract from his justice what disfavour had withheld from me; but my wife, who alone could have overcome my dislike to the step, only confirmed me in holding back. She said once, "Injustice is better than the humiliation of taking as a favour what one has deserved as recompense." So shutting myself in an ill-humour, which was only childishness, I lost once again the opportunity which always escapes him who cannot seize it, and delayed for thirty-two months a promotion which, if I had had it then, would have altered my career.

At one of the sumptuous receptions which I attended in those days, as I looked at the gold and purple throne which seemed as indestructible as it was brilliant, I suddenly thought of the first time that I had seen Bonaparte, then a major-general on half-pay. It was in that garden of the Tuileries which now was his, near the upper end of the Spring Walk, now the Orange-tree Walk. At that time the little man was living at Paris, supported by the father of Junot, his first *aide-de-camp*, and had to solicit on his own account what before long was to be obtained only by his favour. That day he was walking with three other persons as unknown as himself, and was only pointed out to us as one of Aubry's victims. From the spot where I remembered him to that where I now saw him the distance was not more than three or four hundred paces, the difference in level thirty feet at most; yet what vast spaces had he not had to traverse—what heights had he not had to climb to pass from one to the other!

The brilliancy of his Court was something incredible. Hundreds of foreign orders were already worn there, beside the star of the Legion of Honour. Personal and hereditary titles were still lacking, but it was felt that this would not long be the case, and the re-establishment of the terms Prince, Lord, Excellency, for the present filled their place. Those entitled to them wore the richest costumes, as did equerries and chamberlains. Of the latter there were a hundred, the posts being occupied by the most notable and wealthy persons in all the countries united under the imperial sceptre. Even the old families of France solicited employment about the emperor and empress.

But though as Chief of the State he was ready to welcome them, as a soldier he was scandalised to see them thus preferring the livery to the uniform, while as a man he was vexed that they had not been willing to help him in founding the power of which they were now swarming to take advantage. This was what caused him in 1812 and 1813 to institute the Guards of Honour; the sons of the first families in France suddenly received orders to join their corps, and were forced to comply. The same feeling drew from him the remark, so terrible in its truth: "I opened the ranks of my armies to them and none offered himself; I opened my antechambers and they crowded in."

M. Morin, with whom I made friends during the siege of Genoa, was living with a friend of his named Sibuet. They passed the winter in M. Morin's house at Paris, and the summer in a pretty country-house which M. Sibuet had at Soisy-sous-Étiolles. They pressed us to come and stay with them at the latter place, and we went there in August. I had a conversation there with M. Morin, worth recording on account of the remarkable foresight which it showed on his part when one remembers that it took place eight months after Austerlitz. We were discussing the emperor's future. Dazzled by our victories, even as Europe and France were, I could see no possible limit to his omnipotence.

M. Morin replied;

> I admit that the emperor is the greatest general of modern times and our armies the first in the world; but his victories have done more to make him enemies than to add to his fame, and every conquest weakens his position rather than consolidates it. He can subdue, but he cannot reconcile. Neither his successes nor his origin will be forgiven him. There is not a king but is disgusted at seeing him with a crown; not a people who can forgive him; not a nation that is not humiliated by having been trampled on by him; not a soul who is not irritated by his pride or terrified by his ambition. His scheme of re-establishing the Empire, the very names of Grand Army, great nation, proclaim everything small that is not himself or does not emanate from him.
>
> He is insatiable, nothing will limit his greed, and there will be no check in the course either of his prosperity or of his disasters. Thus his enemies have only to wait. Just now they are stopped only by their powerlessness; but their hatred is prolific. Yet I do not say that his downfall is at hand, only that he is marching to it. I do not deny even that he may yet increase his

deceptive power and raise himself yet higher, but it will only be to fall into a deeper depth. Believe me, all that his building gains in extent and elevation it loses in the solidity of its foundations. In spite of truces, there is a struggle between Europe and him that can only end in destruction, because on one side there are twenty nations, while on the other is a single man.

His first reverse will be the signal for a crusade in which France herself, weary and exhausted, as by that time she will be, cannot fail to be involved. And it is impossible but that he will meet with that reverse, because everything comes to an end, and the enthusiasm which deifies him today will wear out like the rest. Shall I finish giving you the whole of my mind? I do not understand how he can have more than ten years to reign!

Struck by his own inspiration, M. Morin asked me to bear the terms of it in mind; and now that the colossal power, which his foresight condemned to ruin, is now only a memory, I set his prophecy on record. Alas! he was only too right. In the rooms which Napoleon occupied at Munich, in either 1805 or 1809, there was a picture of Charles XII. "Take away that portrait," he said; "it is a man with nothing to show." And what results has he himself to show? Or what sort of a comparison will follow, as far as that goes, if beside Napoleon, who made France lose all that she had won, including what she had won without him and before he was heard of, we set Frederick the Great,[1] who, as the head of a weak State, alone against all Europe, without finances or population, doubled the might of Prussia, and put her among the leading nations? Yet who would dare to put Frederick before Napoleon?

We had been a week at Soisy, and I was coming in one morning to breakfast, when we heard a horse gallop up. The messenger brought a letter bearing the stamp of the emperor's household, in which the chamberlain on duty informed me that His Majesty would see me at nine o'clock the next morning at Saint-Cloud. I had never been summoned like this before, and had nothing to prepare me for this favour, for such it evidently was. Morin suggested a confidential mission, Sibuet an embassy. We returned to Paris for dinner, and next morning, by three minutes to nine, I was at Saint-Cloud. In the room leading to the emperor's study I found Murat and a score of persons belonging

---

1. *Frederick the Great & the Seven Years' War* by F.W. Longman is also published by Leonaur.

to the household, all in short green coats, trimmed, like their three-cornered hats, with gold braid, armed with whips, and hunting-knives hanging from broad belts, waiting to follow him to the hunt. Seeing me, the chamberlain on duty said, "His Majesty was just asking if you had arrived." I called his attention to my punctuality, and, knocking at the door, he showed me in.

The emperor was standing up in the costume just described. He accosted me with a pleased air, and said that he had just appointed me general of division. After receiving my best thanks, he spoke of my wound, seemed interested to hear that it was in a fair way to get well, and dismissed me no less kindly than he had received me. As I left his study, Murat came up and asked what the emperor had said to me.

"Prince," I replied, "he was good enough to say that he had appointed me general of division."

"My dear Thiébault, let me be the first to congratulate you."

Others—Duroc, Savary, I think Le Marois—followed his example.

I had not got into my carriage again before the emperor had leapt on horseback and gone off at full speed, all those who had to accompany him racing after. I could not understand this similarity of taste between Napoleon, the busiest monarch in the world, and his predecessors the Bourbons, the idlest of existing princes and the most imperturbable sportsmen. Anyhow, all through that summer he shot and hunted, and everyone racked his brains to vary his amusements in that line. like a good courtier, Alexander Berthier was not behindhand. He had the idea of giving the emperor some rabbit-shooting in a park which he possessed just out of Paris, and had the joy of having his offer accepted. The property possessed everything calculated to make the sport agreeable except rabbits; but rabbits are common enough, and the marshal, being, as adjutant-general, accustomed to think of everything and provide, considered that he was as right as he could be when he had ordered a thousand of those animals to be turned down in the park on the morning of the day.

An order of that kind is not executed by halves, and not a rabbit of the thousand was wanting. At length all was ready; the emperor had been expected, the emperor had arrived, a splendid breakfast had been served. The accessories made way for the principal business; the sport began, and Berthier was in high delight at having been granted the honour of giving his master some healthy pastime with the opportunity of distinguishing himself. But how can I tell it or be believed? All those rabbits, which should have tried in vain, even by scattering themselves, to escape the shots which the most august hand destined for them, suddenly collected first in knots, then in a body; instead of having recourse to a useless flight, they all faced about, and in an instant the whole *phalanx* flung itself upon Napoleon. The surprise was unbounded, as was Berthier's wrath. At once he assembled a force of coachmen with long whips, and, proud of having found a decisive opportunity of protesting against a cruel word which had escaped the First Consul on the field of Marengo—"Berthier is not of the stuff of which they say brave men are made"—he darted forward at their head.

The rabbits put to flight, Napoleon was delivered; and they were looking on the incident as a delay—comical, no doubt, but well over—when, by a wheel in three bodies to right and left, the intrepid rabbits turned the Emperor's flank, attacked him frantically in the rear, refused to quit their hold, piled themselves up between his legs till they made him stagger, and forced the conqueror of conquerors, fairly exhausted, to retreat and leave them in possession of the field, only thankful that some of them had not succeeded in scaling the rumble of the emperor's carriage and getting themselves borne in triumph to Paris.

It only remains to explain the phenomenon, and all was revealed as soon as it was known that Berthier's emissary, not aware that there could be any difference between one rabbit and another, had bought rabbits from the hutch instead of from the warren. The consequence was that the poor rabbits had taken the sportsmen, including the emperor, for the purveyors of their daily cabbage, and had flung themselves on them with all the more eagerness that they had not been fed that day. The laughter which this revelation elicited may be guessed, also the way in which it added to Berthier's despair. In his shame and confusion, regretting the ridicule even more than the fact, he vowed, a little late in the day, that he would not be taken in again.

I told the good news of my promotion to my wife and my father, asking them to say nothing about it till it was officially notified. My father approved, and said nothing; but Zozotte, while equally thinking I was right, confided it, from one intimate friend to another, to nearly all the world. Yet a week went by; I had received nothing. I began to be anxious, and made inquiries of Maret, who was now Secretary of State, only to be taken aback by the answer, "Nothing concerning you has reached me."

Murat, with whom I breakfasted next day at Neuilly, could only suggest that the emperor wished to make a formal distribution of promotions at the festivities which were in preparation to celebrate the peace—an answer that did not satisfy me. It would have seemed simpler and more natural if he had said, "I will speak to the emperor of it." He advised me to show myself at Saint-Cloud at the audiences after Mass.

I did this; but at the first of these the emperor only nodded to me, and occupied himself in conversation with David the painter; at the second, the emperor said to me, "Well, have you received your lieutenant-general's gratuity?"

"Sir, I have received neither the gratuity, of which your Majesty is so good as to speak, nor have I even been advised of my promotion." He cast a glance at my uniform, and, after standing still a moment, passed on without replying.

I cannot now understand how I failed to understand my position; but I did so entirely. The truth was that Berthier, who, with Soult, had hindered my promotion at Vienna, had returned from Munich the very evening after my audience at Saint-Cloud. My appointment had come into his hands, and he had taken upon himself not to send it, waiting for a good opportunity to inform the emperor, who, at the audience just mentioned, knew nothing about this, Murat and Maret not having spoken of my application to them. He did not again speak to me on the subject, which proves that Berthier had succeeded in getting my appointment revoked or postponed. In my exasperation I vowed not to serve again as general of brigade.

Some days afterwards Junot arrived from Piacenza, whither he had been sent as governor. I soon called on him, and was excellently received. Dining with him one day, some one pitied me for my wound.

"I admit," said Junot, "that Thiébault has had a rough time of it, yet I rather congratulate him than pity him. I would give something to have had the honour of being wounded at Austerlitz."

When we returned to the drawing-room, he came up to me and said, "I say, how is it that you are not general of division?" I told him of Soult's dislike to me and of what had happened since.

"It is very extraordinary," he said; "but Soult has nothing to do with it; he is not big enough to make the emperor change his mind. I will do something, and let you know the result."

That same evening, being with the emperor, he took an opportunity of saying, "I thought Thiébault was general of division?"

"Well," said the emperor, "so he is."

"But, sir," he rejoined, laughing, "he has not received his appointment."

"He shall have it."

"That is all I could get out of him," said Junot, when telling me what he had done.

"It is not quite what I should have liked," said I; "but, anyhow, he neither retracted nor denied, so I must have patience." I thanked him for this new mark of kindness; but though I saw a good deal more of him, and Mme Junot made acquaintance with my wife, I said no more about my position, which daily became more unpleasant.

The peace so loudly vaunted and so dearly earned was suddenly threatened. One heard talk of differences with Prussia, of the bragging of that Power, finally of war. The Army of Austerlitz was still in existence, and its principal corps were soon on the march. I could not yet think of serving, so that I was outside of all the movement. I bade *adieu* to Murat and gave him my good wishes, but refrained from taking my leave of Berthier; nor did I appear at the emperor's final audience. As for Junot, there was no leave to be taken of him, for he remained as governor-general of Paris.

Jena overthrew the Prussian monarchy more gloriously and more decisively than the Austrian monarchy had been overthrown at Ulm. The whole Prussian Army was annihilated and the king defeated in person. Thus Jena combined all that could adorn a triumph; and though it did not lead to peace, like Austerlitz and Wagram, or even to a truce like Marengo, it sanctioned a vast annexation, and was therefore second to Austerlitz only.

By an imperial decree, dated Wittenberg, October 23, 1806, the emperor ordered that possession should be taken in his name of all the Prussian states between the Elbe and the Rhine, of the states belonging to the Duke of Brunswick and to the Prince of Orange, and of the territories of Hanover and Osnabrück; that these countries should never return into possession of the aforesaid princes; that they should be divided into five governments; that I was to be governor of the fourth of these, and so forth.

The duplicate of this decree, signed "Marshal Alexander Berthier," reached me on October 29, with orders to start at once. There was a preliminary question—Should I accept? At first I was inclined to say that, as I had not received my commission as lieutenant-general, I could not accept any military office. My friends expostulated, however; and when I spoke to Junot, he burst out laughing, and said that merely to hesitate was not folly, but insanity. My wife also wished me to accept, and this, added to a consideration of the advantages of the post, finally decided me. Fulda was the seat of my government, and I set out for that place a fortnight after receiving my orders.

[General Thiébault held the government of Fulda until May 17, 1807. This part of his career is less likely to interest English readers than that which followed, and we may pass over both his doings at Fulda and a visit to Tilsit at the time when the French and Russian armies were fraternizing there. He saw a dinner given by the Imperial Guard to the Russian and Prussian guards. French and Prussians were drinking freely, but he was struck by the abstemiousness of the Russians. He sent his secretary to ask one of the Russian grenadiers why he declined a glass offered by a Frenchman. The man answered, "Because, if I drank any more, I should be drunk; and if I got drunk, my emperor would say I was a pig, and he would not like that." He also saw *Bashkirs*, with their mail coats and bows and arrows. On his departure from Fulda the inhabitants presented him with a gold sword, in token of esteem.

The question of his rank still remained undecided. Berthier was determined to hinder his promotion, and in July he actually received his appointment to command a brigade in one of the divisions of Davout's army corps. This, however, he succeeded in evading on the plea of not yet being fit for service, and ultimately obtained permission to return to France, coupled with four months' leave of absence to take the waters at Barèges. Meanwhile, the war in the Peninsula was drawing on,]

CHAPTER 10

The Expedition to Portugal

During the campaign of Austerlitz Paris had caused the emperor great anxiety. Public credit was never lower; the funds fell to eight *francs*;[1] and it required all the magical splendour of Austerlitz, with its sudden and decisive consequences, to change the situation and restore to France confidence in the present and hope for the future. Many causes no doubt produced this serious state of things; but the cause to which Napoleon attributed it in a large degree was the want of energy in the government of Paris during his absence. On starting for the Jena campaign, therefore, he had wished to leave in the capital a man of as much vigour and activity as loyalty, and no one could better justify his confidence in these respects than General Junot. The result quite met his expectations, and the general's conduct as governor of Paris, added to his former claims, was bound to call for some recompense that could at once pay for the services he had been rendering and console him for having taken no part in the most recent feats of arms. No one therefore could find it anything but natural and just if the new enterprise which was obviously about to follow the Prussian and Polish campaign was entrusted to Junot, even to the exclusion of all the marshals and of such men as Reynier, Saint-Cyr, Suchet, or Vandamine.

Such was at least the ostensible cause for giving to Junot the command of the army corps of the Gironde—a corps whose destination was not avowed, but was at the same time undoubted. Everyone knew that it was going to become the Army of Portugal and conquer that kingdom, one of the last and the most important of the customers still

---

1. [Napoleon had appropriated 50,000,000 *francs* out of the deposits in the National Bank, which not unnaturally shook the confidence of depositors and lenders.]

possessed by England on the Continent. But the selection was enough complicated by secret motives that it was equally a mistake on the Emperor's part and a way of punishing Junot. A mistake, I say, because Napoleon knew that Junot had not the qualities required for the part assigned to him; and a punishment, because the command, given in anger and accepted with deep vexation, was at the same time one of those pieces of favouritism which, by exciting the jealousy of rivals, form the misfortune of those who are the objects of them and the delight of their enemies. These main causes had concurred to place Junot in this conspicuous yet disastrous position, and this leads me to go back to his early history and make a short digression.

He served at the siege of Toulon as a gunner in the Côte d'Or Regiment, and distinguished himself more than once by his courage, originality, and cleverness. Of the first many anecdotes were told, notably the following. He was supping with some comrades near the batteries, in a tent which I think they shared, when a shell from the fort fell in the middle of the tent, and was about to burst in the hole which it had made in the ground. Everyone had risen and was running away when Junot, seizing a glass, exclaimed, "To the memory of those of us who are going to perish!" How far the wine had any influence on the effect his words produced, I know not; but all stopped, took up their glasses, and remained motionless till the shell exploded. One fell dead, and the others tossing off their bumpers cried, "To the memory of a hero!"

Colonel Bonaparte of the artillery wished to see the author of this freak. He found a young man, full of cleverness and ardour, who had had an excellent education; and from that time he never lost sight of him. Some days afterwards he had occasion to order a reconnoissance of considerable danger; involving a risk of being taken prisoner, Junot offered to undertake it.

"Very well," said Bonaparte; "but go in civilian clothes—your uniform would expose you too much."

"No," said Junot; "I will never shrink from the chance of being killed by a cannon-ball, but I will not run the risk of being hung as a spy."

The duty successfully accomplished, Junot rejoined Bonaparte, who was in one of the advanced batteries, and made his report. "Put it in writing," said the colonel, and Sergeant Junot, using the parapet as his desk, rapidly and cleverly wrote out his report in four pages. As he was finishing the first page, a round shot meant for him struck the parapet and covered writer and writing with earth. "Polite of these English," he said, laughing, "to send me some sand just when I wanted it!"

These and many other similar feats earned him a reputation, and the representatives of the people appointed him sub-lieutenant, and ordered Colonel Bonaparte to hand him his commission. On receiving it, without a word, he tore it up and threw down the pieces. "What are you doing?" said his chief.

"What a man ought to do that is not the sort to take his epaulettes from those beggars. When you are a general, give me them if you think I deserve them, and you will see how I shall receive them."

Soon afterwards Bonaparte, being promoted major-general, got Junot made an officer and took him as his first *aide-de-camp*. He ought to have remained always Bonaparte's first *aide-de-camp*.

When Bonaparte was dismissed by Aubry, Junot and his father contributed largely to his support, the father even selling some land to meet the wants of his son's young general. *Aide-de-camp* and general also at various times saved each other's life. In this way a friendship grew up, based on an almost fanatical attachment and a devotion without limits, such as it seemed that nothing would weaken. But a man who has risen from an unpretending station to almost superhuman heights does not care to be reminded of his humble origin; while he who wishes to make the most of any claim which such reminiscences may give him does best to keep them to himself. Unluckily, the desire of publishing them becomes more acute in proportion to the exaltation of the object of them; and certain indiscretions, maliciously reported or even exaggerated, gave the ex-*aide-de-camp* the character of a troublesome person.

Another point was that some people were jealous of Junot, especially Savary, who was a legacy from Desaix to Bonaparte. There was no comparison between him and Junot in respect of knowledge or cleverness, though Savary was not without ability, nor yet in respect of frankness and affection; but Savary was second to no one in loyalty, and he had moreover a power of self-restraint, a demeanour and behaviour, beyond his rival's capacity. If he had been governor of Paris, he was not the man to play billiards in a public room in the Champs Elysées, quarrel with the markers, and try conclusions with them with a billiard-cue and get beaten—an adventure adroitly turned to account with the emperor.

Again, Junot's extravagance was something fearful, and he had a perfect fever of gambling. There was a story of a game of *bouillotte*, where the stakes were 100,000 *francs* and 500 *francs* a counter. In general, Junot had no idea of discretion. His nickname in the army was "The Hurricane," and it was not in his nature to use his advantages with moderation. Without being proud, he was vain; though good-natured, he could be offensive; his quick temper was devoid of tact in handling people of rank and authority. He was fanatically submissive to Napoleon, but recognised no other subordination. Savary, Le Marois, Clarke, were all annoyed by his arrogance; the last, indeed, he seemed to take pride in insulting and defying. His intrigue with Mme Murat, however far it went, made another powerful enemy to aid the party of his rivals, besides annoying Napoleon.

To these causes he was indebted for his post as commander of the first army corps of the Gironde, then as commander-in-chief of a French and a Spanish army, as governor-general of the kingdom of Portugal and lieutenant to the emperor, with a ministry, an enormous civil list, a vast luxury, and, it may be said, a court. These enabled him to play a part in history, and to attain, in those dazzling days, to the idea of putting on his own head the crown of the House of Braganza, driven from Europe and exiled to Brazil by him.

Junot's nomination had just come when I got back from Tilsit, and I went to offer my congratulations, since one could not speak of condolence. The more furious he was, the more pains he took to make believe he was glad. "It is a fine errand," he said, "and highly confidential. There is not a marshal who did not want to have it, and there is not a general who could not get a marshal's *bâton* out of it. Besides, I keep my present position as governor of Paris and first *aide-de-camp* to the emperor, and therefore the salaries;[2] no one was ever better treated.... But, hang it," he suddenly exclaimed, "why should not you be my chief of staff? If it suits you, and your wounds will allow of it, I will ask for you at once."

"My wounds," I answered, "allow of anything that suits me; that is, of any duty which a general of division may perform. The duties of chief of staff are not incompatible with that rank, and nothing would suit me better. So you may count on me, though my wounds are not really closed."

Next day a servant came to tell me to call on him. As soon as he

---

2. The post of first *aide-de-camp* was presently abolished, and the emoluments with it; and he was superseded as governor of Paris when he was made governor-general of Portugal.

saw me he said, "I have a nasty bit of news for you. Berthier objects to you as my chief of staff on the ground that if you do not need the Barèges waters you have deceived Davout and him, and the emperor himself."

"I have deceived nobody," I said. "No one can force me to serve in my present state, but also no one can set limits to what I may do in my eagerness to serve under you. These are distinctions which it pleases ill-nature not to make. In short, must I give up going with you?"

"Make another attempt, and make it at once, so as to prevent anyone else from being selected. To this end, you should call on the Prince of Neuchâtel when he returns from Saint-Cloud an hour hence."

I had hardly reached the prince's apartments when he alighted from his carnage, and, as I was in his path, he was forced to receive me. When I urged him to agree to General Junot's request, he said, "Your place is at Barèges or at Tilsit."

"My place," I returned, "is wherever I can devote myself to the emperor's service." This answer was somewhat unseemly; it struck me in that light, and, in the dilemma between keeping up the kind of vehemence indicated by it or leaving myself in a worse position than before, I added, "Prince, your persistent refusal and your severity make one thing clear to me: you mean to punish me for not having died of the wounds that I got at Austerlitz."

Berthier was not an ill-natured man; he was even good-natured. The ill-temper with which he pursued me was a special and personal matter, not the result of habitual predisposition; and when one had got him alone, he was accessible to a multitude of honourable feelings. My last words, with the odious interpretation I seemed to see implied in his, had unexpectedly called up the annoyances which were the only reward I had received for the blood I had shed, while they were corroborated by the sight of my arm still in a sling. He was fairly unseated, and, if he only postponed for six years his wish to make me serve under Davout, the terror of all generals, at any rate, he abandoned the idea of making me command a brigade. Nor could he resist the first impulse which made him take me by the left arm, with the exclamation which also he could not repress, "How can you say such a thing to me?"

To which I replied, "It is more painful to think and say it than to hear it."

"Well, well," he rejoined instantly, "it will be all right; you shall go with Junot." And on August 28 I received my orders to go to Bayonne, as chief of the staff to the "corps of observation in the Gironde."

On the day before we left Bayonne to march into Spain Junot took me aside and said:

> We are going on an errand which is bound to offer advantages, even pecuniary, to the generals who have taken a share in it. You shall not be forgotten, and the campaign shall be worth 300,000 *francs* to you. This I promise; and, in return, I ask your word of honour not to have anything to do with what is called 'business,' or at least to inform me at once, if anyone makes any proposal of the kind to you.

I replied:

> Many thanks, sir for the gratuity you are good enough to allow me to accept. I give you my word of honour as you ask; and it cost me all the less to do so, that dirty jobs of that kind are neither in my way nor to my taste.

A note in my *Narrative of the Expedition to Portugal*[3] (Paris, 1817) speaks of the enthusiasm with which our troops were received in Spain, especially in Biscay. It proved, no doubt, that the sound of our fame had reached even the villages of Spain, but still more the degree of the Spaniards' discontent with their government. If our march seemed like a holiday for them, it was a triumph for us. What a contrast was there between their present disposition and the deadly hatred for us which before a year was out animated that same population! What a disgrace to think that that terrible change was the due meed of a score of treacheries! And what a terrible lesson in the fact that Spain, at that time without administration, without strength, so to say, playing no political or military part in Europe, became one of the most potent factors in the destruction of that stupendous man who, in his superb disdain for the Spaniards, had thought that he could with impunity bubble them out of their fleet, their army, their capital, their fortresses, and their king!

Of our march into Portugal, by way of Vitoria and Salamanca, until we reached Abrantès, I need add nothing to what I have said in my *Narrative*. Our journey across the Beira from Alcantara onwards was terrible; General Caraffa's Spanish division lost 1700 or 1800 men from hunger or fatigue, drowning in torrents or falling down precipices. After this, Abrantès seemed to us like a haven of refuge. I need not

---

3. [Readers of Napier will be familiar with this work.]

again relate the details of our arrival, or the exhaustion of our men, who had been marching night and day through inaccessible gorges, living on acorns and honey. I may, however, jot down a few personal reminiscences which would have no place in a military work.

The country through which we had just been passing was comparable only to a chaos, and the weather that we had had on the journey was of the kind to complete the picture. "Not only our vehicles but our led horses had been unable to follow us, so that each was reduced to the tatters which he had on his back and to a single horse, which by the time we reached Abrantès could not carry him. I had endeavoured to set the example of endurance under hunger, rain, precipices, and sleeplessness, as well as to devote myself to the care of the sick and the weak. I may even say that in that frightful labyrinth I preserved a moral courage which occasionally deserted General Junot. At Sobreira-Formosa, for example, not having strength to reach the hovel intended for him, he flung himself into the one marked as my quarters, got upstairs only with us half-carrying him, and on reaching the room in which the staircase terminated flung himself on a pallet and there passed the rest of a terrible night.

Meanwhile, General Delaborde and I, in spite of our exhaustion, went to work to have the big drum beaten and fires lighted, and set men shouting to collect the poor fellows who had gone astray in the mountains. After such sufferings endured in common, I thought that anything which could soften the remembrance of them ought also to be in common. So when on the morrow of our arrival at Abrantès I learnt that the commander-in-chief had requisitioned all the available saddle-horses, and had given one to each of his *aides-de-camp*, after reserving three for himself, I felt sure that, as I was totally unmounted, I could not have been overlooked in the distribution, nor yet the few staff-officers who had followed me, and of whose labour I had not been chary. So I went to the commander-in-chief and said, "No doubt I have to thank you for having thought of my *aides-de-camp* and me in the distribution of horses you have just made."

"No," he said; "you are big enough to look after yourself."

"Up to now," I returned, amazed at the answer, "I have had other things than myself to think of. Besides, as all the horses have been requisitioned by you, I do not exactly know where I could have got any."

"Get them where you like," he said; "for my part, I have not so much as a dog to give you."

I left him, "riled" to the last degree, but taking note of the licence granted and promising to avail myself of it. Reaching my quarters, I sent for Captain Vidal de Valabreque, and, upon telling him how we were looked after, I asked if he was the man to undertake an errand, not exactly dangerous, but possibly involving some risk. As he did not hang back, I told him to cross the Zezere with twenty-five troopers, go to Santarem, requisition the fifteen handsomest horses to be found there, put them together in a stable, and set a sentry over them as for my sole and only disposal. All this was carried out, but as I got near Santarem the commander-in-chief, mounted as well as his *aides-de-camp* on nice fresh horses, cantered past me and got there an hour before me.

I had not reached the first houses of the town when I saw Vidal hurrying towards me. The first words he flung at me were, "General, I am done for!" He complained that the commander-in-chief, having heard of the requisition of horses made by my orders, had been furious with him, and had sent him as governor to the fortress of Castello Branco, with orders to go alone. "And when I observed," said poor Vidal, "that going alone meant ten chances to one of being murdered, he sent word that if I was not off in an hour he would have me shot."

I told Vidal to wait for me at my lodgings and went to the general's. He was at table with his staff, and asked me to join them. I declined. He did not say a word about Vidal, but asked me several questions to which I replied in the most laconic fashion. It was clear that I had come for a serious explanation, and that there was no getting out of it. After a silence, and when the meal was over, I asked him for a few minutes' conversation. As soon as the door of the room was shut he said in an abrupt tone, "You want to speak to me about Vidal?"

"Certainly."

"I have given him his orders."

"Impossible to carry—out even if he were to blame."

"Do you think I shall let him off for having made a requisition?"

"There has been no requisition made here but by my written orders, that is, by me."

"No officer has any right to execute such orders unless countersigned by me."

"In all service matters my signature is yours; when it ceases to be, I shall no longer be your chief of staff. Besides," I continued, "when in spite of my pressing need you left me horseless at Abrantès, when you told me to get horses where I liked, when my officers and I have been riding for the last two days on wretched crocks, changed at every halting-place, which make us the laughing-stock of the troops, and would make it impossible for us to follow you if you wanted us, have not you given us a right to do what in practice you have rendered inevitable?"

"All right," he replied—"do not let us say any more about it; do what you like with the horses."

I hastened to put Vidal out of his perplexity, and he at once took me to the stable where the objects of all this fuss were. He had selected a splendid lot. The finest was at once taken to the commander-in-chief, who accepted it without a word. I took three; two I gave to the paymaster; Vidal had two, and the two other staff-officers present, one each; the other five I restored to their owners.

The state we were in when we entered Lisbon is hardly credible. Our clothing had lost all shape and colour; I had not had a change of linen since Abrantès; my feet were coming through my boots; and in this guise I took possession of one of the handsomest suites of rooms in the capital. My host, M. Ratton, a Burgundian by birth and one of the wealthiest merchants in Portugal, offered me linen; new boots were found for me; I was shaved and cleaned up, and by the end of half an hour, no longer an object of horror to myself and others, I was taken in one of M. Ratton's carriages to the commander-in-chief, with whom I worked for seven hours on end by the clock.

As everyone knows, Junot took possession of Lisbon, of the army that was there, and of the entire kingdom, without having at hand a single trooper, a single gun, or a cartridge that would burn; with nothing, indeed, save the 1500 grenadiers remaining from the four battalions of his advance-guard. Fagged out, unwashed, ghastly objects, these grenadiers had no longer strength to march even to the sound of the drum, and yet the commander-in-chief must needs, by way of a demonstration, walk the poor wearied wretches all over the town, in pouring rain, for six hours. The rest of the army dropped in at intervals of one or two days in still worse condition, some even falling down dead at the gates.

Things were gradually got into order, and, as the soldier's lot is, the most luxurious comfort succeeded the most cruel hardships. M. Ratton and his family treated me with extreme kindness, and after our departure from Lisbon had the honesty, in spite of extreme pressure put upon them, to refuse to speak any evil of me.

General Junot was a man of whims, and you needed to be thoroughly used to his sudden fantastic caprices not to look surprised sometimes. "Did you ever see any of my pistol-shooting?" he burst out one morning.

"No, sir."

"Well, you shall." And, indeed, he gave me a very good exhibition of the art. Another day, after dinner, he said in the most imperious tone, "Follow me." We got into a carriage and went down to the harbour. A boat with flag flying was in readiness, and took us off to a handsome Portuguese 50-gun frigate, which had just been thoroughly refitted and had her crew on board. No sooner were we there than Junot had the anchor got up and the sails, set, and as there was a pretty breeze we were soon under way. After a quarter of an hour of evolutions performed to his order, he told the captain to begin firing both broadsides, and for another quarter of an hour he kept them firing, and made them alter their course back, and so on, in the midst of all the smoke and uproar. The row and the evolutions were fit for a lunatic asylum. We then got into the carriage again and went to the opera.

Another time, Admiral Siniavin, in command of a Russian fleet of nine ships of the line in the Tagus, gave a great dinner to the commander-in-chief. Knowing his guest's tastes, he gave orders that when the health of the two emperors was drunk the flagship and the other eight, mostly 80-gun ships, should fire a salute. All the bottles on the table were upset; the pictures hanging on the cabin bulkheads were shaken from their hooks and fell on the deck; our vessel cracked all over. Such an uproar was never heard out of the infernal regions.

Junot's whims were, however, not always so inoffensive. When I found him in one of his surly tempers, it needed all my attention to keep him in check. After one groundless quarrel I had intended to leave the army and go away unbidden. General Loison told him of it, and from that time, though I could not avoid some rough treatment, he never flew out with me as he did with almost everyone.

Towards the end of February, 1808, I had been considering that, in the event of a general insurrection and the descent of an English army, we should not have a single place in the neighbourhood of Lisbon where we should be in a position to resist superior forces and await either succour or the end of the crisis. I therefore deemed it indispensable to choose a place for general concentration, to fortify and arm it, and to make a store of provisions for a year; and I drew up a proposal developing this idea. Eight or ten days after, having, as my custom was, left this on the general's desk, I received orders to have the neighbourhood of Lisbon explored within a radius of fifteen or twenty miles, with the object I had suggested. I confided the duty to Lieut. Vallier, an officer on the staff, formerly of the engineers, and his report indicated the peninsula of Setubal as fully the best place. It was roomy and healthy, and, moreover, allowed of our holding the fort of Bugia, and consequently defending the entrance to the Tagus.

On the landward side nothing was needed but an entrenched camp. All the warlike stores in the arsenal at Lisbon would have been evacuated on this point, while for provisions the supplies from the Alemtejo would be enough and to spare. All this was undeniable, and was recognised to be so, and it only remained to carry it out. Unluckily, this required a sequence of ideas instead of whims, a firm will in place of vehemence, a continuous effort in place of hesitation and indolence; and for that very reason it was impossible. At first, therefore, the plan was ordered and urged forward—then it was postponed, then forgotten; and, when the regrets came for the time lost, it was too late to retrieve it. Yet if Setubal had been thus occupied, Lisbon held, Elvas retained, the emperor would not have taken four months from the date of our evacuation to reach us or raise our blockade, even supposing we had still lost the Battle of Vimiero, as we never ought to have done.

For seven months Portugal enjoyed undisturbed peace. Commerce began to retrieve its losses. Private fortunes had not been touched; titles, offices, functions, had been maintained; and the best harvest in the memory of man dispelled all fear of impoverishment or famine. Portugal then seemed to be waiting till its destiny should be settled; but our want of faith, let me say our treachery, our want of tact, our insolence, revolted Spain, a country naturally as well disposed toward us as any in the world; while the eternally disgraceful conduct of Dupont and Vedel at Baylen and Andujar put the finishing touch to the annihilation of our authority in the Peninsula. When the news came that a French army had passed under the yoke to the Castilians, the 12,000 or 15,000 Spanish troops forming part of the Army of Portugal mutinied, and all whom we could not at once arrest and disarm went back into Spain.

The Portuguese Army, unhappily, followed this example; insurrection broke out in Oporto, while in the south an English fleet blockaded the Tagus. Finally, an English army, landing at the mouth of the Mondego, opened a campaign against us, and, serving as a rallying-point to the popular rising, the numbers of which it increased tenfold, it soon left us no alternative save total destruction or the misfortune of a treaty, which, though its terms were most honourable to us, none the less marked a new reverse to our arms, and was in its results nothing less than a disaster.

Though I have told the story elsewhere, I ought to say something about the military operations which preceded our evacuation, and that, even though it is an effort to do so, I have painful memories to set down regarding General Junot in his capacity as a soldier. Nor shall I really be inconsistent with what I have said in my *Narrative* respecting that campaign; for, though what I then said may have put certain people off the scent, it can have misled no military man capable of judging. Readers, doubtless, will not find in it the full particulars which follow; but it none the less contains all the facts necessary to support them, that is, a statement of all the blunders made. It will even suggest the significant generalisation that all the actions in which the commander-in-chief took no part were creditable in the highest degree, while the Battle of Vimiero, where he commanded in person, was, by his fault, one of the most deplorable military events that our annals can recall. Why should I have acted so circumspectly in 1817?

No doubt I was led to it by my feelings of affection and loyalty towards General Junot,—feelings which account for the pain it gives me to permit myself these revelations, even today, when the truth can no longer do him any wrong. Then his death was recent; I was writing under the Restoration, and if I had not taken pains, without distorting facts, to cast a veil over all that might lower the part played by a commander-in-chief who under the Empire took his place in history, I should have handed him over not only to the impertinences of the party who had "gone abroad," but to the scorn of the English, the allies at that time, not of France, but of the Bourbons, who were reigning against the will of France. Now that I am free of all these considerations, and am writing more than twenty years after the deplorable end of a general who, especially as a general, was a kind of enigma,[4] I can concede nothing further, even to reticence. Besides, there is all the difference in the world between a narrative which was only a copy of my reports to the Minister for War, and memoirs in which one is placing oneself at the bar of posterity.

Before the insurrection in Spain and the revolt in Portugal, the

---

4. ["Of greater reputation than he could support"...."at one moment a great man; at the next, below mediocrity."—Napier.]

commander-in-chief had displayed the greatest energy. The generals had been able to maintain their defensive, and then to take the offensive at almost all points with advantage, when 200 English vessels, of which we had had information for some time, landed troops, artillery, and stores at Figueira, near the mouth of the Mondego. This convoy was to be followed by others yet larger. No doubt to save Portugal not only good conduct and valour were needed, but genius; and the loss of it, which now seemed almost certain, was to be imputed in the first place to Junot, but in the second to Napoleon. Junot was to blame for not having, as soon as he reached Lisbon, given effect to the proposal of making an entrenched camp from Casillas to Setubal, and then collecting provisions for a year. This would have given time for him to be succoured, and would have caused him to be so; and it would have prevented the English Army from advancing into Spain.

As for Napoleon, the moment he learnt that an English army of from 25,000 to 30,000 men was about to be sent to Portugal, he should have got together all the troops that he had at Madrid and in the west of Spain and sent them to Alcantara, so as to keep his hold on both banks of the Tagus. We should have had news of this movement by way of Portalegre, with which town we were always in communication, and could have reinforced the army, after deducting our sick and wounded, with 24,000 men, including 1200 cavalry, and with a formidable artillery; and in this way we should have remained masters of Central Spain, and been in a position to re-enter Madrid and even keep possession of Elvas.

As it was, we were abandoned, and owed it only to a mere chance that we were not at the most critical moment weakened to the extent of 4,000 men, who by the emperor's orders had left Lisbon for Cadiz. Too weak to detach a strong body in presence of the English army, fanatically supported by all the forces of Portugal; unable to remain at Lisbon; having no supports or resources anywhere else; encumbered by a number of Frenchmen belonging to the administration, and by women—we needed, if we were to escape the necessity of evacuating Portugal, a colossal and decisive success, such as we could not hope for. But there is a considerable difference between taking your chance of a success and missing your chance through negligence.

Flanked on one side by its fleet,[5] on the other by a Portuguese army and levies, the English Army advanced on Lisbon. Our troops were

---

5. [Of transports, that is; and H.M.S. *Alfred* (74). A fleet could not have acted on that coast.]

not concentrated. Loison's division was putting down the insurrection in the Alemtejo, and time had to be given him to rejoin the army. To that end the enemy's march had to be delayed, and at the same time the country on which we might have to fight, to be reconnoitred. This duty had been entrusted to General Delaborde, who discharged it most honourably. Meeting the enemy's six columns, 18,000 strong, he beat them at Roriça by the ability of his manoeuvres and his choice of positions, though he had only 1900 men to oppose to them.[6] By favour of this success, he was able to fall back on Montachique, take up a strong position there, and cover Lisbon, while Loison's division made every effort to rejoin him by marches as laborious as might be expected in Portugal in the month of August.

At last that division was able to join Junot's troops, and marched with them upon Torres Vedras, where they took up position and waited for Delaborde, who had been called back from Montachique. Thus our entire force was concentrated. It amounted to 9,200 men, with whom we had to face 16,000 of the enemy, who were in position between Torres Vedras and the sea, at Lourinham and Vimiero. My *Narrative* puts the number of the army that opposed us at Vimiero at 18,000, but I was wrong; not that, as the emperor thought sometime later, that army consisted of 13,000 English and 6,000 Portuguese—there were no Portuguese there—but the English had lost 2,000 at Roriça. Well, instead of meeting them with 9,200 men, we might have opposed 13,500, for Loison had left 1,000 of the Hanoverian legion at Santarem; 2,000 had remained on the left bank of the Tagus; and 1300 could have been borrowed for the day of battle from the garrison of Lisbon and from the ships.

If the English troops, especially their officers, were not in 1808 worth so much as they afterwards were—as, indeed, the combat of Roriça had brilliantly shown—this was of course no excuse for not equalising the forces when the means of doing so were at hand; but it was still less a reason for not compensating for such a mistake, as far as might be, by acting with calculation and prudence. There should have been a personal verification of the reconnoissances entrusted to the engineer officers, and operations so far as possible should have been

---

6. [Once for all it may be noted here that readers will do well to check French statements of numbers in the Peninsula by Napier, who is never unduly partial to his own side; also that *battre* is not strictly equivalent apparently to our "beat." Delaborde covered himself with credit at Roriça; but his next halt was 30 miles to the rear.]

undertaken to get a thorough knowledge of the ground, of the way in which the enemy's forces were distributed, and of the position of his guns. Yet the commander-in-chief ordered an immediate attack without having seen anything for himself, or knowing upon what and against whom he was marching.

Better to understand how heart-breaking such a course of action was, it should be known that the English general's right, and to some extent his right rear, rested on the sea; that his centre, in front of which a small stream flowed, was established on an isolated mamelon, commanding all the approaches, and itself commanded in rear and on the flanks by heights showing a double range of steep escarpments. These were garnished with two lines of troops and a double row of batteries of heavy calibre, forming four lines of fire independently of the mamelon. His left, which, owing to the slope of the ground, was, as it were, buried, from the very fact that the right was advanced some distance beyond the centre, flanked it; it rested on nothing, did not even reach the slope at the bottom of which Lourinham stands, and was only covered in front by a ravine ending at that slope.

Such was the position in which we found the English Army, when at 9 a.m. we had cleared the defile of Torres Vedras. That position, about which the commander-in-chief disdained to trouble himself, ought to have been as fatal for the enemy if we did not attack it in front as for us if we did; and its occupation might turn out to have been at once senseless and disastrous for the English. Senseless, I say, because no one had any right to suppose that he could meet a general capable of being taken in by it, and disastrous because, if instead of running our heads against it we had turned it, it would, as the sequel will show, have been only a mousetrap.

The reasons in favour of the system of divisions, and the advantage of keeping the troops of one division together, are well known, especially the importance of making them fight in company, and all under the immediate orders of their own chief. Now, quite apart from the craze which made him march upon the centre of the enemy's position such as I have just described it, Junot on approaching that position ordered General Delaborde to continue his direct movement with his second brigade, while Brenier was to make an independent turning movement round the English left—a disposition which was all the cruder that it required Brenier to go three times as far as was necessary, thus in broad daylight giving the English thrice as much time in which to get ready for him. In this way he was outside of the battle properly so called, while Delaborde, when he arrived within musket-range, found himself on ground upon which it was, so to say, impossible to debouch, where the fire of all the batteries converged, and from which with a handful of people he had to carry positions before which 10,000 men would have come to grief.

As Delaborde was losing heavily without anything to show for it, Junot suddenly ordered Loison to support him with his left brigade, while the right brigade was to follow up Brenier's movement. In this way another brigade was rendered useless on our right, while on our left another brigade was devoted to useless destruction. Yet even now, if Loison had marched with his right brigade, we should at least have had a general of division, that is, a centre of command at each centre of operations; while the result of sending him to the ground occupied by Delaborde was that on one side we had, with two brigades, two generals of division not likely to agree well, while on the other, with an equal number of troops, we had two generals of brigade who never could agree.

The arrival of Loison with his reinforcement only caused a most gratuitous addition to our losses. "To get the thing over," as the commander-in-chief said, though in a different sense from that in which he used the phrase, he sent forward the first of the two grenadier regiments forming the reserve, and that unlucky regiment was exterminated before it had fully deployed. The second, under Kellermann in person, followed, and was no less badly mauled. Thus, three of the best divisional generals that France possessed, with six regiments, were all together in a place where none of them and not a single man ought to have been; but, as our position, became every minute more disastrous, the commander-in-chief, followed by me, went himself to this ill-starred ground.

The result was that, while two out of our five brigades were "in the air," with no common understanding or action, and indeed were soon recalled, nearly the whole English Army being free to act against them, on our left, our three remaining brigades, cut up by artillery fire, were led, besides their brigadiers, by three generals of division, a chief of the staff, and a commander-in-chief, and that in a situation where Napoleon himself could have done no more than a corporal,—that is, when there was no choice save to die or to retreat. A volume would not hold all that could be said on the subject, and, indeed, the stream did not run dry. Loison and Solignac were foaming at the mouth; Kellermann, who was entrusted with negotiating after that disastrous scuffle, thought only of bringing them to a successful issue, so convinced was he that under similar leadership we should have no hope save in them. Delaborde was heart-broken, and I was no less so. How often has that worthy general and consummate soldier talked over that deplorable day with me to try and find some explanation of it!

The fact is that Junot was a clever man, indeed very clever; he was a man of education and, when he really applied his reasoning power, a man of sense, and even of great judgement and sagacity. He was now thirty-seven years old, and had had eighteen years' service; for fourteen years he had been *aide-de-camp* to the greatest general of modern times, one of those extraordinary men whose every action, every word, was a lesson and an illuminating flash. He had understood that man's battles and campaigns; he used to repeat his precepts, and, so far as concerned preliminaries, no pupil ever copied his master better. Thus, when the regiments were about to advance, he used to show himself in their front and raise them to the highest pitch of enthusiasm by harangues no less striking than apposite.

Ready to give a hundred lives, if he had them, for victory, he was when kindled with excitement really splendid; and thus till he issued his final order—I mean till he split Delaborde's division into two—we were as hopeful as from that moment we were dejected. Some explanation of this amazing action was needed; and some thought that during the breakfast on the grass of which we had just been partaking, at which the general had drunk various wines and liqueurs, he had taken too much, or, at any rate, too much considering the heat of the day, if not in actual quantity. Others maintained that the sight of the enemy or the smell of powder excited him till he lost the use of his faculties.

For my own part, ever since recalling these incidents two years later at the time of the affair at Astorga, where he sent a storming-party to destruction, I have been unable to avoid the thought that the reasons alleged—fumes of wine or dizziness from powder-smoke—must have been complicated by the beginnings of mental derangement. Some such explanation is needed to account for what would otherwise be incredible, namely, that no sooner was the battle over than Junot got into a carriage with Mme Foy, whose husband had recently been wounded, and in this way went right through our whole column; conduct which would have been offensive after a victory, and after a disaster could not but cause indignation.

Headlong and fiery, Junot had not the perseverance nor the self-control without which mere fire is impotent. Blindly courageous as a soldier, he had no comprehensive view, no foresight, no inspiration. In any kind of struggle against an enemy, the only thing he understood was the shock; of tactics, which alone can lead up to and secure a victory, he had no notion. What he omitted to do at the beginning through over-eagerness he failed to do at the end through discouragement.

Thus in the Battle of Vimiero, as soon as retreat became necessary, Junot disappeared without giving any orders to anyone; while Margaron, yielding to the inspiration of his own courage, continued to show a bold face, and prevent the English from pursuing; Delaborde, acting on his own initiative, rallied our left and brought it out of action; and I of my own accord hastened to the right, which had lost both its generals, and helped it to effect its retreat. A thousand men like Junot could have marched through hell; but a thousand like him could not have planned, directed, and won a battle.

Yet nothing could have been clearer than our right course at Vimiero. Coming in touch with the enemy at 9 a.m., we ought to have spent the remainder of the day in letting the troops rest after their night march, allowing the masses of men who had dropped to the rear to come up and complete the strength of their corps, and learning both the position of the enemy and the distribution of his troops. This would have shown that a frontal attack was ridiculous; but we should have done everything to cause the belief that such an attack had been determined on, by throwing up batteries, covering the ground with skirmishers, making a number of feigned reconnoissances leading to as many skirmishes, showing the heads of our columns.

These demonstrations should have occupied the 21st; and at night, leaving the reserve under Kellermann to look like an advance-guard, we should have pushed Delaborde's and Loison's divisions, plus 600 cavalry under Margaron, and 15 guns, between Lourinham and the enemy's left. Before day we should have been in force on the plateau on which the English camp leaned, and their general, having lost all his advantage of position, would have found himself at grips with an army which was turning his flank.

In that position, what could he have done? Would he have faced us with only a portion of his force, and, as some have suggested, have marched with the rest to Mafra, so as to reach Lisbon before us? In that case, the body opposing us would have been eaten up; our reserve, with which our communications would have remained open, would have taken in flank the column on its way to Mafra. We should have flung ourselves on their track; and as our men march better than the

English, and moreover were better fed and could stand the heat better, we should have eaten up that English army, beginning with the tail. The march to Lisbon would have been disastrous, and the well-known prudence of English generals rendered it improbable.

The only course left to them would have been hand-to-hand resistance; but we should have arrived in force on a point where we could have found but few troops; these would have been overthrown at the first onset. To check us or prevent us from cutting off the retreat of the entire army, it would have been necessary to bring up fresh troops: but the English Army being drawn up in a good many lines, several corps of it would have been a couple of miles away, and would have taken nearly two hours to arrive, out of breath, in small groups. The fate of troops employed in these successive attacks is well known: the part which met us first would have been stopped by us, and followed and harassed by our reserve; and they could have brought only a few guns into action, for most of their pieces were too heavy for easy manoeuvring on the field.

Even though we had no more than 9,200 men, the English Army was bound to have been beaten, if not destroyed, and the unhoped-for success of which I spoke, realised: Portugal would have been left to herself, the insurrection ended, and all her resources thrown into our hands. And this result would have been attained if Junot had been as good at manoeuvring in presence of the enemy as at a distance from him; while, if we had acted with 4,000 more men, the destinies of the world had been changed. General Junot at Vimiero was the arbiter of the most momentous issues; and this, independently of the interest attaching to the accurate relation of so important an operation of war, explains the long digression into which I have been drawn.

It only remained for us to evacuate Portugal. The bases of a convention were arranged, on the 23rd, for, in spite of their important success, the English, not knowing when the expected reinforcements might reach them, did not feel secure of their position; and by the preliminaries we were granted the honours of war. The definitive treaty was signed on the 30th. General Beresford, a man of polished manners, but very firm character, showed great obstinacy in the final discussions before the signature.[7] However, he showed no more energy and less talent than General Junot, who was all the more superb

---

7. [General Thiébault's memory, of which he often complains, seems to have played him false here; for Beresford did not appear on the scene till September 5, when he came to act as commissioner for executing the Convention.]

because it required not a general but a man to save what could be saved in the disastrous circumstances. Thus, thanks to his energy and to some brilliant inspirations, by the force of his reasoning no less than by the vigour of his character, he obtained concessions from the English negotiators which irritated the Portuguese to the last degree. Our situation at Lisbon during the final moments preceding our departure was most alarming. The word was passed of "Death to the French," but I will not recur to those unhappy days.

Upon the ratification of the treaty, hostages were given on both sides. Colonel Dunkin,[8] now Lord Russell, member of the English House of Commons, was sent to us in that capacity. He called on me, and said:

> General, you are the cause of my being here. I translated your *Manual for Adjutants-General* into English. In that work you undertook to follow it up by a complete work on the subject, and I am come on purpose to call upon you to keep your word, and to say that there is a translator all ready for you.

Nothing could have been more obliging or more worthy of so distinguished a man. I told him that his proceeding made me feel more keenly than ever the duty of fulfilling my promise, and that in fact, if he had thought fit to leave us quiet in Portugal, I should before long have had all the time I wanted for doing it. However, as soon as ever I had leisure again, I would employ myself upon a general *Manual*; but if the opportunity never came again, I should hold him in some degree responsible. We parted on the best of terms with each other.

One of the articles of the Convention was to the effect that all objects of art in the possession of any Frenchman belonging to the army should be referred to a commission presided over by General Beresford, and that the baggage of all Frenchmen, including the generals, should be searched.[9] One day when I had been visiting the Castle of

---

8. [This must have been Colonel (afterwards Sir Rufane) Donkin. He appears from a passage in the report of the Enquiry on the Convention of Cintra, to have been at this time on the staff of the army. He was M.P. for Berwick from 1832 to 1837, but it is needless to say that he never bore the title of "Lord Russell." Perhaps Thiébault was misled by his unusual Christian name. If he ever translated the *Manual for Adjutants-General*, the work was never published. Thiébault's large work, *Manual of Staff Officers' Duties*, appeared in 1813.]

9. [No article to this effect will be found in the text of the Convention of Cintra; but the commissioners did make the French disgorge a good deal of plunder, carried off at the last moment.]

Quelus with General Junot, he noticed that I was admiring a Virgin in mosaic on *lapis-lazuli*, in a silver frame ornamented with eight angels in high relief. It was the gift of a Pope to some king or other of Portugal, Unnoticed by me, Junot gave orders that it should be brought to me, as from him; and when I got home I found it there. As it perforce came within the article, I had it taken to General (afterwards Marshal) Beresford, informing him how I had come by it.

I also noticed that my cases were all ready to be closed, and begged him to have; them searched. He returned the mosaic, with the reply that at the time when I had received it General Junot had the right to give it me, and that the gift had been ratified by the Commission. Further, he said that no case or trunk having my name on it would be searched by anyone, and that he was charmed to give his personal concurrence to this mark of public esteem. Few things in my whole life have more flattered me.

Nor was this the only gratification I had. By the force of circumstances, and also in accordance with the promise I had given to the commander-in-chief, I had kept clear of all speculative affairs; and this earned me, during our last moments, special esteem from the Portuguese and the chiefs of the English Army. I have spoken of General Beresford, who as marshal presently commanded the Portuguese army. The commodore in command of the convoy that was to take us tried hard to get me on his ship instead of General Delaborde, but that was not possible. As for the inhabitants, at a time when Loison had to be protected against them by four battalions and four guns in bivouac at his door, they were so kind to me that I could reduce my guard to twenty-four men. I always went out on horseback, followed by a single orderly, and never out of a walk; and in that town, hostile as it then was, I never met, I may say, one man, even of the lower classes, who did not take off his hat to me.

I can only say that in 1831, the Chevalier Suchet, brother of the marshal, coming from a dinner-party of Portuguese, and finding me at the Marchioness of Turgot's, told me some most flattering things about the memory of me which still existed twenty-three years afterwards at Lisbon, and about the unanimous testimony rendered to my conduct. General Taviel about the same time said to the Countess of Sugny, "There was only one general who did not thieve in Portugal, and it was Thiébault."

"I hope," said Mme de Sugny, "that you also exclude yourself from the thieves."

"Why, no," he replied: "there were two occasions in which it was just a little too much for me."

Some goods of a less usual kind that we took back were *émigrés*, of whom there were many in Lisbon at the time of our arrival, and they were scared away by it. Several had to thank us for their return to France, and among them I may mention the Count of Novion and M. de Bourmont. We had found M. de Novion colonel of the police force; and the commander-in-chief had been received at the gates of Lisbon by detachments, both on foot and mounted, of that force in their finest array, who had escorted him to his house. The count had also guaranteed order at Lisbon, and not only had he been able to keep his promise in this respect, but he had also rendered us the greatest services during the whole of our stay. With him he had his eldest son, Edmund, a good and worthy young man, clever, eager, and full of brilliant promise.

This young man was nearly always on duty about me, and was of great service; I loved him dearly, and on many occasions was happy to act towards him as towards a son of my own. He is dead, and has left only one brother, very unlike him. As for the father, there was no attention he did not pay me. Every day he read me his reports to the commander-in-chief. He drew plans very well, and gave me one in Lisbon, executed with the greatest care; and to him I owe the information given in my *Narrative* as to the events which preceded our entry into Lisbon. I have there told how an extraordinary council was summoned by the regent, and presided over by him; but in 1817, when the regent had become king, I did not; think I could add one anecdote which I had from M. de Novion. I give it here, because it admirably depicts that Dom Joao, afterwards John VI, the incapable son of the poor mad Queen Dona Maria, and also because it explains better than pages of history the state of neglect in which we found Lisbon.

Now the meeting of the council I refer to had to discuss the grave question:

> Is Portugal strong enough to take the risks of resistance and war, or should it accept the occupation, and the prince regent leave his European States?

The discussion soon became exciting, thanks to the vigour with which one of the council, Dom Rodrigo da Souza, defended the former course, and the most critical moment of the terrible debate had been reached, when the prince struck a mighty blow on the table. At this signal, which seemed to announce an irrevocable decision, all ceased speaking; and in the midst of that silence the prince exclaimed, "Got two of them!" It was quite true; of three flies which had settled in front of him, he had squashed two. As is known, Souza's noble advice earned him exclusion from the council; and the prince embarked for Brazil, whence he was only to return to be king, at his mother's death in 1816, and to reign ten years from that date. But what is explained by the anecdote I have just related, is how the regency and reign of such a prince could not fail to deal a fatal blow to the power of Portugal, and, by the loss of Brazil, reduce her to a mere province.

To return to the Count of Novion. When we went away, he could not, considering the zeal he had shown on our behalf, remain in Portugal. Besides, he had been nominated major-general in the Portuguese service, by decree of the emperor, of itself a claim to the vengeance of the Portuguese. Thus he was practically obliged to accept from us, that is from the emperor, the favour of re-admission to France, which did not prevent him from becoming at the Restoration one of the most furious of Ultras, and, I deeply regret to say it, arrogant enough to deserve appointment as one of those Grand Provosts who presided over so many judicial assassinations in 1815.

Another of our refugees who deserves special mention is the Count of Bourmont. Upon our entry into Lisbon he paid assiduous court to Junot, and before long he, as well as Mme de Bourmont, shared the commander-in-chief's most private evenings, even those which he passed with Mme Foy. That lady was, doubtless, not Junot's du Barry, but she was even less his La Vallière; and one can understand that a man like de Bourmont must have had more than one motive for his conduct in regard to her. When the English army landed, yielding in part no doubt to his warlike French blood, but also with views which I have no desire to trace, he had asked leave to accompany the commander-in-chief as orderly officer.

Then, having doubtless found no opportunity for treachery of a kind to suit him, and perhaps imagining that in this respect he might be more fortunate in France, he applied for an order to return with us, and it fell to me to give him one, as I had done to the Count of Novion. At what price he obtained the honour of returning as a major on the staff, in the service of a country which he never deserved to see again, is well known; and what payment he made for the grades of major-general and lieutenant-general which in succession he received from the emperor. A traitor in presence of the enemy, betraying all those who were united under the same flag by a community of honour, one may say, that he justified the saying to which he gave rise: "Between M. de Bourmont's face and a convict's shoulder there is no great difference." [10]

Our embarkation began on September 11th. On the 13th the Duke of Abrantès went on board the *Nymphe* frigate, which was to take him; Delaborde on board the *Aimable* frigate, and I on board the *Fylla* corvette. It was with melancholy feelings that I bade farewell to the fair sky of Lusitania. On the banks of the Tagus we left power, glory, honour, and wealth. But we were escaping from a foreign country, and going to retemper our spirits on our native soil; while for my part I was about to see my wife again, and delight her with the rich presents I was bringing back, and to realise some, at least, of my dreams of happiness.

---

10. [Bourmont, after protesting his devotion to Napoleon, deserted to the allies on the eve of Waterloo, taking, it is said, important information with him. In 1830 he commanded the expedition to Algiers. The soldiers had a little rhyme: "*Alger est loin de Waterloo. On ne déserte pas sur l'eau. De notre général Bourmont Ne craignons pas la trahison.*"]

CHAPTER 11

My First Sea Voyage

For the first time in my life I was about to undergo a sea-voyage. Independently of the emotion arising from my first acquaintance with the most beautiful but also the most terrible of the four elements, I underwent the further impression of travelling on board an English ship, and being practically at the mercy of our implacable foes. Our convoy of forty-five vessels added the interest of a fine sight.

On the morning of September 14 we set sail, and soon was out of sight of land. We bore westward at first to clear Cape Finisterre, and then so as not to be caught off a lee shore by the rough weather which threatened at the equinox. We proceeded thus for some days, when a dead calm came on. The sails flapped, the vessels stood still on a sea of oil. It is quite a mistake to suppose that a calm of this kind does nothing but breed *ennui*: it causes the consumption of provisions which have been calculated for a shorter voyage, and justifies the saying that you may sometimes go a hundred leagues at sea on a pound of bread, and sometimes not one league on a hundred pounds.

Nor is that all; a convoy of ships becalmed is at the mercy of currents, which, with no counteracting force, become irresistible, tearing the vessels from their moorings, running them on board of each other and causing most serious damage. We had a proof of this on the second day: several of our craft were very seriously injured; and in spite of all repairs that could be made, they were left in no condition to face the storms that we presently encountered, and perished in them. At length, on the third day there was again a ripple on the water; a breeze sprang up, and the order was given to be under way at 11 p.m.

Just then Lord Stuart, who showed me such attention at Lisbon, and wished to take me on board his frigate, and expressed so many regrets at not getting me instead of General Delaborde, sent me an invitation to dine with him that day. I went with Fontenay, son by her first marriage of the great lady once Mlle de Cabarrus, but better known under the name of Mme Tallien than under that of Mme de Fontenay, or that which she now bears of Princess of Chimay. Fontenay was tall and handsome, a worthy son of his mother in his noble bearing; besides that, he was an excellent and charming young fellow. He had joined us at Lisbon, and I had taken him with me because he spoke English well, and could act as my interpreter. So I set out in company with him, in a boat manned by a midshipman and four sailors.

Lord Stuart [1] was charming during the meal, which was excellent and very lively. I sat by him and we chatted. He regretted that he had not one of our military bands on board. I mentioned that of the 86th, and offered to give him an order authorizing it to leave the transport where it was, and come on board his frigate. He was delighted, and I gave him the order. Why did he wait till the next day to make use of it? He would have saved some lives, for the transport went down with all hands, carrying with her the staff of the regiment, the two grenadier companies, and the band. She was one of those that had suffered damage during the calm, and the storm finished her.

She leaked all over, the pumps being inadequate, and it was soon only a matter of calculation to say when she would founder. At this critical moment a privateer appeared; the colonel leapt into a boat, went on board, and besought the commander of the sinister craft to save his unhappy shipmates. Perhaps it was impossible; anyhow the colonel obtained only a refusal, and was not even allowed liberty to return to his sinking vessel. Bewildered and despairing, he soon saw her sink beneath the waves, with the pick of the regiment that he had been so justly proud of commanding.

To return to our dinner-party. On leaving the table, we went to play, and, thanks to the punch, the second table absorbed us as completely as the first had done; so much so that the commodore suddenly exclaimed, "It is a quarter to eleven, and there is no time for you to go back on board the *Fylla*" During the calm, the two ships of war had kept at some distance from each other and from the convoy, and were a mile and a half apart. The only course to take, therefore, was to remain on board the frigate till daylight; but this looked like nervousness, and I could not show that before the English. The more they foretold

---

1. [Lord George Stuart, son of the first Marquis of Bute, at that time commanding the *Aimable* frigate. The commander of the *Nymphe* was Josceline Percy. It is curious that all the three ships in charge of the convoy seem to have been captured vessels.]

danger and displayed fear on my account, the more determined I was to brave even their own element; and in less than a minute after the corvette's light had been pointed out to us, Fontenay, the midshipman, the four sailors and I leaped into the boat and rowed off.

The boat was small, and only just held us; but it went all the faster over the waves amid a dead silence, broken presently by a cry from the midshipman, echoed by the four sailors.

"What is it?" I said.

"All the lights have just been put out," said Fontenay; "it is the moment for the vessels to get under way, and our sailors do not know which way to steer." Our crew became uneasy; indeed everything pointed to our being lost, and on the point of losing not only our own vessel but the whole convoy. We should be left two hundred and fifty miles from land, without an ounce of biscuit, in a boat as big as a cocoa-nut.

Since then, in reflecting on this adventure, which I have related a couple of hundred times, I have never understood why Lord Stuart took no measures to prevent the danger of which he had nevertheless so fully warned us. Could not his frigate, which sailed at a very different rate from our boat, have approached the *Fylla*, before that vessel had her sails set, and allowed us to leave her deck only when there was a certainty of our safe arrival? Could he not have given us a lantern, so that we should not get out of sight; or follow us, so that in the event of our not finding the corvette we might the sooner get back on board him? Or, lastly, might he not have kept the lights burning till the *Fylla* should fire a shot to announce our safe arrival? I thought of a thousand methods which might have been adopted, and no reason why they had not been; for to explain it by the effect of the wine and the punch upon us all, especially Lord Stuart, though the only conceivable reason, was none the less the most opposed to reason.

Anyhow, having nothing to steer by, wrapped in darkness, and abandoned to a fate which to them seemed already upon them, our sailors, giving themselves up to despair, ceased rowing. Aware of the danger, however, I had paid great attention to our course and remained certain of the direction. It was necessary at the same time to inspire confidence in my five Englishmen, who were standing up, lamenting and gesticulating. Fortunately, in times of peril, he who is free from irresoluteness and takes the authority is always sure to be able to enforce it. At my shout of "Silence, and keep your seats," repeated in English by Fontenay, the sailors sat down and were silent. I pointed out the course to follow and ordered them to row on; they obeyed, and gave way with all their strength. Then I told them that a signal which I would give all seven of us would shout simultaneously.

At the first attempt our voices were lost; there was no echo, hardly any resonance. The second was not more fortunate; nothing answered save the sound of our oars, and all hope of safety seemed to be fading away. I kept up the courage of my six companions; and as my voice had lost none of its strength, they still hoped. Then, mustering all our forces, we sent out a hail still louder than its predecessors,—a hail of distress if ever there was one—and listened, in indescribable perplexity. Frankly, this was my last hope. We ought to have taken half-an-hour to cover the distance; as we had gone fast, we might perhaps have gained five minutes, and we had been going for twenty minutes. Hence our not being heard showed that either we had been on the wrong course, or else that the *Fylla* had got under way sharp at eleven o'clock, in which case it was all up with us.

Thus, in the dismal night and amid that watery desert, we could hardly draw our breath in that protracted mental agony, when a voice, very faint, but distinguishable, was heard. We felt as if emerging from the grave. It will easily be understood how briskly we strained our throats in reply, and with what joy we heard the voice again, and much louder. Soon something showed indistinctly against a dark horizon; the lantern of the *Fylla* was relighted. We had not strayed from our course, and a few minutes later we were climbing up the side of the corvette, which was already under sail. In order to wait for us, when our last shout was heard, she had been obliged to trail up her sails and drop an anchor. A minute later, and we should not have seen her, nor ever been seen again ourselves.

At daybreak next morning a vessel was signalled. She was the packet from England to Lisbon. She bore up and sent Captain Rodney the London newspapers. In one of them was an article on the Battle of Vimiero, ending with the words:

> The field of battle remained in our hands, and General Thiébault, chief of the French staff, was found among the dead.[2]

I was furious. The paper was sure to have got to Paris; the French papers were sure to have given extracts from it, and the article in which I was mentioned was of a kind not likely to be omitted. Thus

---

2. [Sir Arthur Wellesley's report of August 21 to Sir H. Burrard seems to have been responsible for this mistake.]

my wife, my children, and my sister could not fail to have been misled by this news, absurd enough, but for them deplorable. Doubtless Junot's *aide-de-camp*, de Lagrave, who had started for Paris on September 3, with a copy of the Convention, would have contradicted the news; but none the less it was barbarous to play such tricks with the repose of families. I ended by getting into a quarrel with the first-lieutenant, a disagreeable man; he was cursing the English generals and admirals, who in his own phrase deserved to be cut up with red-hot razors for signing the Convention of Cintra. This ferocious person, however, was the only one I had to complain of. Captain Rodney was an excellent man, and the second-lieutenant, named White,[3] was a charming fellow.

But that infernal first-lieutenant, a very sea-wolf, practically commanded the vessel, and, as the English way is, he did it very well. All matters relating to cleanliness and discipline were carried to an extreme. Every day the deck was washed with soap, and the whole vessel cleaned from top to bottom. The discipline was severe to the point of cruelty, the slightest mistake being punished by blows with a rope's-end, administered in the presence of this madman with such severity as to draw blood. The morning was the appointed time for these chastisements, and as three or four took place every day I used to be distressed when I awoke by the cries of the victims. I complained to Captain Rodney, who ordered that all punishments should stand over till I had landed; and when I left the *Fylla*, there were more than seventy out of the crew of 140 awaiting torture. A third of them were foreigners, among them several Frenchmen, who had not ventured to make themselves known, and whose impressment no doubt had been effected with the aid of disgraceful usage.

The packet had passed us about an hour, and wrinkles almost imperceptible, but extending farther than the eye could reach, succeeded each other on the water more and more closely. White warned me that this was a sign of an approaching storm, and that as the ripples came from the north-west in very long lines the tempest proclaimed itself as of great violence. The waves would strike us with all the impetus given by a course of 3,000 leagues, and would catch us in the Bay of Biscay, the worst berth in the world in bad weather. Some whales showed themselves, leaping in the distance, and our vessel was presently in the white foam produced by the creatures.

At the same time, but much further off, we saw a kind of moving

---

3. [In the original, 'Weith'; but the emendation seems obvious.]

mound which appeared and disappeared. The officers judged that it might be a waterspout, and were a good deal concerned. Finally, about 4 p.m., a vast school of porpoises, which always go to meet a heavy storm, were seen coming up, and in fact from the southeast. About six the wind got up, the sea rose, we moved more quickly, and the vessels of the convoy, with all sail set and well filled, formed an imposing picture as the sun went down. We were bowling along at I do not know how many knots, when the commodore signalled Captain Rodney to go about and bring on a vessel that had dropped astern. We tacked, ill-pleased enough at the delay, and made sail after the laggard, even firing a shot to hasten her movements; but the damage she had suffered during the calm prevented her from keeping up. We took her in tow, but unluckily the storm soon rendered us unable to continue this assistance; the unfortunate transport was left to herself, and was one of those never heard of again.

At midnight the storm redoubled its fury, and again at six in the morning; and for sixty hours it grew fiercer and fiercer at similar intervals. When night came on, we had been sailing in a convoy of forty-four or forty-five vessels; day found us all alone, and not a vessel in sight. I do not exaggerate when I say that now and again the waves ran twenty or twenty-five feet higher than the flag at our main-mast, lifting us then to that height to let us down again into the abyss. A corvette is a poor shelter against such waves as these; being short, she only takes one crest at a time, while a frigate takes two, a ship of the line as many as three; one pitches therefore twice or thrice as often, and much more roughly, than in other men-of-war, while the rolling is also greater. Till then I had not suffered from sea-sickness; but at that game I had now to pay up.

The *Fylla*, one of the vessels which the English had captured at the burning of Copenhagen, of which they were so proud, was a solidly built vessel, almost new. Nevertheless, on the second day of the storm, all topsails had been taken in, all courses but one brailed up, the guns shifted to the stern, all hatches and portholes closed, and strong cables taken from one side to the other, though the timbers creaked all the same. The creaking was mingled with the noise of the lashing rain, the howling of the wind, or its shrill whistling in the rigging, the crash of the waves as they broke against the ship; and what struck me most amid this fearful uproar was the profound silence of the whole crew, motionless at their quarters, and ready in the event of a catastrophe to do all that lay in the power of men.

On the second night I managed to get on deck in the pitch darkness and remain there an hour among seventy automatons clinging to the rigging, to which I myself held on so as not to be thrown down or carried away; and I never felt anything more melancholy than this silence in darkness. Except for these few hours passed on deck, I lashed myself to my table, so that I could continue to draw up my general report of everything relating to the end of our expedition, and make out the fortnightly states for the time subsequent to the cessation of communications. These documents with their covering letters were copied out fair and got ready to be sent off. I even added a ballad, of which the music was worth no more than the words.

One evening about ten o'clock we were together in the captain's cabin, which I shared with him, when a fearful noise was heard on deck and a torrent of water dashed down the companion ladder; we thought we had foundered, and nothing could look more like it, but it was only a wave which had swept the deck and carried away the hatch. Except that four poor sailors were washed overboard by the wave, we escaped with the fright; but the pumps had to be manned; as these brought up only dirty water, they reassured us as to the state of the vessel, as indeed they did every morning. "Upon my word, general," said White, "you have bad luck; I have been at sea since my childhood, I have twice doubled Cape Horn, and have been in gales in the most stormy seas, but I never saw anything like this one." It cost us, indeed, seven vessels out of our convoy.

After we had been knocked about in this way for a fortnight the storm seemed to be going down, and one evening the sky cleared, if not entirely, at least sufficiently to allow of an observation. White was very clever at these astronomic operations; he ascertained that we had been driven to the latitude of Madeira, or not far from it. Another night we were carried on to the Roches Bonnes, ill-named because they are the only shoal in the ocean and formidable enough. I had been warned of it by the running to and fro and the shouting; I had seen the captain jump out of his hammock, which hung opposite mine, and run on deck in little else than his shirt, so I called Fontenay, from whom I learnt the news, and as I could do nothing to avert the new danger I stayed in bed, while Fontenay came every other minute to keep me informed. Thus we tacked, we fired broadsides to set us toward the southward, the lead was heaved every moment, and there was some anxiety about what it brought up. Finally, nothing but sand was found on it, and we began again to go ahead.

When we went on board, we had been told that the passage would take ten days; I had accordingly brought on board six sheep, thirty-six fowls, two or three hundred eggs, hams, and I do not know what besides, as well as two hundred bottles of Bordeaux wine. But as Rodney was very ill-provisioned, my stores were drawn upon till at the end of a fortnight everything was consumed. For three weeks I was reduced to the wretched fare of the vessels; that is to say, to salt provisions of the roughest kind. Even the wine gave out at last, and we had nothing to drink except the vilest beer. I say nothing about the water, which had become so bad that one had to hold one's nose when using it, even for washing; besides, it had got so scarce that it was only served out by the glass.

Somebody had somehow managed to keep a few morsels of fresh meat, which were used to make us a last gravy-soup, a nice thing at all times, but all the more valuable at the time when, owing to the danger of fire on a vessel so much tossed about as ours, any hot food had become exceptional. At length we were at table, moored to our chairs; my plate, well filled, had just been placed in the fiddles, and I was about to carry the first spoonful to my mouth, when the worst sea that we had yet experienced gave the vessel such a shock that I had my soup all over my waistcoat and breeches. To my wrath at losing so rare a treat was added that of having my clothes spoilt and being scalded, so that nothing might be lacking to my disappointment and to the mirth of my good friend Rodney. But what made me furious, above all, was that the sea should have played me such a trick in presence of Englishmen.

As we approached Quiberon, the place fixed upon for our landing and for our point of rendezvous in the probable event of our being dispersed, we began to overtake the vessels that had arrived before us and to be overtaken by those that had followed. The commodore had collected some on his side, and we found him tacking about to await us. Thus it was with nearly eighty sail that on October 14 we bore for Quiberon Bay. The frigate went ahead, our corvette brought up the rear; but at that moment the storm came on again so violently that the *Fylla*, which had been the last to reach the entrance to the bay, was no longer able to get in. She was obliged to stand out to sea, and was about to be cut off from the rest of the convoy, the most unexpected consequence of which would have been that the convoy assembled in the bay would have gone to England as prisoners of war. The explanation is as follows.

Being off the port, we were beginning to think that we were free from all further apprehension, when we were told that none of our signals were being answered from the shore, whence we inferred that they refused to receive us. However, as Lord Stuart thought it conceivable that the officer in command of the batteries might have sent to ask for orders, he decided to wait for daylight. Hardly had the sun risen when he repeated his signals, but there was no more answer to these than to those of the day before. Accordingly, on the morning of the 15th he gave the order to weigh anchor and sail for England. Judge of my consternation and anger when I heard the sound of a fife playing the infernal air to which it is customary to weigh anchor on a man-of-war. I had some influence with Captain Rodney, and so, in spite of the rudeness of the lieutenant, who looked upon us already as prisoners and could not suppress his joy, I persuaded him to stand in towards the frigate that I might confer with the commodore.

When we came near enough, a midshipman went on board Lord Stuart with a note, in which, as chief of the staff, and as such representing the commander-in-chief, I requested in the name of the Duke of Abrantès, and on the faith of a treaty which a man of his honour could not infringe, that he would receive me and hear what I had to say. His reply was that the circumstances did not allow him to receive me, that the silence on shore proved that we were not wished to land, that all his vessels were running short of provisions, and that he had no time to lose. He added, however, out of consideration for me, that if I would point out any feasible method that would also permit him to start for England in thirty-six hours at the out-side, he would adopt it. There were two generals of division there, for Delaborde and Kellermann were on board the commodore, but it had not occurred to them to do anything to avert the disaster. If the convoy started for England, we lost, not only all the horses on board as well as an immense amount of material, but more than fifty general and staff; officers, and a whole division became prisoners of war.

My first idea had been to ask the commodore to set me ashore in the *Fylla's* gig. I pointed out to him that he had a whole army as hostages for four sailors and a midshipman. But he replied, "Impossible"; and I was at my wits' end when I chanced to catch sight of a French coaster, which was taking advantage of a lull in the storm to fish under the nose of the English fleet. It seemed like a messenger from heaven, and I told the commodore that after his refusal all I asked was that he would order the *Fylla* to capture the little craft, and I would make use of it to go ashore the next night. I added that, if in the course of the following day I did not succeed in landing the troops, he might do as he thought his duty and honour enjoined.

It may be supposed that I awaited his reply with anxiety. I was in the captain's cabin alone with my *aides-de-camp*, Vidal, Vallier, and Fontenay, and a few servants, notably Jacques Dewint, who was second to no one in daring. In a state of great exasperation, we all expressed the opinion that death would be better than the captivity with which we were threatened. We settled, accordingly, that if we were made to sail for England, and if the frigate, resuming the lead, got out of the way first, we would try to get possession of the *Fylla* and escape, even if we had to run her ashore. After all, there was a good chance of success in this daring scheme. A third part of our crew were foreigners, including several French; all had been thrashed almost to death for the most trifling reasons; a good many were ordered for flogging after I was gone. Besides, the captain was a nonentity, the second-lieutenant a young man of no great influence, while all hands trembled at the name of the first-lieutenant and the master. We had kept our side-arms and our pistols.

Starting from this point, our plan was as follows:—We would call the captain into his cabin, and White also, and lock them in—that was easy; then we would blow out the brains of the first-lieutenant and of the master, and be ready to fire on all who tried to avenge them or take their places. Meanwhile, one of us would be at the magazine, and, while proclaiming that in the event of resistance we should blow up the vessel, I would throw handfuls of gold on the deck. It would be ten to one that all the foreign sailors who were awaiting their turn for a flaying would join us, and that nearly all the English would either be held in check by the fear of being blown up or won over by the gold. If we had succeeded, many of the transports, where there were only ten or a dozen English to four or five hundred Frenchmen, would have followed our example. And supposing us to fail, as the fact of not having tried every means to land us in our own country was equivalent to a breach of the Convention, and put us back into the state of war, our rising would thus have been legalised.

Fortunately, this desperate attempt was not needed. The commodore's reply arrived and was favourable; the *Fylla* shook out her sails, and the English man-of-war, for the moment under my orders, bore down upon the wretched little French hooker, whose capture was just then more important to me than if she had been the finest vessel in the British navy or the richest Indiaman. Seeing us coming towards her, she showed her heels, and, owing to her start, had some chance of being able to run ashore and escape us; but when we came within range, I had a shot fired, and this brought her to. After this fortunate capture we resumed our place in rear of the convoy and waited for night, seeing that by day the little vessel, having been in communication with us, would have been sunk if she had tried to re-enter the harbour. However, on reflection, I had to recognise that, in view of the presence of the English vessels, we must wait for daylight before we could get admission to any of the harbours in the bay.

Two hours before daylight on October 16, taking my chief valuables with me, and accompanied by Fontenay and three other officers, all in full uniform, I went on board my coaster and stood to the eastward, so as not to look as if I was coming from the fleet. At daybreak we all lay down in the hold of the vessel, and thus entered the harbour, the skipper and two sailors alone being visible. The vessel by my orders lay up close inshore, and then we showed ourselves. There was a post of thirty men hard by, and the officer, calling them to arms, tried to hinder our landing. I at once leapt from the head of the vessel into the water and ran up to the officer, crying, "Are you mad?"

"General," he replied, "we have orders not to admit General Dupont's army."

"And how did you find out that we belonged to that army?"

So the riddle was explained. But two things required to be dealt with instantly. We had to get off our dispatches to the Minister for War, and Fontenay, mounting the first screw that could be found in the village of Quiberon, galloped off with them to Paris, where, by good luck, he arrived an hour before the emperor returned from Erfurt. He carried at the same time the general report which I had drawn up in the middle of the storm, and a letter to my wife.

The other matter, urgent to the last degree, was the disembarkation. Stuart had made me renew the undertaking to get it effected within two days. The vessel which had brought me went off at once, followed by all those still remaining in the harbour. The civil authorities were employed to hasten the operation and offer rewards in my name to those who made the greatest number of trips. During the organisation of this work at Quiberon, one of my officers started for each of the other harbours or landing-place in the bay, so as to set all the available vessels to work.

Then I mounted and rode to Auray, called together the town

council, sent orders for all the boats and oars in the river to be sent down to the beach with all the men capable of handling them. Then I rode all along the coast, seeing that the work was done smartly; and, in short, I made such a good job of it that by the evening 15,000 men, all the horses, and the whole of the artillery were landed, and nothing remained on board but some material, to the landing of which Lord Stuart offered no objection. To wind up my connection with the English navy, the only thing left was to send some fresh meat, green vegetables, salad, bread, wine, and two jugs of milk to poor White, who was suffering from scurvy.

General Delaborde was at Auray. I went to him and asked for orders, the commander-in-chief having landed at La Rochelle. "Why should I command?" said he.

"Because of your seniority."

"Are you not in correspondence with the minister?"

"Surely."

"Then would it not be simpler for you to continue to transmit his orders to us, as heretofore, in the name of the commander-in-chief? The detail is in good hands. Kellermann and I have decided to do nothing but executive work here, where, indeed, we should not be but for you."

Therewith he paid me the only compliments that my recent doings were ever to earn; for with the exception of himself, Kellermann, Margaron, and a few colonels who were present, no one ever said a word about them, while, save to a few friends, I spoke to no one of them. I may add that, good-natured and honourable as was General Delaborde's refusal to interfere, it had its compensations for him, seeing that all day and all night were hardly sufficient for my efforts to get the troops ready with all speed to resume their journey.

Among the letters which I had received from the Minister for War was one containing these words:

> The emperor forbids any general or other officer, or any person employed in the administrative department, belonging to the Army of Portugal, to appear in Paris. You will bring this order to the knowledge of all whom it may concern, and see that it is strictly carried out.

I had been as speedy in forwarding copies of this gracious dispatch as careful to let no one remain in ignorance of it. For my own part, in all cases where they did not affect the interests of the service, I was not accustomed to trouble myself about measures of this kind. Seven times in my life I was destined to take similar liberties; this was only the fourth, and as may be supposed, not having seen my wife for fourteen months, and eager beyond measure as I was to embrace my children and to mingle my tears with those of my sister for the loss of our father, who had died during my absence, I did not hesitate to take this. Besides, I was still in a sufficiently bad temper over the refusal of my promotion to feel myself justified in not being over-particular; so I set off for Paris with all the speed in my power.

I had a pleasant journey by the banks of the Loire, from Nantes to Tours. On reaching Paris, I was sitting well back in my carriage, to avoid curious eyes, when in the middle of the Boulevard de la Madeleine, at two in the afternoon, one of my axles broke. The loafers knocked round at once—one might have said that every paving-stone gave up its man; but were there none but loafers? Thanks to Fouché, who, as in treachery so in the matters of spies and information, has "gone better" than anyone else, it was a well-known fact that a secret which three persons shared was no secret to the police. Now I was surrounded not by three persons, but by more than two hundred, and though I at once jumped into a hackney-coach, leaving Jacques to look after the carriage, it was ten to one that some knave had recognised me.

After this, the only disappointment possible was not to find my wife at Paris; and, as the fiend would have it, she had the day before heard of the order relating to the generals from Portugal, and, learning that the Duchess of Abrantès had just started for La Rochelle, she had concluded that I, too, should not venture to show myself in Paris, and had thought she would go and meet me at Tours. To crown all, instead of going by Chartres, she had taken the road by Orleans, which she never used to do. I could only wait, and asked for the children. Naïs was brought, but as soon as she saw me she ran and rolled herself up in the muslin window-curtains, shrieking when I came near her, and remaining unapproachable all the day. On the other hand, Claire, when brought in by her nurse, showed that she was already quite good and amiable. She let me take her and kiss her, fixing her great blue eyes on me. She had been born in my absence, the news of her birth reaching me after I had been a few months in Portugal.[4] About midnight my

---

4. Mlle Claire Thiébault died April 9, 1894, when these *Memoirs*, which she herself had never read, were passing through the press; leaving to those who knew her the memory of a simple and kindly nature, a generous heart, and a delicate wit. Ed.

wife returned and my happiness was complete.

On the Monday after my arrival I had been dining with some friends; just as we rose from table in came an *aide-de-camp* from Hulin, who then was military governor. Amid the enjoyment of the first days I had quite forgotten my accident on the *boulevard*. I saw none but friends on whose silence I could count; and as I went out little, and only in a carriage, I had hoped to escape the police-spies. But at that period of the Empire one did not escape them, and the breakage of my axle had been quite enough to draw attention to me. Hulin's messenger brought a letter from the Minister for War, beginning:

> I am much surprised, general, that you have taken the liberty of coming to Paris, in contravention of the emperor's orders.

And ending with an order to return to my post on the following morning—that is, to rejoin the army, which now, a month after its disembarkation, was about to go back to Spain. The first division was, indeed, in pursuance of the orders I had left, on its way from Auray to Bordeaux.

I had hoped that they would have winked at my coming; but, though mistaken as to this, I was not taken unawares. One thing calculated to develop my refractory mood was that on the envelope of the letter Clarke had clapped an enormous "General of brigade." Now, if I had not had a *centime* in the house, I would not have agreed to serve in that capacity. The campaign in Portugal had added still further to my claims and to my irritation; for the end of it had been that I was the only one in that army who had received neither rank nor money, and I had just saved a division from being taken as prisoners of war to England. So I had vowed never to wear my major-general's uniform again, unless to go and declare that I was giving it up for ever; that is, to get done with the business by an audience which I was resolved to demand of the emperor. My income was sufficient to allow me to choose between independence and a humiliating position; and there was as yet nothing to show that the emperor would not do me the justice I expected of him. I knew that he had been well satisfied with my report of the expedition, and I had heard on good authority that I was to be made general of division and count.

All these considerations determined my line of conduct. As the minister's letter required a written reply by the bearer, this went at once, to the effect that none of the motives for the prohibition could have any application to my case; that, as regarded the moral effect of our evacuation of Portugal, I could not fail to carry out the views of the government, and that in this respect my presence for a moment in Paris could not fail to be of use; that to have gone round by Paris would not prevent me from reaching Bordeaux at the same time as my effects, for I had no orders to post thither, and should have marched like the other generals; and, moreover, that I had been called to Paris by serious family reasons, having had the misfortune while in Portugal to lose my father, I added:

> Finally, I start next Saturday, because that has always been the day fixed for my departure.

I felt that the last sentence was indecorous; but the more I had restrained myself in the rest of my letter, the less control I had over my final words. My wife was frightened; but I would not alter it, for I could not let them think I was going next day, and lay myself open to a fresh letter for not having gone. Next morning I went to pitch into Hulin, to whose espionage I ascribed what had happened. I told him that nothing in the world should make me start before Saturday, and bade him go and tell the Minister that, if they pushed things to extremities with me, I would not go at all. Poor Hulin tried to soothe me, with no great success; but, to cut the story short, I heard no more of the matter from anyone. I have always attributed this moderation to the emperor's satisfaction with my report forwarded from Quiberon.

As soon as he arrived from Erfurt, he had sent for Clarke and said, "Have you any news from the Army of Portugal?" On his reply, "I have just received a long report from the chief of the staff, which I have not read," the emperor had added, "Go and fetch it." And he at once fell to, and read once and again the eighty or hundred pages without laying it down. Under these conditions it was not easy for Master Clarke to come down heavily on me for a breach of orders which did no harm to anyone. So I had the benefit of his silence, and owed him no thanks.

On the Saturday I duly left Paris. My wife went with me as far as Tours, where we passed two more days together. Then we had to part; she to go back to her children, I to return to the Peninsula. I reached Bordeaux on the morning of November 25, and went to call on the Duke of Abrantès. "Here you are at last," he said when he saw me.

"Yes, sir, in accordance with my marching orders, which I lay before you, and which fix today for my arrival."

He began to laugh. "Look at these two papers," he continued, taking them from his desk and showing them to me. "According to one, I have to punish you"—this was a sharp complaint of me from the minister—"according to the other, I have to congratulate you. The first may amuse you it gives a good picture of Clarke's character; as for the second, over the terms of which I may embrace you, it confirms your promotion to general of division."

Thus for the second time the much-desired step, so anxiously awaited, was gained. My ill-temper was dispelled, and all uncertainties respecting the continuance of my career, now secure, were at an end. It was amusing that the announcement of it should come simultaneously with a fulmination from Clarke, who had doubtless denounced me to the Prince of Neuchâtel as he had to Junot, and who must have been annoyed that his denunciation—the ten-thousandth, perhaps, that he had made should be answered by my promotion. Less pleasant was the letter from his Highness the chief of the staff, dated Burgos, November 19. Here it is:—

> To Major-General Thiébault,
> Chief of Staff to the 8th Corps of the Army of Spain.
> Sir, I hasten to inform you that the emperor, by decree of this day, has appointed you general of division.
> His Majesty authorises me to give you this information provisionally, in anticipation of that which you will receive officially from the Minister for War.
> (Signed) The Prince of Neuchâtel,
> Vice-Constable,
> Chief of the Staff, Alexander.

I defy anyone to imagine anything drier. Not a word of courteous opening, and the term "sir" substituted for "general"; also the title "major-general" retained in the address, though when the letter was written it no longer belonged to me. The tone of the letter portended no more goodwill in the future than in the past. None the less, I had obtained justice from the emperor, and for the present that must suffice; and I felt pretty well satisfied, in spite of Clarke's wrath and Berthier's ill-temper.

This was the last I had to do, from a military point of view, with the Duke of Abrantès, one of the three men for whom I have felt most attachment. I have long since forgiven him for not keeping his word about the 300,000 *francs*, though the fulfilment of it would have meant a secure existence for myself and my family.

I remained eleven days at Bordeaux, getting together the troops who came from Auray with the small number who, like the commander-in-chief, had landed at Rochelle, not to mention the detachments arriving from the depots. Regiments, brigades, and divisions had to be definitely re-formed, furnished with what they needed, and sent forward to Bayonne. We remained there from the 12th to the 19th of December. The year before we had been kept there for fifty-one days; but we had now many fewer hopes and illusions, many more regrets and apprehensions.

It was no longer a matter of adding laurels to laurels, of giving new life by new triumphs to the lustre of our arms, of adding by dint of conquests to our preponderance in Europe. Now we had reverses to tone down, insults to wipe out; we had entered upon that road of misfortune which was to lead, at the end of a long and convulsive death-struggle, to the invasion and splitting-up of France, and to the downfall of the mighty Empire.

On December 20 I crossed the Bidassoa for the fourth time in my life, but this time with no certain destination, and in a position no less false than that in which General Junot found himself. He had become Duke of Abrantès; but he was no longer senior *aide-de-camp* to the emperor, or governor of Paris, or commander-in-chief. As for me, who, when major-general, had been chief of the staff to an army, including Spanish and Portuguese troops, of 51,000 men, in whose doings the whole world took an interest, I now found myself, as lieutenant-general, merely chief of the staff to a corps of 20,000 men, numbered "8," and so reduced to an obscure fraction of the whole that it once had been. For the duke and myself, it was a case of having been exalted to be abased.

My position soon seemed to get worse, for Junot, whose sympathy alone rendered it tolerable, received orders to leave the 8th Corps and go to take command of the 3rd in Aragon. For the moment no chief took his place, so that the various portions of the corps, now really a body without a soul, continued their movements under command of General Loison. On January 6 we reached Leon. But all this did not satisfy me. It was too far from the functions I had been performing and those which were left to me. Therefore, as soon as I heard that the emperor was or was just going to be at Valladolid, I went and told Loison that I was leaving the 8th Corps and going to the imperial headquarters, and I asked him kindly to see to the provisional supplying of my place. "Is all that out of your own head?"

"Yes," I said, and added, laughing, "Acting as my own commander-in-chief, I have just decided on this disposition of my forces, and charged myself with carrying it out."

"But do you remember the passage relating to you in the order in compliance with which the duke left the army—'Your chief of staff will remain with the 8th Corps'?"

"Quite well."

"And you go in spite of that?"

"Certainly."

"And to Valladolid?"

"Just as I left Vannes for Paris."

"You are playing pretty high!"

I started; but, by an extraordinary coincidence, on the way I received the very order which I was executing, and all that remained of a step something more than audacious was an act of submission. The promptitude with which I appeared, the result of my insubordination, seemed a proof of my zeal.

I reached Valladolid a little before noon, and went to the march-past, which the emperor held every day himself. I had hardly got to the ground when he appeared. After the inspection he caught sight of General Legendre, who had been chief of the staff to Dupont's corps. Instantly, with a look of thunder, he addressed him in these words: "You are a bold man to show yourself before me!" A terrible scene followed, in which Legendre vainly tried to find excuses for the conduct of the generals at Baylen. Napoleon would hear none of them. His invective became fiercer and fiercer, until he ended by saying:

> And your hand did not dry up when you took the order to Vedel to lay down his arms! If, instead of giving way to sordid interest or disgraceful panic, you had fought instead of capitulating; if you had formed attacking columns instead of deploying; if you had kept your troops concentrated instead of breaking them up you would have beaten the Spaniards and kept our retreat open. The insurrection in Spain would not have been so unprecedently successful; England would not have had an army in the Peninsula; and what a difference in the way things would have turned out, perhaps in the destiny of the world!

As he uttered the last words he turned his back on General Legendre, who at once left the ground and, soon after, Valladolid. Thus ended that memorable scene, which for any other than Legendre would have ended more than his career.[5]

Though General Legendre's position and mine were far from being identical, there yet was some analogy between them. I had, indeed, been struck by the fact that in the whole of his crushing peroration the emperor had avoided all allusion to the Army of Portugal. He had no doubt honoured me only with a nod, but there had been no frown on his face at the sight of me. He had even sent for me to Valladolid. Yet I, like Legendre, had been chief of the staff to an army which had given up to the enemy the country it was appointed to defend, and in relying on him for its conveyance back to France had only saved appearances. If I felt quite easy as to anyone reproaching me with having sacrificed anything whatever to save my filthy gold, I none the less knew that in the matter of theft, extortion, profits or partitions, Portugal left Andalusia no ground for jealousy.

I was therefore glad to have remained unperceived at that parade, and not to have to appear before the emperor immediately after such a violent outburst of wrath. As I went back to my quarters, I was congratulating myself to my *aides-de-camp*, when I heard my name called. It was Savary, running after me to say, "The emperor sends orders that you are to be with him in a quarter of an hour." A quarter of an hour was doubtless not a long time in which to appease the wave after such very rough weather, though Frederick II had taught my father that it was enough. Anyhow, I had only to prepare seriously for the audience to which I was summoned.

One thing I was determined upon; I would do nothing to injure the Duke of Abrantès with Napoleon. The emperor greeted me with a simple "Good morning, sir," and continued: "So you capitulated to the English and evacuated Portugal!"

"Sir," I replied, "the Duke of Abrantès yielded only to necessity, and he extorted an honourable treaty from people who, if he had been in command of them, would not have granted us even a capitulation."

"What passed at Lisbon," he returned, "was only the consequence of what happened at Vimiero. That, sir, is when you ought to have beaten the enemy, and when you would have beaten him if great blunders had not been committed."

I saw, on the one hand, that he had made up his mind not to pronounce Junot's name, and that his "you" was a turn of phrase with

---

5. [This, and the following scene between Thiébault himself and Napoleon, have been merely summarized, owing to considerations of space. The latter has already been given pretty fully by the Duchess of Abrantès in her *Memoirs*.]

which I need not trouble myself; on the other, that as mistakes had as a matter of fact been committed both on the field of battle and on the way thither, I had better avoid picking up the glove,—that is, defending what was indefensible. We had a long discussion as to the forces at the disposal of both sides. He compared our action unfavourably with that of Soult, who had driven the enemy out of the Peninsula. I pointed out that Soult had as much failed to hinder the embarkation of the English Army as Junot to carry the position of Vimiero. He laid his finger on most of the weak spots in our disposition; and I was amazed to find that he really remembered the contents of my report better than I did myself. I was, however, able in some cases to show justification, in others to demonstrate that measures which it now appeared as if we ought to have taken would, at the time when they could have been taken with effect, have been obviously premature.

He put a number of questions to me upon the nature and degree of the difficulties which the various provinces of Portugal presented to a hostile force, and took some notes. Here I had no hesitation; no one at that time knew Portugal better than I did. The new campaign upon which he was about to employ Marshal Soult was the theme of inquiries for which he might not have another opportunity. With regard to the marshal's route, he said, "It is a case of crossing rivers instead of crossing mountains;" and in fact, in marching within reach of the coast from Galicia to Lisbon, one has to cross the Minho, the Douro, the Vouga, and the Mondego. But, as I observed, if they were more in number and larger, it would be better than going through the Beira and Tras os Montes.

"Marshal Soult," I added, "will only have to act along practicable roads; he will march through a land of plenty; he will be able to operate everywhere, and in order to cross the three chief rivers he will have at his disposal the resources of Tuy, Oporto, and Coimbra." He relished this reply, which justified his plan, and everything made me think that the interview had satisfied him. A few questions served to extract the remaining information which he wanted from me.

Then he stopped, and, turning toward me with the manner and tone to which he was so well able to impart an air of kindliness, and to which the power of his gaze and the wonderful expression of his mouth gave an indefinable, let me say irresistible, charm, he said, "Well, General Thiébault, have you any request to make of me?"

"Yes, sir," I answered; "the Count of Novion, who was commanding the police when we arrived in Portugal, and who opened the gates of Lisbon to us, and did so much to prevent any resistance being made to us; whom your majesty appointed major-general; who during the recent events threw in his lot with us, and returned to France with the army was arrested as an *émigré* the moment he landed, and is now in prison at Nantes. I consider it my duty to appeal to your Majesty for his release, and to commend him to your favour."

"Can you give me a written statement of what you say?" he returned, with a half-surprised look.

"Certainly, sir."

"In that case, let me have your memorandum as soon as it is ready. I am sending a messenger to Paris at four o'clock, and I will see that your request is carried out."

A week later the Count of Novion was at liberty. After that, with equal kindness, he resumed: "Well, General Thiébault, have you any other request?" Destiny, spiteful destiny, willed that in the teeth of, or on account of, my bad luck, which had already lasted so long, I should look upon myself as having too many claims to condescend to a request. In spite of my five years in Italy and my services at Austerlitz although I had been appointed adjutant-general on the field of battle at Naples, and general of brigade under similar conditions at Genoa honours, orders, titles, and gratuities had not fallen to my share. I had, I repeat, so many claims to put forward that I knew not where to begin; and to be reduced to humble myself was a thing that always scared my pride.

Convinced that my service spoke loudly enough, I replied, "No, sir." Instantly the emperor's brow clouded, and he dismissed me with the words, "In that case, sir, I wish you good morning."

As I passed through the waiting-room, where from the length of my audience it had lasted over an hour and a half—they had all been thinking that my fortune was made, Savary came up to me and eagerly asked, "Well, what have you got?"

"Nothing."

"Why, did not the emperor give you a chance of asking for anything?"

"Yes, twice."

"D—— it all, that's too much!" The strength of his language meant a good deal, but it came too late. I wished that Savary had given me a hint before my audience. However, I understood how all that was kind and honourable in the emperor's first impulses gave way to the pride of power, and this made him tolerate any importunity, any audacity, any want of respect on the part of suppliants, just for the satisfaction of being invoked or prayed to like a deity. These requests and supplications were abasements that had to be submitted to if one would obtain even the best-earned rewards. What was in every sense a matter of mere equity had to be received as a favour, and to him who did not know how to solicit his reticence was imputed as a crime, when it ought to have contrasted favourably with the shameless beggary of others. Anyhow, I missed the last opportunity that destiny offered me of grasping fortune, and perhaps of preventing the misfortunes which ruined the end my career and made my life torture; and that because I was not thoroughly imbued with the idea that with all sovereigns you must ask, and *à fortiori* never refuse; while with Napoleon, in regard to favours, the only thing needed was just to fatten.[6]

However, the emperor was not inclined to neglect the interests of his service, and continued to employ me in high functions. The next day, in fact, I was appointed governor of the three Basque Provinces. Five days later, being disgusted with the condition of Burgos, and finding Vitoria well enough commanded by one of the three generals of brigade whom I was to have under my command, the emperor, as will be seen, changed my destination and appointed me governor of Old Castile. The command was important, and involved the conquest of various difficulties which it took unprecedented efforts and labour to conquer. However, the first order reached me that evening, and on the morrow I was off for Vitoria.

I was drawing near the last place where I was to sleep before reaching Burgos (on January 17); I was in my carriage *aides-de-camp*, secretary, servants, escort, riding after. My servant Jacques suddenly said, "Here is the emperor, I think."

I was on the point of alighting when I heard someone call, "Who is in that carriage?" Jacques had hardly time to reply, "General Thiébault," when the party tore past me. Savary was first; after him came the emperor, simultaneously lashing the horse of his *aide-de-camp* and digging the spurs into his own. He was upon that incredible ride in which he covered the distance from Valladolid to Burgos—some seventy-five miles—in three hours and a half. A good minute after them Duroc and the emperor's Mameluke[7] galloped by, and at a like distance after

---

6. "I never give unless I am asked; the empress herself gets nothing without asking for it," said Napoleon on one occasion.
7. *Mameluke Ali,* with Napoleon from the Tuileries to St. Helena by Louis Étienne Saint-Denis is also published by Leonaur.

them came a guide, exhausted with the effort to make up his lost ground, and four more brought up the rear as they best could. The journey was not more extraordinary for its speed than from the fact that the emperor accomplished it with as a rule only one person at his side, in the teeth of the *guerrilleros*, who were already organised, and of the exasperation prevailing among the proud Castilians. It was Caesar and his fortune again a fortune which both Caesar and Napoleon had to pay for.

At Burgos the emperor had occupied the archbishop's palace, and I was lodged in the rooms which he had just left. Everything recalled his presence. His bed, in which I slept, had not been made; his table was covered with fragments of paper, pens, and dust; the chairs were standing about; half-burnt tapers were in the candlesticks. All the disorder said, "For twelve hours this was the centre of the world."

When I was in Masséna's division, I had known a major in the 32nd who came, I think, from Marseilles, a regular "*Troun de Dious*."[8] In Egypt he had been made colonel—rightly enough, because at the head of a regiment, especially the Provençals of the 32nd, he could be trusted to act with the certainty of a battering-ram. Later on he was made general of brigade, which was less necessary, and, finally, general of division, which was not necessary at all, and governor of Old Castile, which could not fail to be disastrous.

This man, Darmagnac by name, having his headquarters at Burgos, asked me to dinner as soon as he heard of my arrival. My *aides-de-camp* were included, and I went with them. Directly we got there news came that a soldier had been murdered. There was, unhappily, nothing unusual about this. Darmagnac had been sixty days in command at Burgos, and for sixty days pillage and devastation had been going on with a frenzy that can hardly be imagined.

The inhabitants were beside themselves with rage and despair, and the scarcity of everything, amounting to famine, increased the epidemics which were eating up our troops. The town was a horrible, the country a pitiful, sight. Instead of coming to terms, peasants and soldiers killed till either side could conjugate every tense of the verb "to assassinate." But, with a character like Darmagnac's, there could be no idea of remedy or conciliation, only of vengeance, and of a vengeance sure to be fertile of reprisals. Thus, after reading the letter which announced the soldier's death, he began to stride up and down the

---

8. [Provençal for "*Tonnerre de Dieu*," an expletive equivalent to the stage Irishman's "*Tare and 'ouns.*"]

kind of drawing-room in which he received us, and treated us to the following monologue:—

> Poor beggar! I will avenge you, if it were on a hundred innocent persons. I feel my anger getting the better of me, and blood calls for blood.

It would have been a scene from the transpontine drama had it not been one of real savagery. I was disgusted, and my *aides-de-camp* no less so; and we were indignant at having to spend two hours with this ex-cook, ignorant as a kitchen-boy, brutal as any boor, who treated men as he had been wont to treat, turkeys and rabbits; a man of the Terror, into the bargain, like Canuel or Donnadieu, and destined like them to enjoy the favours of the Restoration and wear the trappings of the Bourbons.

Next morning my carriage was ready at eight, and the luggage was nearly all in. My people were all mounted, and I was taking a last look at a bivouac fire burning in the little square before the palace, upon which the soldiers in the joy of their hearts had just thrown a whole *pianoforte*—in short, I was about to get away from that town, the scene of all these abominations, when an imperial messenger, coming from Vitoria on his way to Valladolid, where the Prince of Neuchâtel still remained, asked for me and gave me a letter from Duroc. It was in these terms:

> My dear general, the emperor bids me write and tell you to wait at Burgos for further orders from the Prince of Neuchâtel.

I shuddered. It meant losing a government which I liked all the better because my wife could have come to Vitoria at once. I was evidently to replace this Darmagnac, who, if he was leaving everything to be done in the way of good, had done a consummate amount of harm; instead of being in contact with a population who had so far shown no great hostility, I should have to do with nearly 800,000 exasperated and ruined inhabitants, and, instead of living at the gates of France and in one of the prettiest towns of Spain, my residence would be not only in the centre, but in one of its most miserable cities. So it was with a heavy heart that I sent an *aide-de-camp* to give Darmagnac Duroc's letter to read, and had my luggage again brought indoors, while my horses and I resumed the quarters which I had hoped never to see again.

However, I felt that the emperor had excellent reasons for putting me in Darmagnac's place; and to pass the time until my appointment was confirmed and escape from useless regrets, I abandoned myself to the pleasures of imagination, which have always done more than reason to make me forget my troubles. From one subject to another I passed to that of the ballads which I loved to hear my wife sing, and thence to that of ballad-music generally. The idea of writing a little work on the subject came into my head. I fell to, and wrote all that day and part of the night; and not half an hour after I had finished the emperor's messenger came back, with orders for Darmagnac to go to Madrid, and for myself a nomination as governor of Old Castile.

CHAPTER 12

An Attack Impending

As soon as I had received my nomination I visited Darmagnac to arrange about taking over the government. He asked to stay for three days longer, but I declined to hear of this; and it was settled that he should call on me next evening in plain clothes with a general report on the state of the province. After leaving him I went round the town, finding a most melancholy spectacle. Deserted by part of its population, it looked like a desolate solitude—in parts a sink of filth. Famine, ruin, despair, pestilence prevailed, with death as the sole remedy. The hospitals, established in deserted convents, were filthy and neglected. The service was utterly disorganised. Passing troops supplied themselves by pillage, and the garrison lived on what they brought in. Force, violence, brutality formed all the law there was, and no redress was to be had even for the gravest crimes.

The day after my orders came, as I was again going round the town, I saw a peasant holding a letter with which he seemed not to know what to do. I made him give it me; it was addressed to one Astulez at Palenzuela. I knew that much grain had been and still was being carried off in that direction, and that this Astulez was one of the agents most frequently employed in operations of the kind. This was quite enough to make me keep the letter, which was written, though not signed, by General Darmagnac's *aide-de-camp*. Here are some extracts from it:

> As you know that if we do not help ourselves others will, it would suit me very well if you would send me 200 *fanegas* [1] on our joint account. I rely on you . . . But silence We have no need to blame ourselves, since the corn is not for the general.

---
1. [A trifle over 300 bushels.]

Farewell; make a good job of it.

And by way of postscript:

You will understand that the corn on our account is not to be addressed to the general.

So General Darmagnac, speculating on the rise in the price of corn caused by his own criminal maladministration, and on the dearth which he had brought about, had been having corn stolen on his account; the thieves had been taking the opportunity of stealing for their own profit, and the *aide-de-camp* had been going shares with them. Chance having revealed this abominable traffic to me, I at once made hue and cry after all grain coming from that quarter, and met with no opposition and no risk, since the matter could only come before my tribunal. Thus I had an unexpected resource to meet the first need.[2]

With this and a quantity of other information, by the time I received the civil and military authorities of Burgos, I knew enough about the state of affairs to be able to administer to each the reprimand he required. It soon became known to everybody, and especially to the military governor and the commissary, that faults and disorders would no longer go unpunished. After the receptions came the inspection of the troops, and, having called the officers into a circle, I told them how disgusted I was to find that their soldiers had under their very eyes been reaping the fruits of sixty days' plundering; adding that in future I should hold them responsible.

The first meeting of the governing body took place in the evening of the day of my installation. I began by saying that I meant to change the state of things. "Your Excellency is undertaking to cleanse a more than Augean stable," said the respected *prefect*, Blanco de Salcedo.

"I am undertaking nothing," I replied, "that I am not certain to accomplish with your co-operation. It is our business to find the means." My hearers were not all convinced, for next day the director of finances, named Casa, wrote to his chief, Count Cabarrus:

We have a new governor, who says he is going to change the state of these provinces; what he is undertaking is beyond human power.

---

[2] The original of the letter referred to was found among the papers left by General Thiébault. There is another postscript: "I enclose a letter for the lieutenant of hussars who is placed at your disposal, and who will withdraw when the job is done." Ed.

Six weeks later the same man wrote—I saw the minute of his letter:

What is going on here is something like a miracle.

But during those six weeks I had only three times taken off my clothes and gone to bed.

On leaving Valladolid, the emperor had entrusted the chief authority to the Prince of Neuchâtel. He exercised it, or rather failed to exercise it, for a few days only; and when he departed to rejoin the emperor at Paris, he left Marshal Bessières as commander-in-chief of the army of Northern Spain, occupying the whole space between Rodrigo and Irun. The marshal in his turn only stayed in the Peninsula long enough to send off the various corps of the Imperial Guard, and was replaced after an interval by General Kellermann. I had nothing but good to say of either, both understanding that the way to stimulate my zeal was to leave me a free hand.

The Duke of Istria approved whatever I did, authorised whatever I proposed, and gave me the means of procuring the funds indispensable for the works I was having carried out. But as soon as I began to incur financial responsibilities, I replaced my governing council, which was no longer needed, by an administrative Junta, composed of the prefect, the director of finance, and the *corregidor*. Three times a week all business, all expenditure, except the most urgent, was taken three times over, first for proposal, then for discussion, lastly for decision; sometimes a fourth time for revision.

With the support of this assembly I was getting ready to reap all the benefits of peace in Old Castile, when suddenly General Ballesteros flung himself into the Asturias with 17,000 men. It was said that he meant to wait there, and facilitate the landing of a body of English troops. We were seriously threatened, and Kellermann received orders from Marshal Jourdan, Joseph's chief of staff, to concentrate at once all the troops at Salamanca, Burgos, and Valladolid, and then in conjunction with Ney, who was to come, I think, from Gallicia, to march against Ballesteros. They did in point of fact attack him and drive him out of the Asturias, but the operation placed me in a most annoying position. In pursuance of the orders received, I had sent my men, to the very last, away.

The chief of the staff had indeed advised me that Marshal Mortier, on his way from Aragon to Madrid with his army corps, had orders to leave me as many men as I had sent away. I thought I might reckon on this compensation, and was, therefore, no less surprised than disgusted when in reply to my inquiry the marshal said:

> I hold the command of my army corps from the emperor, and no one has any right to break it up. My troops will be commanded only by my own generals, and I declare to you that I will not allow you a single man.

I returned:

> Marshal, there is no granting or refusing till a request has been made, and I beg you to observe that that is the case here. It is no question of myself, but of the authority by whom the orders you have received were issued; namely, that of the king, the emperor's lieutenant and substitute in Spain. Burgos is from every point of view the most important place between Irun and Madrid, to say nothing of the fact that it contains 12,000 sick and wounded. Moreover, the construction of a fort, intended to be a citadel, is just begun, and the very workmen want watching. Now on the arrival of your first troops every man, even to my very guard, left this place; and if you leave no one here, there will be no one. As my responsibility does not extend to the use of the only sound arm I have left, it will not be I that will have to account to the emperor for any disaster that may result from the abandonment of this place.

I thought that he might be struck by what I said, and ashamed of what he had said to me, according to the dictum of one of our moralists "*Nothing is so stupid as a clever man in face of sound reasoning.*" But Marshal Mortier was imperturbable. I always considered this marshal's elevation as an instance of those little ways in which the great ones of the earth are fond of showing their power by misusing it. In spite of the energy he displayed at Krems,[3] Mortier was none the less one of the most wretched marshals appointed by Napoleon for one moment is not enough to make a man. Yet if I speak of him as a poor creature, I do not deny that he may have been a good fellow and a very brave man; nor is my opinion to this effect founded alone on his feat of arms at Krems, brilliant as that was. Mortier, always brave, was brave at Krems in an exalted degree, and raised to heroism what in another

---

3. [On the march upon Vienna in 1805, when Mortier, with the divisions of Dupont and Gazan, was isolated on the left bank of the Danube, and had to cut his way through Kutusoff's army, three or four times outnumbering his own force.]

would have been only the courage of despair. However that may be, I was convinced that his obstinacy, which he considered firmness, left me no hope, and I parted with him, saying, "As you please; but today's messengers will take my reports to Paris and to Madrid."

On leaving him, I met Girard, the brilliant officer who had formerly been *aide-de-camp* to General Monnier, and who, being then a general of brigade in the marshal's corps, was provisionally in command of the division which Suchet had just quitted. He told me that the marshal had spoken to him of his determination not to defer to the king's order, while he himself, using the same arguments as I had done, had ended by proposing to leave me at least one regiment; but with no result.

Early the next morning, just as the last division of the army corps was about to march out, I received a letter from the chief of the marshal's staff, informing me that the colonels had orders to leave the post occupied, for it was notorious that I had no one to relieve guard. So Burgos remained in charge of some 250 men; but even then the colonels, finding themselves able to choose the men, left me only 250 sick, who ought to have been in hospital. For three days and nights these poor fellows were forced to remain in guard-rooms, where several died.

This state of things had lasted for thirty hours, when the prefect came running in to tell me that Ballesteros, who had been driven out of the Asturias, but was not pursued, had just arrived with 17,000 men within ten miles of Burgos, and intended to attack and carry the place with the bayonet next day. "Very kind of him," I said, "thus to postpone what it would be so easy to do at once." Still, while unable to advise the prefect not to take such measures as seemed desirable for himself and his family, I asked him not to spread any alarm. In spite, however, of my precautions, the town was soon in a state of active agitation. I went all over it, and then went to inspect the works at the fort; that is, to show myself to the numerous Spanish workmen who were employed there.

As I went round, accompanied by the military governor and the commissary, I enjoined all the necessary measures to ensure that at the first tap of the drum all the Frenchmen in Burgos, including all in the hospitals who could stand, should be assembled and armed. On my way home I looked in on the commissioner of police, and told him to send some safe men in the direction of Ballesteros' camp, so as to keep me informed of any movements which might go on in that direction.

Still, do what I might, I was at his mercy; and in my anger I was still looking after non-existent ways out of it, when a deputation from the inhabitants was announced.

The deputation was composed of honourable men, several of whom were unknown to me, while some were known as no friends of mine. One of these latter was spokesman. He said in effect that, in gratitude for what I had done for the town and district, the whole population constituted itself my protector. While he was speaking, many thoughts assailed me. If the town was under obligations to me, was it seemly for me to accept the value of them at the hands of the inhabitants? To allow myself to be protected by people who ought to look to me for protection was a kind of surrender, and I saw that that moment was decisive of my future. As one of the emperor's generals, I had to account to him for the powers he had entrusted to me, all the more so that the authority which I exercised was his. It was with the manner and tone of one who is offended but tries to check himself that I replied:

> And what should make you think that I am in want of a protector? Gentlemen, I appreciate the motives under which you have acted, but I cannot approve the step you have taken. To begin with, you are mistaken as to my resources; and, further, you know nothing as to the movements of troops which are going on around this town, or of the progress of the troops which are on the point of arriving, and may soon teach General Ballesteros that he has more important business on hand than to trouble himself about Burgos or me. Lastly, even if he were by any possibility to win a few hours' success, I may tell you that the town of Burgos and all that is in it would instantly be blown up. As regards that, I assure you that my measures are taken and my resolution is irrevocable.

The immense mass of powder which to everyone's knowledge was at my disposal, and the firm intention which I showed to make use of it, disconcerted my interlocutors. They at once withdrew, doubtless to make use of what I had told them; for Ballesteros, after remaining for two days in his camp, left it suddenly and marched towards Santander, without touching what Marshal Mortier had put so completely at his disposal. From a remark of his which was reported to me, I learnt that he had feared universal condemnation if I carried out my threat; and, in fact, he would have got neither glory nor profit by fighting a handful of sick men to take a town which he would probably have been unable to hold. I have spoken of General Suchet; I said that he had left the division that he commanded in Marshal Mortier's corps. He did so because he did not find it suit him to serve under so incapable a chief, because he felt that he had talent to play another part, and, finally, because, having nine years before been lieutenant-general in command of an army, he had no idea of remaining any longer at the head of a mere division. He had given notice of this, and in order to cut the matter short he had resigned his place just when interest was being made at Paris for him to get Junot's place in command of the 3rd Corps.

Knowing that I was governor of Old Castile, he had come to stay with me while awaiting fresh orders, and had even asked that they might be addressed to me. In this way he passed five days at Burgos, and nearly all his time in my company, for he had been kind enough to accept my table as his own. Expressing his desire to take a lesson of government in a conquered country, he examined all the measures I had promulgated, discussed my motives for adopting them, read my proclamations, visited hospitals, prisons, forts, magazines. He was, above all, struck by the results I had obtained and the affection shown me by the people.

Just then an order had been given to the *guerrilleros* to stop nothing that was travelling in my name or was addressed to me, a compliment which only General Thouvenot and General de Tilly at Segovia shared with me. At length I received General Suchet's appointment to the command of the 3rd Corps. On receiving it, he asked me if I would serve with him. "I can offer you," he said, "the command of one of my divisions; I need not tell you that I should think myself happy to have you, and that it would be no fault of mine if you were not compensated for what you leave."

If I could have accepted this kindly offer, which I have so often regretted having refused, I should have gone with an army which not long afterwards became the Army of Aragon, and which was destined to have the only honourable part played by our troops in Spain. I should have served under a chief who was my friend, and who would have given me full credit for my conduct, and at the very least I should have found myself under the command of a deserving man instead of under that of an incapable mountebank like Dorsenne, or a brainless peacock like Caffarelli. But my wife was on the way to join me at Burgos; I had not the heart to do no more than go and spend eight days with her at Bayonne, and for her sake alone I remained in that town, which I was unable to make endurable for her more than a month. This was for me the beginning of a long series of vexations, while General Suchet began those glorious campaigns with which it would have been at once a pride and pleasure to me to be associated.

It was half-past three in the morning and I was fast asleep, when I was roused with a start by the creaking of my door as it was thrown suddenly open, by the disorderly noise of boots, spurs, and a trailing sabre, and by hearing some one shout, loud enough to split my head, "I am sleepy, I am thirsty, I am hungry!" It was that amiable lunatic La Salle, who had galloped in advance of his equipages to pass a day with me, accompanied only by his *aide-de-camp*, De Coëtlosquet, who in those days acted as joker and humorist to people whose assassin he was one day to become.[4]

Before my servant had time to bring candles, I had leapt out of bed and embraced poor La Salle, who was on his way to join the Grand Army. Interested in all that could interest me, he must needs visit my quarters, my hospitals, the fort—not like Suchet, for his own profit, but out of pure friendship for me.

When he heard how I had got rid of Ballesteros, he congratulated me on the result which the course of events had given to the base conduct of Marshal Mortier, maintaining that if Mortier had left me a regiment no one would have thought of the deputation of which I had made use to correspond with Ballesteros; if I had had any troops, I should have thought only of defending myself, and, being too weak to hold out, I should have been done for. Thus all was for the best in the best of worlds.

That day gained me another visit—from M. Roederer, who was on his way from Paris to Madrid. He dined with us, and the meal was remarkable for certain discussions upon high topics, in which La Salle was magnificent. On leaving the table, M. Roederer took me aside and said:

"I was acquainted with General La Salle as the most brilliant of our light cavalry generals; I knew that he was witty and valiant, but I was miles from crediting him with the high ability which distinguishes him. He is a man of surpassing talent; his mind and his learning are no less deep than brilliant."

---

4. Thiébault always expresses himself with great severity in regard to those who, having served the Empire, were afterwards mixed up in the reprisals of the Restoration. Ed.

Nor was there anything exaggerated in this eulogy.[5]

We had hardly left the table than we must have punch, and that in great bowls in rapid sequence. Then the fun began, and De Coëtlosquet's turn came. I do not know how many scenes he performed, or how many Bacchanalian verses he did not sing us, but he acquitted himself to the delight of all. Towards ten o'clock La Salle's equipages arrived; he had given his orders, and post-horses were harnessed to his carriage. After the most affectionate embraces and wishes which Heaven was never to grant, as he had his foot on the step, "What's all that?" said he, seeing five mounted *chasseurs* of the Nassau Regiment. "It is an escort, which will accompany you as far as Celada."

"I told you I wouldn't have an escort" (we had had a dispute on the subject during dinner).

"And I choose that you shall be escorted."

"*Donnerwetter!*" he exclaimed, addressing the *chasseurs* in German. "If you escort me, I jump on the postilion's horse and charge you." So I told the *chasseurs* to follow him fifty paces behind.

Thus we parted and he left me, rejoicing in the idea of adding to that harvest of laurels which he had already gathered on so many glorious battlefields. Exalted by his good luck, he was hastening to a death no less premature than deplorable; that day was, indeed, the last of his existence for me. Alas! when the terrible bulletin of the Battle of Wagram reached me, it brought me the first but also the last news which I was to receive of poor La Salle. He had died a hero's death, leaving to me a grief which will only terminate with my life. Yet that loss, no less irreparable for France than for me, was rendered still sadder by other losses less harrowing but still sad enough.

Pouzet, whom I had seen so brilliant on the field of Austerlitz, had similarly paid with his blood for the laurels gathered amid the

---

5. [Roederer, as the French editor points out, took notes of the conversation, and his report of it will be found in the Appendix at the end of vol. viii. of Sainte-Beuve's *Causeries du Lundi*. Not much trace appears of the "discussions *d'un ordre élevé*," but as a picture of bright table-talk it is admirable. The friendly dispute between Thiébault and La Salle on the question of the escort is duly recorded. The meeting took place on April 28, some days, therefore, before Ney and Kellermann entered the Asturias, and some weeks before Ballesteros had left that province and marched upon Santander; so that the rumour as to that general having been close to Burgos, previously to this must have been unfounded. In any case, Burgos would hardly have been on his way from Oviedo to Santander, though, knowing that the place was defenceless after its troops had been summoned to Kellermann, he may have detached a force to look at it. But this cannot have been till May, so that in any case Thiébault's recollections here must have got confused.]

chances of that struggle; the worthy Saint-Hilaire had not survived it; and, lastly, Gauthier, whom I loved next to La Salle, and who in respect of eminence and of valour was in the first rank of the warriors that France ever possessed, completed the sum of three who made that day for me a day of bloodshed and mourning; and what tells a tale of incredible injustice is, that that officer, fit as he was to do honour to the marshal's baton, died a general of brigade, after holding that rank for eight years, to the disgrace of those to whom the disgrace is due.[6]

---

6. [It is curious that Thiébault seems to speak of Aspern (or Essling), in which Pouzet and Saint-Hilaire were killed, as if it was one and the same battle as Wagram, in which Gauthier and La Salle fell. It looks as if the defeat had been kept dark till it could be reported together with the victory. For La Salle's death and some estimate of him not quite so admiring as Thiébault's see Marbot's *Mémoires*, vol. ii.]

Chapter 13

As Good as Dismissed

All at once serious and vexatious news began to spread. Marshal Soult, who had taken upon himself the reconquest of Portugal, after the fashion of a master undertaking a job of which his pupils had made a mess, had, it was said, been attacked, beaten, cut to pieces by Sir Arthur Wellesley, losing, it was further said, the whole of his material and his hospitals, and saving only by a miracle some rags of his army. Doubtless all this required confirmation; yet it was easy to read in the faces of the Spaniards that we had recently undergone a real disaster in Portugal. Before long, indeed, we had certain intelligence that the marshal had retreated into Galicia, and this was as far as our uncertainty and anxiety had brought us, when General Delaborde, who had been serving in the marshal's army, arrived at Burgos on his way to France. From him I had the following account of affairs.

As we knew, Marshal Soult had got as far as Oporto. There he halted—an extraordinary thing to do, since, having no reinforcements to wait for, he should have crossed the Douro without the loss of a day, pursued the English at the sword's point without giving them time to look round, found an opportunity of beating them, and, as the result of his victory, tried to enter Lisbon. This would have been in conformity with the rules of war, and with the dictates of honour and duty. Instead of this, he settled himself at Oporto, scattered his troops, and, presuming that no one would venture to cross the Douro under his nose, tried to get some advantages for himself out of a state of things, which in another would have stimulated his zeal, loyalty, and fidelity.

The emperor had just escaped a serious overthrow. Thanks to Marshal Masséna, a large part of the army had avoided destruction at Essling; but the bridges over the Danube had been carried away. If the situation was short of threatening, it was full of doubt and difficulty, and it seemed as if it might be long before the emperor would be in a position to attend actively to what was going on in Portugal. On the other hand, the loss in men and money which the Spanish war was causing us began to grow appalling. To Marshal Soult the disagreeable turn which the emperor's affairs seemed to be taking suggested the idea of profiting by the opportunity to make himself King of Portugal.

Meanwhile Sir Arthur Wellesley, learning that the marshal was taking but little thought about war, but was dreaming, in profound security, of the delights of a throne, concentrated his forces, advanced to the Douro, bringing some boats with him, and succeeded under cover of night in passing some picked regiments to the right bank of the river.[1] These formed up, concealing themselves in a spacious building to the east of the town. By daylight, 3,000 men were assembled, and they remained in concealment while other troops were crossing the river further up. At length, about 11 a.m., the English general having assembled all the troops required for his attack on the right bank of the Douro, set them in motion against Oporto. General Delaborde, learning of their sudden appearance, hurried to the marshal to let him know of it. He had just sat down in all tranquillity to eat his breakfast. On seeing the general, he invited him to share it, but soon learnt that there was something more urgent to be done, namely, to fight the English.

At the same moment the musketry was heard. The first idea was to defend the town; but the vigour of the attack was of itself enough to render defence impossible, and other English columns had so manoeuvred as to cut off the garrison of the town from the other divisions of the army. Soon all was disorder and confusion; though he had a river to cover him, the marshal had been surprised in broad daylight and in his own headquarters. No means remained of saving anything beyond the men and a few horses. It was quite true that everything had been abandoned,—hospitals, treasure-chest, guns, tumbrils, baggage, even the equipages. Even to get out of Oporto cost infinite trouble, and assembling the divisions was yet more difficult, for not one road fit to be called a road remained free. The army had therefore to throw itself into the wildest mountains and take as its road of escape one of the most frightful paths. It would have been all very well if, once engaged in those formidable gorges, the army could have proceeded in securi-

---

1. [Of course the statements that Wellesley brought boats with him, and that the army crossed the Douro in the night, are equally unfounded.]

ty; but in front of it was a torrent flowing in a deep gully, only passable by one wretched little bridge. This bridge was held by the insurgents; a hundred men could have barred the passage to a thousand times their number, and it might be destroyed with one stroke of an axe.

Yet a failure to take it meant the abandonment of all hope of saving a single man. In default of open force, the only chance lay in the cleverness and daring of one brave man. The choice fell upon Colonel Dulong, and never was a choice, though inspired by terror and despair, more fortunate. Dulong, an intrepid and shifty man, went forward with 500 picked followers, and came in sight of the bridge at nightfall. Lying flat and crawling through the brushwood, he examined the approaches and noticed some carelessness on the part of the men who were guarding it. There was not one on the bank where he was, and a single sentry was on the bridge. Darkness came on; and then, followed by some fifty of his men, with the rest ready to support him, he went forward, still on all fours, as far as he deemed it prudent. Then he halted and remained lying down till midnight, the right hour for a surprise, had arrived.

Then, at the head of his whole force, he flung himself on the guard of the bridge without giving them time to resist, and still less to cut away the bridge; in this way preserving for France such colours and men as were left.[2] It was a heroic feat of arms, and will always honour the memory of a brave and excellent officer, whom a fatal destiny drove to destroy himself by his own hands, or rather the only hand of which the use remained to him.[3] Thus Marshal Soult's army made its way out into Galicia.

Such was General Delaborde's tale. He ended with a statement which it is painful to record. Marshal Ney was occupying Galicia, and possessed more artillery than he needed; enough indeed to be an embarrassment from its disproportion to the number of his troops and their requirements. Marshal Soult asked if he could spare him some batteries,—a request which there were a score of reasons not merely to comply with but to anticipate. Ney did not let him have a single gun.

"And you are returning to France?" I said to General Delaborde when he ceased.

---

2. General Marbot's version [which is merely translated from Napier] of Dulong's feat (*Mémoires*, vol. ii.) differs in several particulars from that here given. Ed.
3. [Colonel Dulong, then lieutenant-general, committed suicide by shooting himself in 1828.]

"Yes, my health requires it, and disgust at the state of affairs compels me."

"And have you settled what you will say in regard to the marshal and the catastrophe?"

"My mind is irrevocably made up on that head. If I am questioned, I shall tell everything; if not, I shall say nothing."

Curiously enough, no questions were asked him; but Loison, a clever man and a spiteful dog, followed soon after, and went straight to Schönbrunn, where he had an audience of the emperor on his arrival. He told the whole story, but extracted nothing save jokes about King Nicolas, or, as the emperor amused himself by calling him, King Nicodemus. Napoleon, who never liked to have made a mistake, seldom struck at those whom he had raised. In the present case he must either have the marshal shot or laugh at him; unluckily for himself, he took the latter course.[4]

As our conversation ended, an *aide-de-camp* from Soult called on Delaborde. He was on his way to the emperor with dispatches; and as he would travel faster than the general, he offered to take news of him to Mme Delaborde on his way through Paris. His courtesy and deferential manner did not save him from a volley of banter, which the general's stern look and big voice rendered supremely comic. "What a lot of luck and of trouble you have lost!" he said. "Your zeal would have earned you at least a chamberlain's place, and I should never have seen you again without a great gold key. Lucky you had not got it on when the upset came, or it might have hurt you."

Old Castile had long been unravaged by civil war; no bands had been formed or had appeared throughout the district in which I commanded; but though I had been able to keep a hand on those under me, my influence stopped at my boundaries. The province of Soria, which I had tried to get added to my government, and which I would have guaranteed to keep quiet with two more regiments of infantry and a hundred cavalry, had remained within the territory of Madrid, though too far off to be in touch with the troops occupying the capital. It soon became a focus of insurrection; guerrilla bands were

---

4. [The story of the intrigues at Oporto is told by Napier (Book vii. ch. i.). He briefly puts aside the story of Soult's aspirations to royalty as erroneous; for which he incurs the sarcasm of Mme d'Abrantès. Thiébault's animosity against the marshal makes his testimony of little value, and much of what he says has been omitted; but it may be noted that Marbot confirms the story, on the authority of Soult's generals, and sees no reason to blame the marshal's proceedings.]

organised and recruited even within my provinces; and when they ventured to take the field, they appeared in the Rioja, and reached my communications with Valladolid, Aranda, and Vitoria.

One day, as I was sitting down to dinner, a messenger brought word that a band of 500 men had just attacked Celada, a village ten miles from Burgos, the first stage on the road to Vitoria. A quarter of an hour later I was on the way, with four picked companies and the Nassau *chasseurs*, leaving orders for a battalion of the 118th to follow me. I reached Celada, whence the insurgents had made off at my approach. I halted there to await the remainder of my troops, and started about eleven at night to make a sudden incursion into the Rioja and try to surprise the band or drive it back into the mountains of Soria.

I had thought it as well to take the chief commissioner of police along with me. While the night slackened the speed of our troops and even of our own immediate attendants, we let our horses take their own pace, and presently found ourselves some way ahead of the column. Wrapped in our cloaks, we were chatting in Spanish as we went along. At a moment when, luckily, the commissioner was speaking, a man emerged from a thicket, came up to us, and said, "Gentlemen, where are the French?" It was a scout belonging to the band, left there to report our advance. Seeing three men alone on the road at that hour, one of whom was wearing a brown cloak and speaking Spanish, he had taken us for some of their men.

No doubt the incident revealed our imprudence to us, but it gave us an opportunity of which I took advantage. While the commissioner was making some sort of reply, I had seized the man by the throat, and whispered, "Silence, or you're dead." We remained motionless till my advance-guard had joined us, when I had my man tied up. As soon as it had been made clear to him that he was not going to escape, I questioned him. He was an inhabitant of Rioja, and had been, he said, forced to join the troop. He heaved many sighs, and I assured him that his only chance of saving his life was to confess the truth, and reveal the place where the troop was. He named the village where it was to pass the night, some three miles from the point of the road where we were.

As he knew the way to the place, I told him that he was to act as guide to the detachment, and that on getting near the village he was to march at the head with a few men singing one of the songs of the country to obviate suspicion. Then I promised him that when the expedition was over, in order that he might not be compromised, he should remain bound as though he were a prisoner taken on the road, and I would procure his pardon. This being explained and settled, I formed a detachment of 400 infantry and 20 cavalry, handed the man over to the major commanding, and went on my way towards Santo Domingo, where I arrived about daylight. At noon my detachment rejoined me; the men of the band had been surprised in their sleep scattered among the various houses of the village. The number of those who had perished was estimated at about 150; the rest had escaped under cover of night, but had left almost all their arms behind. In order the better to disguise the part played by his guide, the major brought back three new prisoners, one of whom, known to be a fanatic, was tried and shot on the spot, while the other two were pardoned by me on condition of not taking up arms again. As for the first prisoner, I gave him some money, and gained one more spy.

Another time I heard that a pretty numerous band was established to the west of Santo Domingo, in a little town possessing several cloth factories. To drive them out was easy enough; but to make my way there unexpectedly enough to surprise them, or at least to compel them to fight, was all the more difficult that the little town is covered on the side towards Burgos by a mountain which cannot be crossed in less than sixteen hours' marching. In order to keep my plan concealed as long as possible, I sent four detachments of 300 men apiece to right and left of a village which stands at the north foot of that mountain. These four divisions countermarched, so as one evening to join the Nassau *chasseurs* whom I brought up. The village was at once surrounded, and parties were pushed quickly forward on to the first slopes of the mountain, so that no one might get in front of me.

At 3 a.m. we started, and, though we made only the indispensable halts, we did not reach the summit till one in the afternoon. As soon as we caught sight of the valley in which the town stood, I made the men lower their arms and ordered the cavalry to dismount, so that we might not be perceived before it was inevitable. We halted behind some evergreen oaks to conceal our concentration, so that when we emerged into the valley, after half-past seven, we had been seen by nobody. Four hundred men in line marched upon the town in double-quick time; two columns of like strength followed them. The cavalry, making their way round to the left, gained the rear of the town, and the men of the band, 800 in all, had hardly begun to retreat when we were upon them.

They were at once overthrown and charged by the cavalry; but, as they fled into the mountains, they lost not more than a hundred men. During the night, however, I learnt that the band had retired towards Cavaleda, in order to take refuge in the forest of that name, and I decided to pursue them thither. One league from Quintanar we found an armed Spaniard hidden in a hole, in order to spy on us. He was seized by my scouts, and, as there was no way of saving him, the poor devil was tried on the spot and shot; which did not prevent the band from getting warning of our approach and flinging itself into the forest.

That forest is certainly one of the most extraordinary in Europe. Five miles in breadth and twenty in length, it is shut in among rocks and mountains so high and so steep, that not a tree of it has ever been felled, unless for the needs of the inhabitants of Quintanar or of Palacios de la Sierra. It is therefore such as the ages since the creation of the world have made it, and, as the soil is excellent, nothing can be compared to the beauty of its trees or the thickness of its undergrowth. I had been told that over wide spaces no light could be seen even at mid-day, and I had been told truly. I had been warned that, as nobody had ever had occasion to make a road through it, the smallest vehicles were useless there, and that it was pierced only by narrow paths, which also was correct. Lastly, it had been pointed out to me as the surest and most formidable hiding-place for the guerrilla, bands, since one might pass within a hundred yards of 10,000 men without seeing a soul; while one might be fired at through the underwood almost at point-blank range, without any means of defending oneself.

But the more the inhabitants of Quintanar were in agreement as to the danger, the more I thought it my duty to face it; for anything was preferable to the disgrace of having come so far only to turn back. On the morrow at daybreak, therefore, having provided myself with three good guides, I penetrated into the forest. The impression that fifty men would be quite enough to hold us at their mercy was so keenly felt by our soldiers that, in spite of the inspiration of that virgin forest, the march took place in the deepest silence.

Three hours passed thus, when suddenly the undergrowth grew thinner, and we beheld a vast space filled, with gigantic oaks which stretched their colossal branches all around us. The ground was carpeted with a fine turf, without a plant or shrub, for the giant trees had stifled all vegetation under their shade. No such temple had ever formed the pride of any druidical rites, and before this wonder of creation a single cry burst from the mouths of all. Here I halted the column, and ordered the men to rest for two hours and cook their food. Rather than raise a sacrilegious hand against the branches in that spot, they fetched firewood from some distance.

Our march was really of the nature of a bravado. I had undertaken it only to show that there was no place to which we could not penetrate; nor had I the least hope of catching the *guerrilleros*, or even any wish to try conclusions with them at so dangerous a spot. When evening came on, as I had not traversed two-thirds of the forest, I left it, and went in a northerly direction to sleep at Palacios de la Sierra. Next day I reached Viniegra de Abajo, a fine village enough, standing in a place that looked like the end of everything, and yet commanded at an immense height above by another village, Viniegra de Arriba. Finding myself in these wild regions where no troops had as yet appeared, I was glad to show myself in as many places as possible.

I also wished to hear of another band, of which this was the habitual refuge; and, in point of fact, I learnt from one of my spies that when the chief of this band had become aware that I was coming into the mountains, he had put himself on the further side of masses of rock through which a few torrents alone had cut their way, no man having ever thought of making use of the passage so formed. The spy had added that the band was at that moment resting at Anguiano. "Why," said I, "according to my map, Anguiano is quite close by."

"Ten miles away, but they are impassable miles."

"The Viniegra torrent passes, however."

"No doubt; but they say it runs between inaccessible cliffs, and falls in cascades, so that its bed is impracticable."

"How far is it by a practicable road?"

"Fifty miles," I think my man said.

Nothing ever attracted me like a feat reputed impossible; so to get fuller information I sent at once for the *corregidor*, to inquire of him about the course of the torrent, and to know if any attempts had been made to get along it. "There have been such," he replied, "but they have not been fortunate. One man only, accompanied by his son, a boy of eleven, did succeed in getting to Anguiano that way, but he went fifty miles round on his return. He would never try it again, and his account deterred everyone else from imitating him."

"Is the man dead?"

"Yes, long ago."

"And his son?"

"He is still alive."

"Take me to him."

We went to him; and when the *corregidor* had explained what I wanted, the son, now an old man, but still with all his wits about him, said with a smile, "An awkward business." He remembered the passage perfectly, and answered all my questions; the result being to show me that the most dangerous part of the affair was not having to follow the bed of the torrent, bristling everywhere with rocks that had to be climbed, nor yet the almost continual necessity of walking in the water and upon rolling or cutting stones, but having to run the chance of a storm, which in those high mountains may get up at any moment. If this occurred, the sudden rise of the torrent would be such that 10,000 men, if caught by it, would perish without a chance of escape for one of them.

I looked at the sky; it was clear, and the sun was sinking to a cloudless horizon. We were near the end of July; the time of harvest is not usually one of storms. It had not rained for a fortnight, and the torrent was nearly dry. I asked if there was a barometer in the village; there was one, and it marked set-fair. I had it taken with the utmost care to my room, so as to see if it moved, and to be able to consult it up to the last moment, with the certainty that no one had touched it. Then, without coming to an irrevocable decision, I ordered the troops to be ready to start at three next morning.

After a final consultation of my barometer, and finding it unchanged, I went to the front of my lines. There I found the *corregidor* waiting for me, and some inhabitants who had heard of the plan which I had dared to form were there also, whispering among themselves. All eyes were fixed on me, and the men seemed to be anxiously consulting each other's looks. However, having secured a guide for so long as I should need one, and decided by a splendid sunrise and the purest and most tranquil air possible, I ordered the drums to beat, and knowing that no one could get in front of me, I cried, "Road to Anguiano!" The soldiers at once began to laugh, and soon followed me singing; for I went in front of the column with fifty picked men.

For half an hour we marched over a lovely meadow; then this suddenly contracted, and an imposing mass of rock offered no passage save by the bed of the torrent. This soon grew more hollow, the banks getting steeper and steeper; while the stream rolled over with more noise and impetuosity. At last the trees that grew in the cracks of the rocks crossed their dense foliage over our heads, and added darkness to our other difficulties. The songs had ceased, and the only laughter was caused by the falls repeated at every step. As soon as it became impossible to retreat, faces grew gloomy at the thought that we must get out of that before night, if only to escape the deep holes in which there was danger of being drowned.

It was weary work to climb without respite to the top of rocks, only to scramble down them again; the troopers especially, having to take care of both their horses and themselves, were exhausted with opening up the road, and they would have had to give up if I had not had them helped by one hundred infantry, who were relieved every hour. Halts were indispensable, to rest men and animals, and to allow those in the rear to come up. Picturesque, indeed, in the extreme those halts were, owing to the way in which the men grouped themselves on every projecting rock.

The day passed thus. In spite of everything, three horses broke their legs and had to be abandoned, with their loads. However, we were approaching the goal of our foolhardy enterprise; but night was coming on. Luckily the torrent bed opened out and became less dangerous; not before it was wanted, for the last mile or so of the march, which for the head of the column had been one of nineteen hours, was done in the night. At last I found myself on the little meadow which on this side lies in front of Anguiano, and is not more than 300 yards from it. As I had already enjoined the strictest silence, I re-formed my sections without noise; though as the soldiers only came up one by one, it was nearly eleven before I had got 500 men and three or four drums.

This was all I needed to carry out my bold stroke; especially as my antagonists were scattered among the houses, the greatest part of them no doubt in bed, and so perfectly secure that it had not occurred to them to set a post on that side of Anguiano, though they knew that I was about the head-waters of the torrent. Accordingly I left to a field-officer the task of collecting the men as they came up, and started with those I had got together, marching with arms at the trail and in silence. A hundred paces from the first house we were spied by a sentry, who called to us. No one answered, and he called again; then, as we only quickened our pace, he fired and gave the alarm.

Our drums at once beat the charge, I kept 100 men with me in reserve, while 400 dashed into the village, where they effected a terrible discomfiture. The slaughter was great; all who did not perish escaped in their shirts and without their arms. Thus my expedition was as successful as it well could be. It cost me only one man lost in the torrent, one killed, and three wounded at Anguiano. I had to remain at the place till the next day, as many men only turned up in the course of the morning. The effect of the march was therefore extraordinary, and, the survivors of those insurgents who had paid so dear for taking things so coolly called my route "The Pass of the Demons."

However, on the day when I left Anguiano, the remains of the band had a kind of little revenge. I had to follow for half an hour a path bordered on the right by vertical rocks, and on the left by the chasm in which the Anguiano torrent flows. This is 200 feet in width, and on its left bank is a hill covered with thick wood. As soon as my column was fairly in the road it received a smart fire of musketry from the other side. It replied, no doubt, and with a brisk fire; but the assailants were hidden by the branches, and my men could only fire at the smoke. Still, as the column replied by a dozen shots to every one that it received, it may be believed that the other side lost some men. Anyhow, it did not last long, though long enough to cause me a loss of eight killed and wounded.

As I was approaching Burgos, I was joined by one of the spies whom I kept always going, and who used to hurry up with news whenever I was on an expedition, never giving me any except in the forest. From him I learnt that the Marquis of Villa-Campo, to whose family I had shown much kindness, though he none the less made war upon us at the head of a band which he had organised, had just been levying contributions in the direction of Reinosa, and was now on his way back to the mountains and intending to sleep in a village some three leagues to my left. At once I changed my direction for that in which he was. Thanks to the guidance of my spy, I seldom left the woods, and avoided villages as much as possible.

When I was obliged to go through one, I sent a *chasseur* forward to the further side, to allow no one to get in front of me; nor indeed was there any reason why anyone should do so, as nothing was known in the district of Villa-Campo's march. Thus I arrived in sight of the village where he was without his suspecting my approach. He had set guards in military style, and his advanced posts began to fire on seeing us. At once a light company advanced in skirmishing order, supported by another light and two grenadier companies. These went forward in line, followed by two columns formed of the centre companies of the two battalions of the 118th. In this way we came to within 600 paces of the village; then the charge was beaten, and the Nassau *chasseurs* tried to turn the enemy's flank. Unluckily at the back of the village was a pretty thick wood, and the cavalry was of no use. However, with my four picked companies I overthrew the rear-guard of the band, pursuing it some distance into the wood; but I was not able to come up with the main body, which had a quarter of an hour's start of me and retreated at the double.

However, night was coming on, and there was no object in pursuing; it was indeed an unimaginable piece of luck in this one expedition to have caught and beaten the only three bands which were disturbing the peace of Old Castile. Finally, after killing about thirty of Villa-Campo's men, on returning to the quarters whence I had driven him, I saw the house on fire. My first idea was to set it down to some soldiers of my column, and I at once told off a fatigue-party of fifty men to help in putting it out. But the inhabitants showed so little zeal, and the *corregidor* seemed so resigned to the loss of the house, which he said could not be saved, that it was left to burn; and next morning when I left the village at daybreak the ruins were still smoking. I had not the least suspicion that I had been the victim of a trick, of which the explanation is as follows.

When the first shots gave warning of my approach, the Marquis of Villa-Campo perceived that he would not have time to get his treasure away. He would barely have been able to load his mules, and the loaded mules would have had no chance of escaping us, had he even sacrificed his whole band in their defence. So he sent them off, as if they were loaded, and had the casks containing the 250,000 *francs* that he had levied, thrown into the cellar. Meanwhile the owner of the house moved everything out of it that he could, and, under promise of compensation, set it on fire. I was completely tricked, seeing in the fire one of those accidents only too common in war, and in the conduct of the inhabitants only a proof of apathy and resignation. Villa-Campo's treasure therefore remained intact under the cellar-vaults; and it was only some days after my return to Burgos that I learnt how I had been taken in, and what mirth my lack of penetration had excited. It was too much pleasure not to be worth paying for; so I had the *corregidor* arrested and sent to prison, with the five principal inhabitants of the village. I also imposed a fine of 25,000 *francs*, and gave notice that if they were not paid within a week, the village would be burnt to the ground.

Always beaten, never conquered, and when broken up at once reconstituting themselves, these bands had begun to hold the Rioja and the surrounding districts to ransom. I established new garrisons and increased the old ones, relieving them frequently, so that I had troops constantly moving about the province. On one occasion I had started before daybreak, and on the strength of some information which turned out to be false had gone to Najera. It was a hot day in August, and when we had reached the place we had travelled nearly thirty miles. The troops were exhausted, so occupying the town with my cavalry and two grenadier companies I made the rest of my infantry bivouac along the stream under a row of fine trees.

We had been there two hours and a half; I had finished dinner, and I was about to agree to the wish of the officers and men to pass the night there, when I saw from the balcony of the house where I had alighted some Spanish horsemen showing themselves beyond the stream on the little hill which is crossed by the road to Logroño; gradually their number increased, and soon there were some sixty of them, who fell to blackguarding us, and that from so short a distance that we could hear them plainly.

Captain Hagen, of the Nassau *chasseurs*, an intrepid officer as ever was, a very Ajax in build and in daring, cried, "General, give us leave to go and chastise those ruffians." Some troops have to be led in order to stimulate them; but these *chasseurs*, the grand-duke's own guard, needed my presence only to restrain them. They were, in fact, a picked corps: no man was admitted without paying 1,000 florins caution money, and the only punishment known was expulsion. They were no less steady than brave, and I know of nothing in the world that one might not have attempted with them. I did not wish to send them into danger, to reply to insults which affected me but little.

What concerned me more was to see in this neighbourhood some well-mounted and equipped troopers, who must certainly be the advance-guard of a body of Spanish cavalry. As it was impossible to find out to whom they belonged, I called my men to arms. The colonel of the 118th objected that his soldiers were tired—a reason that could no longer be accepted; so, as soon as my *chasseurs* were mounted, I started at the head of them, bidding the infantry follow me with all possible dispatch.

The Spanish troopers no sooner saw me issue from Najera than they made off, not, however, getting out of sight, but maintaining a distance of 500 or 600 yards between themselves and me. Now and again, those who were best mounted would halt, and, waiting till we were within hearing, would fling fresh insults at us and bolt at full speed. For my own part, neither quickening nor slackening my pace, I contented myself with trotting after them, and in this way they drew me on to little more than half a mile from Logroño, to the beginning of a wood, whither I had at once made up my mind to advance. Then I suddenly saw 800 Spanish cavalry drawn up in line, all well-mounted, equipped, and armed, forming under the light of the setting sun a picture no less fine than impressive.

I halted my little troop, and advanced with my *aides-de-camp*, and with Hagen and the major of the *chasseurs*, a cool but none the less firm officer, in full view of the legion. The insults began again, and were poured forth most furiously by two young Amazons, splendid with embroidery, beautiful as angels, ferocious as demons. Mounted on dainty horses, they came and challenged us in a hundred ways, even firing their pistols at us. Hagen was foaming at the mouth. "For Heaven's sake, general," said he, "let us charge, and it will be very bad luck if I don't bring back one for you and one for me. You shall have first choice."

I laughed, but it was really no matter for joking: we were in presence of eleven times our number; nor had we to deal with a collection of peasants, but with genuine cavalry, with regular troops, disciplined and quite fresh, while we had already done thirty-five miles in the heat of the dog-days. We could not even get at them in line, seeing that the ground which lay between us and them was full of pits, and did not allow us to pass more than four abreast. I had no great desire to make a mess of it, and I cared about it all the less that the walls of Logroño and the roofs of the houses were covered with people, and our struggle was about to be witnessed by the whole population. My infantry was five miles to the rear, and therefore I could expect no support.

Yet, on the other hand, the thought of having come three leagues to overtake this force and then not to dare to attack it was humiliating, at a moment when in the presence of so many spectators no means had been spared to challenge to a combat; and, moreover, would there not be a risk of my prudence looking like timidity to my German chasseurs who were spoiling for a fight? So I took the major aside. "Never mind Hagen's nonsense," I said; "you know your men better than I do; you are an officer of experience and! ability; you understand my position in regard both to myself and to the Duke of Nassau; now what is your opinion as to the possibilities?"

"As your Excellency asks for my opinion," he replied, "it is that we shall beat them."

This was decisive. I made my troopers dismount, half of them at a time, in order to tighten their girths, adjust their bridles, and let their horses get breath. This took a quarter of an hour, during which the Spaniards continued to blackguard us. Then the trumpet sounded, and we emerged from the wood. A perfectly ferocious yell arose at once from the whole Spanish force, while the chiefs and other officers, aided by the two ladies whom I have mentioned, caracoled in front of their men, stimulating them with voice and gesture. We started at a walk, then trotted, and, continually quickening our pace, were soon at full gallop, and fell upon the horsemen with a general cheer. Having made the double mistake of waiting for us halted and formed in a single line, they were broken in an instant.

A panic set in among them: a hundred or so to our left, who were cut off from the main body, fled headlong towards Logroño; the rest made off at full speed to the mountains, ridden down and sabred by us. After pursuing for a quarter of an hour, I halted with my *aides-de-camp* and orderlies, and then, sending one of the Nassau officers forward with orders to bid the major fall back on me, I went towards Logroño with the intention of waiting for my infantry; but the *corregidor* and some of the leading people were already on their way to present me with the keys of the town, on a silver dish, and to invite me to enter. Thus I took possession of an enemy's town, in which undoubtedly the *guerrilleros* had their associates, attended only by my *aides-de-camp*, four orderlies, and my valet.

I was at the mercy of the inhabitants; but I showed sternness proportionate to the dangers of my position. Thus an hour passed; a very long one. The next three-quarters were no less so, seeing that I had no news of either my infantry or my cavalry. Night came at last, and I was getting pretty uneasy at the delay, when I heard the drums. But what had become of the cavalry? It was allowable to fear that it had got entangled among the mountains in its pursuit of the Spaniards, and fallen into an ambush; so that when by the time it did turn up I was properly anxious. That madman Hagen had taken it along in a charge of six or seven miles, in the course of which it had killed or wounded some sixty men, itself losing only three wounded, who were being brought back in a cart. "And the lady that you promised me?" I said to Hagen.

"Ah! general," he exclaimed, "I was within two paces of her for a whole hour, but my horse was too blown to let me catch her, and I had not the heart to fire, even to bring her down. Anyhow, I gave her a bit of my mind, and she will remember me."

This brilliant little affair delivered Old Castile from the corps of Spanish cavalry which had come I know not whence, and did not reappear. As may be supposed, I highly eulogized the conduct of my *chasseurs*, and even wrote to the grand duke, who allowed me some honours for them. For my own part, all the thanks I got for these raids was an expression from General Kellermann of his satisfaction at seeing me back; for he thought it useless to pursue the guerrillas into the heart of the mountains, where the roads had to be guarded, and the removal of the troops deprived these for the moment of their regular protection. He was wrong, however. In every conquered country, and above all in Spain, if you want to maintain your authority you must impress people's minds; and thus the breaking up of the guerrillas, on which the hopes of the Spanish partisans relied, had a considerable moral effect within my government.

About this time overwork began to tell on my health; I became subject to hallucinations, which, while not preventing me from distinguishing real objects, used to call up, sometimes for a period of twenty-four hours together, the most unreal and often the most fantastic images. To give an idea of them, I will mention one. In one corner of my room I saw a carpet of turf forming itself. It spread and became a charming meadow, which was presently surrounded by magnificent trees. Gradually a whitish spot developed in the middle of the meadow; it grew, took the hue of flesh and blood, and in a few moments presented to my view a magnificent woman.

As I gazed in a sort of rapture, the fair body became covered with spots, turning into wounds, from each of which emerged so hideous a monster that in horror and fear I turned away. I was in truth reduced to the state of the neophytes whom the Egyptian priests used to prepare by long fasting and maceration to receive the impressions they wished to give them. If my mind had shared in the disorder of my imagination, or any other senses in that of my sight, it would have been insanity.

When this crisis was at its height I had written to Jourdan, the chief of the general staff, giving an account of my condition, and explaining the impossibility of my attending personally for some time to the reports sent him from Burgos. The reply to this letter was that the king had learnt with regret that the state of my health did not allow me to continue my functions as governor, and that he had consequently selected General Solignac to succeed me. Even in the case of a Darmagnac, this ill-concealed dismissal would have been scandalous;

in my case, no name was bad enough for it.

On the part of the king it was sheer impudence, for he was misusing a power which he had no right to claim. I had been appointed by the emperor, and could be removed only by him, But for the weakness of my condition, which did not allow me to master my temper, together with the tendency I always had to take advantage of every opportunity of seeing my wife once more, I should have appealed to the emperor, and Solignac would have left Burgos without having time to make a mess of the authority which he so scandalously misused. But I acted otherwise, and I was wrong. A few hours after Solignac's arrival I gave up my functions; but I had held a meeting of the governing committee, and handed over to the prefect 27,000 *francs* which remained out of the fund which the Duke of Istria had put at my disposal for public works. "Hang it," said Solignac, when I told him why I had called the meeting, "it would have been much simpler to hand it over to me." That was precisely what I did not want to do.

After settling this matter, and thanking all present for the way in which they had helped me, I bade them farewell; and at daybreak next morning, without waiting for orders or leave, and forgetting the possible effect on the emperor's temper of abandoning his service and letting the King of Spain trample on his sovereignty, I started on my return to France, or rather to Paris.

Chapter 14.

My Work Undone

As I entered Tolosa I noticed two carriages; reaching them, I saw the Duke and Duchess of Abrantès emerging from the house where they had passed the night, and ready to continue their journey towards Burgos. The surprise was equal on both sides; as for the duke, after I had handed the duchess into her carriage, he took me by the arm, went back with me into the room where he had slept, and, embracing me, said, "I know how you defended me to the emperor, and I want to tell you how much I am touched. It is you, to whom I did not keep my promise, who alone have shown yourself my friend, while it is the people that I heaped with kindness and loaded with money who slander me in a hundred ways." As he said this he stretched out his hand, and as he grasped mine his eyes filled with tears. Both his outburst and the suffering of which in such a man it gave evidence moved me equally.

At Irun I halted for a few days for the following reason. I had written to my wife from Pancorbo to tell her what had befallen me, and announce my departure for Paris. Upon reflection, I had added a postscript to this effect:

Feel the ground as to the effect produced by my supersession, and which may be produced by my arrival, and send me an answer at once. I will wait for it at Irun.

I had to wait eleven days for the letter, and I learnt from it that the emperor had been as much displeased by the selection of General Solignac as by my supersession, and that orders were on the road to give that general another employment and send me back to my post. My wife further announced that she was starting in consequence of these orders, with a view of at least passing a few days with me at Bayonne.

No doubt my pride was flattered, both by the reason for these orders and by their nature. I was as thoroughly avenged as I could be by the snub inflicted upon Marshal Jourdan, General Solignac, and the king; but the orders could not repair the mischief done, nor restore to me what I had lost. There are some things which cannot be begun over again, and among them were the efforts which I had made; all the more so that a few days had undone their result. The discouragement of the men who were devoted to our cause was only equalled by the exasperation of our enemies, as letters received from Burgos left in no doubt. The soldiers were compensating themselves by fresh excesses for those which they had so long been prevented from committing. Solignac's rough ways had upset all my organisation, making the present evils irremediable, the future inevitable. The precautions that I had taken for the safety of the troops were neglected, on the ground that they indicated fear, and that under his command nobody ought to fear anything.

However, others than I must see to the re-establishment of my system; it was quite enough for me to have succeeded Darmagnac. Consequently, the sole effect produced by my wife's letter was to inspire me with a desire of anticipating the orders announced in it. I started immediately, after taking the precaution of writing to the Prince of Neuchâtel to the effect that, though I might have referred the matter to him, that is to say, have disregarded the order in virtue of which General Solignac had been sent to Burgos, I had thought that the respect due to the king and the inconvenience of setting up a contest of authority in the eyes of the Spaniards should decide me to obey; that, as my position at Burgos was no longer tolerable, I had left it for Irun, where I had been awaiting orders for twelve days; but that, as none had reached me, I should lose no time in coming to Paris to give account of conduct, and to receive any orders with which the emperor might deign to honour me.

Having thus arranged for my flight, I decided to ride the distance from Iran to Bayonne, where my equipages were to rejoin me. They arrived twenty hours after I did; while awaiting them, I had looked out for a carriage to take me to Bordeaux; I discovered and hired one so light that I could draw it with one hand. As soon as it was possible to harness it I leapt into it, with my *aide-de-camp* Vallier, while Jacques hastened forward to order the horses. In this way, thanks to liberal "tips," five-and-twenty hours sufficed me for the journey from Bayonne to Bordeaux—a feat at that time unprecedented, for in those days the wheels would sink into the sand up to the axle, and one usually took more than forty hours over the journey. I expected to have met my wife on the way, and, as may be supposed, I carefully examined all the carriages that passed me, and made inquiries at every posthouse. On arriving at the entrance to Bordeaux a clerk at the barrier handed me a note, in which my wife informed me that she had been obliged to halt there by an attack of fever. Fortunately, she was better, and in a couple of days I started with her for Paris.

One circumstance was as useful to me as I could have wished; it was just at this moment that the emperor's marriage with Marie Louise was taking place. Generosity is an ornament to good fortune, and gives a sanction to its greatness, so that one can venture on a good deal with a fortunate chief. My impunity, to which after all I was getting accustomed, was a proof of this. As a matter of fact, as people had other things to do than to pick a quarrel with me, they spoke to me only of the justice with which I had recently been treated, and how completely I seemed to ignore it.

On the day of the great ceremonies of that august alliance, when the daughter of the ancient Caesars allied herself to the modern Caesar, seeming for ever to unite the eagle of France to the eagle once of Rome, afterwards of Germany, I was seriously unwell; but, as soon as I had at all recovered, I thought it my duty to go and pay my respects to their majesties while they were still at Compiègne. I stayed there three days, with the idea of having an audience of the emperor or an explanation with the Prince of Neuchâtel; but this was impossible. The hours during which the emperor was visible were taken up with State affairs and intercourse with the high personages who surrounded him. As for the Prince of Neuchâtel, he was always the first to go to the palace and the last to leave it, and was quite unapproachable. Thus, except for one dinner with Masséna and another with Duroc, my days were passed in attending the Mass in the morning, the receptions and presentations later in the day, and the general circle in the evening.

My second day was ending in this fashion. I happened to be in the card-room at the end of the apartments devoted to the receptions. The empress was playing her game; kings, archdukes, princes, foreigners of the highest rank, and a host of illustrious Frenchmen were following the emperor with their eyes and watching his least movements, while he exchanged a few words with one, honoured another with a nod, went from one table to another, and addressed remarks more witty than polite to the ladies.

Having gone round and got back to the door which separated the card-room from that which preceded it, he passed through, and in an instant a vast crowd poured after him. Lounging along, he reached the centre of the room. Then he halted, crossed his arms, stared at the floor a couple of yards from his feet, and remained motionless. The kings, the Archduke Ferdinand, uncle to the empress, and the other eminent personages who were following stopped at once; some backed, others moved aside, all drew closer together, until a widish circle was formed round the emperor, he standing in the centre motionless. Everyone copied his immobility, no one broke the silence.

At first people even avoided looking at each other; but gradually eyes were raised and everyone looked about him. Another few moments, and the glances assumed an interrogative air, as if all were asking themselves to what this bit of acting was the prelude, the tacit inquiry in presence of so many foreigners of that rank making all the French people ill at ease. And, in truth, such a sudden lapse into contemplation, no less eccentric than out of place, might for the first two or three minutes have been attributed to a need on the emperor's part of working out some important idea which had unexpectedly occurred to him; but when five, six, seven, eight minutes had passed, no one could discover any meaning in it. Yet it remained clear that, in the case of a haughty master at a moment when he thought fit to make so singular an exhibition of himself, the thing to do was to do nothing. Unluckily, Marshal Masséna, who happened to be in the front row, while I was just behind him, formed a different opinion.

Indeed, I have always been convinced that, being as he was a man on the field of battle of happy inspiration and accurate observation, and lacking all these advantages at court, he thought he would be doing a service to Napoleon by affording an opportunity of putting a natural ending to a ridiculous scene, the most ridiculous of its kind that I ever saw. He did not understand that, by furnishing a chief to whom his own reputation was an insult with the means of snubbing him, he would at the same time give him a way of escape by simply substituting a piece of cruelty for a piece of affectation.

Consequently, at a moment when not a soul had any idea of moving he left his place, went into the circle which a malevolent genius seemed to have traced in order that he might come to seek an affray there, then advanced slowly towards the emperor. Astonishment and curiosity were depicted on all faces, though mine could have expressed only fear. However, we had not long to wait, for scarcely had the marshal uttered a few words in too low a tone to be heard, than, without raising or turning his eyes, indeed without moving, the emperor said clearly, in a voice of thunder, "What business is it of yours?" and the old marshal, who, in spite of his renown and his rank, had been humbled in the face of all Europe, instead of departing at once and going home to hide his shame, returned to his place without answering, and to my complete amazement returned to it backwards.

Never have I felt more mortified, never did the despot in Napoleon appear to me in a more arrogant and shameless light; for it was an insult, no less gratuitous than cruel, to France in the person of one of her oldest and most illustrious defenders. As for Napoleon, after awarding such a prize for great services, he continued to act the statue for a few moments longer; then, as though waking from a dream, he raised his head, uncrossed his arms, cast a searching glance on all those around him, turned round without saying a word to anybody, and re-entered the card-room.

At a sign from him the empress threw down her cards and rose, all the games ceased, and everybody stood up. As he passed Marie Louise he said to her in a sufficiently dry tone, "Come, madam," and walked on while she followed him three paces behind. As he approached the door of the inner room it opened, and, as soon as the empress had passed through it, it shut on them. It was not yet half-past nine, but Napoleon was coughing a good deal and seemed wearied. Such is the picture which I shall never cease to have before my eyes; I am still wondering what it meant.

Next day the Prince of Neuchâtel came up to me as we came out from Mass, and the following conversation took place.

"The emperor means you to go back to Burgos."

"What was an honourable selection will now be only a chastisement."

"How so?"

"The government is no longer in the state to which I brought it."

"All the more reason for going back there."

"What I did there cannot be recommenced, and what has been destroyed cannot be repaired."

"Zeal will furnish you with means, and the emperor counts on yours; besides, once the insurrection is stamped out, all will be safe."

"Stamped out?—yes; but it keeps increasing and spreading."

"And for that reason we are going to put an end to it by doubling the forces."

"No doubt more forces are indispensable, but that's not what will finish this war."

"What do you mean?"

"That in order to conquer the Spaniards you have got to convince them."

"You have got to beat them and reduce them."

"To beat them is easy, but how are you to reduce people who have information about everything, are never betrayed by anyone, show nothing but skirmishers, never masses of men, whom an army cannot get at, while individuals or weak detachments escape them only by miracle; against whom you cannot manoeuvre, who resist no more than they submit, and who, favoured by the most broken ground, limit their warfare to alarms, excursions, surprises, and assassinations."

"People only continue a war when they do not have to pay the expenses of it; the way to sicken the Spaniards of it is to make them pay dear. Populations offer so much hold that it is impossible for us not to succeed in curing them of rebellion."

"Fanaticism puts aside repugnance as well as interest; the fanaticism of the Spaniards is at once political, national, and religious. Day and night a hundred thousand apostles are preaching it furiously to ignorant enthusiasts, sober, resigned, brave men. And again a struggle of this kind, if it looks like lasting, demoralizes troops and toughens the people. So few commanders understand it that it is bound to occasion many mistakes; lastly, armies are used up while populations renew themselves: it is like the hydra devouring and springing up afresh."

"The Imperial Guard will succeed in giving an account of all these difficulties."

With that he left me; half an hour afterwards I was on my way to Paris, and I hastened to return to my wife, wondering whither the pride and blindness of all these people was going to lead them.

A few days after this, I went to pay my respects to Masséna. I found him alone, walking about his room. He was in an excitable state, and, as he never minded what he said before me, he let himself go. Marshal Jourdan's portrait had just been removed from the Hall of the Marshals; and he said some things about its removal that were no less forcible than to the point. We spoke of other soldiers who had been ill-treated; and, hoping to calm him, I said in reference to one of them, "It was an unlucky job about him." Thereupon he seized my arm and shook it, saying, "And how do you know that there won't be an unlucky job about me before six months are out?"

In truth he was struck with the notion that the object of the rude and harsh treatment to which he had been exposed was to place him in so irksome and unpleasant a position that he would be unable to decline the task which was intended for him, or even to attach any conditions to his acceptance of it. And the command of the Army of Portugal, at the head of which Soult had just received a most well-deserved and smarting defeat, a command given to Masséna without the means of making it a success immediately realised his foreboding in the most cruel manner possible. He started at once; I not till three weeks later.

One last reminiscence is connected with this visit to Paris. I was buying something at a bookseller's when I saw a man enter whose face, figure, manner, and voice struck me. It was M. de La Fayette, whom I had not seen for sixteen years, and then only in uniform; so that at the first moment I failed to recognise him in the plainest clothes and with no decoration. Besides, I had been told that he was dead, so that it was a complete surprise for me. We chatted for some time. "Why are you not in the Senate?" I asked him.

"I declined to be," he answered; "this government is too arbitrary for me to take any share in it!"

"Yet, my dear *Marquis*" (I said to myself as I left him), "under this government which is too arbitrary for your taste you are living in freedom in spite of your opposition, while in the days whose freedom you regret, if when you threw yourself into the arms of the Austrians they had sent you back to your own country instead of shutting you up for five years at Olmütz, it is a hundred to one that your brethren and friends would have cut your head off; while a good many patriots who went further than you only escaped by a miracle the sword of their own chosen government."

But the time was come for me to set out for Burgos. Though I often dawdled about getting off, I never did so when I had once fairly started; I went straight to Bayonne, only stopping there for one night. While I was on my road, the emperor had returned to Paris, and brilliant parties were being given in honour of the new sovereign, on whom France relied for a successor to the mighty Empire. But these marks of public rejoicing were marred by one portentous disaster I mean the burning, on July 1, of the ballroom which Prince Schwarzenberg, the Austrian ambassador, had built on to the house occupied by him. In connection with the grief that resulted from this fatal event, one terrible coincidence struck everybody. Just as the marriage of the Archduchess Marie Antoinette had been the occasion of an alarming tumult, so that of the Archduchess Marie Louise seemed to form its counterpart.

Some superstitious presentiment caused that fire to be regarded as marking the end of the Emperor's good fortune. When I heard at Burgos of the disaster, I confess I could not help feeling a touch of this weakness; but, at the first moment, all my fear and anxiety was fixed on my wife, who was to have been at the ball. The newspapers came twenty-four hours sooner than the letters, and I passed a night of horrible expectancy; but the letter came at last. A slight indisposition had prevented Zozotte from going to the ball, where she had arranged to meet the poor Princess of La Leyen, who actually did lose her life there. So she had been in no danger; but everyone thought that she had been there, and she added in her irrepressibly comic fashion: "My drawing-room has never been empty since the burning. People come in crowds to know if I have not something about me that has been roasted."

Painful as it was for me to reappear at Burgos, discouraging as it was to recommence a task that had once been done, I was back again there. The emperor had spoken, and all wills submitted to that omnipotent voice. With resignation to it, my zeal had returned, and, by dint of meditating on what might still be possible, I had devised measures for spreading sound views and inducing their acceptance, calculated in my judgement to win back the country. Yet I was none the less very anxious. For the success of my efforts I needed an absolute authority, as the only way to create resources, enlighten the inhabitants, punish or reward individuals; but this authority no longer existed. The title of governor, though borne upon my instructions, was now only a worthless stamp. The Imperial Guard had preceded me into Spain; its headquarters, which I thought were to be at Valladolid, were at Burgos; and as the general in command of it could take his orders only from one of the colonels-general of the same corps, he had been invested with the supreme authority, and lodged in the rooms where I had had my quarters, which was enough to put me out of currency. Moreover, though my junior, he was my superior officer.

As a crowning disaster, this officer was General Dorsenne—a splendid man, once: the sumptuous lover of Mme d'Orsay. His foppery made him ridiculous, but the emperor liked him for his swagger and pluck—very good qualities in an officer of hussars; but what is an arm with no head to direct it in the case of a commander-in-chief? A single interview was enough to leave me no doubt as to Dorsenne's character and his value. From that moment there was no more to be said; I had no longer a position. I had no notion of squabbling over the rags of authority; and as 'the Guard was to settle finally all the difficulties of the war in Spain,' I renounced every kind of initiative.

Just as the Prince of Neuchâtel had been unable to comprehend that in order to conquer the Spaniards you needed to convince them, so it was thought that a rod of iron would answer for everything, and that it would be possible to subdue by terror the most fearless people in the world, and the most capable of taking reprisals on conquerors who did not shrink from such methods. Though "brigands," "vile and abject rabble," were thought good enough names for the *guerrilleros*, and it was implied that they were highly honoured by being killed, the Imperial Guard, with its reputation for invincibility derived from so many victories, must needs be matched against these nobodies.

Of course everything fled before it; but that very flight, while a necessity for the guerrillas, served them in the tactics which they had adopted against us. What was their game? To kill. Well, it cannot be denied that a hundred shots fired in a volley often fail to wound a single man; while ten shots fired individually kill or wound several. Besides, with them it was no longer a case of combats limited to a certain time; it was a continuous struggle, without rest or respite. No opportunity for trap or ambush was missed; advantage was taken of every hour of the day, every kind of weather, every position, and it always ended in the pursuers becoming the pursued. They never killed or wounded many men at any one time; but, as their blows were constantly renewed, the only possible end was to use up, with nothing to show for it, a picked army whose preservation was of so great importance.

Then anger stepped in, and caused random arrests of inhabitants in their own houses, or poor fellows found in the fields. They were then questioned; and whether they were unable or unwilling to say anything, or did not give satisfactory answers, they were put to the torture. One major, Dorsenne's worthy *aide-de-camp*, was especially well-suited for horrors of this kind. He generally began by tying up the wretched people by their thumbs; then he had them hoisted up and jerked till their bones were dislocated. Old men and priests were thus put an end to. Those who survived were taken to the dungeons of Burgos, which for them meant condemnation to death without trial.

Dorsenne had put up three huge gibbets on a hill in full view of the house which I had *furnished*, and which he occupied; and on these the bodies of three alleged accomplices of *guerrilleros* were always hanging. One morning there were only two, the family of the third victim having carried off the body in the night in order to bury it. Dorsenne at once ordered the military governor to have a man fetched from the town prison and hung on the gibbet which was disengaged.

The governor was a Swiss colonel named Traxler, a kind-hearted and brave man. His hair stood on end at the receipt of this order; and thinking that there must be some mistake, he hurried off to the general to have it cleared up. He was received with the utmost harshness; the order for the assassination was repeated, and that so angrily, that lacking courage to resist, he resigned himself, went to the prison, made the best selection of the unhappy victim, and sent him off, unconfessed it may be added, to the gallows. Then in perfect despair he came to me, and, with tears, told me what had been done. I was disgusted, as I well might be; but if some strong language escaped me, I abstained from any criticism. Indeed, what was there left to say? If before obeying Traxler had consulted me, my answer would have been that the order was a crime in which he ought never to take part, and an insult to himself to which the only proper answer was the resignation of his post.

This was the kind of man to whom the emperor had entrusted not only the destinies of that important part of Spain, but also the fate of nearly a million of men, and interests of appalling moment. He could not have made a greater mistake, for the Guard were, of all troops, unquestionably the least adapted to this kind of warfare; a kind which Napoleon never understood, and thought he could finish as he had finished his wars with Austria, Prussia, and Russia. In those cases to beat a general was to vanquish a sovereign; here, in order to reduce Spain, it would have been necessary to beat the whole country in the person of each one of its children.

CHAPTER 15

I am Made Governor of Salamanca

As I have said, Marshal Masséna had preceded me into Spain. When I reached Burgos, it was a fortnight since he had passed through the place, and he was preluding his Portugal campaign by the sieges of Rodrigo and Almeida. Alike as a Frenchman, as a devoted friend to the marshal, and as one interested in seeing the English army which had forced us to evacuate Portugal driven out in its turn, I was led to draw up a statement of my ideas as to the most suitable mode of regaining that kingdom. The occupation of it was essential if we were ever to retain any but a very precarious footing in Spain; and I made out the plan of campaign which I published in 1817 among the documents at the end of my narrative of Junot's expedition.

As soon as I had finished it, I sent it to the Prince of Neuchâtel and Masséna. The latter thanked me, the former confined himself to an acknowledgment; but as I afterwards learnt from Canouville, one of Berthier's *aides-de-camp*, the plan was at once taken to the emperor, who, after two perusals of it, asked for it to read it once more, and did not return it. Thus the emperor was in possession of all the conditions necessary to success; namely, that in that country what was wanted was an expedition, not a campaign; that it should be undertaken with sufficient forces to be checked by no obstacle; and that we ought to be in a position not merely to beat the English Army, but to drive it into the sea, retaining the power, after striking the great stroke, of sending half or two-thirds of our force back to Spain.

What conclusion is to be drawn from his action in the teeth of this demonstration? That he expected Masséna to work miracles? But the marshal was no longer at an age, nor had he the health, for that sort of thing. It was known that he was but a survival of himself, and that he had become one of those heroes of the past who ought not to be exposed to the caprices of that fortune of which he had once been the brilliant master.

Must we then admit that the emperor could face without much repugnance the notion of failure, were it only as a diminution of the glory which Masséna had won by his own efforts? This view had its supporters; though it was a possible answer to them to say that before long there was an idea of giving the marshal a force nearly equal to that which I had thought necessary, namely 100,000 men. On the other hand, one is compelled to recognise that the manner in which the collection of these was prescribed revealed more charlatanism even than dishonesty; for it must have been quite plain to those who gave orders to that effect that they could be only partially executed, and that, given as they were only when Lord Wellington had had time to complete the lines of Torres Vedras, which saved Lisbon, they were no longer of avail to produce the end desired.

As a matter of fact, what was done to reinforce Masséna's army? The decision was taken to arrange for it simultaneously both by adding to it Marshal Soult's army corps, and by the creation of a new corps which was to join the Prince of Essling at Santarem by the right bank of the Tagus, while Soult, coming from Badajoz, was to cross that river also in a line with Santarem, and join him similarly.[1] But here, again, the emperor neglected to sow in such a way as to produce a good crop. He had spoilt the expedition by not giving Masséna at first the means of bringing it to a prosperous end, and by placing under his orders both Marshal Ney, one of those men who can take their orders from none but themselves, and the Duke of Abrantès, who, having commanded our Army of Portugal, was for this reason no less than from his own character an awkward subordinate. And now he might have felt that, if in the interest of his country Masséna was capable of rising superior to his just indignation, Marshal Soult would act only in pursuance of his own culpable hostility; for, when his worse feelings were once called into play, nothing could be hoped for from him on the score of obedience, patriotism, or even honour.

Everything had to be sacrificed to rivalry and ambition by this man, who in the course of eleven years of marshal's rank, or even merely

---

1. I speak with full knowledge of the facts, since Berthier, being unable to communicate with Masséna, kept me informed of all intelligence that came and all orders that were given with regard to the Army of Portugal. He sent me for instance a translation of everything relating to it in the English newspapers. In this way, too, he sent me copies of all the orders given to Marshal Soult; notably that which directed him to make for Santarem by the left bank of the Tagus.

as commander of an army corps, never succeeded in doing honour to his profession by any feat of arms.[2] Marshal Soult, therefore, found reasons for not going further than Badajoz, and the non-execution of that part of the emperor's plan rendered the rest of it nugatory. In this way, by letting off the English Army, Soult paved the way for the series of disasters which led to our expulsion from the Peninsula and to the invasion of the South of France.

I return to the subject which gave rise to this digression; namely, to the plan of campaign which I drew up for Marshal Masséna. Once it was finished, General Dorsenne not being more disposed to give me work to do than I was in the humour to do it for him, I had nothing demanding my attention, for I was in very truth governor *in partibus*. Meanwhile, thanks to the confidence placed in me by the inhabitants, no detail of the brutality and barbarity which went on remained unknown to me; so wishing to deaden both the depression caused by inaction, and my regrets for the good I might have done, I clung for salvation to the work of compiling my *General Manual for Staff-Officers*.

I have mentioned how I had kept this work in view, and how in Portugal I had been urged to do it by Colonel Donkin. So I set to work on that treatise, which but for this period of unexpected inaction I should never have had an opportunity of writing. The disasters which followed so rapidly rendered the popularity obtained by the *Manual* of little advantage to me, but the edition was rapidly exhausted. I did not take any trouble to have it reprinted, though the last copies of it were sold at 25 or 30 *francs* apiece, and it was bought and used for the training of staff-officers in Paris, London, Berlin, and St. Petersburg.

Meanwhile, Marshal Masséna having reached Santarem pretty rapidly found himself, as I have said, checked before the formidable lines of Torres Vedras, defended by the English Army and the whole Portuguese army, as well as the militia and part of the population. Not only was he unable to force them, but he would not even have remained in front of them with impunity had not the strength of his character and

---

2. Out of respect for established opinion, I have often investigated the marshal's career to see upon what his reputation rests. No one could ever quote to me anything but Austerlitz, Corunna, and Toulouse. As we have seen, on the occasion of the first he had ophthalmia, and never showed himself on the field. [For English readers who have been accustomed to think that Marshal Soult was beaten at Corunna and Toulouse, it is perhaps unnecessary to reproduce General Thiébault's arguments against reckoning those battles to his credit.]

the power of his name rendered it possible for him to hold for some time a position which no other could have held for a week. It was then that the emperor at last comprehended that it was possible to pay too dear for the pleasure of tarnishing the glory of a soldier who still held a great military reputation.

As I have said, he had given orders to have it reinforced by Marshal Soult's corps, which never came, and by the newly-formed corps under the Count of Erlon.³ In this latter there was no one who knew Portugal, but it was felt, nevertheless, how necessary the knowledge of it had become; and the emperor, who punished me for not having begged his favours, did not at least deprive me of the honour of deserving what I was not allowed to have, and bethought himself of me to supply what was lacking to the commander of the new corps.

The Count of Erlon was certainly one of the most estimable men I ever knew, but so thoroughly established was the opinion of his weakness as a general that, without noticing it, everybody spoke of him as the Count of Erlon, nobody as *General* d'Erlon.⁴ It should be added that he did himself perfect justice, and being consistently with his excellent nature quite incapable of making "side" do duty for a total lack of talent, he adopted every useful proposal with perfect good humour, never appearing to be hurt by one's taking the initiative, and never trying to claim what did not belong to him, even though it took effect only under his name. I might, therefore, be regarded as necessary to that army corps, and the emperor ordered that I should be employed as chief of the staff to it.

This was indeed putting my loyalty to a pretty severe test, for it was bringing me down from the Duke of Abrantès to the Count of Erlon, and from an army in which I had been the second personage to a corps which only formed the quarter of an army. But there was appended to my orders the following, written on note-paper in the hand of the Prince of Neuchâtel:

> The emperor bids me tell you, General Thiébault, that on this occasion he counts upon your zeal in his service and your devotion to his person.

---

3. [Better known, perhaps, as General Drouet. He was son to the famous postmaster of Varennes.]
4. In the same way Louis XVIII, of witty and spiteful memory, said one day in my presence to the Count of La Roche-Aymon, "Good morning, general," and to General Lauriston, "Good morning, *marquis*."

Hesitation was impossible, and in no case should I have hesitated; besides, it was a question of substituting war for inaction, and of leaving a hateful man, who could not fail to be as glad of my departure as I was glad to be no longer a witness of his atrocities, for one whom I esteemed. I was about to rejoin Marshal Masséna, from whom I could not fail to obtain a position which was certain to suit me in permanence, while I was equally certain of it in the event of the Duke of Abrantès replacing the marshal. In presence of a man of a thoroughly good nature one has spontaneous sympathies and unexpected points of contact which serve to shorten the preliminary stage. My first visit to the Count of Erlon proved this; it lasted nearly three hours, and when we parted we had reached a degree of intimacy and confidence which with some chiefs scarcely results from several years of intercourse, while with others it never comes into existence.

Attached to the Count of Erlon was an officer of whom equally I could not speak too well. This was Colonel de Salaignac, a deserving man, possessing much more ability than his general, and in consequence of this superiority coming very near to commanding the army. I do not know what opinion he held of me, but he at once subordinated his influence to mine; and as it was impossible to have better intentions than he, while in that respect his general was inferior to no one, and I could claim equality with anyone, we found ourselves from the first day in perfect agreement. The initiative of proposals devolved on me, and the licence allowed me went so far as to permit me to take upon myself arrangements beyond my authority. As no proposal which I had occasion to make was rejected, and no order that I gave was repudiated, there was no longer any limit to my efforts, seeing that such treatment has always been enough to convert my zeal into enthusiasm.

The 9th Corps had been rather scratched together than formed, the troops composing it had been collected on the march, the administrative officials and generals had joined it how they could. So far as regarded the organisation of the service, nothing had been done when it arrived at Burgos. Nevertheless, when it reached Salamanca, it was all ready to march upon Ciudad Rodrigo, and afterwards to take up a position between Santarem and Almeida. The rainy season was over; we could not fail to find some resources; moreover, every soldier was certain of entering Portugal with bread and four days' biscuit; lastly, each division was to be followed by a herd of cattle. We were thus about to leave Salamanca fully convinced of a prompt junction with Masséna, when on the eve of the day fixed for our departure I was seized with one of my attacks of inflammation of the bowels. I was therefore obliged to remain at Salamanca, and allow the Count of Erlon to go without me, sincerely attached as I was to him, and deploring the necessity of leaving him just when I was about to be most useful.

An incident, serious in itself, scandalous in its consequences, took place almost immediately owing to my being out of the way. A consequence of the mixture of inadequacy and kindness which made up the Count of Erlon's nature was that with him power did not result in authority. He might be exactly compared to some material which needs a lining stronger than itself, and, unluckily, the *aide-de-camp's* solidity was by no means sufficient to redeem the commander-in-chief's want of backbone. When the army reached Burgos, I had found that some officers had reached the point of getting orders given as they liked and of disregarding when necessary the orders that they had received. One of the things that I had the greatest difficulty not to establish in principle, but to put into practice, was inducing the general to discuss with me all the orders to be given, to give them only through me and to insist on their punctual execution; that is to say, to back me up on this point in such a way as to prove to the subordinates that they had a commander.

But as soon as I was no longer there Salaignac was left powerless, and General Claparède, who commanded the first division of the 9th Corps, was quick to draw a splendid profit from my absence. He succeeded, in fact, in persuading the Count of Erlon that in order to secure his route it was advisable that he, Claparède, should be ordered to cover the right; that is, to beat and drive across the Douro all the insurgents or partisan corps who were on the left of the river in the direction of Coimbra. The order, drawn up by himself, gave him full powers of action, without any restriction as to the time he was to remain separate from the army or the distance which he was to keep from it; communications soon ceased, for he kept too far off for orders to reach him; he fought for his own hand.

On the strength of hypothetical engagements, such as can be invented with impunity in a popular war out of a few shots fired in the air or against walls, he levied enormous contributions of which he never rendered any account, and he sucked a parish dry before leaving it to make his profit out of another. In this way he made money enough to meet the extravagance and luxury of the remainder of his life, without any hindrance to his road towards the House of Peers, of which he is at this day an honoured member.

By order of the Count of Erlon, as indeed by the fact of my rank and position, I had, on remaining behind at Salamanca, received the command not only of all the men belonging to the four army corps then in Portugal, so far as they were included in detachments which had already arrived or were expected, but also the chief command of the district. Just when I was getting quite well again the Duke of Istria, Bessières, arrived at Valladolid. He commanded in chief the Army of the North of Spain, with a territory extending from Irun to Alcantara, and composed of Navarre, Biscay, Old Castile, and the province of Valladolid, being four out of the six governments formed in Spain. Having heard that I was at Salamanca, he wrote in haste to inquire as to the circumstances which kept me there.

I replied that it was the result of illness, but that I was ready to rejoin the Count of Erlon and Marshal Masséna as soon as possible, with the detachments intended for the Army of Portugal which had successively arrived at Salamanca. By return of messenger I received from him an autograph letter to the effect that, as d'Erlon had joined Masséna, the reasons which had chiefly caused my nomination as chief of staff no longer existed; that it was well known that I had only accepted the post from a laudable point of self-devotion, and that it could not suit me to retain it; that for his own part he could not forget what I had done at Burgos, and that he accordingly offered to create for me a seventh government, composed of the provinces of Toro, Zamora, Salamanca, Ciudad Rodrigo, and Almeida, which he much hoped I should accept. He would undertake to obtain the emperor's approbation, and he thought the post would suit me all the better from being of importance; since, although governor, I should be *de facto* commander of the advance-guard of the Army of the North. The detachments would be taken on by General Gardanne.

Thus I found myself a governor for the third time. I have just said what was the effect on me of kind treatment; and if the Duke of Istria, the third and last commander-in-chief under whom I was to congratulate myself on serving, had shown unlimited confidence in me, I was bound to do as much in respect of zeal by way of justifying it.

By a fresh piece of good luck I was even better backed at Salamanca by the Spanish authorities than I had been at Burgos. The excellent prefect of the latter place, Blanco de Salcedo, had been no less recommended by his intelligence and devotion than by his personal qualities; but the prefect of the seventh government, named Cacaseca, was even superior to him as an administrator—I may almost say as a man. Active, honest, firm, able, he knew with incredible accuracy the amount of supplies that the smallest hamlet of Estremadura could furnish; he was acquainted with the special points of every functionary and of the chief persons under his administration; and for every duty—hostile as the mass of the inhabitants were—he could lay his hand on the right man to undertake it.

Thus he never required or enjoined anything that was not fair or possible, and I never gave an order that was not carried out. We went along in undisturbed agreement, in consequence of which order combined with economy to lighten the burdens as far as that was possible, and, in spite of the presence of so many troops, to maintain a balance between requirements and resources. In spite of all obstacles, his orders brought all that was required punctually to the day, without its being once necessary to have recourse to military execution, or even to hold one of those councils which had been so useful to me at Burgos. But, indeed, I do not know whom among the local authorities I had not reason to praise.

I had not long been holding the seventh government when General Foy arrived at Salamanca,[5] having, by miracle, escaped two Portuguese corps and the bands of Don Julian Sanchez, one of the two or three most formidable guerrilla chiefs in Spain, with the loss of only ten stragglers out of his small escort. He was bearing dispatches for the emperor, and orders for General Gardanne, who had been left behind in Spain with a view to a mission, about which, from the time that I took possession of the seventh government, he had no further occasion to trouble himself. Now he was to rejoin Masséna with all the troops that he could collect, intended for the Army of Portugal.

This Gardanne was not the general of whom I spoke in connection with the Roman campaign, who was called Moustache Gardanne. He had before this died of vexation, in consequence of an unjust reprimand given him by some marshal or other,[6] and, above all, of the uselessness of the remonstrances addressed by him to the emperor, upon whom that brave officer had claims which ought never to have been

---

5. [This would be about the middle of November 1810.]
6. [General Antoine Gardanne died at Breslau in 1807. The one here in question (Claude) seems to have been employed again, if he be the Gardanne whom Marbot (vol. iii.) refers to as serving in Eugène Beauharnais' army in 1813. He died in 1818.]

overlooked. The General Gardanne of whom I am now speaking—a small, lean, weakly-looking man—is the one who, at the beginning of the blockade of Genoa, behaved so finely in the action of the 20th *Germinal* before Varazze, when he was in command of Marbot's division, and had his leg smashed by a bullet. At Tilsit he had been intended by Napoleon for a mission to the Shah of Persia; later on he became governor of the imperial pages; and now, still as general of brigade, he was employed in the Army of Portugal.

I had no less regard for him in private life than as a distinguished soldier, and, though he could not at that moment get together more than about 2,000 men, I felt the more at ease about his operation from the fact that Masséna was master of both banks of the Zezere; that the Portuguese General Silveira, who had threatened General Foy, was at that moment marching towards Coimbra; and that, consequently, there was nothing on General Gardanne's road which could endanger him. My amazement, then, may be imagined when, ten days after his departure, I heard that, after losing 1,000 men, who were never heard of again, he had returned to Rodrigo with his troops utterly disorganised. To confirm this deplorable news, he arrived at Salamanca. I hastened off to him.

"Great heavens!" I said, "what is the meaning of your retreat—effected in this manner, too?"

"General, when I got near the Zezere I found an enormous force in front of me."

"An enormous force?"

"Yes, general—the united army."

"Marshal Masséna was between you and it."

"It had, apparently, turned his flank."

"But that's impossible."

"It is true, however."

"And you saw that army?"

"I saw the advance-guard of it."

"And you ascertained its presence by an action?"

"I did not think it right to commit myself so far."

"An advance-guard action in a country of that kind commits nobody to anything. At all events, you reconnoitred the advanced posts of the advance-guard that you saw?"

"No, general; it was useless. The inhabitants assured me that I was in presence of the enemy's army; that the French had evacuated the left bank of the Zezere; and that the bridge of Punhete had been carried away by a flood."

"And you took their word for it?"

"They all told the same story."

"And you withdrew without any verification?"

"I should have been lost if I had stayed, seeing that I was on an island which I had to make haste to get out of."

At the word "island," I looked at him without answering, and he went to fetch his map to show it me. Presently, the *island* appeared to be only a peninsula, formed by the Tagus [7] and two affluents near their source, which finally made it clear to me that the poor man had gone out of his mind. That day's messenger took the report which I had to send upon this serious matter to the Prince of Neuchâtel and the Duke of Istria. Without concealing what I thought of Gardanne's condition, I confined it to the simplest statement of the facts.

But all the moderation that I could put into it did not prevent me from receiving by the return messenger a crushing paragraph to be put into the general order of the day, containing poor Gardanne's dismissal, with orders for him to go back to France and go home. Grieved as I was at seeing so cruel an ending to so honourable a career, I went at once to impart to him the order that I had received, and ask him to leave Salamanca before daylight, so that he might not be there when the severe treatment meted out to him became generally known. He yielded to my wish, and I had a sad parting with him.

Now what was the enormous force before which General Gardanne had, not withdrawn, but run away, without giving himself time even to collect his troops, abandoning the whole number of men who were scattered about in their craze for marauding, to which a large number always devote themselves when a column is badly led? One shudders to say that that force, that united army—if, indeed, he did see anything, which I doubt, seeing that I have been assured that he never got near the Zezere—was, and could be nothing but one of the marshal's posts. Thus, it must have been some fifty of our own troops before whom General Gardanne fled. It was in fear of these fifty men that he abandoned 1,000, who, scattered as they were, had been massacred by the inhabitants, or by the Portuguese guerrillas, and he had actually reached his object when he missed it in the most disastrous manner.

By coming to live at Salamanca I had put another 150 miles between myself and my wife; but I was lucky enough to find some

---

7. [*Sic*, and the Duke of Wellington seems to agree, but it is hard to see how Gardanne can have reached the Tagus in the time. The Zezere must be meant.]

people there with whom I could at least talk of her. Among these I may mention the Duchess of Abrantès. The presence of that lady at Salamanca was certainly extraordinary; but it was due to a domestic difficulty, the settlement of which had involved the condition that she should accompany her husband as far as she could go with him, and, in the event of her being obliged to remain behind, should fix her residence only in some place assigned by him. It must be owned that the conditions could not have been more rigorously carried out.

The duchess followed the duke to Rodrigo, being within a month of her confinement. Being compelled to remain, she gave birth amid all the disorder of a siege, under every circumstance of privation, and with a frightful epidemic raging, to a son, who is now called Alfred, but was then named Roderick.[8] As this seemed an impossible place of abode for her, she started for Salamanca as soon as she was able to travel, which was soon after my arrival there; and I do not know that she would ever have reached it but for me. I had received information of her coming; and simultaneously, that Don Julian, at the head of his terrible force of insurgents, had formed the plan of carrying her off in the forest of Matilla. She was to be already at Alba de Yeltes, and the very next day her inadequate escort would be face to face with the redoubted leader.

There was not a moment to be lost; I at once sent two columns to right and left of Matilla, ordering the commanders to be past it before daylight, and giving them instructions to keep near the road and to join the escort of the duchess, as soon as a shot was fired. Lastly, I set out myself with two squadrons of cavalry to meet her. When I fell in with her, night was coming on, and she was just entering the forest. It was a dramatic moment; but I said nothing about the danger she had been in or my precautions, and attributed my sudden appearance to the desire of meeting her sooner. As soon as I had seen her surrounded with troops I took my leave and returned to Salamanca, where I received her next in the least uncomfortable house that the town could boast.

To have the society of so distinguished a lady was an unimaginable piece of luck at the far end of Estremadura. Anywhere her company was desirable, but it was inestimable among the Spanish provincial ladies, the smartest of whom came in point of education and manners nowhere near ladies' maids in a good family with us. Here then was a person as amiable, literary, and brilliant as our age could produce; here

---

8. [He fell at Solferino, in 1859.]

was one of the leading hostesses of Paris transported into the midst of a population which seemed to belong to days long gone by. Besides her social qualities, she was a lady whose firmness of character was equal to her merits; of which I hasten to give a proof.

Don Julian continued to keep the province in a state of trepidation; Portuguese detachments from Silveira's corps had shown themselves on the left bank of the Agueda, and I deemed it useful to march against them with such forces as I could dispose of. I reported this to the Duke of Istria, and called upon Mme d'Abrantès to let her know of my approaching departure and convince her of the necessity of moving to Valladolid.

I said:

Salamanca can no longer be safe for you, since I am taking away all my troops, except the men required for the defence of the fort; and in that there is no place where you could be lodged. Moreover, I must tell you that all the guerrillas have their eye on you, attracted by the ransom which they would be sure to get; and it would be a match between them who should make prisoners of you and your son. So take advantage of the moment when I can assure your safe journey as far as Valladolid. If you wish, I will state all this in writing; my respect for you and my attachment to the duke make it a duty.

She was not to be moved by anything I could say or do; she had only left Rodrigo for want of food and shelter; when she announced to the duke that she was going to Salamanca, she had promised him not to leave that town without him, and she was determined to keep that promise happen what might. If she could at a pinch have one room in the fort, it would quite satisfy her. Lastly, thanking me for my advice, and for pressing her to accept it, she begged me not to leave a single man more at Salamanca on her account.

One must have been there to appreciate all the courage that this resolution implied; and I was much struck by it. By thus placing herself above the considerations which would have swayed any other woman, the duchess rose superior to her sex, and showed that she was able to place her strength of mind on a level with all the other qualities of which the world has formed its opinion, and to which posterity will render homage. After all, my proposals to the Duke of Istria had no more result than those I had made to her. He did not sanction my departure, and Salamanca did not lose its garrison.

The duchess concerned herself a good deal about religion, and was compiling a commentary on the Apocalypse. She did me the honour of thinking that my soul was not entirely that of a reprobate, and undertook my conversion. At first I thought it was a whim, but she persevered in it. One evening in particular, which I finished alone with her, she carried the matter so far that I felt it on my conscience to be causing her to waste so much trouble on me. When I went home, about eleven o'clock, I put my hand on a copy of one of my proclamations to the Spaniards, which contained a highly orthodox passage. This I sent her at once, with a letter in which I complained that she had made me melancholy by her remonstrances on my lack of piety. I added that indeed I did not always show myself to be guided by the highest light; but if she would be good enough to cast her eye over the enclosed proclamation, she would see evidence that at all events at certain moments I found my way back to the right path. "You are incorrigible," she said, with a smile, when I met her next morning; and there was no more talk of religion between us.

One evening, just as I was finishing my game of chess with the duchess, a servant announced M. de Canouville. An instant of silence testified to our astonishment and our curiosity; after which a piteous voice besought food and admission for a poor worn-out and famished traveller. Then as a face worthy of the voice came through the doorway, that face, which indeed was that of Jules de Canouville, was greeted with a general shout of laughter. With an instinctive movement everyone rose and went towards him, with exclamations appropriate to the doleful get-up of this dandy of the court, this most fashionable of the young men of the day, to the mud with which he was covered, to the disorder of his dress, to his beard, which nowadays would be too short, but at that time was regarded as untidy.

After the first outburst and many repetitions of his name, after disconnected words uttered at random, everybody having ejaculated in his own way and in different keys, "Canouville!—you!—he! Is it possible?—how?—why?"—it became possible to frame a sentence, and a dialogue on the whole as comic as the entrance was succeeded by something resembling a conversation.

After having told us that he was the bearer of dispatches for the Prince of Essling, with orders to discover an army which in Paris was supposed to be lost, he came to the real motive for his journey, and repeated to all of us twenty times what he declared he could not tell anybody once, what everybody knew, what he was all on fire to tell us. Being *aide-de-camp* to the Prince of Neuchâtel, he had recently become the lover of Pauline Bonaparte, Princess Borghese. In order to put a stop to the intrigue the emperor had had this duty entrusted to him with orders to start at once, and the crazy fellow, in order to get back quickly, had galloped without rest or respite. While he related the details of his adventure he mingled them with alas's and sighs fit, as the duchess said, to blow the candles out.

Nothing equally melancholy could have been more comical or more lively. His supper was another comedy, for complaining all the while that he was being left to starve, he did not hear or did not notice when his meal was announced, and at the table, where he took his position like a man ready to eat up everything, he went on talking and forgot to eat. At midnight I wanted to retire, but he begged me not to go without him, and it was striking one when I succeeded in getting him to adjourn the meeting. At the duchess's door such of the party as had remained till then separated; I thought that he also would take his leave and make his way to wherever he was staying, but he stopped, and resuming his lamentable voice there in the middle of the road, said to me, "General, would you have the heart to desert an unhappy young man?"

"Surely not," I replied; "and if you do not breakfast or dine with the duchess, I am sure I hope that you will look upon my table as your own."

"But for tonight?"

"For tonight? Why, you're going back to bed and to sleep."

"What bed?"

"Why, hang it, the bed at your lodging."

"I haven't got any lodging."

"What, didn't you get a lodging when you arrived?"

"No, general, and if you desert me I don't know what will become of me;" and, roaring with laughter, I took him along to my house.

There we had another display. When I ordered my servant to get a bed made for him in my sitting-room, he went on, "General, you are so kind."

"Well?"

"Well, I am too unhappy to sleep alone."

"Oh, indeed; you don't want to sleep with me?"

"No, general, but pray have a bed made for me in your room," and I did so. Instead of going to bed, I had to hear the whole story of his happiness and his misfortunes, a panegyric of the excellent qualities and the charms of the princess, and the confession of his passion for her. The poor lad had lost everything, his heart and his head alike; with the exception of a few minutes my night was equally lost, but one does not often have a more amusing one. However, I did get to bed, and finally to sleep. As for him, when I woke up he had gone out; by eight in the morning he had presented himself at the duchess's, and had her woke up to get a letter from her to the duke. She sent answer that he was mad; indeed, I had given him the day before all the reasons to show that as communication with the Army of Portugal was interrupted it would be no use for him to continue his journey, and that he must wait for a more propitious moment to discharge his errand.

After he had left the duchess I saw him again; he wanted to push on at least as far as Ciudad Rodrigo or Almeida, but I made him see that even if he got there, which appeared impossible without an escort—and with that I had no excuse for furnishing him—he would be none the less cut off from the Army of Portugal; while if, contrary to all probability, a column of that army succeeded sooner or later in cutting its way through to one of those towns, it would not go away without communicating with me and receiving my orders and dispatches, so that there would be nothing gained for his errand by leaving Salamanca. "But in that case," he returned, "what would be the good of my staying here? My dispatches will go just as well with yours as by themselves. And what impropriety would there be in my handing them to you?"

"I should not receive them."

"And if I left them on your desk?"

"Well, I should have to have them taken up. But you would not get any receipt for them; you would remain responsible for them, and I should report the matter."

No one can imagine what these simpletons after Berthier's sort were, charming young people, all in good style and possessed of some fortune, in some cases of sufficient distinction and position to attain to anything, and of whom none ever played any part unless in ladies' *boudoirs*. Canouville was one of the most agreeable of them. He got more and more excited till he persuaded himself that he would be bearing an important piece of news if he went to Paris and said that it was impossible to communicate, although I represented to him that twenty dispatches of mine had informed, and were still informing, the Prince of Neuchâtel of the fact.

Although I repeated to him that it was ridiculous to ride 600 or 700 leagues in order to get a blowing up and perhaps something worse, he declared that for him an hour passed at Paris was worth a whole lifetime. Finding this a sublime reply and reason, he departed on the strength of them, crossed all the north of Spain without taking a single man to escort him, reached Paris at night, was run down at once, and forced to decamp at daybreak. Three weeks had not passed when he came back very melancholy, and begged me to give him back his dispatches.[9]

After these trivialities I come to more serious matters, namely to the events connected with my government of Estremadura. Salamanca was crowded up with detachments, squadrons, and battalions which were collected there to join Marshal Masséna. Orders could no longer reach them, and thus I was in a position to handle more than 18,000 infantry and nearly 1700 cavalry. I considered how to make them useful, and the only way which presented itself to me was to employ them against Don Julian, who was alone within my reach. As regarded forces, although his amounted to 6,000 or 7,000 men, I had eight times as many as I needed to beat him. But the difficulty was to get at him, and do something more against him than execute the movements of which the guerrillas were everywhere the object, and which generally ended only in seasoning them while tiring the troops.

In order, therefore, to guard myself beforehand against any reverse, I began by reinforcing my garrisons, and increasing the escorts of my convoys and messengers, while neither placing nor leaving a single man in the country. I even made a show of believing that the war of insurrection could be ended only by the help of justice and persuasion, and remained inactive. The Spanish authorities, those who took the French side, and even some of my own officers, complained of my system; while Don Julian's *partidas*, who were supreme in the country districts, and pressed me closer and closer, congratulated themselves on it. At last the Duke of Istria wrote to me about it; but the only answer he got was, "As for the fifth paragraph of your letter of yesterday, I entreat you to allow me to keep the contents of it perfectly dark."

While everyone was thus attributing to me every intention except the right one, I had completed my arrangements. Suddenly one day, ten columns, each of 1,000 men, issued at midnight from Salamanca,

---

9. [The rest of the story will be found in General Marbot's *Mémoires*, vol. ii. Canouville, with the dispatches, reached Masséna at Guarda about the end of March, some two months after he had originally been sent from Paris. He appears to have been killed in the following year at the Battle of the Moskowa.]

Ledesma, and Alba de Tonnes, while 4,000 who had gone out the day before under pretext of reinforcing the garrisons of Ciudad Rodrigo and Almeida, having slept at Matillas, broke up suddenly into four columns, acting in concert with the others. In pursuance of their orders two of these columns passed along the Tormes, one to the east, one to the west of Salamanca, destroying all boats and guarding or breaking down all bridges, while the other twelve flung themselves into the wooded mountainous country which lies between that river and the Agueda, tracking Don Julian's scattered bands in every direction through their cover in the woods, and driving them out into the plain, where nine columns of cavalry, which had unexpectedly arrived under General Founder, cut them to pieces.

Two of the bands were surprised in the villages occupied by them, and destroyed; others suffered more or less; and such was their loss and terror that nearly 2,000 men made their submission, abandoning Don Julian. He had another 1200 killed or wounded, and was reduced to 3,000 men, and those a good deal shaken.

Unprecedented as was such a success against the guerrillas, it corresponded only to the first part of my plan. When Don Julian's consternation was at its height, one of the emissaries whom the prefect had given me, a man of great tact, had approached him and said, "I was talking about you yesterday to the governor." Thereupon he reported an alleged conversation, in the course of which I was supposed to have expressed my regret that a man of Don Julian's worth, of such high capacity and noble courage, should consent to serve so deplorable a cause and increase the misfortunes of his country, when he might have contributed so powerfully to bring them to an end. Everybody would render him the justice he deserved, and the governor more than anyone. Having enlarged on this theme, my man added:

> If, then, you will rally to the only cause which can bring happiness to Spain, and leave a side on which you will never be considered anything more than the head of your peasants; if, in short, you are willing to play a part worthy of yourself and take advantage of your good fortune in still being able to set a good example, the governor will undertake to get you appointed major-general—(this had been arranged with the Minister of War)—to get a ribbon given you—)this was known to be the object of his highest ambition)—to have a regular corps of 6,000 men, infantry and cavalry, organised under your com-

mand to keep you near him—to retain within this government only so many French troops as may be necessary for garrison purposes, and to entrust you with the carrying out of such orders as may be given to the small towns and villages, which will make you the second person in these provinces.

This proposal astonished him. He was flattered by the offers made and touched by what he was told about my personal esteem for him. What he knew of my character, my conduct, of the manner in which I treated the Spaniards, added still further to his confidence; in short, shaken as he was by the terrible lesson he had just received, he entered into negotiations with the *prefect*, who was quite the man to bring this important business to a good conclusion.

It was just at this time that General Foy returned from Paris, making forced marches to rejoin Marshal Masséna. He required for his escort both the remains of the force which General Gardanne had so unexpectedly and unluckily shown himself incapable of leading, and the whole of the remaining troops which belonged to the Army of Portugal. This reduced me to about one-third of the force which I had hitherto had at my disposal, and that at a somewhat inconvenient moment however, the loss of 12,000 men going to the front is less weakening than the arrival of 40,000 in retreat.

A reinforcement of this size, taken to the Army of Portugal just before the news came that a fifth corps was about to follow it, combined to support the idea that the Portuguese would be beaten and the English compelled to re-embark. This idea discouraged any hostile attempt on the part of the Spaniards, and, consequently, strengthened my position more than the reduction in the number of my troops injured it. The negotiations between Don Julian and myself were not interrupted; still, as there were necessarily many points to be discussed, and as Don Julian of course needed time to win over his most influential officers as he had been won over himself, several weeks elapsed.

At length we had come to an agreement under all the heads. Don Julian had succeeded in assuring himself of the concurrence of nearly all his people. The terms of the agreement were drawn up, and we had only three days to wait for the meeting of all those who were to sign it with us. I was rejoicing, therefore, at the success of a plan conceived by myself alone and conducted with the greatest secrecy and good fortune, the aim of which was to employ Spaniards in fighting Spaniards, with the moral conquest of Spain as its possible result.

I was even considering the ways and means not only for putting forward the re-organisation of Don Julian's troops, but of levying a second Spanish division, and making plans to employ these troops, mixed with some French corps, in reducing the neighbouring provinces. Indeed, I know not whither my sanguine schemes were not leading me, when the news arrived that the Army of Portugal, pursued by the English and Portuguese, was in full retreat and falling back on the province of Salamanca. Here was an end to all my dreams.

A few days later there arrived Marshal Ney, returning to France, and the eldest son of Marshal Masséna, on his way to Paris, ostensibly to congratulate the emperor on the birth of the King of Rome, but mainly to bear the marshal's report upon the evacuation of Portugal. As it chanced, they met at my house, when Marshal Ney did me the honour to call upon me on his arrival. Both confirmed the terrible truth by melancholy details.

The mere announcement of that terrible retreat had restored to the insurgents the hope of seeing their cause triumphant. Besides that, some men of Don Julian's band had soon found plenty of money upon some soldiers of the Army of Portugal whom they had killed, and greed put the finishing stroke to their elation. All those who had laid down their arms took them up again. Assassinations and skirmishes began again. Such an overthrow, no less unforeseen than decisive, put me out of the running just at the moment when I was about to play an important part. I may add that I held my peace with regard to it. I mentioned it only to the Duchess of Abrantès at Salamanca, and later on to the duke, while I reported it only to the Duke of Istria. To impart it in any other quarter would only have looked like swagger.

As is well known, what made Masséna's retreat necessary was the impossibility of living any longer on the banks of the Tagus; but it is less well known under what circumstances the army was reduced to famine, or how want of food, by making retreat inevitable, caused the failure of that expedition, the last of the three which we were to make against Portugal. My plan and Dulong's for the campaign of 1810 had made it clear that, in order to attack Portugal again, it was necessary to act with sufficient troops to get possession of the country and of Lisbon by forced marches; that is to say, to make it impossible for anything or anybody to stop us. If this advice had been followed at once, success might have been regarded as certain.

But although the emperor knew those plans, and, as I have said, after reading mine wanted to read it again, the 2nd Corps, under

General Reynier, was not put into communication with the Army of Portugal till July 10, before which date it had been reduced to the 6th and the 8th Corps, and was in no condition to pass the Coa. Besides this, it was considered that, as a preliminary to his entrance into Portugal, Masséna ought to take Ciudad Rodrigo, which surrendered on July 10, Fort Concepcion, which was evacuated on the 22nd, and Almeida, which, thanks to its powder-magazine blowing up, capitulated on August 24.

These delays, which were forced upon Marshal Masséna, and in no way depended on his own wish, allowed time in Portugal for completing the means of resistance which might have been anticipated and prevented if the previous operations, which occupied nearly four months, instead of being reserved for the Army of Portugal, had been entrusted to some corps from the Army of Spain. Of these months, lost by us, Lord Wellington was able to take colossal advantage. He received a fresh division of English troops, he increased the Portuguese army, he doubled the militia and summoned the whole country to arms, he had the crops burnt, which if we had come sooner we should have found standing; he prevented the sowing of the land, and caused whole masses of the population to leave their homes, even in some of the most considerable towns, like Viseu or Coimbra—extreme measures, and frightful enough to be matched a thousand leagues away by the burning of Moscow.

Moreover, taking advantage of local conditions, formidable enough in themselves, he had time to arm and complete the lines of Torres Vedras—a series of natural curtains or abysses which he bastioned with 114 redoubts. These were revetted on the front and flanks as well as at the gorge, and could no longer be carried with a rush, nor could any impression be made on them except by cannon-shot. They could be retaken only by breaching and assault. These works, testifying to great ability, were completed by inundations, by vertical escarpments, by trenches, abattis, *chevaux-de-frise*, and pitfalls, and were supplemented before Lisbon by two other lines of works, to the strength of which 25,000 workmen were daily adding.

This threefold place of arms, this new Gibraltar, of which Lisbon and its fort became the citadel, was defended by 30,000 English and as many Portuguese troops, by the militia, and, as a reserve, by a population of 400,000 souls; and, further, by the inhabitants and refugees who had taken shelter in the towns and villages within the lines. Lastly, Lord Wellington, with his boundless prudence, going so far as even to admit the possibility of our reaching Lisbon in spite of all these obstacles, had assembled thousands of vessels there, partly loaded them, and was prepared to send on board all that he required, including provisions.

In face of these defensive forces, what was our position for the attack? Almeida and Rodrigo having been taken under Lord Wellington's nose, the Army of Portugal, after a further delay of twenty days, which I have never understood, had left the former place on September 15 to plunge in with half the necessary force—action which, as I have said, can only be explained on the part of those responsible for its inadequacy, either by an absurd confidence due to the intoxication of the moment, or by intentions rather antagonistic to the marshal's reputation than suited to the interests of France.

On the 27th took place the unlucky affair of Busaco, which may be imputed to the ignorance of the Marquis of Alorna and the other Portuguese who had been given to the marshal to enlighten him as to roads and localities. It might have been avoided if, instead of attacking the front of that formidable position, they had followed the road which turned it, and which a peasant pointed out the next day. That failure cost us 364 prisoners, 521 killed, and 3,160 wounded. These last reached Coimbra with the army on October 2, and were massacred there on the 7th.[10]

On the 6th the army moved, always driving Lord Wellington before it, to Pombal, and on the 11th to Alcoentre, whence the marshal employed the 12th and 13th in reconnoitring for himself the whole front of the lines of Torres Vedras, and in collecting information from which he learnt their full strength. He had at his disposal for the attack of this unattackable position some field-artillery and 50,000 to 55,000 men, while he would have required a battering-train to demolish the redoubts, and for the attack of such works a force two or three times

---

10. The poor creatures had been placed in some neighbouring convents under the charge of a deputy-inspector-general, two commissaries, two doctors, twenty-two surgeons, eighteen officials; all these shared the fate of the wounded. The crime remained unpunished; it ought to have been avenged by the burning of Coimbra, and a village for every man. A war of armies has its laws, a war of peoples has none. [This falsehood as to the massacre of the wounded at Coimbra by the Portuguese, which every French writer seems to repeat, has every time to be "nailed to the counter." Napier expressly states that Colonel Trant succeeded in repressing the disorder before more than ten lives had been lost, and gives a letter, signed by several French officers (including the very deputy-inspector-general here mentioned!), in which Trant is thanked for his care of the prisoners.]

as numerous as the defenders.

The position was hopeless, and the expedition, as it had been devised, had failed. It had failed from the slowness with which the Army of Portugal had been collected, by the time wasted in siege, but, above all, by the insufficiency of the force employed. What can be said further? If the lines of Torres Vedras, which there were no means of forcing, were not attacked, it was equally impossible to withdraw, because retreat would have worn the look of flight, and would have brought the Anglo-Portuguese army into Spain. Yet how was the retrograde movement to be avoided in a country where nearly all the resources had been destroyed, and from which the population had fled, leaving famine behind it, while the only thing to be found was, so to say, earth in which to bury the dead? To face so perilous a situation, two things were needed in a very high degree—inspiration and energy; and Marshal Masséna realised all that could be expected of his character and genius.

He resolved therefore to make Santarem his centre, and, in order to subsist his army in that position, he organised a system by which part of the army should scour the country to a considerable distance and bring in whatever provisions had escaped destruction; he had mills and bakehouses set up, the hands for them being supplied by the army, which also furnished iron-founders, carpenters, blacksmiths, for the repairs necessary to the material. This involved the erection of workshops, the training of workmen where deficient, the manufacture of tools, and the demolition of useless houses to provide iron and timber. He succeeded, ultimately, in building boats, throwing a bridge over the Tagus, even making powder; and by the help which he obtained especially in the artillery corps, and also in the various regiments, he was able to hold out for nearly five months, and thus solve what might have been considered an insoluble problem. His stay there was of itself a memorable event, only to be recorded with admiration.[11]

Meanwhile, as Lisbon could not be the prize of a sudden rush, the marshal had devised two plans for making himself master of it. The first consisted in trying to draw Lord Wellington out of his lines, beat him in a pitched battle, cut him off from Lisbon by forcing his left, break up the combined army, and, once master of the open country, to march on the works, which could no longer be defended, and upon the capital, which, thrown upon its own resources, would be unable to offer any further resistance. The other was to blockade Wellington

---

11. [Napier, it will be remembered, more than once expresses a similar opinion.]

on the side of the Alemtejo, as he was already blockaded on the right bank of the Tagus, by occupying the whole left bank to the mouth of the river; leave no subsistence within his reach on either bank, and reduce by famine the population of Lisbon, including that of the towns and villages within the lines, and the English and Portuguese armies.

To feed such numbers by sea, at the mercy of a gale of wind, would have been very difficult; and, besides, batteries placed on the Tagus might sink or burn nearly the whole of the vessels employed in the service. The English would then be reduced either to evacuate Lisbon, when the object would be gained and the lines become useless, or to march upon the marshal in order to beat him off, taking their chance of attacking him in his entrenched camp, or else to offer battle in the open field. In order, however, for the execution of this plan to be possible, it was necessary that fresh troops should come to occupy the left bank of the Tagus, and, of course, that they should arrive while the Army of Portugal was still able to live in its position at Santarem. It was for the purpose of carrying out this new plan of campaign that General Toy had been entrusted with the duty of submitting to the emperor, besides his dispatches, this scheme which I have just explained, and that Marshal Soult had been ordered to proceed to Santarem, where Masséna had already succeeded in erecting a bridge.

This last news, I mean the order given to Marshal Soult, I had learned both from General Foy and by a letter from the Prince of Neuchâtel, who, as I have said, considering that of all the troops in Spain I commanded those that were nearest to the Army of Portugal, thought it well to keep me informed of the projected operations, and sent me all the news that was then to be had of that army.[12] General Foy confided to me fully the arrangements decided upon by the emperor with regard to the operations that the army was to carry out, and these all the more deserve to be recorded that the failure to carry them out was a cause of our disasters, which would have been avoided if the emperor had only been more severe with his marshals, and had hung Soult after his treasonable conduct at Oporto.

Having lost all hope of seeing Lisbon taken by a rush, the emperor had taken his stand on Marshal Masséna's plan, that is, on the double idea, either of procuring the evacuation of that city by famine, or of continuing to hold the English army in check and push it backwards; in order, so to say, to strengthen the hands of that party in England

12. [A letter of Napoleon's to Berthier, dated February 6, 1811, given in the Appendix to vol. 3 of Napier, shows that this was done by his special order.]

which blamed the expedition. To this end he had decreed:

First, that the Army of Northern Spain, under the Duke of Istria, the district of which comprised all the country between France, the territories of the armies of Aragon and the Centre, Portugal, and the sea, and contained the 3rd, 4th, 5th, 6th, and 7th governments, should if necessary assist the Army of Portugal, and act as reserve to it:

Secondly, that the 9th Corps should continue to hold the line behind that army, so as to combine with it and back it up:

Thirdly, that his Catholic Majesty should employ part of the Army of the Centre in maintaining the communications between Madrid and the Army of Portugal, by way of Alcantara:

Fourthly, that after the capture of Tortosa, he should send fresh reinforcements to the Army of Portugal:

Fifthly, that in the meantime Marshal Soult with the 5th Corps should proceed as far down the river as Santarem, in order that Masséna might be free to operate with two of his army corps on one bank of the Tagus, and with three on the other. In this way Lisbon would no longer be able to draw provisions from the Alemtejo, and our army would be fed from the resources of that province, the granary of Portugal.

In discussing this subject with me General Foy said:

> You see the emperor's intention is that before all things we should hold on to Santarem, construct *têtes-de-pont* on both sides of the Tagus, continue to harass the enemy, and, in order to maintain that line of action, live on resources from the left bank of the Tagus, thus incidentally depriving Lisbon of them. Meanwhile, in the event of being forced to quit Santarem, we should establish ourselves on the Mondego; every position which would be effective to hold the English army in check being suited to his wish and to the interests of his policy. But, if we do quit Santarem all is lost, seeing that it is impossible to subsist the army behind the Mondego, and I could not succeed in convincing the emperor of that.

"So much the worse," said I; "and further, if Marshal Soult's co-operation is necessary to enable Marshal Masséna to remain at Santarem, you may reckon on an early retreat." Of this he seemed no less convinced than I. "But," I resumed, "you have just left the emperor. Even though it be only semi-official, a letter from you in such circumstances cannot fail to have something official about it; and if I were in your place, in order to have a clear conscience I would write to Marshal Soult, inserting one of the emperor's own phrases, which you remember with such extraordinary accuracy." [13]

He adopted the idea; but as he was just about starting when our conversation took place, he promised to write the letter on reaching Ciudad Rodrigo, and sent it to me open in order that I might acquaint myself with it and copy it out before forwarding it. In point of fact I received it on January 25, and sent it on by the same day's messenger, but, as the copy which my *aide-de-camp* made of it shows, it lacked vigour, and I told General Foy as much. Accordingly, being pressed by a dispatch from Masséna which reached him at Almeida, and pushed on by my remarks and my urgency, he wrote a second letter to Marshal Soult, dated the 27th. This was worth a good deal more, although it pitched its requirements in a lower key, no doubt from a fear of seeing none of them complied with. This letter, the dispatch of which I hastened as much as I could, bore with it but a very feeble hope on our part; for if we had our doubts as to the efficient co-operation of Northern and Central Spain, we felt sure from our knowledge of Marshal Soult's character, of his jealousy and rancour, that he would manage to slip out. What he did, I may add, was as follows.

He was at Seville when he received the order to proceed into Portugal. On receiving it he did in point of fact leave Seville without delay, but he left two battalions there, a faulty arrangement, seeing that nothing more certainly paralyses a movement or more certainly leads to great losses than the division of troops into small parcels, and, moreover, these two battalions had nothing to guard at Seville other than the National Guard of that town. Having brought about this first split, he went to attack Olivenza, which surrendered after nine days' siege, but this necessitated a second split; that is to say, a second garrison. Having taken Olivenza he marched on Badajoz, and began a fresh siege, during which he fought on the banks of the Gevora one of those battles the result of which against Spaniards can be neither doubtful nor glorious, except indeed in a case like that of Kellermann, near Alba de Tormes, when, with two regiments of dragoons, he beat the entire army of the Duke of Parque.

---

13. General Foy once said to me: "I never forget anything, and I have so much memory left that I would, with a certainty of whining, back myself to write down, without stopping, every place where I slept during my twenty years' service." All his great speeches in the Chamber were delivered by heart, and he knew them much better when he had dictated them than when he had written them himself.

As for the siege of Badajoz, it lasted fifty-four days, ending only on March 11; that is to say, forty-three days after the date of General Toy's second letter, and five days after famine had compelled Masséna to commence his retreat. From these figures it may be calculated that if he had marched as he ought on Santarem without these fancy stoppages, he would have been fifty days sooner in co-operation with Marshal Masséna; and if he had co-operated entirely with him, I mean by coming up with his whole force, the Army of Portugal would have been saved. But having, as we have seen, left two battalions at Seville and a garrison at Olivenza, having lost I do not know how many men at the Gevora,[14] being obliged to place a garrison in Badajoz, and detach others to escort his prisoners, he would only have joined the marshal with fragments of his army.

One may further rely upon it that, if after the capture of Badajoz the Army of Portugal had still held its ground at Santarem, he would have discovered fresh sieges to undertake, fresh battles to fight, fresh occasions for detaching troops—in short, fresh opportunities for wasting time and for leaving men on his route. But will it be maintained, according to the rules of ancient warfare, that before advancing it was necessary to secure his rear? There was no reason for this with the Spaniards, no justification for it in a war in which one's rear could never be secure, no object in it when he was on his way to join a powerful army. I ask again, Did the question of the Peninsula lie at Seville, at Badajoz, at the Gevora, or even at Olivenza? It lay at Lisbon, and in the defeat of the principal English Army and its expulsion as a consequence.

This would be rendered certain by the immediate junction of the 5th Corps, and *à fortiori* by that of the two army corps under Marshal Soult, and it would have brought about the pacification of Spain and of Portugal; the insurrection of which countries, at Cadiz and in the west alike, was ultimately sustained by the English troops alone. In this decisive situation, therefore, Marshal Soult showed himself as much to blame as at Oporto he had shown himself incompetent, and one may say of him that he betrayed all those who trusted in him. This is the man in regard to whom Madame d'Abrantès was so far deceived as to uphold his cause against Marshal Masséna.

To go back to Masséna. The return of General Foy, so far from diminishing his perplexities, had added to them. His plans came back to him, their adoption confirmed by the emperor's order; but the more

---

14. [Nearly 2,000, says Napier, in the two sieges and in the battle.]

essential it was that they should be carried out by Marshal Soult, the more he feared they would not be. Nor, indeed, was it long before he was certain; and in order to leave no doubt, the guns at Badajoz, which could be heard from Punhete, completed the revelation of the shameless way in which the main operation was being sacrificed to subsidiary undertakings.[15]

Meanwhile he was getting near the end of his resources. Little remained but a reserve of biscuit, prepared for the sustenance of the army in the event of its having to be led back to Spain through devastated provinces. The rations had been cut down some time ago; everything that could be swept up within four or five days' march was eaten. In this state of affairs they had reached February 18. On that day General Loison gave a final breakfast to the commander-in-chief, the commanders of the three army corps, General Solignac, and General Foy. Masséna took advantage of this meeting to ascertain the opinion of the generals as to the best thing to do, if it became impossible to remain at Santarem; it was, in fact, a kind of council of war, held without having recourse too obviously to that sign of distress. It appeared that there were two courses open: one was to march on the Mondego, and this was in conformity with the letter of the orders received; the other was to throw themselves into the Alemtejo, where the army could live and prolong the war in Portugal, and this seemed to agree better with the emperor's intention, seeing that without provisions they could only reach the Mondego to leave it at once and return to Spain.

However, the former movement would cover Spain, while that on the Alemtejo would leave Spain wholly uncovered, and leave Lord Wellington free to march as far as Salamanca, and get possession of the whole of Spanish Estremadura. Thus it was on these two courses that the discussion took place, as it were, casually. The majority were of opinion that they ought to hold out to the last extremity, reducing the rations still further, and if necessary drawing on the reserve of biscuit, so as to wait for Soult as long as possible, and also to await a final decision for which they had referred to the emperor on January 20, and which it was calculated might be expected about May 1. The marshal agreed so far as concerned further waiting, but rejected the suggestion as to the reserve of biscuit, the last resource which might save him from the most frightful consequences—perhaps even from the loss of half of his army.

---

15. [Napier quotes General Pelet as taking practically a similar view of Soult's proceedings.]

The agony was therefore prolonged, by unheard-of efforts, for another seventeen days. Then all was over; the last word was said. The guns of Badajoz continued to roar, and it was necessary to submit to evacuating Portugal. Thanks to Masséna's foresight, all was ready for that step. But Lord Wellington, too, was ready to follow, seeing that he knew our situation as well as we did ourselves. It had, indeed, become inconceivable to him how a situation could be prolonged which his army could not have endured for a week, and which our men had been bearing for 141 days.

I am not writing the history of that campaign in Portugal; but having been in a position to know the principal events of it, I have not hesitated to record them in these reminiscences, the more so since they rectify numerous errors, and brand sundry discreditable calumnies. Secondary matters have had to be omitted, and I need merely call to mind the series of reconnoissances and combats connected with Masséna's march from Almeida to Santarem, the long halt which he made there and the learned and ably calculated dispositions, thanks to which he was always in a position, in spite of the enemy's superiority, to check any enterprise of Lord Wellington's over so large a field.

I confine myself similarly to mentioning his retreat from Santarem to Rodrigo, the ability with which he made use of the precepts of the art of war, turned to account the resources of his genius, and drew profit alike from his own daring, the might of his name, and the prudence—one might say the timidity—of his adversary. Wellington limited his audacity and eminent genius to the business of taking advantage of our misfortunes and mistakes; and he gratuitously threw away three-fourths of the advantage secured to him by his superior forces and by the good fortune of never having to wait for a piece of useful information.

The retreat of the Army of Portugal gave occasion for only one noteworthy action; and this took place at Sabugal on April 3. It might have been avoided if General Reynier had had faith in Masséna's foresight; but in the conviction [16] that he had in front of him only a fraction of the Anglo-Portuguese army, he let himself be brought to an engagement with nearly the whole army, and unluckily was not aware of it till about 11 a.m., when the fog cleared off and he found himself outflanked and attacked in front by forces which he could not resist.

---

16. [He was perfectly correct, as a matter of fact. Nothing like the whole Anglo-Portuguese army was ever engaged, and at first Reynier had to deal with one battalion and four rifle companies.]

Unluckily, too, the 2nd Light Infantry and the 36th of the Line, having won a momentary advantage, gave way to their impetuosity and lost more than they ought to have done. Thanks to the return of General Reynier's coolness, a vigorous resistance and clever manoeuvre saved his corps, and it was able to effect a retreat in the most imposing style, with a loss of only 250 killed and wounded, while the enemy, though remaining in possession of the field of battle, lost far more heavily in Erskine's and Picton's divisions.[17]

Almeida being victualled for six weeks, Marshal Masséna decided to give his army a much-needed rest. Leaving the left bank of the Agueda to the enemy, he distributed his corps as follows: the light cavalry at Alba de Yeltes, the 9th Corps at San Muños, the 2nd at Ledesma, the 8th at Toro (which took the Duchess of Abrantès away from Salamanca), the 6th at Alba de Tormes and Salamanca, at which place the general headquarters were fixed, and the heavy cavalry between the Tormes and the Douro. The 9th Corps went to the Army of the South, under Marshal Soult. It was madness to go on employing that marshal, who served only for his own hand; but the latter years of the Empire offer the most amazing mixture of genius and insanity.

---

17. [The total loss of the allies was 200 killed and wounded. Napier puts that of the French at 300 and 1200 respectively: probably too high. Picton's division was hardly in action at all: so its loss cannot have been great.]

Chapter 16

On the March Again

From the moment of the arrival of the Army of Portugal within my government, my position became difficult in the extreme. I had had a presentiment of this, and had confided it to the Duke of Istria, to whom I had written:

> The return of the army makes all administration impossible. Requirements will be out of all proportion to resources; waste and disorder of every kind will go on, and all efforts will be powerless. Do you wish to remain responsible for such a dismal state of things? or do you not think that it would be more seemly to abandon the seventh government to the Army of Portugal?

The duke adopted this idea at once, and wrote to Masséna; but Masséna was not the man to be led off on a false scent. He replied:

"The Army of Portugal is not a territorial army. Its business is to face the English Army, and fight it wherever met with. It has retreated to Salamanca in order to save Rodrigo, and if possible, Almeida, and to cover the Army of Northern Spain itself; and therefore it ought to be fed by the Army of the North, since Spanish Estremadura is part of that army's territory."

All this was sufficiently well-grounded to be unanswerable, and we had to submit; I to keep things as regular as still was possible, and the Duke of Istria to send convoys of money and provisions, for which I at once formed a committee of management. If my position became painful, I owe to the Duke of Istria my compliments for doing all that he could to lighten my burden. Whatever I did, suggested, or asked, was sanctioned, confirmed, and adopted; and when I insisted on having my responsibility for the smallest details covered, I received a letter in these terms:

> I approve all that you have done, are doing, or are going to do.
> (Signed) The Marshal Duke of Istria.

The first sitting of our committee was marked by a scandal. General Lamothe had collected forty or fifty cattle, and dared to ask that they should be bought of him for the consumption of the army. "During the campaign," he said, "I was much out of pocket for my spies, and I want the value of these cattle to recoup me to some extent. As the Army of the North has now to feed the Army of Portugal, it has got to buy my herd."

We were very angry, and I ordered the beasts to be at once sent back to their owners; but before anyone arrived to take them, the general had sold three-fourths of them cheap to some peasants.

One morning, when I went to pay my respects to Marshal Masséna, I found him with the wife of a captain of dragoons, who had become his mistress, and who had been with him all through the campaign. I had heard of this folly and regretted it, since it had the worst possible effect in the army;[1] besides, the marshal was really old enough to be able to dispense with this kind of camp furniture. My interest in him and his reputation made this person's presence painful to me, and it was awkwardly enough that I allowed myself to be presented to the fair dame, who was in truth nothing much to look at. "I say, Thiébault," he said, after a few words had passed, "when are you going to give us a dinner?"

"Why, sir, whenever you like," was my answer to this unexpected question.

"All right; the day after tomorrow."

"And whom may I ask to meet you?"

And he filled up five-and-twenty places. The lady had the place of honour. Could I have acted otherwise towards the marshal, considering gratitude and old memories?

However, I was glad to be in a position which gave me an opportunity of again showing him respect, though unluckily it gave rise to a dispute which caused me real unhappiness, inevitable as it was. One day, when I had just received from the Duke of Istria 300,000 *francs* for the insatiable demands of Masséna's army, the marshal sent for me and said, "My dear general, here is a statement of 80,000 *francs* arrears of pay due to me. Kindly have them paid to me out of the fund that you

---
1. [See General Marbot's *Mémoires*, vol. ii., chap. 33, for some details as to this.]

have just received. On this occasion I reckon upon your old friendship." The perspiration stood on my forehead.

"Prince," I replied, "this fund is destined for a special purpose; it belongs to the subsistence of your army."

"It belongs to its wants," he returned, with an air of surprise and impatience; "and what is owed to me forms part of its wants."

"If you had taken over the command of these provinces, it would have been for you to judge of these distinctions, and no one would have been more forward or more happy than I to carry out your orders in this as in all other things. But you chose that they should remain under the Duke of Istria, and he is now the sole arbiter."

"I undertake to get it confirmed, and what you do will be right."

"I am distressed beyond words, but what I ought not to do will not be done by me."

"And it is you, Thiébault—you that refuse to pay me this?"

"Each "you" went through me like a knife. It broke my heart to have to refuse anything to that great soldier who had so many claims to my reverence, whose least words had been such absolute orders to me, whom I loved as much as I respected him; never did my conscience exact a more painful sacrifice. I may add that, owing to the way in which the marshal at last raised his voice, it was heard by persons in the adjoining rooms, and the scene became public property. The paymaster who had charge of the 300,000 *francs* was told of it, and an expression which I had actually used to the marshal was repeated to him:

> Pray, sir, instead of asking me for what is impossible, send your secretary with a few grenadiers to the paymaster, and bid him exchange your statement, duly receipted, against the 80,000 *francs* due to you.

And this paymaster, Jullien by name, who has now retired to Blois, and himself reminded me of the incident a few months ago, was seized with such a panic at the idea of the adoption of this means, which could not compromise him in any way, and which the marshal did not adopt, that he left Salamanca at once and fled to Valladolid.

Meanwhile the time which the marshal had thought it right to devote to resting his army had expired. It became necessary to think about the provisioning of Almeida, and to endeavour to throw back the Anglo-Portuguese army into the rocks of Portugal. Accordingly, and in pursuance of the emperor's orders, he called upon the Duke of

Istria for the co-operation of 1500 cavalry, fifteen to eighteen guns, and a division of infantry as reserve, the whole to be drawn from the Army of the North; then he broke up his cantonments and proceeded in person to Ciudad Rodrigo. Two days after his departure, the Duke of Istria turned up at Salamanca about eleven in the evening.

He was perishing with hunger, and I ordered supper for him; and as he was tired, he let me put him up. "You see, my dear Thiébault," he said, "I am come in person and of my own proper motion to fight under the orders of the senior and the most renowned man of my rank."

"The example, sir," I said, "is worthy of you, and after such dismal precedents as we have had you could not better serve the emperor than by setting it."

"And for that reason I am come, like a French cavalier, at the head of a handful of heroes."

At these words I looked at him; it did not need his accent to remind me of his origin, and I feared to detect some second thought concealed behind his chivalrous *gasconade*. Next moment he betrayed it by saying that to collect the infantry division of which Masséna had spoken would have taken too much time.

Arriving thus, as a marshal in command of 1500 cavalry and six guns, he hoped by this bit of bounce to put me off the scent of his settled intention not to lend the division which he had promised. Now for an operation which was to last a week, if an important action was foreseen in the course of it, a solitary marshal, even with his plume, could hardly be regarded as equivalent to a division; and when it was a question of stopping the English Army from following us, or to roll them back in a decisive battle, what could be more obvious than to set the division of Séras in march, and even reinforce it with 1500 of the Guard from Valladolid and 1,000 men from my government? But so simple a conception did not fit in with the rival ambitions of the marshals. These marshals, even when the emperor in creating them had lowered the value of his own creations by the commonplace selections he made, gave him at first nothing but satisfaction, so long as he required only fine names, fine titles, fine clothes, and fine fortunes.

His court was brilliant, and sixteen marshals' batons might well seem a subject for pride in it; but when he wanted men, he found himself less well provided, and able men like Masséna and Lannes, who deserved their promotion, had been insulted by association with unworthy colleagues; those who would have deserved it no less and had not obtained it were furious, and those who obtained it without deserving it were drunk with pride, and thus became even less worthy than before.

In every way the emperor had succeeded only in making malcontents, and in giving rise to the jealousies, hatreds, and conflicting ambitions which ended in such treasons in the service, in such derelictions as those of which the wars in Portugal and Spain furnished examples. This explains the conduct of the Duke of Istria towards Masséna. In spite of all his good personal qualities, he was no more able than others far less well-disposed than himself to make up his mind to aid the military success of a chief who, though equal to him in rank, was his superior in merit.

To return to the *gasconade* under which he masked with some effrontery his refusal to co-operate effectively, no sooner had I heard it than I saw that a refusal of this kind would jeopard the last warlike operation which the Army of Portugal was to attempt against the English army. I had at first congratulated the Duke of Istria on the generous way he had come to put himself under Masséna's orders; but when I learnt the nature of the betrayal concealed under this apparent generosity, I could but hold my tongue. Perhaps my silence may have seemed too significant; but I was unable to get out a word.

Anyhow, the trifling reinforcement so pompously heralded was not to arrive till the next day. The duke passed that day at Salamanca, and, wishing to take advantage of his presence to get something out of him in the interests of my government, I presented to him the officers of the garrison and the head of the administrative department; also the Spanish authorities, ending up with the rector and dean of the university. When these last appeared, I took occasion to speak of the ancient glories of the university of Salamanca; the disastrous effect that the war had had upon it, and the fame which would await anyone who could succeed in restoring it to its former position, and bring its statutes into harmony with modern requirements, pointing out that no one was in so good a position to do it as himself.

The Duke of Istria was pleased by the suggestion, and after addressing some complimentary words to the authorities, and praising this new proof of my zeal, he asked what he could do. "Why," I said, "you can order me to hand you on your return from Rodrigo a general memorandum on the subject, and allow these gentlemen to hope that you will consider it."

"Certainly," he said; "I promise them to do what is in my power, and you as well as they may rely on my word!"

My object in the proposal was of course to produce a moral effect on the inhabitants, and to win partisans to my side who would take an interest in the preservation of order and the maintenance of my authority; but the memorandum I had undertaken to draw up involved no small labour. As my days were wholly occupied, I had to give up my nights to it, and for the necessary information I decided to apply to the remaining members of the university. We used to meet at ten in the evening; I questioned them and noted down such information as they could supply on the spot, while they undertook to make any researches that were necessary in archives and elsewhere, and bring me written reports. In this way twelve sittings finished the work; and when the Duke of Istria returned to Salamanca, a fortnight after his departure, a statement of the present condition of the university, with a scheme for reviving it, the whole filling two hundred folio pages, was to his astonishment duly laid before him.

He was, however, presently superseded as a punishment for his conduct in the short campaign, and his place was taken by Dorsenne, from whom nothing in that line was to be expected. So the only result of my labours was the translation of my report into Spanish and its presentation in a printed form to King Joseph, his ministers, and other persons concerned. I was also granted an honorary doctor's degree, a compliment paid to no one else, save, a little later, to Lord Wellington.

Meanwhile the last operation of the Army of Portugal had been going on. Masséna had left Salamanca on April 25. On the 26th he was at Rodrigo; on April 30 he received the 6th and 8th Corps, arrived the day before, and on May 1 the 2nd and 7th. These four corps made up 35,000 men, including 1800 cavalry; [2] but they had only twenty guns. The Duke of Istria, arriving on the 2nd, brought the number present under arms to 36,600; and as he brought thirty teams for the artillery, and six guns with their teams, it was possible to increase the number of pieces by sixteen.

On the same day the marshal issued an energetic order of the day; and leaving to Clauzel's division—I forget for what reason—the duty of guarding the communications between Rodrigo and Salamanca, he crossed the Azava to give battle to an enemy occupying entrenched positions, with 30,000 English, 35,000 Portuguese, and all Don Julian's

---

2. [The 2nd, 6th, and 8th Corps contained over 37,000 under arms; and there were 7,800 cavalry, of whom Napier estimates that 4,000 were in the field.]

partida posted at Nava de Aver.[3]

The affair began by an attack on Fuentes de Oñoro on the morning of the 3rd. That village was carried, and its occupation cut the enemy's line in two; but three English divisions occupied the high ground at the back of it, and one of these charged into the village and retook it. It was again attacked by Ferey's brigade, supported by four battalions from Marchand's division, and again occupied by our troops. A desperate struggle for it was maintained throughout the day; towards night we again lost the upper part, but remained in possession of the lower village.

During the night of the 3rd, Lord Wellington, seeing the necessity of not allowing us to regain possession of the higher part of the village, filled all the houses with troops, garnishing with them the walls and the neighbouring rocks, so that the marshal judged it too costly to force the enemy at that point. He accordingly employed the day in reconnoitring the front and flanks of his positions. As a result of this, the army was by daybreak on the 5th in the position of having refused its right, without losing hold of Fuentes de Oñoro; then, having by a magnificent movement turned the enemy's right flank, it became master of the fairly accessible ground lying between Nava de Aver and Pozo Velho, and was in a position to take Wellington in flank and rear, and throw him back into the *cul-de-sac* formed by the Coa, the Agueda and the Douro.

In this situation, among the crags with which the banks of those torrents bristle, the English army would have been certainly lost, its only means of retreat being one small bridge hardly practicable for horses. The opening of the fight at Pozo Velho was worthy of the way in which the manoeuvre had been conceived. General Maucune with his brigade attacked that position, routed the English division which held it, killing 300 men, taking 250 prisoners, and entirely overthrowing it.

Soon afterwards, the English 50th[4] regiment was cut to pieces; the enemy was walked back a league, and the movement was distinguished

---

3. [This is of course an enormous exaggeration of the numbers of the allied armies. The total English force on the Coa did not amount to 24,000, and some were blockading Almeida. The entire number engaged, including Bon Julian, was estimated by Napier at about 35,000. The Duke of Wellington, however, puts his total force, inclusive of those forming or protecting the blockade, at under 30,000.]

4. [Marbot says the 51st; but neither of these regiments appears to have been present. No regiment lost so severely as the language employed by both writers would imply.]

by some fine cavalry charges. General Fournier, among others, drove in the lines and broke the squares; supported by Watier's brigade, he overthrew all that came in his way. In the middle of one of these scuffles an English general [5] had already surrendered, and his whole regiment had been taken, when by bad luck General Founder's horse was killed, and this disaster was at the same moment accompanied by another. General Montbrun had surrounded three English squares, and they would have been captured if General Mermet's division had, as it should have done, followed up the movement; but for want of this co-operation they escaped.

However, these little disappointments need only have caused a few moments' delay; the inequality of forces [6] seemed to have disappeared in face of the marshal's compensating ability, and the Anglo-Portuguese army was on the brink of a frightful disaster. But it has to be said, painful and humiliating as the remembrance may be, that when victory was secure and all that remained was to finish defeating the enemy, when the men, elated in the highest degree by the ability of the dispositions and the result of their brilliant charges, asked for nothing more than to come to close quarters, and were panting to emulate each other in working wonders, French generals refused to fight.

As a result of that incredible disobedience, which Masséna had no longer the energy required to punish by blowing out the brains of one of the generals who were defying his authority—as a result, too, of that unwearied good luck which has made the Duke of Wellington a hero, and in the eyes of a few silly people a great man[7]—our troops stood still with success before them and recoiled from victory; just at the moment, too, when General Ferey was recapturing the upper part of Fuentes de Oñoro, which, owing to the inaction of the rest of the army, he had to abandon afresh.

As we had failed to profit by the movement which had brought us in rear of the enemy's right wing, he had recovered all the advantage of his superiority in numbers, and of his position, favourable almost everywhere to the defence. His whole army was once more rallied and united; one night was enough to make all the assailable points of his line bristle anew with entrenchments, and no further attempt was

---

5. [Colonel Hill of the Guards. "*Tout son corps*" must be taken to mean fourteen men, the number captured with him.]
6. ["The enemy never had such a superiority of numbers opposed to the British troops as in this action." Duke of Wellington.]
7. ["*Wellington n'éblouissait personne, mais il nous battait.*" Lanfrey.]

possible. The marshal had, however, two reasons for remaining in presence of the enemy—the one to show that he held possession of the field of battle, the other to carry out the emperor's orders in regard to Almeida; namely, to blow up the defences, spike the guns, and destroy everything which might be of use to the enemy from a military point of view. In order to ensure the execution of this he had to hold his ground, and to that end have the means of meeting any attack on the part of the enemy. Having only five cartridges per man still left, he decided to send General Lamothe to Rodrigo for ammunition, which in point of fact arrived that evening. As for Almeida, the marshal sent orders directly by letter to General Brenier, who commanded that fortress, adding:

> Give me notice that you have received this letter by firing at ten o'clock tomorrow evening in the direction of our position, four salvos from twenty-five of your heaviest guns, at intervals of five minutes. Having executed your orders, withdraw by Barba de Puerco.

To write the letter was easy enough, to get it delivered was less so. The promise of 6,000 *francs* to the man who would manage to do so, produced three volunteers. All three were accepted; three copies of the dispatch were made, each on a piece of paper two inches by one; lastly, the bearers were told to swallow them if they could not get them through, and, if captured, to pass themselves off as deserters. The three men set out at eight in the evening; only one got in, a man named André Tillet of the 6th Light Infantry. At ten in the evening of the 7th the four salvos were fired. In the course of that night, after worrying the enemy with constant reconnoissancee, the marshal left Pozo Velho, and brought all his force back in front of Fuentes de Oñoro, making Lord Wellington believe that the attack was to be renewed upon his centre or left flank, and forcing him to keep his troops under arms all day.

On the 9th the marshal maintained his position, continuing to harass the enemy, who did not venture to leave the rocks or his entrenchments, with fresh reconnoissances; and by the morning of the 10th he was in full retreat, followed by the enemy, whom by this movement he drew away from Almeida.[8] The garrison of that town was therefore

---

8 [This seems to be quite incorrect. The English were at least unconscious of the operations supposed to be giving them annoyance, and Wellington did not pursue Masséna. The escape of the Almeida garrison was due to a blunder.]

likely to be saved, and, in fact, he had the satisfaction of hearing at midnight a muffled and prolonged report, announcing that the fortifications were destroyed. Soon he learnt that General Brenier and his garrison had succeeded in joining the 2nd Corps before daylight. In this way the only orders which the emperor had given to the marshal had been carried out.

On the 11th Masséna heard that Marshal Marmont, who had arrived on the 7th under colour of replacing Ney at the head of the 6th Corps, was really come to take over from him the command of the Army of Portugal. He handed it over to him at once, and departed for Paris the same day.

This was Masséna's last feat of arms in his last campaign. Now was he, during that expedition, below his level? Some people have felt able to say so; no one has proved it. And in point of fact, from the beginning of the campaign, he was constantly disserved: first by the emperor, who only gave him half the troops required for success, and, to assist him, men who knew nothing of subordination, while making him delay four months in an expedition which ought to have been rushed through; secondly, by those who had to guide him, and who, headed by the Marquis of Alorna, led him all astray at Busaco; then, as has been explained, by Marshal Soult; lastly by his generals, above all by Reynier, one of the most able men whom we had left, but who at Sabugal took no notice of his warning and previsions, and at Pozo Velho forgot his own past and his position as a French general, and never fired a shot. Yet those very actions of Fuentes de Oñoro and Pozo Velho, which recall the desertion of his generals, recall also the daring with which, in spite of his age and infirmities, Masséna assailed a greatly superior force, and the genius which was able to conceive and carry out a manoeuvre calculated to neutralise the advantages of position and numbers, and snatch victory out of Wellington's hands, destroy the English army, and restore Portugal to us.

Masséna then showed himself in Portugal a chief no less clever and daring than in old days. The facts are there to prove it, and all that we can justly say is, that while morally equal to himself and worthy of his past, he was physically much enfeebled; and that in order to maintain his flashes of genius he perhaps lacked that elevation of his powers those supreme spurts of energy, which at times succeeded in forcing destiny itself to change in spite of the treachery of men and circumstances.

However, when Masséna was gone, the Duke of Istria returned

with his escort to Valladolid, where to my misfortune and that of the army, he was, as I have said, replaced by General Dorsenne. Marshal Marmont, who replaced Masséna, took up his position at Plasencia with the three corps of the Army of Portugal, in observation of the Anglo-Portuguese army. The Duke of Abrantès and Generals Loison and Solignac returned with others to France; I remained at Salamanca, at once as governor and as commander of the advance-guard of the Army of the North, while the Count of Erlon, with his corps reduced to six regiments, crossed the Tagus, and in conjunction with the 5th Corps helped to raise the siege of Badajoz, which Marshal Beresford was investing with 15,000 Portuguese and I know not how many Spaniards.

The course of the to-and-fro movements connected with Masséna's latest operation had brought the Duke of Abrantès with his army corps to Salamanca. As soon as I heard of it I had written to offer him board and lodging with me, which he accepted both coming and going. As he was leaving me, he said, "I say, are not you a count?"

"Nothing in the way of favours," said I, laughing, "falls to my account."

"What, have you neither title nor endowment?"

"Neither one nor the other."

"That is absurd; it can only be due to forgetfulness. However, I shall not forget."

Three weeks afterwards I received from the arch-chancellor the announcement of my nomination as baron, which I found more absurd than forgetfulness itself. My first idea was not to accept a title which carried no endowment, but I was told so often that I was going to create a fresh cause for complaint by advertising my contempt for a title which emanated from the emperor, and I was so much lectured on the subject, that I accepted it, though without thanking anyone or even acknowledging the letter announcing it. Nor, though it would only have cost me 300 *francs*, did I apply for the usual patent, or take any further steps in the matter till 1830. Then a decision was given to the effect that whoever had not taken out his patent of nobility at the end of six months would forfeit his rank; and as there was a good deal of difference between not caring for the title and being officially declared to have forfeited it, I went through the business, though the fees in similar cases had by that time risen to 500 *francs*.

Thanks to my neglect, the Revolution of July took place before the patent was made out, and in order to get it it was necessary to take the oath of allegiance to Louis Philippe. This I have not done up to the day when I write these words, July 2, 1836, so that I have no more patent than if I had not paid the expenses.

The Army of Portugal having taken position in front of Plasencia in order to cover Madrid and operate on the flank or rear of the Anglo-Portuguese army if that should cross the Agueda, and the cavalry of the Army of the North having returned to Valladolid, a period of repose and expectation seemed to be opening, and I found nothing to think about except the needs of my troops and the observation of the enemy. Having my time free, I made an effort to smooth over the traces of all these disorders, confiscations, and devastations, to restore some balance between requirements and resources, lastly to comfort the inhabitants by showing some marks of interest in their condition.

Under the first head the difficulties had greatly increased. In point of fact, Lord Wellington's army being collected between the Agueda and the Tagus, did not allow of my drawing anything from that part of Estremadura; while Don Julian, who had established himself afresh between the Agueda and the Tormes, interfered with our smallest consignments, all the more actively because he needed to get his negotiations with me forgotten. He was overlooked and kept up to the mark by the Marquis of España, whom the Cadiz Junta, not thoroughly trusting Don Julian, and not wishing to leave him to himself, had sent with superior command into Estremadura.

Being unable to carry out plans which these difficulties rendered impossible, I started with what remained possible. I devoted myself to making tranquillity reign at Salamanca, to putting justice on the side of conciliation, and to getting all interests respected. The city was kept perfectly clean and lighted; all the houses were numbered, and the names of streets and squares put up. As I had done at Burgos, I forbade further interments in the churches; and on the strength of a measure passed to that effect by the Council of Castile in 1799, I devoted to burials a large piece of ground belonging to some monks, and to make things complete I had hearses and mourning coaches built, and brought all the management of funerals within the functions of the town council.

When I was at Salamanca in 1801, the bishop, Don Tavira, had been fruitlessly attempting to open up the view between the Episcopal palace and the cathedral; that is, to form a handsome square in place of the hideous houses and narrow, filthy street which lay before those two buildings. Ten years later, having all the authority at Salamanca in my own hands, I remembered this and resolved, mere *infidel* that I was, to carry out a project over which the Fénelon of Spain had been baffled. But in order not to be stopped in my scheme by the complaints which would certainly be raised by the members of the chapter—to whom the houses belonged—I made all my preparations with the greatest secrecy. Then I published my decree, founding it on sanitary grounds, on the wish constantly expressed by the inhabitants of Salamanca, on the authority of one of the most justly honoured prelates in Spain, and so forth. I gave the canons, or their lessees, five days to clear out of the twenty or thirty houses to be pulled down, and ordered that a valuation of the property should be made within two days, that it might be entered on the public debt.

No sooner was my edict published than a deputation of the most prominent members of the chapter came to me demanding that it should be recalled or postponed. I received this demand as I generally received such, and they decided to appeal to Madrid; but they had to send a special messenger, and they had only three and a half days left—a time in which I knew that it was impossible for the matter to be considered in council and an answer to be brought back. By the third day an official valuation had been made, the canons refusing to be parties to it; and four days after publication of the notice, the demolition began, at 4 a.m., under the superintendence of an engineer officer; two local masons and six soldiers working at every house. Some of the canons who lived in the houses declined to stir; but foreseeing this, I had put on a double number of hands to their houses, and it may be guessed that they cleared out with some promptitude.

It was as well that I made haste, for two days later an order came from Madrid to suspend the proceedings, but by that time there was nothing more to do but to clear up the rubbish. Opposition ceased when there was no more interest in keeping it up, and I ended by getting the sanction of Madrid, just as, except for a few canons, I had the applause of Salamanca. No sooner was the square marked out than it received my name, and an order of the town council confirmed what the public voice had demanded.[9] The! order was formally presented to me, and, having thus become the godfather of the square, I was naturally led to beautify it.

One evening, as I was walking outside the Valladolid gate with Vega, the excellent chief commissioner of police, discussing some matter of

---

9. [It is now the Plaza del Collegio Viejo.]

public utility, the prolonged tinkle of a little bell diverted my attention. The commissioner told me that it was the distress-bell of a little convent, inhabited by Trappist nuns vowed to perpetual seclusion and isolation. They lived only on provisions bestowed by the charitable, and sometimes they got forgotten. When their hunger became too acute, they rang the bell that we heard. It may have been going on for an hour, and I walked quickly towards the convent, Vega following me. He rang; the wicket was opened and he announced the governor, adding, "Open, by his orders." Hasty steps told us that the one who had first spoken to us was rapidly retreating; a few minutes of perfect silence followed. Then a fresh voice questioned us again, and received the same answer.

At the words, "But who are *you?*" the commissioner declared himself; the door creaked on its hinges and opened. I passed the threshold beyond which eternity commences, pain forms the whole of existence, and death the sole remedy, and, crossing a sort of little lobby, followed a low narrow passage black with age, which received its light only from a cloister used as cemetery, overgrown with brambles, save where places had been cleared for recent graves, and surrounded by cells, very coffins, dark and stifling. From one side of this cloister opened a little church with no ornament but an altar of worm-eaten wood, in the centre of which a lamp, throwing out a flickering flame, seemed to be lighting up the way to annihilation.

Finally I found myself in presence of ten or a dozen women, or rather spectres. Shod in sandals, without stockings or linen, clad in rags of black serge, with veils of the same material falling to the waist, these poor creatures seemed of no age and of no human shape. Their sepulchral voices, weak from want of food, their look of annihilation and misery, their forms still living and vegetating on the brink of the graves which themselves had dug. That place, where every complaint is a scandal, every regret a blasphemy, every sigh a crime, filled me with indescribable sadness.

However, having saluted the poor things respectfully, I said in Spanish to one who was a few paces in front of the others, "It is the desire, sister, to render you more speedy help that brings me into your presence." She merely bowed, and I exclaimed, "Tell me at what moment you will require food?"

"None of us has eaten since yesterday," she replied; and informed me that their nutriment was limited to bread, dried fish, vegetables, and oil. I sent Vega off at once to fetch on the back of a porter what was wanted to meet such urgent wants; and I announced that I should not leave the convent till the provisions came.

While waiting I got full information about all that concerned the dwellers in the place; their terrible rule, their numbers, how much stuff was required to clothe them fully, their daily consumption of food, their other wants, including those of their chapel. When the provisions came, and I took my leave, I promised not to forget them, requesting them not to forget me in their prayers. Having thus become the objects of my special care, they not only had bread, fish, and fresh vegetables brought to them every morning, but were provisioned with dried fish and vegetables, with salt and oil, and received any quantity of black serge to repair or renew their dismal garments. Just before I left Salamanca, I sent them a double allowance of provisions and commended them to the care of the prefect.

After these administrative reminiscences, as I may call them, I note some facts as to the relations of my government with the army. They have no great historical value, but the reader may take them for what they are worth. General Reynaud had lately become governor of Ciudad Rodrigo, in succession to one Cacault; and having some important requests to make of me in respect of the needs of the place, it occurred to him to send his *aide-de-camp*, Chambure, with the letter, in order to get things more properly and thoroughly done.

In my case this means was superfluous. I was sorry that General Reynaud had adopted it without my authority, and I evinced some fear as to Chambure's safe return. He begged me to have no anxiety on that point, for with the 400 men of his escort he would back himself to face all Don Julian's forces. I knew his valour, but that was not enough to reassure me. A thousand infantry and 200 cavalry were therefore ordered out to support Chambure as far as Matilla; but as they could go no further, I ordered him to fall back with them if he heard that Don Julian had collected his bands. Before his departure could give rise to rumour, he left Salamanca one evening at eleven, reaching Matilla next morning at daybreak. There his force rested for two hours.

After passing the village, some of Don Julian's horsemen showed themselves a long way off, and soon disappeared. Another five miles was covered in perfect tranquillity; but having gone that distance, Chambure's advance-guard found itself attacked by two columns of a thousand men each; and the fire becoming very lively, he deemed that an immediate retreat on Salamanca was indispensable. He began to retire in perfect order, but his retreat was already cut off by two columns similar to those in front, and all Don Julian's cavalry.

Thus he was enveloped by forces ten times greater than his own, and any other than he would have been done for. But while a quarter of his people checked with a brisk fire the advance of the two columns that had barred the road, he himself, at the head of the remaining 300, charged all those in his rear, overthrowing all whom he could get at. He did wonders, killing and wounding three times as many of Don Julian's people as he lost of his own; but he was reduced to 200 men and himself severely wounded in both arms, most severely in the left. By this time the 1200 men who had supported him, and who had orders not to leave Matilla for three hours after his departure from it, marching on the sound of his fire, saved him with the remnants of his column and returned with him to Salamanca. On hearing of his disaster and his arrival, I went to see him, expecting of course to find him in very low spirits.

He was in despair, and, say what I would, I could not get him out of the notion that this unlucky encounter had broken his career and ruined his future. I had to report the affair to the Prince of Neuchâtel, and so pained was I by Chambure's condition that it inspired me, in composing my dispatch, to finish by requesting the Cross of the Legion of Honour for him. I based my request on his honourable antecedents, on conduct which partook of heroism, and upon his state of despair, which indicated that the life of this brave officer depended on the granting of the favour. I did not, however, disguise from myself how little could be hoped for from such a request, for the emperor's way, as is usual with conquerors, was justifiable enough indeed, both in itself and on the score of example, to reward successes and punish reverses. It was, therefore, with no less joy than surprise that I received by return of messenger poor Chambure's nomination as member of the Legion and the cross bestowed on him.

At once I went to his house. Luckily, he was lodged with an excellent lady, who had three very pretty daughters, no less good than their mother. They helped to dress his wounds, and looked after him as if he had been their son and brother. Thus, before going to his room, I always used to look in upon the ladies to learn how he was. That day I was struck by their sadness, and, in point of fact, they said that his depression was becoming extreme, and that the doctor and surgeon, who had just left him, were growing uneasy. "*Señorita,*" said I to the eldest of the young ladies, "will you help to save his life?" She seemed eager to do so, and I continued: "Take this cross and ribbon and conceal them in your hand. Then go casually into his room, and, under the pretext of seeing something to be put to rights in his bandage, get near him, fasten the ribbon to his shirt without his noticing it, and leave his room immediately." She fulfilled her task admirably.

As for Chambure, owing to his dejection he at first noticed nothing, and it was not till he was alone that he caught sight of something red on his shirt. Being unable to use his arms, he called. At that moment I appeared, followed by his hostesses. With a smile, I said, "Well, what is the matter with you? What can you want more, when you have received the prize of your devoted service, and it has reached you, too, by the hands of a charming young lady?"

"Add—when I owe it to you," he replied, in an excited tone. Indeed, he was beside himself; it was a real crisis, which restored his tone and saved him. All the same, he remained crippled in his left arm, but was able to continue in the service and distinguish himself. How he did at Dantzig is well known.[10] He was made colonel at the Restoration and died in 1830. I have never known a more energetic man.

Talking of Don Julian, one of my spies brought the news one day that that terrible chief was assembling his bands to surprise the garrison of Avila during the next night but one. That garrison had been furnished by the Army of Portugal, and so had nothing to do with my government; but it consisted of Frenchmen, and the question was how to convert a possible success on the part of our enemies into a certain failure. This was more than enough to stimulate my care; but what was to be done? Avila was twenty-four leagues away, and I had not time to get there with my troops. Nor could I without orders abandon my position and leave Salamanca for four or five days at the mercy of Don Julian, or it might even be of an English division. Still less could I send a weak detachment. Failing any help, I must at least manage to convey information and put the *commandant* on his guard. Others might have been content to send this by a spy; but I did not like to stop short at this means, as nothing could be less depended on than the arrival of a man of whose conscientiousness, moreover, I had no firm guarantee.

In this state of uneasiness I went to the *prefect* and asked him for the names and addresses of two of the wealthiest and most determined among our enemies at Salamanca. Then I went home and wrote my dispatch to the governor of Avila. This, when rolled up, was as thick as a crow-quill. While I was writing, the richer of the two men whose

---

10. [See General Marbot's *Mémoires*, vol. iii.]

names the prefect had given me was, by my orders, brought to my house. As soon as he was shown into my study, I said, "Sir, you are one of the greatest enemies that we have at Salamanca."

"I, governor? I assure you—"

"Well, never mind the fact of it. You have the reputation of it, and that is enough for the commission I have to give you. You see this little roll. Take it. It is a letter for the governor of Avila. Within twenty hours it must be in his hands, and within forty the receipt for it in mine."

"But, governor, how is that to be done?"

"That is no affair of mine. But from this moment you are in the custody of two *gendarmes* who will not lose sight of you. If the orders are not literally carried out, I send you to General Dorsenne as a traitor; and you will understand that the least thing which can happen to you will be to be escorted into France and shut up there till the peace."

The name of Dorsenne took him aback, and not without reason. To restore his spirits I rang. The two *gendarmes* entered, and, having already received their instructions, collared him and led him home. As he was going, I assured him that it was the first and last time that I should employ such methods towards him. Thirty-eight hours later I received a reply to my letter. Don Julian's attack took place, but no one was taken by surprise, and he was beaten off with loss.

Meanwhile, Ciudad Rodrigo, which had been besieged for a month past, was getting to the end of its provisions and needed revictualling. Covered to the eastward by inaccessible rocks, it was blockaded on the north by Don Julian, on the south by the whole Anglo-Portuguese Army, to the west by an English division holding both banks of the Agueda—that is, by 50,000 troops in all. It was dependent on the Army of the North, but that could not put more than 26,000 men in movement; and, naturally, this seemed an insufficient force for an operation which involved the covering of an immense convoy. The Army of Portugal, 24,000 strong, received orders, therefore, to join the Army of the North for the operation of revictualling. It was, in fact, all the more interested in the matter from the fact that, if once the enemy became masters of Rodrigo, the position of the Army of the North on the Tormes would be rendered very precarious, while no motive for holding Plasencia, no possibility even of so doing, would be left to the Army of Portugal.

The Army of the North consequently assembled at Salamanca. It was composed, first, of Séras' former division, the first of that army of which I received the command while remaining governor of Estremadura; second, of Souham's, the second division; third and fourth, of two divisions of the Imperial Guard fifth, of a brigade of the Guard forming the reserve; sixth, of a cavalry division under General Watier; seventh, of fifty guns.

On the morrow of its arrival at Salamanca, General Dorsenne reviewed this army, small in number but in splendid condition, and in the evening he assembled at his house all the generals belonging to it. I learnt from him that my new division had a detestable fault—that of disorderly marching. "Do what General Séras would," said he, "he found it impossible, on the march, to prevent his corps from leaving half their people behind."

"That, however, is a breach of order which it is easy to prevent."

"Easy?" he rejoined, with a grin; "you'll have something more to tell me about that."

"I should be surprised if it were to be anything but good," replied I coldly, "for no troops ever marched badly under my orders."

"Besides," put in General Dumoustier, "we will help each other; and, as I do not wish your men to have the trouble for nothing, please announce to your division that I will pay one *napoleon* per head for every straggler that it brings back to me." And we agreed upon the same price for any that his division might bring back to me.

The departure of my division, marching at the head of the army, was fixed for 7 a.m., and I gave orders that it should be under arms at six. I arrived at the same moment, inspected them, and was very sharply down on the smallest matters. Then I called together all the field-officers and captains of the nine battalions composing the division, and, having said to them how much it grieved me to have to begin with finding fault, I told them of the reputation that their troops had, and announced my determination to change it from that day forward. To this end I ordered steps to be taken which I had found successful on a former occasion—for instance, that no man should leave the ranks except at the hourly halts, and then only from absolute necessity, and not without handing his musket to his right or left hand man, and without being accompanied by a corporal, who was not to lose sight of him; that colonels and majors should keep always riding to and fro from rear to front of their regiments and back again, and that nine sergeants and eighteen corporals, under a captain and a lieutenant, should follow the division and rummage all houses, coppices, and so forth, near which it passed. In order to enforce my regulations, I made a rule that any battalion from which a single man had succeeded in remaining in the rear should march for an hour in sections, while the officer commanding his company should be put under arrest.

In spite of these measures one man of the 31st succeeded in escaping the vigilance of his officers. He was arrested by my squad of non-commissioned officers, and his battalion, no less than his captain, underwent the threatened penalty. It was a good lesson. I was careful to keep my division in such order that, if a hostile corps had dropped from the sky, it would have found me all ready to fight. No division marched as well as mine, and the result was that, in the evening, I was able to ask General Dumoustier how much I owed him? I was complimented all round, and even General Dorsenne, happening to ride past me about three in the afternoon, had called out as he galloped by, "It's impossible to lead troops better, General Thiébault!"

On September 21 the Army of Portugal came into line with us on the other side of San Muños; 46,000 to 47,000 infantry, marching with 3,000 or 4,000 cavalry and eighty guns, did not leave much opening for Lord Wellington, who accordingly did not stir. Thus the revictualling of Rodrigo took place without any opposition, and was completed at nightfall on the third day after our leaving Salamanca.

After that, what more was there to do? We might either confine ourselves to the revictualling and retire at once, or else cross the Agueda during the night and fall upon the Anglo-Portuguese Army at daybreak. Neither of these courses was adopted, and we passed the night and the following day in consuming, with no advantage whatever, since we were culpably inactive, 60,000 rations of the provisions which, of all things in the world, ought to have been most carefully economised. While deploring this halt,' which its uselessness rendered absurd, and while saying to ourselves that with other commanders it would perhaps be all up both with the English Army and with Lord Wellington's unintelligible reputation, we had made up our minds to this new bad luck, and were conceiving nothing save a prompt return to our respective positions, when we received the order to cross the Agueda at daybreak the next morning, and to follow the Army of Portugal, which was to take the lead.

In spite of thirty hours' delay, under circumstances in which the loss of a single hour ought to have been made a crime, fate still offered us the possibility of a conspicuous success. The wise and prudent Wellington had not thought that we should march upon him. He had made no arrangements with this view, and, by our march on Fuenteguinaldo, two of his divisions, particularly that of Craufurd,[11] were cut off from the rest of his army and forced to throw themselves into the valleys which lay between our left and the Agueda. Out of those valleys, thanks to the rocks through which the torrent dashes itself, and which render them impracticable, there is no possible exit, and the English divisions which had got into them could only be saved by carelessness on our part. And in truth, a single reconnoissance on the left bank of the Agueda, and on our left, would leave those two divisions at our mercy.

But among us there was no less incapacity and negligence than there was pride and vanity; Lord Wellington was no less lucky than he was unskilful and improvident, and the two divisions, concealing themselves while we marched forward—the two divisions whose destruction would have disabled the Anglo-Portuguese Army from acting for some time to come, and might, perhaps, have been for us the beginning of a series of successes—emerged from their retreat during the night, passed between us and Ciudad Rodrigo,[12] and rejoined Lord Wellington unmolested.

In no condition to resist us, even if he had had all his forces united, and having no chance at all when deprived of two of his divisions, he manoeuvred with some luck through the whole of that day. He threatened our right, causing me to be sent to a point where, by the time I got there, no one was to be found. His cavalry, supported by two divisions of infantry,[13] held their ground against General Montbrun long enough to give us the impression that it was a serious engagement, but not long enough to compromise him. Thus our illustrious chiefs were so much taken up with what was passing in front of us, and on our right, that it did not even occur to them to trouble themselves with what might be taking place in rear of our left; to which fact, as I have

---

11. [The "two divisions" probably mean the 60th and 74th regiments, which got separated from the rest of the 3rd division, and had to cross the Agueda and make their way for some distance up the right bank, and Craufurd's light division, which was posted in observation beyond the Agueda, and got back to the main army later by the same route.
12. [This is hardly correct. The French army was by this time across, *i.e.* on the left bank of the Agueda. Craufurd, as has been said, made his way back by the right bank, passing behind the French, but in no sense between them and Rodrigo. Rather they had passed between him and that place.]
13. [If, as seems probable, this refers to the combat at El Bodon, the "two divisions" were the 5th and 77th regiments.]

said, two divisions owed their escape.

Owing to the false movements which that day I was caused to make in order to fight an enemy who wanted only to gain the time that he made us lose, and kept drawing us to one point only to get us away from another, I was the last to reach the position which our two armies had taken. It consisted of two hillocks, on one of which the Imperial Guard and its enormous artillery was extended in three lines, lighted up by the last rays of the sun, and offering, I may observe, a splendid picture.

In front of this position was a detached hillock, still occupied by the English troops, which certainly ought to have been taken as soon as we had come up. General Dorsenne had, however, arranged otherwise. On my return, after hearing my report on the English corps which I had driven in, he said, "You see that hillock; it is the position for the advance-guard of the two armies, and I have reserved it for your division. So you will turn out the enemy's corps, which is still there, and establish yourself on it." Night was coming on and there was no time to lose. When my first brigade came up, I marched on the hill at the head of my light infantry, and, fortunately carrying it without much trouble, I bivouacked there with my troops.

As we had thus taken the place of advance-guard, I thought that we should resume our attacking movement at daybreak, putting our time to all the better use for having already wasted a good deal of it. Accordingly, I was at the front of my lines well before daybreak; but I was wrong again. Six, seven, eight, nine struck, and I had no news of anyone. At length Marmont and Dorsenne appeared at the head of their gorgeous staffs, and my troops at once stood to their arms. Hardly, however, had these gentlemen come up than they dismounted and began to examine through their field-glasses the English camp covering Fuenteguinaldo. I had known it by heart for the last two hours, and the proper way to examine and reconnoitre it now would have been to march upon it, across the two miles that separated us from it.

However, if from a military point of view nothing could have been more unsatisfactory, there was a doleful comicality about the scene. "Yes," said the marshal, making efforts to see what was not there through a telescope supported on an *aide-de-camp's* shoulder—"yes, my information is correct; the right of the English line rests upon an impracticable escarpment." Thereupon I again took up my own glass, which was an excellent one, and could discover no indication of such an escarpment.

General Dorsenne was equally unable to see it, and told the marshal so. He made no answer, but continued, "That camp is covered with revetted works." After exchanging one or two words and looks with me, General Dorsenne further observed that it was all he could do to see a few places where the ground had been thrown up. At length the marshal finished his examination, adding, as though no one else had spoken, "And, as I was informed, those revetted works are armed with heavy guns brought from Almeida, so there is nothing to be done." Thereupon he called for his horse and made no answer to General Dorsenne, who assured him that he did not share his opinion. Before riding off with the marshal, Dorsenne said to me: "I mean to have another go at him, but I wish first of all to have the opinion of all the divisional generals in my army, so I shall have them all to dinner with me, and I reckon on you."

The meal took place at the bivouac, a handsome carpet being spread on the ground, and covered with pies and other cold food of the best kind, served on silver dishes. We dined standing up, but that was not enough to give the luxurious repast a sufficiently military character. The end of the meal coincided with that of the day, and then General Dorsenne collected Souham, Dumoustier, Roguet, Watier, and myself under a great ilex, and, after a few words of explanation, asked our Opinion as to the alternative of attacking the Anglo-Portuguese army or retreating. We replied that all discussion of the point seemed to us useless; that our opinion, as the regrets we had expressed might show, was unanimous and decided, that we all deprecated the misfortune of losing a second day in so deplorable a fashion, and that, without stopping to consider what the marshal professed to have seen and heard about the strength of the English camp, we ought, in order to retrieve what still might be retrieved, to march upon the enemy an hour before daylight the next morning.

"I am delighted to hear you," returned Dorsenne. "Your opinion is mine. I shall maintain it with all my power and repeat my proposal to the marshal to undertake myself the attack which he does not care for." He left us.

Hardly had he gone to the marshal when Montbrun came out from him, and, seeing us under the oak, came up to us, saying, "What on earth are you doing there? You look like conspirators."

"Well," I returned, "we are conspiring, but it is in behalf of the honour of our arms."

"Oh, come! "he answered; "after all these campaigns, and all these years of fighting and glory, the honour of our arms does not depend upon an affair at Fuenteguinaldo."

"It depends," retorted Watier, "upon not missing a chance of an important victory which is more than necessary to us."

"The essential point," continued Montbrun, "is that we should not lay ourselves open to a false move. The English camp cannot be attacked, and the final proof of it is that Wellington is awaiting us there. Now to run into danger without any result is not the way to be done with him."

"We are still in hope," said Dumoustier, "that the marshal will go back upon that opinion, which we do not believe to be yours." He tried to maintain that it was his. We made no further reply and he left us. Half an hour afterwards General Dorsenne came back.

We ran to meet him, but his first words were, "We are to retreat." None of us made any answer, he continued:

"I have done what I could, but with no result. All the same, I had the best of the argument, so long as we consider the question only from a military point of view. But directly I declared to the marshal that I should attack alone, and that he might find himself responsible for the consequences, he said: 'Pray do you know what private instructions the emperor has given with regard to that English Army—whether it suits his policy that it should be destroyed, or whether, on the contrary, he has not an interest in keeping it in Spain, on account of the position which he holds with the English Parliament, so long as he has English troops in front of him.' When the question became political and ceased to be military, and when the marshal observed that as our orders were limited to the revictualling of Rodrigo, we became doubly responsible for everything unconnected with that operation, I insisted no longer.

"Thus we withdraw. The Army of Portugal starts first, marching on its rear. The Guard will go at eleven this evening, General Souham at midnight, while you, General Thiébault, will march at 1 a.m. and cover the retreat of the two armies with your division, and the cavalry under General Watier."

This was the end of it. It will never be thoroughly known how much mismanagement there was in these Spanish affairs.

Whenever I had an important movement to carry out, I was always on the ground more than an hour before the time. It is, indeed, the only way in which one can be sure of removing all difficulties, of anticipating omission, neglect or delay, of stimulating the slothful, of rewarding the diligent; in short, of securing that everything is in good order. By half-past eleven I was on the front of my lines, and, as I walked about, was watching the English camp-fires, when suddenly one of them went out. This struck me. I watched more closely, and thought I saw a good many others dying down. I spoke of it to my *aide-de-camp* Vallier, who was beside me. He formed the same opinion. Furious at the part that we were playing, and fearing that for the second time in my life I might be in danger of having to beat a retreat, an idea which I could not bear, I sent with all speed for a captain of the light company of the 31st—a good officer, at once courageous and sensible. I told him to call his company to arms, and, as soon as it was ready, I made the men take off their sacks, leaving a few men in poor health or bad marchers to guard them, and said to the officer, after making him compare his watch with mine:

> It is now a quarter to twelve. You will march upon the fires which face the road, with your men in light order, as they are. You will reach those fires in three-quarters of an hour. You will ascertain whether the enemy is still occupying his camp or has left it, and, in an hour and a quarter, you will come back to me at this place. You understand of course that you must in no case run any risk, and, at the least appearance of resistance, you must retire and fall back with the battalion which I shall send to back you up.

He started. The minutes passed slowly, and I anxiously scrutinised the English fires, which meanwhile continued to diminish in number and in brightness. At length, before an hour had elapsed, my captain hurried up to me, crying out: "The camp is abandoned, and there is not an Englishman left in Fuenteguinaldo."

"Follow me," I replied, and ran off in my turn in order to reach, as soon as possible, the house where General Dorsenne lodged. He was mounting his horse when I told him my news. At first he would not believe it. I had to explain to him what I had done, and to call forward the captain who had just come from Fuenteguinaldo. He was amazed.

"Halt your divisions," said he to me, and I replied that no one had stirred. He at once went off to the marshal. The disillusion was great, and I am by no means sure that the little lesson which I had given their Excellencies was to their taste. In order to leave an opening for a little swagger I was directed to march with my two divisions on Fuenteguinaldo, and *aides-de-camp* galloped off to fetch Souham and the Imperial Guard and the whole Army of Portugal back with all speed. The last-named troops were only overtaken at the gates of Rodrigo, and had to march back twenty miles. That was the way the men were knocked about, just as the opportunities which fortune still offered were missed, by men who were too incapable to owe such opportunities to their own combinations or to any feeling for their duty, but who none the less rose to honours and fortune. I may add that on reaching Fuenteguinaldo I hastened to verify the marshal's statements, and found that the impracticable escarpment was a slope gentle enough for cavalry to gallop up, that the revetted works consisted in an entrenched camp barely marked out, and that, as for great guns, there was so far no place in which a 4-pounder could be mounted.[14]

How is this incredible way of performing military duty to be explained? Alas! in the present instance the blame cannot be thrown on incapacity. Marmont was no doubt not a great warrior, still less a great leader of men, but he was surely soldier enough to understand that the English general, not having foreseen that we should cross the Agueda, would have been broken up and annihilated, if we had marched boldly upon him on the night when we reached Rodrigo. He knew equally well that at Fuenteguinaldo that general, being separated from two of his best divisions, would again have been beaten if, instead of looking at him with field-glasses at nine o'clock, we had attacked him at daybreak. No, the answer to the question must be found exclusively in Dorsenne's vanity and Marmont's pride. The Army of the North was a stronger and finer force than that of Portugal; its artillery was more numerous, better horsed, better served; and there seemed no doubt that on the field of battle it would play the leading part. But this army was commanded by a lieutenant-general, that of Portugal by a marshal of the empire; and the general said, "I am as much a commander-in-chief as the marshal is, and no one but myself shall dispose of my troops or command them."

Thereupon the marshal had no idea of exposing himself to the risk of having to play a part second to that of a general of division; and neither had so much patriotism or loyalty to a master who had heaped them with favours, or so much honourable feeling as would have enabled him to sacrifice these wretched personal considerations to the safety and glory of the army, and be done once for all with the English Army, thus preventing the disasters which ended in our being

---
14. [There was a little more than this, but the works were by no means strong.]

driven out of the Peninsula.

But to return to Fuenteguinaldo. After so benevolently losing two of the finest opportunities for beating the English army, first in detail, then all together, it was thought as well to devise some means of converting into a ground of boasting, what ought only to have been spoken of with shame and confusion, and making it possible to print: "The enemy did not accept battle. He fled before our eagles. We have hurled him back into the rugged rocks of Portugal," and suchlike rubbish. In pursuance of this object, though nothing was to be gained by a demonstration of that kind, I was ordered to advance with my two divisions to Aldea da Ponte, a village just short of the point at which the lofty mountains and deep gorges of the Beira begin, and thence to attempt a reconnoissance in the direction of Alfayates, by the road on which the English Army was retiring.

General Watier led; I came up with him at Casilla de Flores, where he had halted; and as I equally needed a halt to re-form my corps, which had got disordered in passing through a marshy wood where the enemy's artillery had quite spoilt the ground for mine, I bade him continue his movement on Aldea. Before I had collected more than my first brigade, an *aide-de-camp* from General Watier came with the news that Aldea was occupied by some English infantry, and that the cavalry division was taking a position at the further end of the defile which terminates three-quarters of a mile short of the village. At once I went off to rejoin Watier, leaving orders with the rest of my division to follow with all possible speed.

Independently of the defile which precedes it, in which it would have been easy enough to stop us, the village of Aldea was readily defensible. Built in a narrow gorge through which a torrent flows, it was flanked to the south by strongly marked wooded hills, and to the north by sharp and impracticable rocks. If these northern and southern points which command the village had been held by troops, I should have been forced to wait for my artillery and for the rest of my division. But as the village alone was occupied, this could be only by a single regiment. At once, in spite both of the infantry which backed the position to the south-west, and of large masses of cavalry which covered a plateau towards the north-west beyond the village, I resolved to carry it without waiting for my troops.

Accordingly, having deployed the 31st Light Infantry by battalions, I ordered the colonel to turn the right of the village with his first battalion and the major commanding the third to turn it by the left, while I myself at the head of the second advanced at the double along the road which passes through the place, and carried it. I was not mistaken; there were only two English battalions there, and the fear of being cut off induced these to retreat promptly, so that we occupied the place in double-quick time without loss or trouble.[15]

As soon as I was in possession of the village, I ordered General Watier to seize the plateau of which I have spoken; .and with his 1800 cavalry he drove from it the 3,000 Anglo-Portuguese horse who were there, and established himself on it. My right flank being thus covered, and steps taken to secure the position we had won, I advanced with the three battalions of the 31st along the road to Alfayates, which a little beyond Aldea turns to the south, and captured the first bank through which that road passes from the troops defending it. But having got so far, I found that I had in front of me not merely some thousand skirmishers, but two lines of infantry, eight guns in position, and behind these, crowning a second line of banks, a whole line of battalions in close order, 10,000 infantry in all.[16] To meet this force, I had 1300 men engaged, but the ground bristling with scattered rocks sufficiently prominent to cover them, my men found shelter behind which they could, with a good deal of damage to the enemy, maintain a combat, which, in spite of a brisk fire, cost them a very small loss.

However, in this position I was running a very real danger; namely, that Lord Wellington, who was commanding in person this strong rear-guard composed of picked troops, the right of which extended beyond my left, might think of taking advantage of his superior forces, and masking his movement by help of the wooded hills, might suddenly bring 5,000 or 6,000 men round by my left, seize the defile of Casilla, and thus cut off my retreat. Foreseeing this possibility, I hastened to post the whole of my second brigade so as to baffle any movement of this kind; and being secure on that side but in no position any longer to hope for anything from an attack, I resolved to go on simply keeping in touch with the English rear-guard, and in readiness to assume the offensive in the event of fresh troops joining me in time, or of the enemy making any movement of which I could take advantage.

Two hours passed, and I received neither orders nor reinforce-

---

15. [Napier, it will be seen, is mistaken in supposing that Aldea da Ponte was taken possession of by cavalry only.]
16. [This imposing appearance was presented by one brigade (Pakenham's) of the 4th division.]

ments nor intelligence; the expectant attitude to which I was reduced could not fail to betray my weakness to the enemy, and I had no doubt that he would try to make me withdraw, both as a sort of revenge and in order to continue his retreat in peace. In fact his fire increased, and I went back to the colonel of the 31st. Alone with him, I reached the front of his skirmishers, and presently I pointed out to him those attacking columns of about 1,000 men each forming in rear of the enemy's skirmishers and ready to advance covered by them. "General," said he thereupon, "I shall want reinforcements directly."

I rejoined:

> This attack heralds another which will be too much for you, even with such reinforcements as I could detach in your favour. Your part, therefore, will be limited to holding your ground long enough to do the enemy all the damage possible, but not long enough to endanger yourself; when you are compelled to retire you will do so, but at the ordinary pace only, upon the second line now formed by the Neuchâtel battalion and the artillery, which I am going to reinforce with a battalion of grenadiers."[17]

I at once gave an order to this effect, and was on my way towards the plateau occupied by the cavalry, when I was stopped half-way up the bank, on the reverse side of which the three battalions of the 31st were still fighting, by General Watier. He was looking for me to say that the enemy's 3,000 cavalry, who since he had dislodged them had nevertheless continued to show a front to him, had just been joined by an infantry division with a battery of artillery.[18]

All this showed that, as I had foreseen, I was about to be attacked both in front and in flank; so I communicated to General Watier the dispositions I had made with a view to such an attack, and added:

> Call in your advanced squadrons, and be ready to pass to the rear of Aldea before your movement can hamper the infantry or the artillery, basing your estimate of time upon the fact that,

---

17. I had posted the Neuchâtel battalion and my five guns in reserve between the village and the cavalry, so as to form a second line which the grenadiers could reinforce if required. It was in a position to sweep the entrance of the Alfayates road and support my cavalry in an emergency. With a view to contingencies I had also detached the picked battalion to cover the left flank of the cavalry and the right of the 31st with which I meant to act.
18. [The 7th Fusiliers supported by two Portuguese regiments.]

if no fresh troops join us, the enemy will be where we now are in half an hour's time.

Hardly had the half-hour elapsed when the three battalions of the 31st were descending, in good order, the bank which the enemy was recapturing from them. Thinking that this movement in pursuance of orders given beforehand was a defeat, he charged the three battalions; but at that moment I passed, with the Neuchâtel battalion and the grenadiers, through the intervals between them, and pushed him back upon the bank, and while my five guns proceeded to hold him in check there, the two battalions which I was leading threw themselves back, moving by the left, on the village of Aldea. In this way the fire of the 31st, which, in pursuance of its feigned retreat, had been drawn up in the second line, and now reappeared for a moment in the first, was unmasked, and the enemy's advance was stopped.

At that moment General Watier's cavalry reached the rear of the village and formed a third line. Two of my guns followed at once, to take up the second line in rear of the village, and were soon joined by the other three and by the 31st, which thus passed once more into the second line, leaving the Neuchâtel and grenadier battalions to show in the first. These retrograde movements had allowed the enemy to continue the attack, and to bring up a battery with which he played upon us. Then, protected by its fire, he marched resolutely to capture the village. But he found me strongly posted in three lines, within a space proportioned to my force, and with my wings resting on good positions. His rush carried him up to my first line, which was barring the village, and it repulsed him. Reinforced by fresh troops, he returned almost immediately at the double. At that moment two battalions were detached from my second brigade, and, charging the right flank of the attacking columns with the bayonet, helped me to throw them back upon the bank which I had abandoned to them. By the time that they reached it again they had lost all desire to renew the fight.

I was very proud of having taught these English how far they had failed to recognise the advantages which Aldea da Ponte might offer for defence, and in point of fact their last attack was a mistake from the moment when I had baffled their devices, just as it had been a mistake, and a principal mistake, to abandon the village, unless indeed Lord Wellington hoped that, carried away by a first success, I should let myself go in pursuit of him without securing my rear. As everything indicated that the combat was at an end, I re-formed my lines, after which I allowed the men of my division to make their soup.

Such was the action of Aldea da Ponte. I have related it in detail, not so much because I was in sole command there [19] as because, being conducted like a well-played game of chess, it was one of those combats of manoeuvres in which everything has been calculated and foreseen, until there is no room for hesitation, till no movement can be made without a motive, no orders given that have not been explained beforehand and cannot be justified.

It was a combat during which none of my troops had occasion to step out, except to march on the enemy, while not a single section of my force was endangered; in which 5,000 French, less than 2,000 of whom were really engaged, contended for five hours against 17,000 English or Portuguese, manoeuvring all the time within little more than a square mile of ground against a chief with the reputation of a great captain, baffling his calculations and escaping his traps, to remain, at the end, masters of the village we had captured from his troops; which cost us 150 men, including 120 wounded, while, as we were told by some prisoners, it cost the enemy 500 and a general officer.[20]

Lastly, and this is unanswerable, it was a combat with which my troops were delighted, and in regard to which General Dumoustier, with his imperturbable frankness, said in my presence to General Dorsenne, thanks to whom I was always on bad terms with all members of the Imperial Guard in Spain:

> From the hill on which I was posted I followed all General Thiébault's movements with my field-glass, and I declare that he manoeuvred in presence of the enemy as one might do on the parade-ground.

Meanwhile, at the moment when I was re-forming my lines after the battle, and General Watier was beginning his movement on Casilla, General Souham turned to me. "My dear general," he stammered, from his height of six feet one or two inches, with the assurance natural in speaking to a man whom he had nearly had for his *aide-de-camp* eighteen years before, "make your division stand to their arms again

---

19. [It is extremely interesting, it may be added, to compare all this detailed description with Napier's briefer account of these operations. In the main features they agree, but the divergencies on particular points are enough to show how little either side in a battle knows about the other.]

20. [The total loss of the allies in the three days' operations was only 300. No general seems to have been among them.]

quickly, and let us attack the enemy again." I divined his motive. As the senior general of division employed in our armies, he could not be in a fight anywhere without playing his part. He was only just coming out of disgrace, and, in order to obtain the favours which he coveted, he needed to fire a few rounds. But these considerations, very strong for him, had nothing to do with my duty; therefore, without even taking notice of the fact that I could not act with him without putting myself under his orders, nor come under his orders without giving him the credit of what I had just done by myself, I replied:

> Night is coming on, the enemy is retreating across mountains, where one can only hope to succeed by flank movements which cannot be judged or carried out save by daylight; so nothing more can be done. My troops are tired; they have just been fighting for five hours and on the march for nineteen. Besides, they are hungry, and are just putting into the pot the last meat which they will eat between here and Salamanca; therefore they will not stir any more.

"Very well," he replied. "I am going to ask General Watier for a brigade."

"His division is under my orders," said I, "but tell him that he is free to do what he likes."

He did in fact apply to that general, and got neither a brigade nor a regiment; then he acted for himself, and, with his four grenadier battalions and the two guns he had with him, he marched upon the enemy's last remaining vedettes, fired five or six rounds at them, followed them for a quarter of a league, skirmishing in the most useless manner, and returned to bivouac I do not know where. His part in the affair could not, and did not, exceed the proportion of a mere amusement; still it was enough for a long story to be made about it in Dorsenne's report, where I was only slightly mentioned, and for him to be made count and receive an endowment, while I, though I had been the only one of the generals in the Army of the North who had really fought, and had fought too with some advantage, got no remuneration but hard words.

Doubtless, in order to avenge himself for the way in which I had given the lie to his assertions before Fuenteguinaldo, and had shown the ridiculous nature of the retreat on which he had insisted, Marshal Marmont, who went the next day with General Dorsenne as far as Aldea, thought fit to say that my fight of the day before had been a blunder. The phrase was after all regarded as it deserved to be, and quickly forgotten, and I only recall it to show the arrogance of one of those men whom their title of marshal forbade to allow any merit in others than themselves.

So much for these melancholy recollections. The presence of Dorsenne and Marmont was as useless at Aldea as at bottom my movement itself had been; in fact, there was nothing more to be done but to withdraw. The two armies fell back, and Marshal Marmont returned to Plasencia, while Dorsenne went back to Valladolid by way of Rodrigo and Salamanca. The result, however, of three days so deplorably wasted was that the English Army was not destroyed, and more than 200,000 rations of the provisions which had just been convoyed to the besieged in Ciudad Rodrigo were eaten.

CHAPTER 17

Fall of Rodrigo

My division numbered only 3,200 bayonets, far too small a number to furnish even the garrisons required within my government, to say nothing of holding the country against Don Julian, or rather against the Marquis of España, who had been placed in general command of all the *partidas* of Estremadura.

Rodrigo therefore received a special garrison, and a brigade from Souham's division was detached to reinforce me. Unluckily, it was commanded by General Bonté, than whom no man was ever worse named, for he had no good points. He was for ever complaining, until I was forced to ask the commander-in-chief to remove General Bonté and his brigade from my government. In their place came a brigade of the Guard under General Mouton-Duvernet. Fresh annoyances arose from this change, since, owing to the pride of the commanders and the pretensions of the most junior officers, all who served in the Guard had always to be placed in an exceptional position. Thus Mouton-Duvernet was specially charged to act against Don Julian, or, as was then said, to destroy him. It was an absurd idea, but anyhow he lost no time about taking the field, surprised an outpost, took eight of Don Julian's men prisoners, and had them shot on the spot.

Next day I received a letter of eight pages from the Marquis of España. He began by saying that my father's honourable reputation, and the opinion which I had caused people to form of myself in those provinces, had convinced him that they would not be the scene of acts worthy of cannibals. Nevertheless, one Mouton-Duvernet, the offspring no doubt of the sties of the Revolution, had just repeated one of those crimes that are unknown among civilized peoples. Immediate vengeance had been taken, and eight French soldiers, selected from the prisoners in his hands, had just been shot in the same place where the eight Spaniards had been, and similar reprisals would be taken whenever occasion was given for them. The marquis added that he knew the independence of the officers of the Guard; he did not blame me personally for what they had done, but he warned me none the less that he was in a position to bring whatever he pleased to the knowledge of my emperor, including the contents of his letter. He ended with the formula:

May God preserve you for many years, but outside of Spain.

I wrote an answer at once, but, not liking to send it without Dorsenne's consent, I referred it to him. He judged that such communications were useless, and explanations might be embarrassing for the Imperial Guard, and the Marquis of España's letter had to go without a reply.

Unluckily, his indignation was just. At first we might fairly have considered the guerrillas as bands of insurgents or brigands, and in that way treat them as outside the law; but one cannot so treat a whole nation, and from the moment when the whole Spanish nation took up arms against us the character of the *partidas* had changed. The rights of special repression which we claimed to draw from our qualities of auxiliaries to King Joseph were fallacious enough. Joseph, the first and the last of the name, had no people; while the Spanish people, who had their own king, no matter whether free or in chains, and England and Portugal as their allies, constituted a belligerent State.

The massacre of prisoners would therefore have been butchery, even if it could have gone unpunished, but, since we were at their mercy in this matter, barbarity was coupled with crime, since the murder of Spaniards involved the murder of Frenchmen. After this affair, Mouton-Duvernet, whom, by the way, I did not suspect of having acted of his own free will, could not stay longer at Salamanca; he was recalled to Valladolid, and his brigade replaced at last by troops who took their orders only from me.

In the account I have given of the revictualling of Rodrigo, we saw two armies making useless demonstrations for five days in a country without resources, until, by consuming part of the provisions which they brought, they had destroyed nearly all the profit of their operation. We have seen them missing the opportunity of crushing the English army, and by this neglect anticipating the criminal mismanagement by which, a few months later, their commanders, Marmont and Dorsenne, put Rodrigo into the hands of Lord Wellington. The result of all this was, that at the end of two months Rodrigo was on the point of running short of bread. My reports had given warning beforehand of the necessity for a second revictualling at an early date. I had pressed the matter more and more, till I got to the point of renewing my importunities every day; but, instead of attending to Rodrigo, no one even answered such of my letters as referred to that place.

Yet, though in itself a place of little importance, at that moment it played a decisive part. If we remained masters of it, we compelled the English army to tarry in the barren mountains of Beira; while, if the place once fell into the hands of the English, Lord Wellington could establish himself in Estremadura and carry the war into the north of Spain. Nevertheless, I suddenly learnt that General Dorsenne was making arrangements for an excursion into Navarre, and that he was going to take with him all the available troops, so that from Salamanca to Pampeluna there would not be a single battalion left to support me in case of necessity.

At this juncture the measure was filled by a disaster no less serious than unexpected. General Reynaud, who was in command at Rodrigo, having still a small herd of sheep and cattle, thought he might send them during the day into the pastures on the left bank of the Agueda, a little more than half a mile from the fortifications. He even deemed it possible to go there himself every morning, with the double object of taking a walk and seeing how his herd was looked after. But Don Julian, ever intrepid and ever indefatigable, very soon discovered a way of making repentance follow upon this over-confidence, and one fine day he carried off herd, escort, and general.

Thus Rodrigo suddenly found itself without fresh meat, without a governor, and almost without bread. The event was the more melancholy that in General Reynaud we lost a commander who was, so to say, wedded to the fortress, who took delight in his adventurous position, and, being no less capable than energetic, allowed us, in the event of an attack, to look for a resistance which would have been impossible with anyone else. I received the disastrous news by express messenger, and at once sent a messenger to General Dorsenne, carrying the original document that I had received, and a dispatch in which I called loudly for his attention to a fortress which was our last stay; for it alone prevented the Anglo-Portuguese army from emerging into Spain, beating the Army of Portugal, and compelling the Army of the North to evacuate the province of Salamanca.

Dorsenne was at table when he received my dispatch. It did not prevent him from finishing his dinner in peace. When the meal was over, he imparted its contents to M. Volland, the commissary-general of his army. Pressed for his opinion, Volland answered sharply, "Why, there can be no hesitation. You must return with all speed to Valladolid, and proceed to Rodrigo with all the troops and provisions that you can collect, calling upon the Army of Portugal to aid you as before."

A sardonic smile was Dorsenne's only reply; it was called forth by the idea of putting me to the test of an awkward position. He therefore continued his journey, did not reinforce me with a single man, did not even ask that the Army of Portugal might so much as make a demonstration; but in lieu of all this wrote me a letter to bid me revictual Rodrigo and replace General Reynaud:

> The provinces of my government could furnish provisions and all necessary means of transport. The operation must he feasible; and my talents, with the zeal that we should all have in the emperor's service, would suggest to me the measures adopted to ensure success and the preservation of the troops entrusted to me.

When I read this letter my hair stood on end. It was impossible to conceive such an enterprise without the destruction of all whom I could employ in it; while, if a disaster occurred, a way had been left open for saying that the operation had been desired only in so far as it was feasible, and power was reserved to ascribe the most fatal results to such or such a step, which I should not have taken, but which would have been presumed after the event. In this way I was made responsible both for the place of which the loss seemed a joke, and for the troops in whose company I appeared to be doomed to sacrifice myself.

And what means of action had I? No doubt my government could find the necessary provisions and transport. So far as regarded a substitute for General Reynaud, some false information had brought to Salamanca General Barrie, whose destination was the Army of Portugal, and I at once laid hands on him, much to his consternation. But in the matter of forces, I had, after deducting the garrison of Rodrigo, 4,500 infantry, six guns, and rather over 600 cavalry, with which to meet the Anglo-Portuguese Army nearly 45,000 strong, not to mention Don Julian, who was occupying the fifty miles between Rodrigo and Salamanca with 5,000 to 6,000 men. Moreover, I could not denude either Salamanca or Alba de Tormes, nor yet the road to Valladolid; so that, in fact, the total of the troops available for the revictualling of Rodrigo amounted to 2,800 or 2,900 infantry, four guns, and 600 cavalry.

In these circumstances my first thought was that, loss for loss, it was better to be lost fighting even hopelessly, than not fighting at all; and I decided that, happen what might, I would try this operation. My second thought was, that being unable to effect anything by force of arms, my only hope lay in rapid movement and in artifice. But on what artifice could I rely to deceive the enemy as to an important assemblage of transports and provisions, when this could have only one object? However, as each hour of delay only prolonged useless tortures, I made up my mind; and as my only hope lay in what was called "Lord Wellington's prudence," I wrote to the *prefect* that 12,000 men marching with twelve guns and 1,000 cavalry were coming to take up a position at Trades, where they were to be subsisted by means of convoys leaving Salamanca every two days, and that he must therefore within twenty-four hours collect a quantity which I named of sheep, oxen, grain, and flour, and at once organise a system of replacing them at Salamanca. I added that I should verify the execution of the first part of the order next day, and the replacement in a week.

A quarter of an hour later the prefect called on me. When we were alone, he said, "Governor, I am sure you would not play any trick on me; I have had a letter from you that makes me anxious."

"I was about to come and tell you what I could not have written." And, in truth, he was an able and devoted man without whom nothing could have been done in the country, and whose zeal deserved to be encouraged by marks of confidence and sympathy.

"I am much obliged to your Excellency," he replied; "so Frades—?"

"Is Rodrigo." And I handed him Dorsenne's letter.

As he returned it, he said, "That is an errand which makes me shudder for you."

"Zeal and secrecy," I continued.

"You may count on both."

"I do so, and shall start the day after tomorrow."

What complicated the difficulties of the operation was that we were entering the rainy season, and the torrents were swelling, rendering it very difficult, if not impossible, to march. When I woke the next morning, a sound which I feared to explain struck my ear. I leaped out of bed; it was raining in torrents. I dressed hastily, and was starting for the *prefect's* when he arrived. He said, "I understand your anxiety; and if I cannot dispel it, I can give you some clear notions. Tomorrow

you will not be able to pass any of the three torrents between this and Rodrigo. If the rain stops before midday, you may be able to get off in two days; if it last till evening, it will be no good attempting anything."
It cleared about midday and became fine.

With an enemy who had all the population on his side, and knew all our movements beforehand, while able to conceal his own with a facility that was our despair, twenty-four hours' delay might be fatal. However, I gave out that I had heard that the movement of the troops on Frades was to be postponed one day, and at the same time that a detachment of the Imperial Guard under General Dumoustier was to arrive next day at Salamanca. Having taken all possible precautions, and made my plans to meet every possible contingency, I left Salamanca at 6 a.m., and was at Matilla by half-past eight; starting again with my troops and my convoy, which had reached that place by a circuitous route, at nine.

As we could only go the pace of the oxen, and the torrents were still hard to cross, it was three in the morning before we reached the forest of Alba de Yeltes, where we bivouacked. Teams, pack animals, oxen, were all exhausted, and needed seven hours' rest; and it was 3 p.m. by the time we were at the point where the woods and mountains end, and the plain, some four miles wide, which lies in front of Rodrigo, begins.

Then I halted the bulk of my force, and, with my 600 cavalry and one picked battalion, myself led the convoy to the glacis, whence the carts and animals were sent back as fast as they were unloaded. The troops bivouacked there, and not a single officer was allowed to enter the town. My unexpected appearance, and the execution of the revictualling operation with a handful of men, caused an indescribable astonishment, and a joy which the inhabitants did not share.

At seven in the evening, accompanied by the principal officers of the garrison, I took General Barrié all over the place; and at eight I called together the same persons and the Spanish authorities, and installed him with all the pomp I could manage, as successor to General Reynaud. Then I held a council, at which I drew up all the orders and instructions which the circumstances could require; and by three in the morning I was with my troops again and on the march for San Muños. We covered the nine Spanish leagues which divide that place from Rodrigo, almost without a halt; passed through it, and at once took up the position which lies to the north of it, so as to place the torrent between the enemy and me, and myself between Salamanca and him. Rodrigo victualled, and my troops out of danger, my task was accomplished. It was high time, for two English divisions were already marching on San Muños, but too late; they did not halt till they knew I was beyond it. Thus as General Barrié wrote to me:

> Two hours' delay in your march, or mistake in your calculations, and you were lost.

Emboldened by this movement of a part of the English Army, Don Julian harassed my rear-guard, which had been strengthened. It faced about, and he received a lesson which sufficed to rid us of him.[1]

I returned to Salamanca at 9 p.m., after eighty-seven hours' absence. The true cause of my departure had become known, and I was welcomed with an outburst of joy. Indeed, they had believed me lost; and I hardly understood my own escape. Everything had been accomplished without the loss of a sack of corn, an ox, a man, and that against the luckiest man that ever was a man whose business it was to hinder the revictualling at any price, who was there for that purpose, and in a position to do it ten times over. The prefect of Salamanca maintained that it was one of the most fortunate operations that had been carried out in the Peninsula.

General Dorsenne's only remark was, "I was sure that you were in no danger save from the bad roads;" which drew from one of my *aides-de-camp* the following reflection: "It must want a zeal like iron to stand such an ill-conditioned chief." However, I had a compensation. The Marquis of España, exasperated at the way in which Rodrigo had been relieved, and perhaps irritated by the trap into which his lieutenant Don Julian had fallen, wished at least to see if some blame could be thrown on my procedure. He assembled the mayors of all the villages which I had passed through, to hear any complaints they

---

1. [Napier, it would seem, imagined that Dorsenne had undertaken an expedition on his own account, and that it was his rear-guard with which Don Julian came in contact. Thiébault's narrative makes it clear that he has expanded one expedition into two. As to the revictualling of Rodrigo, his words are worth quoting, as showing that the bad weather cut both ways. "A large convoy was collected at Salamanca by General Thiébault, who spread a report that a force was to assemble towards Tamanes, and that the convoy was for its support. This rumour did not deceive Wellington, but he believed the whole Army of the North, and one division of the Army of Portugal, would be employed in the operation, and therefore made arrangements to pass the Agueda, and attack them on the march. Heavy rains rendered the fords of the Agueda impracticable. Thiébault seized the occasion to introduce his convoy, and, leaving a new governor, returned on the 2nd of November, before the waters had subsided."]

had to make against me or my troops: but he found on the evidence of these men, whose instinct was to accuse us, that I had been the first to enter every village, the last to leave it; that not a fowl, not a cabbage, not an egg had been touched; that no inhabitant had an act or a word to complain of. His inquiry had to suffice him, and he ended with a phrase which had been said before, reported by two mayors to the prefect, who at once informed me of it: "It is impossible to manage troops better."

Rodrigo being provisioned for five months, I was beginning to think that I should not have to trouble myself about the place for a long time, when I heard that Lord Wellington had given orders for the construction of fascines and gabions in large quantities. I at once reported the matter, expecting of course a prompt answer, but I received none. Meanwhile, every day confirmed the news with the addition of fresh details, and by every messenger I forwarded the corroborative information I had received, but always without result. At the end of a fortnight, anxiety was added to indignation; and though in no way obliged to do so, I sent an abstract of all the reports forwarded by me to General Dorsenne to Marshal Marmont, whose headquarters were still at Plasencia. His army was in presence of the English Army and threatened its right flank; it could prevent the English from crossing the Agueda and attacking Rodrigo, which stands on the right bank of that river; but my second appeal had no more success than my first, nor did I succeed in shaking the confidence of either of their two excellencies.

In the meantime the facts reported to me became even more urgent, nor did they leave any further doubt that the attack of Rodrigo had been resolved upon. Thereupon, quite as much to shelter my own responsibility as to omit nothing that could prevent a great misfortune, I took upon myself to address to the Prince of Neuchâtel an abstract of all my dispatches to Dorsenne and Marmont; placing it, though this was unusual, at the end of my fortnightly states. I had just sent off the third of them when M. de Richemont, the marshal's senior *aide-de-camp*, arrived at Salamanca, coming from Plasencia to join the marshal at Valladolid. He had been sent to judge for himself of the situation of the provinces through which he passed, and to inform me that the sixth and seventh governments had just been made over to the Army of Portugal. "It is a great pity," said I, "that all this was not done a month ago; they might, with advantage, have taken some thought for Rodrigo."

"For Rodrigo?" he replied; "you may be quite easy about Rodrigo, general." Something more than astounded by his confidence, I showed him my reports, but nothing could persuade him. At last he took me aside and said: "No one could be on better terms than the marshal is with Lord Wellington; they are in constant communication and often write to each other, and there are few days on which we do not know what is going on in the English army. Well, general, the preparations of which you speak, and which are to some extent real, have no other object but to lead us into making false movements. The English army is not ready for any important operation, and will undertake none before the spring." I saw that he would not hear reason; and when he departed, after telling him that the statements on which he founded his opinion would not change mine, I gave him a letter confirming the contents of all that had preceded it, and begged him to lay it before the marshal. He undertook to do so with the air of one deferring to authority.

Reaching Valladolid at seven, he found the two commanders-in-chief still at table; my report amused them, and I formed the subject of their pleasantries till ten o'clock. When at length their Excellencies had just parted in high good humour at my ridiculous obstinacy, one of my staff officers, sent off post-haste, arrived with the news that the whole English Army had crossed the Agueda, and that after nightfall a division of it had approached Fort Marmont,[2] which must have seemed supremely humorous. It had filled the ditch with the fascines about which we had just been joking, and had carried the fort with the bayonet. In the course of the same night the parallels which we had made two years previously had been re-opened with great ease, siege batteries had been at once mounted, and the guns were heard without intermission.

My messenger's tale caused the scene to change; faces were drawn up otherwise than with laughter, and, amid a general turmoil, officers started for all the points at which there were available troops, and handed them the order to proceed by forced marches to Salamanca. Before daybreak the armies of the North and of Portugal were in movement; my messenger was sent back to me in all haste, with a letter from the marshals saying that within a week 60,000 men and 100 guns will be under the walls of Rodrigo. In a postscript were the words:

---

2. [This appears to be the fort better known as San Francisco.]

Herewith a note for General Barrié: promise 6,000 *francs* to whoever brings a receipt for it.

But these belated efforts were useless. Master of Fort Marmont, making his way by our parallels which he had only to sweep out, making use of the very platforms of our old batteries, reopening with ease the breaches that we had made, Lord Wellington was able in thirty-six hours to assault, and, while he was storming the place on one side, Don Julian, who knew it perfectly and had correspondents in the town, escaladed it on the other, so that it was taken with incredible rapidity.[3] The news of the surrender reached me just as Marshal Marmont entered Salamanca in advance of his columns, and I treated him to it just as he alighted. General Dorsenne, who was following him at the distance of a league, learnt it at the gate of the town, and retired with his troops.

This apparent serenity, or rather this inexcusable carelessness on the part of the two chiefs with regard to Rodrigo, must be explained as follows. Feeble as General Dorsenne's capacity may have been, and with whatever vanity Marmont may have relied on himself, neither one nor the other can have believed that my reports were unfounded. But the two commanders detested each other. Marmont, whose reasoning about war was as brilliant as his practice was bad, was offended at seeing a divisional general so mediocre as Dorsenne playing a part equal to his own; while Dorsenne, taking his own grenadier's courage for the qualities of a commander-in-chief, thought much more of himself than of Marmont. Each of the two wished some great misfortune to happen to the other, and was watching for an opportunity of helping it to come to pass.

Thus, with regard to Rodrigo, Marmont said to himself, "Until General Dorsenne has handed over to me the command of the sixth and seventh governments he is responsible for the place; and if he loses it for want of calling in my help, it will be a fault of which it will be no concern of mine if he never recovers." Dorsenne, on his side, could say, "I am about to hand over these provinces to the marshal; a fortress like Rodrigo cannot be taken with a rush. I shall have preserved it so long as I had any concern with it. Consequently, it is the marshal who

---

3. [The siege began on January 8 by the capture of Fort San Francisco. Nothing, however, was heard of it at Salamanca till the 15th, and then the information must have been very imperfect, for the place was not finally taken till the night of the 19th. Nor did Don Julian take any hand in the affair, for he was in observation on the Tormes. The escalade referred to was effected by Pack's Portuguese.]

will be responsible for it." But the place fell at the very moment when one was giving up the territory and the other receiving it, so that they were both responsible for that too disastrous event.

It is, of course, needless to say that the fall of Rodrigo was a heavy blow to any energetic inclinations on my part, and a final discouragement in the exercise of my command. All that I had done and devised for the good of the country seemed doomed to perish, and I could not bear to see so much effort end in nothing. As for the marshal, I was a standing reproach to him, while he was for me only a chief who recalled deplorable memories. I was convinced that he would be glad to see me depart; but in this I was mistaken. As a general in the Army of the North, I had done the commander-in-chief of the Army of Portugal the wrong of having been three times in the right; but, as a general in his army, he looked upon me as a man to whose zeal Fuenteguinaldo, Aldea da Ponte, the second revictualling of Rodrigo, bore testimony. Moreover, it would not be easy to replace me without detriment to Salamanca, where the inhabitants showed much regard for me. Thus, when I presented myself to the marshal a few hours after his arrival, he bade me sit down, and said, "Of course, I need not assure you, General Thiébault, that you retain under me both your government and the command of your division."

"I beg your Excellency's pardon, but I belong to the Army of the North, and I start tomorrow to rejoin its headquarters."

"When the emperor handed these provinces over to me," he said, with an air of surprise, "he equally made over to me the generals commanding in them, especially those who are, like you, in command of the troops which are left with me."

There was no reply to this, and yet I did reply, "My orders are to serve with the Army of the North, and I am obliged to adhere to them."

He saw that my mind was made up, and added, with some annoyance, "At least, I suppose that you will remain long enough to give some instructions to your successor?"

"In that case," I replied, "I will remain till the day after tomorrow"— and thirty-six hours after his arrival I had left Salamanca.

Before long, General Dorsenne was replaced in the command of the Army of the North by General Caffarelli, and the headquarters of that army had been moved to Vitoria. My first visit to my new chief did not give me a very high opinion of his ability, but in other respects I had no fault to find with him. He gave me to understand that, in the event of his being called away by any exigencies of his duty, he would leave the temporary command to me; nor was it long before an occasion presented itself of putting this into effect. Although Lord Wellington took months to do what a man worthy of his good fortune would have done in a few days, he could not help profiting at last by his advantages and by all that our generals were good enough to do for the benefit of his reputation. Accordingly, he marched on Salamanca in order to turn us out of that province.

Marshal Marmont, whose headquarters were now established at Valladolid, brought up his cantonments, marched to the Douro, and manoeuvred in front of Lord Wellington, with sufficient ability to check him and compel him to manoeuvre in his turn. This was all the more fortunate, since the Army of the Centre was on its way to attack the right flank of the Anglo-Portuguese Army. Now, if ever, was the time to be content with holding it in check, to do everything to prevent its retiring, and to remain in a position to follow it; but if Joseph came up and beat Lord Wellington in concert with Marshal Marmont, it would be the king who would naturally play the chief part.

Now Marmont, who at the first revictualling of Rodrigo let the English Army off rather than share with Dorsenne the credit of defeating it, had no more desire to leave all the merit of a great action to Joseph. Consequently, having been rejoined by a weak division of his army, and taking no thought of the fact that the enemy had received a still more considerable reinforcement, he resolved, single-handed, to attack an enemy before whom he had been forced to fall back behind the Douro. He recrossed that river, by which he had been covered, marched back to the Tonnes, traversed it between Alba and Salamanca, reached the Arapiles while Lord Wellington was waiting for him, and fought, no less criminally than unfortunately, the battle in which, according to the English newspapers, we lost twenty-five guns, several eagles, and 15,000 to 18,000 men.

Having won this victory, Lord Wellington was in a position to complete the destruction of the Army of Portugal, but the inconceivable slowness of his operations saved the remnants of that army, and allowed time for marching to their aid. With this object General Caffarelli advanced with 10,000 to 12,000 men, and started so hastily that, while leaving me in chief command of the Army of the North, he had no time to give me any instructions.

About this time I had a last gleam of hope for the glory of our arms. Dispatches came from the Minister for War, dated August 22 and

26, to the effect that "the arrival of the Prince of Essling to command the Army of Portugal, with reinforcements which are on the march, is about to change the aspect of affairs;" and "the arrival of the Prince of Essling with 10,000 men is about to give the Army of Portugal the accession of troops demanded by it." From these dispatches it appeared that Marshal Masséna was resuming the command of that army, and this at once suggested to me the idea of obtaining a division in it, and leaving that perfect Bedlam, the Army of the North.

Unfortunately, the announcement was premature, and Masséna did not accept the appointment. His son-in-law, General Reille, was appointed in his place, while I continued to wait at Vitoria till the hour of my deliverance struck. About the end of the year the twenty-ninth bulletin from the Grand Army reached us, and we learnt the disasters that had befallen it. I applied to the Minister for War for a post in that army; and, as at that time most generals were seeking employment elsewhere, my wish could not fail to be granted. I had at the same time demanded six months' leave on full pay, and I received it, by return of messenger, on January 24, 1813. A regiment of Polish lancers on their way back to France reached Vitoria the same day, and I started with them the next day but one. We made our way with considerable difficulty, and at great risk, to the frontier. We were blockaded for three days by Mina's forces in the town of Villareal, escaping only by the fortunate circumstance that General Dumoustier was at Vitoria, and obtained permission from Caffarelli to send his first brigade to our aid. General Mouton-Duvernet, who commanded it, protected our march till we were in sight of Tolosa, and other troops escorted us almost to the Bidassoa, marching all the way under a continual fire from Spanish skirmishers.

Thus I left the Peninsula for the last time after seven years in succession passed in it. Though I left behind me many men who were attached and even devoted to me, and was well-esteemed by many who had fought with me, the farewell of the Spaniards was conveyed to me in the fire of musketry.

Chapter 18

I Join the Grand Army

Re-entering France after an absence of more than thirty months, while the world was yet ringing with the disaster that had befallen us, deeming our cause almost lost in the country which I was leaving, and which in five years had devoured the equivalent of what the snows of Russia had just annihilated in five weeks, I could not fail to gather the opinion of the departments through which I passed. Everywhere in the country was grief and terror, in the towns apprehension and discontent, while I found Paris ringing with complaints, and yet we were far from knowing the extent of our losses.

The full horrors of the retreat were as yet unknown, and people clung, especially in the country districts, almost superstitiously to the hope that those who did not return were no worse than prisoners. In Paris, indeed, people knew too much to be able to allow that Cossacks could have become humanised; a few moderate spirits alone came anywhere near the truth, and this truth, though less appalling than the legend which had already sprung up about that terrible campaign, was cruel enough to induce the examination and criticism of the mistakes that had been made, and people's exasperation increased as they reckoned up the worst of them. Enthusiasm had given place to a severe and unjust estimate; some people, through self-esteem, others through patriotism, were hurt or humiliated at finding only a man where they had been accustomed to see a hero and a demi-god. In the first flush of this reaction friends no longer hesitated to foresee new mistakes and new disasters, while enemies let themselves run riot.

Among the latter was my friend Rivierre, who yielded to no one in the fury of his Bourbonism. Being so clever a man as he was, he had proclaimed his hopes a little too spitefully and prematurely, and had been arrested and taken to La Force, whence he came out just as

I returned from Spain. A good many other arrests of the same kind had been made; this was a distinct return to the days of persecution, but, as in Rivierre's case, the matter really turned only upon a remark, and as he was a charming and kindly fellow with many friends, Savary, who then was Minister of Police, was attacked by all kinds of people demanding the release of the prisoner.

Considering the hazardous state of affairs, Savary thought it his duty to appear inexorable, and it was only a circumstance of the most trivial kind that decided him to abate the sternness of his rigorous methods. Our common friend Lenoir, happening to dine with him, made the same request to him as they left the table, and could make no impression; but the conversation led them into the billiard-room, and Lenoir, always a quaint and original person, was inspired by the occasion, the consciousness of his own skill in the game, and Savary's claims to be a great performer, with the idea of replying to his refusal as follows: "Well, let us leave it to luck to be the arbiter of his liberty, and agree at least to play for it the best of three games." Savary began by laughing; then, rather than allow that he was afraid to lose, he ended by accepting the challenge. Never were games better fought, but at length Lenoir won, and Rivierre left La Force.

On the day after my arrival, which happened to be Sunday, I went to the palace, attending the morning audience after Mass and the empress's reception in the evening. At the morning audience the emperor asked me, "How long have you been in Paris?"

"Since yesterday, sir, and in the full hope that your Majesty will deign to make use of my zeal."

He looked at me kindly, gave an approving nod, and replied, "I shall bear you in mind."

But, good heavens! what a difference between these receptions and the last at which I had been present at Compiègne! What had become of the kings, the archdukes, the foreign princes, the ambassadors—even the ambassador of Austria? All that luxury, all that glory, the homage of the world had disappeared; the emperor was grave, Marie Louise. embarrassed, all faces gloomy, and, if a few people made an effort to smile, it was by the help of grimaces that signified more than ever the sincere expression of the sentiments which they were intended to conceal.

On March 21 I received from the Minister for War an order to post to Mainz, and be there by the 26th. Being delayed by indisposition, I was not able to start till that day. Up till then, whenever I left my wife, the pain of parting from her had been, in a way, alleviated by dreams of glory and hopes of sharing in new victories; but at the time of which I am speaking these had altogether vanished. Like so many others, I had the impression that fortune was weary of Napoleon. France still obeyed his call, but it was only with reluctance that she now delivered up to him her gold and her children. The legislative body was alienated; the Senate, too weak to resist, was, for that very reason, incapable of giving support.

Our commerce was annihilated, the produce of our fields—wine especially—was valueless, suffering was universal, individuals were in mourning; the finest army that France had ever put in the field was destroyed; our very frontiers were ill-defended by wretched recruits against the veterans of Europe thirsting for vengeance. Thus, to whatever hopes I might endeavour to cling, I did not escape the most cruel apprehensions. A divisional general of some reputation, I looked back with regret upon the feelings which had inspired the obscure soldier of 1792, and it was in a melancholy mood that I journeyed towards Mainz, and reached that town on the evening of the 29th.

I expected to find my orders there; none had yet come, and several days went by in painful expectation, all the more wearily because I might have passed them happily in Paris, Everything was making ready for the reception of the emperor, and I had some hope of obtaining employment in a corps that would fight under his eye. But by the same messenger who announced his arrival for the next day I received orders from the Prince of Neuchâtel to take command of the third infantry division of the Grand Army, consisting of the sixteen third battalions of the regiments belonging to the 1st Corps, and to proceed at once to Wesel, where it was being organised. Of course this destination, which put me on a footing with many celebrated generals, was bound to give me some pleasure; but the 1st Corps, which just then became the 13th, was that of Marshal Davout, and Wesel brought me near Hamburg, where his headquarters were. Thus my request to leave the dullest and least estimable commanders in the Army of Spain resulted only in bringing me under the orders of the most detestable commander in the Grand Army.

My first duty at Wesel was to take part in the trial of Count Bentinck, accused of having fomented an insurrection in his little state of Varel. Le Marois, who was then governor-general of the district, acting under instructions from the Duke of Feltre, Minister for War, wished for a conviction and a capital sentence, and General Lemoine, who presided over the court, did his best, under pressure from Marshal Davout, to secure them; but, by a majority of five to two, the Count was sentenced merely to imprisonment until the conclusion of peace, without confiscation of goods.

On May 31 I received orders to join my division at Bremen, and by a later dispatch I was put in supreme command of all the district between the left bank of the Elbe, from Harburg to Cuxhaven, and the frontier of Holland. I reached Bremen on June 6, but my stay there and my command of the district in question were short, for within a week the Prince of Eckmühl summoned me with all my troops to Hamburg, to take the chief command in that place, pending the arrival of General the Count of Hogendorp. I reached Hamburg towards noon on the 13th; and thinking that it was as well, considering the marshal's character, to pay my respects to him with some promptitude, I alighted at his door before even taking any steps about my quarters. All the communications I had had from him so far had been expressions of content, and I expected a good reception.

My disappointment was therefore great when I saw his brow pucker, his eye grow gloomy, his face sullen. With one hand he raised his spectacles, with the other he rubbed his bald head. Before, or rather without, any greeting, but in a very angry tone, he addressed me with these words:

"So you let off a traitor? You were to have made a much-needed example of Count Bentinck, and you preferred to make the case into a triumph for the emperor's enemies!"

It may be supposed that my surprise soon gave place to indignation. Neither of us would yield a point, and, while he went on adding to his odious assertions, I repeated till I was hoarse:

> The sentence depended on the facts, not on me. Four conscientious men deem it an honour to have shared my opinion, just as I deem it an honour and a consolation to have shared theirs. I explained myself pretty plainly beforehand as to what would be the result if he were brought to trial, and if I had behaved otherwise I should look upon myself as an assassin.

They could hear us shouting all over the house and even in the street; it was scandalous and disgraceful. This scene lasted half an hour; it might have lasted ten times as long without our coming to an understanding. I was talking of honour and conscience to a man who in this case had no notion of what either one or the other was. So I took advantage of a moment when, instead of answering me, he began to puff, to say, "Prince, I have no lodging, and I must go and look for quarters."

"Your lodging is taken," he said, "and the governor will show it you." After which, as I was taking my leave, he said, "You will come and dine with me, and I will talk about the orders that I have for you." May I remark that he never said another word to me about Count Bentinck? That ugly budget was exhausted, but a good many other budgets of controversy were to be filled before long.

An hour later I was with General de Laville, a man distinguished in all ways and an excellent officer, whom I had known when he was on the Duke of Istria's staff at Salamanca. "What a devil of a fellow your marshal is!" said I, when we were alone.

"I own that it is a serious matter to serve with him," he replied; "he forms prejudices easily, and never gets over them. No considerations of humanity have the least value for him. For instance, he is a good husband and father, and in his own home hardly has any will of his own; yet he would without hesitation sacrifice his wife and children in the performance of what he thought his duty. He is quite paternal to the men, kind to the subalterns, but strict with commanding officers, and often more than harsh with the generals. This has what has made him the most enemies; but there is nothing to be done with him; it is an affair of character first, then of habit."

"Well," I said as I left him, "if to what your official position allows you to say we add private information, it will be clear that, in order to be worthy to serve under him, one ought to have killed one's father and mother."

A few days afterwards I got on the same topic with General Dumonceau, under whom I had served as a captain when we attacked the lines of Breda in 1794. Though he spoke with all possible moderation, it was clear that he pitied me for taking his place, and that General Fezensac, one of his brigadiers, agreed with him in congratulating himself on leaving the 13th Corps.

At dinner-time a score of persons assembled in the marshal's drawing-room; he came in himself just as I entered, but he began at once to walk up and down, and, as he said nothing to anyone, no one spoke save for a few brief remarks. We sat down almost immediately, but at table he showed no more disposition to converse. For this he had several reasons; being a very commonplace person, he had nothing to say, and, as no one else cared to start a conversation which he did not keep up, it was limited to a few inconsecutive sentences. Being a great eater, he had something else to do than talking, and, sitting at his right hand, I was amazed at the amount he swallowed. Finally, having the ardour of a fanatic for everything connected with his duty, he meditated about his course of action even during his meals, and rarely lifted his great head, but kept it over his plate, while his eyes only strayed in furtive glances.

After dinner I went with the marshal into his study, and he told me that to the command of my division he was adding the government-in-chief of Hamburg. He gave me information about the place—in some measure no doubt too minute—but none the less important. While swamping himself with details, he furnished to anyone who was capable of selecting and classifying them the materials of rapid information and means to complete it. I repeat, he had neither elevation in his views nor breadth or depth in his ideas, but whatever was within his range he knew with a precision which, though consistent with some disorder, kept him well informed of everything. As may be supposed, everything relating to the question of keeping an eye on the inhabitants, that is to say, to the employment of spies, was very fully dealt with.

On the 23rd Count Hogendorp arrived to take my place, and the same day I received orders to leave Hamburg next day and go to Lubeck, as governor of the town and country and commander of the advance-guard of the army.

During this time an armistice existed which was ultimately prolonged until August 15. On that day a messenger reached me with the information that hostilities would recommence on the 17th and orders to leave Lubeck in two hours with all the French and Danish infantry and artillery. I was to pass the night at Oldersloe and to start the next day for Wandsbek, there to await further orders. At the same time, any statement as to an evacuation of Lubeck was to be contradicted; various officials were to remain there as well as all gendarmes, custom-house officials, and the whole of the Danish cavalry.

Everything that could be got ready in view of a sudden departure had been so, but some things must not be done beforehand for fear of arousing suspicion, while others, from their nature, cannot be. Among these was the distribution of five days' provision for the troops; the provisions were ready, but the distribution of them had to be organised, which, with twelve battalions, could not be done in a moment. Besides, the day happened to be Sunday, and at three in the afternoon on Sunday, unless repeated orders have been given for each man to remain at his post, a certain amount of dispersion is inevitable. Further, it was raining in torrents, and nothing causes so much delay as bad weather. Lastly, as my ordinary dispatches, reaching me at nine o'clock that morning, had informed me that up till then there had been no news of the armistice being denounced, I did not expect to receive any marching orders that day; I was therefore no less perplexed than astonished, but I was struck with the idea that there must be some important reason connected with this abrupt order for a retrograde march, and, by doing everything imaginable to hasten their departure, the troops were able to be started between five and six that evening.

I must mention one among the arrangements which I had to make in carrying out the marshal's orders, because it gives so good a picture of him. When communicating various arrangements to the prefect, I was to order him at the same time to bring up immediately all the money that was to be found in the counting-houses, and to inform the inhabitants that there would be no more amnesty for acts of revolt, that we should henceforth be as severe as we had hitherto been merciful, and that they would no longer get off with a fine.

The terms "amnesty" and "mercy" were comic in the extreme in the mouth of the prince, who had exceeded all the limits of severity; and, however dear they had paid, the inhabitants were far from having hitherto got off with fines, seeing that 644 of them had been banished and a good many shot. One last phrase in the marshal's order respecting them was no less ridiculous: "Let them give their good wishes," he said, "to whom they please, but they must confine themselves to that." This was one way of securing friends for his sovereign, and that in a city which then formed part of the French Empire.

After a forced march through the rain, and across country by ground all poached with three days' downpour, my troops were weary when I reached Oldersloe at 4 a.m. on the 16th. At six we were on the march again, and reached Wandsbek towards evening. So far as troops went, I found there only the third and fourth battalions of the 33rd Light Infantry; General Delcambre, however, the commander of my second brigade, a man whom for all reasons I was glad to have in my division, was waiting for me. He handed me an order to proceed to the camp at Glinde with the whole of my second brigade, giving me information at the same time which showed me clearly enough that we were marching by way of Lauenburg towards the Stecknitz.

I thought I must be dreaming. The Stecknitz, a kind of natural canal, joining the Elbe at Lauenburg, runs into the Trave a short league above Lubeck. It has a course of about seventeen leagues, a distance about equal to that between Lauenburg and Hamburg, whence it followed that, in order to arrive the last with exhausted troops at a point which I might have been the first to reach without any trouble, and with my battalions in good condition, simply by following directly the course of the Stecknitz, I had covered superfluously the whole distance from Lubeck to Wandsbek. Will it be said that the enemy was manoeuvring in such a way as to compromise me?

But, in the first place, the marshal should have known that the number and quality of the enemy's troops were not of a kind to render him very dangerous, and that, as I could be supported by the Danish corps, I ran but little risk; in the second place, if this combination did not offer enough security, and if the marshal was afraid that I might be overmatched, ought he not to have sent me the ten battalions left at Hamburg, or else march as far as Oldersloe with his whole force to meet me, in order to manoeuvre in strength upon the enemy's right, which would have been sufficient both to check him and, as we soon proved, to make him retire?

But neither Delcambre nor I could admit that in any case it would have been other than absurd to send us off along bad roads upon a useless retrograde march which caused me to send 110 men into hospital, cost my troops 2,000 pairs of shoes, and caused serious damage to my artillery, even if the movement had been justified by the circumstances; that is, to collect us with a view to a grand combined movement. But the latest reports had confirmed the successive withdrawals of many of the enemy's corps which we might pursue, so that on that point the marshal could have no uncertainty. To allow of any on other points, it must be supposed that he was unaware of the respective situations of the armies, and of the operations with which the emperor calculated on opening the new campaign; but this cannot be admitted, as a few words on the emperor's position and plans will suffice to show.

The emperor's assailants amounted to 600,000 men, of whom 500,000 had been brought up. To meet these he had 300,000, not reckoning the 100,000 so deplorably distributed among fortresses, 21,000 left in Bavaria with Augereau, 37,000, including 12,000 Danes, under Davout—all wasted forces which would have enabled him to collect 400,000 men under his command. No doubt he had won with greater odds against him but all was changed. Our once invincible soldiers were now only weakly children, plucky enough no doubt, but devoid of strength or experience. In front of them they had the picked veterans of the world, kindled to fanaticism by popular exasperation, while at the same time France was by her cries for peace chilling the zeal of her last defenders. Our chiefs reserved all their vehemence, all their energy, for complaints of the war; while those of the enemy, emboldened by our disasters, could not keep up with the incitements of their hatred or with their desire for vengeance.

It seemed, too, as if the enemy's generals had acquired by a long series of defeats what many of ours had unlearned in the days of prosperity. Napoleon himself was no longer what he had been. Besides, the arena of this gigantic struggle had increased in an alarming fashion. It was no longer the kind of ground of which advantage could be taken by some clever, secret, sudden manoeuvre, such as could be executed in a few hours or, at most, in one or two days. Napoleon was not overlapped as at Austerlitz; he could not turn his enemy's flank as at Marengo or Jena, or even wreck an army, as at Wagram, by destroying one of its wings. Bernadotte to the north with 160,000 men, Blücher to the east with 140,000, Schwarzenberg to the south with 190,000, while presenting a threatening front, kept at such a distance as to leave no opening for one of those unforeseen and rapid movements which, deciding a campaign or a war by a single battle, had made Napoleon's reputation. The man was annihilated in presence of the space.

Again, Napoleon had never till then had more than one opposing army to deal with at one time; now he had three, and he could not attack one without exposing his flank to the others. Once more again, all these masses obeyed the impulse, the thought of one man; and by a supreme stroke of destiny it was a Frenchman—one, too, without the apparent pretext of such men as Bernadotte or Langeron—who impressed this military coalition with the stamp of his genius. History will recount the infamy of Moreau by recording the advice with which he guided our enemies' march, more disastrous as it was to us than all the forces heaped against us. I have already referred to that advice, but it was so faithfully followed by those to whom it was addressed, and played so important a part in our disasters, that I will venture to repeat it.

He bade them expect defeat wherever the emperor gave battle in person, and make their arrangements to mitigate and repair the disaster; to avoid as far as possible coming to an engagement with him, that is, with his Guard or his picked corps and commanders, and with this object to retreat when he advanced and follow when he retired; to attack and fight his lieutenants whenever they could get at them; and, lastly, when these had been beaten and enfeebled, to unite all the forces possible to those already existing, to march against him, snatch victory from him no matter at what cost, and allow him no further respite.

Such was the formidable plan of that fatal campaign, and nothing which could contribute to its success was lacking blunders, bad luck, defection, baseness. Yet it must be said that the blunders of which the bad luck and defections were the consequences emanated, and could only have emanated, from Napoleon. It has been said that his plan for this second campaign of 1813 was the occupation of Berlin by the combined armies of Davout and Oudinot, of Breslau by the Army of Lusatia under Ney, and of Prague by the Grand Army, commanded by himself. But can it be supposed that with an army thus divided in the presence of colossal forces, and forming a salient angle more than sixty leagues wide at the base and of more than 110 leagues in the side, a single man of those who reached Breslau would ever have returned? However, we have no evidence that all these expeditions were to go on simultaneously, and it may be allowed that Napoleon wished to conduct abreast only those to Berlin and Prague, and that was indeed too much.

Anyhow, he opened with a false movement, but succeeded, nevertheless, in getting Blücher out of the way. He did not, however, beat him, and found himself obliged to leave him alone before he had been defeated. Arriving before Dresden, which Moreau and Schwarzenberg—relying on his being at a distance—were besieging, he won a victory, rendered all the easier by the absence of Klenau's corps, in which Moreau's death avenged his country on him and called an anathema down on the traitor's very memory. But bad luck and blundering had already borne their fruit. Macdonald, puffed up by the command of 80,000 men, who never ought to have been entrusted to him, began by infringing his orders, which were to do no more than hold Blücher. In spite of his generals' advice, he attacked him, was crushed and secured, or, at least, hastened the junction of the three hostile armies which he was commissioned to keep apart.

Oudinot left Bayreuth on August 19 and 20 to march on Wittenberg, left the road to Torgau, which he should have followed on the 21st, and on the 22nd, having sent the 4th Corps towards Blankenfeld, the 12th towards Ahrensdorf, and the 7th towards Gross-Beeren, was defeated at the last place by Bernadotte, who, with his 100,000 men, needed only to force the centre of the army in order to beat it. Owing to the enormous blunder of checking the movements of Mortier, Marmont, and Saint-Cyr, before ascertaining whether the corps most in advance and most endangered had halted and secured its rear, Vandamme, who commanded it, proceeded to Kulm and remained there, again contrary to the wish of his generals. There he was surrounded by the whole of Schwarzenberg's army and taken with half his corps.

Finally, Napoleon, not enlightened by Oudinot's disaster as to the danger of breaking up his army, and not understanding that nobody could take his place, and that the part of all his lieutenants together should be limited to giving him time to reach any spot where a serious engagement was to be fought, sent Ney to replace Oudinot, and ended only in connecting the name of Rohrbruck with a new disaster, for which, though it resulted chiefly from the treason of two Saxon divisions and the refusal of two of our cavalry divisions to fight, Napoleon is none the less to blame. In truth, we were being pushed by fate towards the abyss, and were now marching only from mismanagement to misfortune, and from misfortune to humiliation.

To resume my own story, which I interrupted at the point when, on arriving at Wandsbek, after an exhausting march from Lubeck, I received orders to proceed the same evening to the camp at Glinde; but my troops, who were following me, could not reach Wandsbek till nine, and they would come so utterly wearied that it would have been impossible to make the men or horses do another twenty miles. I confined myself therefore, while reporting everything to the marshal, with sending on General Delcambre and two battalions of the 33rd to that camp, where he only arrived, and that with extreme difficulty, at two the next morning. I did not start until the next morning was well advanced.

On the 17th I was ordered to proceed with my second brigade to Bergedorf, in order to support General Pécheux in a reconnoissance on Lauenburg; but, as I was better placed for this purpose at Glinde than at Bergedorf, I was obliged to make a fresh retrograde movement. I was utterly puzzled; but all these inexplicable movements were explained the next day, when the marshal appeared at Bergedorf, and our movement on Lauenburg was finally decided upon.

I arrived before that place on the 19th. The enemy had covered it with redoubts, and was occupying it with 1800 men and ten guns. An attack was at once resolved upon, and, as the redoubts faced the road which we were following on the right bank of the Elbe, the marshal ordered the two first battalions of the 30th to carry them—an order which was carried out with the vigour and confidence of the most veteran troops. With shouts of "Long live the Emperor!" a charge of the bayonet in a few moments placed in our hands the redoubts, the place itself, all the enemy's artillery, and 400 prisoners, forming with 100 killed a loss of 500 men; while, thanks to the rapidity of our attack, our own loss amounted only to two killed and seven wounded.

So far the result was good enough, though it might have been better. The force entrusted with the defence of Lauenburg was enclosed within a triangle formed by the Elbe, the Stecknitz, and us. It was not strong enough to cut its way through our columns, and, in order to retire, it had neither boats nor bridge across the Elbe—only a single bridge across the Stecknitz. We ought to have reached that bridge at the same time as the redoubts, and two battalions would have been enough to cut off the retreat of 1300 men. As it was, the bridge remained clear and they escaped; when I received orders to pursue them, they had got half an hour's start, and I could not catch them, the marshal not having discovered that I could not do it without 500 cavalry. And this was all.

This first action, which might have been better managed, was not followed up. Hardly was it finished when scattering and indecision began afresh. Never did a commander dislocate divisions and regiments more grotesquely. To mess his troops about was a mania and a passion with him, thanks to his perpetual condition of mental indigestion. With him one never knew what orders were or were not given. Not only did he break up divisions, but he detached generals of brigade in such a way as to make them independent. Thus I never saw General Gengoult after he unquestionably formed part of my division, nor did I catch a glimpse of a single man of the 61st.

As I have said, we were not marching in order to fight the weak forces left in Mecklenburg simply with a view of keeping us amused. We were marching, as we knew, in order to join Marshal Oudinot, whose business was to beat Bernadotte's army and capture Berlin. As that marshal was to advance by the left bank of the Elbe, my only uncertainty was whether we should go forward towards Dömitz to threaten the rear of Bernadotte's army and force him to divide it, or cross the Elbe in order to effect our junction on the other side of Magdeburg before Oudinot had been compelled to fight; or to constrain Bernadotte to detach a large body against us before he could put his whole force in action against Oudinot.

It must be further observed that, operating as we were with 27,000 French and 12,000 Danes, we could not afford to make a false movement or lose a day. On the evening of the 20th I marched on Boizenburg, which I had reconnoitred during the previous night, and which the enemy had evacuated, withdrawing in the direction of Wittenburg. As I have said, the ascertained aim of our march being given, it had seemed to me impossible but that we should either follow our road as quickly as possible towards Berlin, by marching on Dömitz, or cross the Elbe to join Oudinot at Magdeburg. I was therefore stupefied when I received an order to turn aside from both these directions in order to go off in one opposite to the wake, of the enemy, whom I had pushed in front of me as far as Zahrensdorf.

I thought at first that the object of this movement was to draw the enemy away, and I was expecting to have to turn back again and to resume my march to the succour of Oudinot, when I got an order to continue our march in the. contrary direction; that is to say, by Mastow on Goldenhow. The marshal took the head of my advance-guard. If he had not been present, I should have been more likely to get ten guides than one, and to march with my advance-guard, verifying my direction at every step. But, as the marshal took this place, I confined myself to keeping at the head of my column, and, knowing his Excellency to be careful in the extreme about details and precautions, I contented myself with making my division march after him.

However, it happened that marching in front even of the scouts, never halting, and putting the troops out of breath with the labour of following him, the marshal forgot what he. was doing on the high road to Wittenburg, and did not take the cross-road leading to Mastow, only finding out his mistake when he was three or four hundred yards past the turning. He returned on his tracks furious and pitched into me, saying that I ought to have attended to my orders only, and seen that they were carried out. I replied that as he was marching at the head of the column I did not think it permissible for me to criticise his leading, which seemed to me to override my previous orders. We had a pretty lively scene—the second and last I had with him. After all, it was not worth so much fuss, for the marshal's mistake had only caused a few moments' delay.

Having got on to our right road, we presently entered a forest, and soon came to a brook too muddy to be forded. There was a wooden bridge over it, to which the enemy had just set fire. But for the 30th we should have been stopped at that point the whole day; but that regiment, always worthy of its old days in the armies of Naples and Rome, extended to right and left of this bridge, and while its fire kept the enemy at a distance three companies from it dashed through the flames and succeeded in crossing the bridge. Once masters of the further bank, they dislodged some squadrons of the enemy's cavalry, and even pursued them eagerly. Thanks to this daring performance, carried out entirely without orders, for there was no time to give any, the fire was put out, and we proceeded.

Our road was winding and sandy; marching became laborious. The guns and especially the reserve battery of 12 -pounders advanced with indescribable slowness, and, as the marshal went always at the pace of his horse, the column soon occupied twice the space it should have done. These prolongations of a column have always annoyed me. Not only do they lead to straggling and bad discipline, but they always involve the risk of exposing the troops to a sudden attack. All my life long I have devoted myself to preventing them, and on this march I was all the more vexed because we were in presence of the enemy, entangled in woods which we did not know, and which had not and could not have been reconnoitred.

The fir-trees offered no obstacle, and we might at any moment be attacked, with no warning save from the scouts whom I had thrown out on my flanks, and I had not been able to place them more than a short distance off. Now if any disaster, any serious loss, or even any useless scuffle took place, the blame would have fallen on Thiébault's division; that is, on its general. It was all very well swearing privately to General Delcambre, but I could not go and tell the marshal, "You are leading like a lunatic." The truer the remark, the less welcome it would be. However, as the underwood gradually got thinner in a way to make me think the end of it was coming, I galloped forward to take my chance of begging for a halt. Just as I came up with the marshal, emerging from the forest, some sixty of the enemy's cavalry appeared, crowning a wooded hill which faced us half a mile away; and the way in which they were prancing seemed to show that they were supported.

Save for the officers and sergeants, our troops, as I have said, consisted of recruits who had had only these three days' experience of war. The infantry had had little instruction, the artillery still less, while the cavalry had nothing of that arm but the name. By the marshal's fault, the column was spread over a distance at once absurd and dangerous, doubling the time required for deploying. At last we emerged upon a little plain with a hill in front of us, on which we saw that the enemy had battalions and batteries in position. The first necessity impressed upon us was to avoid everything that could shake troops as raw as ours; then we ought to have halted the head of the column, closed up the infantry and artillery, and deployed the 30th as best we could by solid battalions, while the cavalry, marching through the wood, parallel to the rest of the column and flanked by the light infantry, was advancing to the edge of the forest in such a way that the troops who wore arms might debouch simultaneously and in good order, for which purpose the occupation of the forest was an advantage to us.

These simple precautionary steps, which I am almost ashamed to point out, having been taken, there would have been plenty of time to see whether we should do better to attack the corps in front of us on the hill, or limit ourselves to a defensive combat with no particular result. The first course was evidently the best. When we came out into the plain, we had to our left a great space of enclosed ground surrounded with walls, and on one side resting upon the forest; to our right a little wood, thrown out like an advanced sentinel on to the plain. To throw some skirmishers into the enclosed ground, to take possession of the opening, occupying it in force and making it the point of the first movements, then, covered by our artillery fire, to march on one of the enemy's wings—this was the obvious plan, and easy to execute. What did the marshal do?

Without having experienced and shared the astonishment and vexation of all who witnessed it, one would not venture to say that, at sight of the sixty prancing troopers, the marshal, instead of giving me his orders, or even discussing what had better be done, fell to rushing about and shouting like a man beside himself, "There is the enemy! Where's the infantry? Where's the cavalry? Where are the guns?"—on which all the *aides-de-camp* galloped off to bring the troops up at full speed. It was enough to shake and demoralize veteran troops; and if an officer of what rank so ever had done anything of the sort, the marshal would have cashiered him on the spot, and he would have been right a hundred times over.

But what was worthy of this opening was that, as each battalion emerged panting from the wood, it was immediately broken up, and, without any need, one company was thrown into the little wood, another into the enclosed ground, a third sent forward to skirmish, the result being that, with the exception of the 111th, three of whose battalions remained entire, the other seven present were all in companies, shuffled like a pack of cards. The men who had fallen behind did not know where to find their companies. During the action they did what they liked, and, as almost our whole force was in the front line, we had not a single man in reserve. Luckily, the enemy was no less weak in numbers than in quality. He only brought up four guns, and they fired as badly as ours. I never saw a slacker combat.

Such as it was, it had been going on for an hour, and nothing enterprising had been done, when six squadrons charged those of our troops who were forming a kind of line between the enclosed ground and the wood. It was a ridiculous charge, and the squadrons were repulsed as they deserved to be, but the fourth battalion of the 111th, making it clear at last what we might have done, formed square at the double, pursued the cavalry, flung it back upon the hill, attacked a battalion of the enemy with shouts of "Long live the Emperor!" broke it, and forced it to retire upon the guns which were playing on us. It was a brilliant manoeuvre, and did all the more honour to Major Lesbrossier, commanding the battalion, that the marshal, who looked on without seeing anything and commanded without giving any orders, had not sent any orders to him; nay, instead of supporting him by a forward movement, instead of taking the hill, and perhaps the guns, he confined himself to recalling the battalion.

About three quarters of an hour later, while the musketry was continuing along our front, and every round from our guns was driving me wild by the badness of its aim, from 1500 to 2,000 cavalry suddenly came round the little wood and fell upon our horse. They would have broken it, and even reached the reserve park and the equipages, had not seven or eight companies of different battalions posted at the outer edge of the little wood, and one battalion of the 111th, the right of which rested on the forest, helped to check them. At nightfall the enemy retired; we did not send a single man to reconnoitre the hill which he had occupied, and passed the night on the ground where we had halted at sight of him.

In view of the possibility of a surprise, it was urgent to disentangle the inconceivable muddle which the marshal had made of all the regiments, and to re-form them, for the companies had been so scattered that there was no one left as intermediary between the general and the captain. It was no easy matter, especially with night coming on, to put a little order into the chaos; but I wished to see all my corps re-formed before anyone rested, and, in order to leave no one any excuse for shirking, and to get the field-officers to help the captains, General Delcambre and I set the example. I had been on horseback since daybreak.

At night I had dismounted, and it was midnight before order was restored. Worn out, dead beat, I had just thrown myself on some bundles of straw which had been spread for me under a shelter of branches in the little wood where I had fixed my bivouac, and I had hardly fallen asleep, when an *aide-de-camp* woke me to say that the marshal was asking for me. It was a long half-mile from my bivouac to that of the marshal, in the middle of the enclosures. The night was dark, the ground uneven. The *aide-de-camp*, who thought he was certain of the right way, mistook it, and made me go twice the distance, and when I got there his Excellency was snoring like a cracked organ-pipe. Thinking that a summons of this kind must have a serious reason, I woke General Cesar de Laville to inquire what the marshal wanted of me. He had no idea. "Well," said I, somewhat irritated, "wake him."

He called him, pushed him, shook him. At last the marshal opened his eyes. At the words, "Here is General Thiébault, whom you sent for," he raised his heavy head, and, having at last got into a sitting position, he opened his eyes wide, suddenly shut them again, then, looking at me drowsily, muttered, "How does the public spirit of the troops stand?"

"The public spirit?" I returned; "do you mean the spirit of the troops?" I was about to add that their spirit was as good as could be, but the marshal had already fallen back in a lump on his straw. General de Laville, as much perplexed by this absurdity as I was in a bad temper at having been sent for to listen to it, advised me to lie down between him and the marshal and wait till he woke, as the sole means of ever finding out what was wanted of me. I agreed, even yet not believing that after such a hard day I should have been made to come so far at one in the morning without a grave reason. However, when at daylight the marshal recovered such senses as he had, it turned out that he had nothing at all to say to me, except that we were to march again at seven in the morning information which any drummer might have brought.

The next day, August 22, we moved on to Wittenburg, and the day after to Schwerin, where we remained till September 2 with no apparent object, and, save for a few reconnoissances, doing nothing. On some of these two battalions with fifty cavalry were employed, under the command of Colonel Holtz, of the 111th, and General

Delcambre. Happening to be at the camp of the 111th on August 31, I saw the marshal and his escort coming. "I am going to reconnoitre myself," said he. From what I had heard of reconnoissances made in his company, thinking too that some amusement might be afforded by an operation of this kind executed by a man who could not see a bit, I was curious to see what sort of job he would make of it; so I proposed to go with him, and we started. Instead of following a road, we went across country, skirting a wood which was habitually full of Cossacks. This detail the marshal knew as well as I did, and some people would have paid attention to certain knolls which lay along our road. "We, however, did not trouble ourselves about such a small matter, but continued to gallop straight ahead, like wolves. We had gone good five miles in this way when the marshal caught sight of a poor pedlar, going along with his box of wares on his back, and made a dash at him.

Meetings of this kind were his delight. It is impossible to imagine anything more minute than his questions, more horrible than his threats, more cruel than the means he employed. Whatever answer the poor wretches might give, they were carried off and locked up, while, in spite of their tears, their prayers, their despair, what became of them and their goods Heaven only knew. The marshal was always inclined to suspect the worst; and as with him suspicion was tantamount to proof, all these poor devils were spies, and only escaped with their lives by miracle. In the present case, two troopers at once took off the man's load and brought him up. All this time the marshal had been looking in an absent way at each of his companions, ending with me. "It would be a funny prize for the Cossacks," he said to me; "just one officer of every rank"—which was true—from himself to a sub-lieutenant, and even to a sergeant and a corporal in command of the escort.

"Your Excellency is well aware," I said, "that the capture would not be complete. You are admirably mounted, and I not badly; but our suite would not share that advantage." He dropped the joke, and taking me for interpreter began his questions. The first personal inquiries the man answered clearly; but when I asked him if he had seen any troops where he had been, of what country and what arms, who commanded them, where the Crown Prince of Sweden was, if there was any talk of a battle, what was said about the result of it, nothing could be extracted from him but "*Ich weiss nicht—ich habe nichts gesehen.*"

"Oh! he knows nothing, he has seen nothing, has not he?" returned the marshal in a rage. "Tell him that that is because he does not choose to know, and has been paid to say he has not seen. He is not prowling about Schwerin for trade; he is a spy, and I shall have his package burnt and himself shot." These threats only produced a fresh denial. "Tie him to a horse's tail and bring him along!" roared the marshal, putting his own horse into a trot and taking the road back to Schwerin, But to tie up the man, who would have struggled, somebody must have dismounted; four or five minutes would have been lost, and we should have to make up our minds to going rather slowly. Taking him up on a horse would have had the same result, and circumstances led to his being left behind—that is, escaping; for just then the marshal seemed to perceive that he was not on very secure ground. From a trot he rapidly passed into a full gallop.

Never did an escort keep closer to the person it was escorting. The two generals, the six staff-officers, the troopers and all formed a single group round the marshal; but before long I was his only companion. We reached the camp at the full stretch of our animals. That we had escaped was a wonder, for we had gone more than a mile beyond a forest which was a haunt of the Cossacks, and I do not know how it came to pass that our retreat was not cut off.

On September 2, in the midst of perfect tranquillity, Davout got the first news of Oudinot's defeat at Gross-Beeren. It might have been thought that he would also have been told that Ney had taken Oudinot's place, and was going to try his luck once more against Bernadotte; in which case our co-operation was more called for than ever. But my orders were to start at two o'clock and cover the retreat of the army, returning by another road to the point where we had started. I marched by Gadebusch to Ratzeburg, where the marshal's headquarters were fixed, and there found orders to take all the reserve park at that place, and return by Mölln to Lauenburg. Here I found General Gengoult and the 61st, and for the first time had all my division under my orders. I took up a position with them on the right bank of the Stecknitz and on the heights of Büchen, across the Schwarzenbek road, and not far from Lauenburg and Boizenburg.

CHAPTER 19

Back to France for the Last Time

The instruction of my division made daily progress, and the campaign, short and miserable though it had been, had accustomed the men to war. I had fourteen battalions under my command; and when I remembered what Masséna had done in 1797 with a division of almost similar strength, I thought I might profit by the lessons of that great captain to extend the field of possible strategic calculations, and began to think over all the combinations, whether for attack or defence, of which the ground admitted. But it was written that never again should I have an outbreak of zeal, a hope of success, an opportunity of showing what I could do, without its being snatched from me. I had accordingly enjoyed my enviable position for barely fifteen hours when I received orders to hand over the command of my troops to General Vichery, in exchange for his, and go and resume command at Lubeck.

I could recall nothing in my conduct during our inroad into Mecklenburg which could justify a snub, if my recall to Lubeck was to be regarded as such. I had, as the marshal desired, carried out the evacuation of Schwerin in such a way that the enemy did not become aware of it for twelve hours; and the marshal had written to express his satisfaction. There was, therefore, nothing to account for his taking a step disagreeable to me; nor, indeed, was he the man to gild a pill. With him, the absence of blame was equivalent to praise, so I could but take as good value the words of the order which implied that I was sent there because I was wanted there. Still, I was none the less dissatisfied with the change, and determined to have it out with the marshal before I proceeded to Lubeck. He merely paraphrased his order, and added, "You know the country by heart. You are appreciated at Lubeck. No one will be so useful there as you."

When about to mount on my way back, I met General Loison. He was furious, and his wrath was no less energetic than eloquent. Of all the generals I have known, Vandamme and Loison were the two who spoke most fluently and forcibly. "If you see me here again," he said, "it is not the marshal's fault. If I had followed his orders, my division would have been lost. To have evacuated Schwerin without securing my retreat is disgraceful—infamous! But," he resumed, in the sardonic tone habitual with him, "what can you expect of a chief who cannot be made to see that he would have sacrificed me?"

I reached Lubeck on September 6, and occupied myself with the defences of the place and other matters, including the execution of the marshal's orders to send vast quantities of provisions to Hamburg. Before long I began to be more concerned with the fear that the marshal might give the enemy time to cut off his retreat, and even form the idea of shutting himself up in Hamburg. The recent disasters had made it obvious that the time had more than come to give up the system of dispersing troops which had been so fatal to us. It was urgently necessary for us to fall back, either to unite with the emperor or to cover his flank. Nothing, however, gave any indication that the marshal troubled his head about the matter, but it was so important that it was a positive duty to take some kind of initiative.

The perplexity was to know how to enter upon questions of such a delicate kind with so touchy and rough a man. Loison was the only person who, from his seniority, his power of ready and nervous expression, and the kind of habit of free speech which he had retained, could undertake at a pinch to bring the marshal to discuss what the interest of the army, of the emperor and of France enjoined, and I resolved to have some talk with him on the subject. I obtained leave to go to Ratzeburg on the morning of the 22nd; three hours later I was with Loison. We had an exhaustive discussion of the subject which had brought me, and we decided that he should allow me time to talk to the marshal about the matters which formed the pretext for my excursion, but that at the moment of my leaving him, he, Loison, should take my place, and that I should not go back till I heard the result of his confidence.

All this was carried out, but Loison could do nothing.

"I do not interpret orders, and I form no opinion as to intentions," had replied this creature, as we called him. "The emperor has ordered me to keep Hamburg, and I shall defend that place till the last extremity; besides, so long as Magdeburg, Hamburg, and Dantzig hold out, the emperor has lost nothing."

"But," returned Loison, "do not circumstances seem to you sufficiently serious for you to set forth your doubts and ask for fresh orders?"

"The emperor does not need anybody's advice; as for orders, I wait for them—I never invite them." Seeing it was impossible to produce any impression on the marshal's well-tried obstinacy, I thought I might at least press the matter upon Loison.

"Do not you yourself," I rejoined, "think that you ought to write to the Prince of Neuchâtel, telling the marshal when you have done it?"

"Oh, dear, no! Let them settle the matter—it concerns them more than us. You will see, however, that we shall end by being blockaded at Hamburg, and that for want of food we shall be captured without honour or glory."

On October 18 the Battle of Leipzig took place. The terrible news of this last gigantic struggle which Napoleon was to wage reached us with all the rapidity which our enemies secured in the spreading of it. If anything, even at that moment, had happened to the marshal, Loison would have taken command of the army; in two days we could have fallen back upon Hamburg, and by the 25th we might have been at Bremen with over 30,000 men; the whole garrison of Magdeburg might have joined us, and we could have retired either to Wesel or to Antwerp. But Napoleon's madness was complicated by Davout's stupidity.

All the fires of the infernal regions would not have sufficed to enlighten the marshal upon what was obvious to everybody, and the question which everyone was uttering all around him, "What business have we to be here?" was for him only evidence of inadequacy and cowardice. Imperturbable in his thick hide, he still remained convinced that so long as Magdeburg, Dantzig, and Hamburg held out, the emperor had lost nothing; doubtless, too, he still dreamt no less confidently of the throne of Poland as the reward of the fresh services which he fancied himself to be still rendering, when he was consummating Napoleon's ruin.

On November 2 the order of the day informed the troops that, communications with Wesel being cut, the corps could no longer rely on their depots, and that the generals must at once hold inspections to ascertain the state of clothing and shoes. On the 4th I received a dispatch containing orders to go at once to Hamburg, where I should receive further instructions. The command of the troops and the governorship of the country I; was to hand over to General Lallemand.

I cannot refrain from the admission that since the collapse of Leipzig my ideas had undergone a change. The army which the emperor had succeeded in remaking had been split up, beaten, and cut to pieces till it had no longer a fifth of its number with which to face enemies elated by victory. Could France, in spite of her exhaustion and with all the confidence and dash gone out of her, still undertake a national war? Such a war could have no result unless protracted, and of this the strength and fury of our enemies allowed no hope.

Lastly, considering that Napoleon could not have any more losses or commit another mistake without being done for, while the allies could still commit plenty with impunity, I despaired for the first time of the success of our arms and the safety of our country, while the possible interests of my family took, for the first time in my life, the first place in my thoughts. At the moment of shipwreck the individual separates himself from the crowd until nothing remains which he is not ready to sacrifice to his own interests.

To return to the command which had been forced upon me at Hamburg. As the result of the personal feelings which had suddenly taken possession of me, I could only resign myself to it by force, and, resigned as I was, I wished for some further opinion than my own to decide what I had to do. Accordingly, after having made all my arrangements for leaving Lubeck the next morning, I went off in the evening to Ratzeburg, *incognito*, to see Loison, whom I thought I had better consult as to what I owed to my rank and to myself, he said:

> Confidence for confidence I have had something to do with this decision; and, if I did not advise it, I at least suggested it, for it was not the marshal's own idea. But you may be sure that he has adopted it so fully that he will not abandon it, and what greater mark of confidence would you have him show you or to whom could he show it better than to you? Our safety or our destruction will not depend upon musketry or cannon-shots, now that the marshal has left us no other part to play than that of garrisoning a useless town. They will not attack us in Hamburg with 36,000 men to defend it, nor will they burn a town of that importance.
>
> We shall not, however, be delivered unless we can wait till some one comes for us, and no one will come unless we are worth

an effort. So we must manage to live there and to keep enough men to make a good show. The whole question of our future is, therefore, wrapped up in that of subsistence, and this cannot remain in the charge of a commissary-general and his subordinates. None of the existing officials are capable of the task, and the marshal came back from Hamburg in much perplexity where to find a man possessing zeal and intelligence as well as strength of character and rank sufficient to make an impression; in naming you I put an end to his uncertainty.

There was no more to be said, and on the next day but one I was at Hamburg. My thoughts on the way thither were melancholy enough as I reflected on the recent events, attended as they had been by the annihilation of all our glories. I made an effort to review them without undue favour or severity. Napoleon was too gigantic to admit of the one and too much identified with France to justify the other. My conclusion was that if General Bonaparte, the Bonaparte of Italy, Egypt, Marengo, had passed judgement on Napoleon's campaign of 1813, he would doubtless have approved its opening, but would have condemned, and have been shocked at, the whole sequel of the operations. If one may exhaust this fancy by applying it to subsequent events, one might say that Bonaparte would have found himself again on the plains of Champagne, but have failed to recognise himself immediately afterwards; while at Ligny, Quatre Bras, Waterloo, Paris, Lorient, he would have deemed himself to have outlived his own identity.

Thus I journeyed, sorely discouraged, towards Hamburg, while the heroic remnants of the Grand Army were illustrating their disastrous retreat to the Rhine by one more victory at Hanau. I was only to leave that city under the standard of the lilies borne by princes mounted on Cossacks' horses princes who, in their desire to stifle liberty, were to do for licence all that Napoleon, while respecting equality, had done for authority.

[The details of the blockade of Hamburg must be passed over for want of space; nor are they calculated to interest the general reader. It may be mentioned that General Thiébault was president of this "Committee of Subsistence," with special charge of the stores of grain, flour, etc.; and was also in command of the defences on the north-east front of the town. The Elbe front was under the charge of General Vichery, the south-west front under that of General Loison, who also looked after the distribution of provisions. Food never ran short, nor were there any military operations of importance. The theatre was open and operas were often given, the principal performer being Mme Fodor-Mainvielle, who afterwards had some reputation in Paris. After the performances it was Davout's custom to hold a council of his generals and other officials. Thiébault describes one of these:]

The marshal walked up and down the room without saying a word, the rest of the company being seated round the room on chairs, a little distance apart. He looked at no one, and made no movement save occasionally to lift one hand to his bald head and scrub it vigorously, apparently with the object of stimulating his always refractory thoughts. Then he would stop in front of one of us, push his spectacles up on his forehead, and ask a question. A few words would be exchanged, and he would resume his walk. When, as usually happened, he had no subjects for discussion and no orders to give, he would fall foul of either the commissary-general of the 13th Corps, or the prefect, Baron de Breteuil. In the case of the former, we were only distressed by the marshal's bad manners; but M. de Breteuil was an excellent man, in general esteem, and it made one indignant to see the marshal plant himself in front of him and say, "Now, M. de Breteuil, of what use are you? Pray tell me what I can do with a prefect? A drummer would be of more use to me. You eat the soldiers' bread and do nothing for it."

The baron was too polite to put him to confusion with any of the obvious repartees, and did not like to go so far as to say, "I am paying my share for your blunders"; but his attendances became fewer and fewer.

However, if he made an exhibition of others, he sometimes made one of himself. I remember one of these meetings when he afforded us a most perfect comedy. I quite forget what the business was, but an order had to be drawn up. After restating the subject ten times over, eliciting a good many observations or objections which he perhaps understood, perhaps did not, which he forgot, remembered, or distorted, and finally making up his mind, he wished to dictate the order—did dictate it, indeed, but in such a fashion that when the secretary read what he had just written there was no sense in it. Even the marshal himself noticed this, and cried, "That's not it! Tear up what you have written, and take another sheet of paper."

A fresh dictation followed, which came to rather less than the first.

The third was even worse. At first we had looked at each other out of the corners of our eyes; presently some furtive smiles played on our lips. At the third test of our gravity we began to bite them. Then the marshal stopped, and, pointing to the table, said to me, "General Thiébault, sit down there. You know what I mean; but you know too that out of every twenty things I say nineteen are always stupid." I hastened to the table to avoid exploding, and, bending over my paper to conceal or suppress my feelings, I drafted for him the order which he meant to give. He signed it, and so this most ridiculous but most diverting meeting ended. That speech was a lasting joy during the rest of the siege, and long afterwards.

Loison, Watier, and I never met without the first speaker saying, "But you know quite well that out of every twenty things I say"— and another would complete it straightway— "Nineteen are always stupid."

I relieved some of the tedium of the siege by finishing a novel which I had begun to write in Spain,[1] and by having my portrait painted by the professor of painting at the Hamburg Academy. Two years ago I heard that this portrait was still in the private room of a member of the Hamburg Senate.

Meantime, while shut up in Hamburg, we were depriving France of so many defenders. The marshal continued to appear quite satisfied with the course he had taken, and his mistakes lasted until the arrival of a spy, who had been delayed overlong outside the town, bearing a letter from the Minister for War. At that moment Loison was with the marshal. The fact of his being present when the dispatch was received, made it necessary to confide in him, and, besides, the marshal was quite capable of not suspecting the nature of the message sent him with so much difficulty and danger. It is possible even that he expected compliments on his determination and on his conduct. Anyhow, when alone with Loison he began to read the dispatch aloud. After that there was no stopping, and Loison had to be put in possession of the whole of Clarke's composition, enjoining in very harsh terms a retreat which had now become impossible. It began with these words: "What are you doing at Hamburg, marshal, while the enemy is at the gates of Paris?"

The marshal seemed quite cast down. Loison, who on the former occasion had not been able to vanquish his self-willed pride, and in-

---

1. [No mention of this novel is to be found in the list of Thiébault's published works.]

duce him to take the step which he was now blamed for not having taken, was obliged to cheer him up by representing that no one could hold him responsible for the non-execution of orders that he had not received, and that the only thing to be done now was to make the best of the irrevocable.

One extremely important recollection is connected with this period. Bernadotte was dissatisfied with the way in which the heads of the Coalition treated him. In spite of his own victories, and the part he had played at Leipzig, he was afraid that, after having helped to dethrone Napoleon, he might be turned off the throne of Sweden. His army was no longer in the front line, but was dragging along in the rear of the armies which had crossed the Rhine. This was an ignominious position, and moreover it was dangerous, and, under the influence of fear or ill-humour, suggested to him the idea of collecting under his command all that was left of our garrisons in the north or on the Elbe and Rhine, uniting them with his own troops, and raising the standard against the Coalition. Then, returning to France at the head of his own Swedes and 100,000 French saved by him, he would take the hostile armies in rear and annihilate them; afterwards, as his reward for this great service, taking the place of Napoleon on the throne of France.

But, in order for the execution of this plan to be possible, it would have to be adopted by Marshal Davout, since not only had he the strongest force under him, but also because he was the only person of sufficient rank and reputation to carry with him the other commanders of army corps and fortresses. But where was anyone to be found who would venture to approach the marshal with a plan of this kind? How was he to be got at?

Now the person to whom Bernadotte applied for this important business was one Rainville, formerly an *aide-de-camp* of Dumouriez, now a hotel-keeper at Altona. He accepted the post of go-between, went to Hamburg, and called upon Loison. Feeling strongly the seriousness of our position, and considering the profound impression which Clarke's letter had made upon the marshal, who had been reprimanded by an obscure general of division for his conduct as commander-in-chief, Loison advised Rainville to carry out his errand, promised to support the proposal if the marshal consulted him, and added that, as no one belonging to the army could take the initiative in such a matter, he, Rainville, as a naturalised Dane, was the only person who could undertake to open the subject. Thus encouraged,

Rainville presented himself to the marshal.

He began by what was merely an introduction; but, when it became necessary to touch on the real subject of his errand, he suddenly began to think of the marshal's short way with people, his fancy for executions of this kind, his terrible provost-marshal, and I know not how many instances of persons shot without trial. Terrified by the idea that his fate depended on a moment of ill-temper, on a whim, on policy, and shuddering at the idea of taking his life in his hand against such an adversary, this diplomat, whose daring was not equal to the excellence of his catering, ran away from, rather than look his leave of, the marshal, and left Hamburg, hardly giving himself time to tell Loison, who was waiting to hear the result of the confidence, that the marshal's character and reputation had prevented him from breaking silence. Thus vanished that hope, if such it might be called.

As the news became more grievous, Loison's anger against Rainville increased. When we heard of the abdication, he spoke of the errand which Rainville had not had the courage to discharge, and the marshal exclaimed, "Rainville is an ass!" But this proved nothing. It requires more foresight and judgement than Marshal Davout possessed to seize the right moment for such plans. At present he was the emperor's enthusiastic servant, and before he would have changed sides it was necessary, as indeed he showed, that he should have seen no further chance of escape, either by victory or by a treaty, and that he should have been in no danger of being compromised, not only by having rejected Bernadotte's proposal, but also by not having shot his enemy. These considerations mitigated the regret which Rainville's pusillanimity or prudence caused me.

There were also insurmountable difficulties in the way of the execution of that scheme. Bernadotte, no doubt, would have played a heroic and decisive part, which would have identified his name for ever with that of Trance if he had undertaken, on her behalf alone, what he had planned to do for himself. In that case he would have been certain of success against the allies, but not sufficiently so against Napoleon, who would never have forgiven him for saving France from the perils, the misfortunes, the disgrace into which he had himself dragged her. But it was not in Bernadotte's nature thus to win the title of "the greatest citizen of the world "any more than it was in Napoleon's nature to recompense such a service. Bernadotte thought only of himself. He only wished to exchange the throne of Sweden for the possible reversion of the crown of France, and from the moment that he appeared merely as an ambitious usurper he was not of sufficient calibre to take the place of his rival.

Reduced thus to a mere dream of ambition, the only chance for Bernadotte's plan seemed to me to have been that a majority of the heads of the Coalition might have been willing to sacrifice their resentment against him in order to get rid of Napoleon. But then the "King of Rome" came to the front; the Emperor of Austria would have been all the more disposed to support the rights of his grandson, as promising a prolongation of his daughter's regency, and France would have as much preferred a Napoleon to Bernadotte as she would have preferred a Cossack to one of the leaders of the Emigration. If I may judge of others from myself, we should have been only too glad for Bernadotte to get us out of Hamburg and take us back to the aid of France; but, once within touch of the armies that were covering Paris, no power on earth could have prevented us from joining them.

When day broke on May 9, 1814, the enemy's lines on the Harburg front were draped with white flags. No sooner did the marshal hear of this than, in spite of the rumours which were spreading and gaining credit, he gave orders to fire on these flags. In less than a quarter of an hour they were all down; and if some men in the army maintained that the hoisting of these white rags was a dodge to deceive us and sow dissension among us, the greater number were by no means reassured. Moreover, fresh flags soon appeared, out of range of our shot, and this seemed significant.

We began to think that it might not have been wise to knock over the first lot, if what they portended really came to pass. Anyhow, this manner of teasing us went on till one in the morning of the 10th, when we were ordered to meet at once at the marshal's for a communication of the highest importance. We went, as may be supposed, with promptitude, and found him striding about, his agitation so natural that it was clear something extraordinary had happened. As soon as the last general of division had arrived, the marshal said:

"Gentlemen, the emperor has abdicated on behalf of himself and his family. France returns to the sway of the Bourbons."

After a silence which no one interrupted he proceeded:

"This news is certain. A relation of my own whom the provisional government at Paris has sent with a message to me has just brought it, together with an order to communicate it at once to the troops, to make them take the white cockade, recognise Louis Xavier de Bourbon as king under the style of Louis XVIII, and to make the army sign an act of allegiance. On this table lie copies of the *Moniteur* relating to these events; read them and then we will confer."

Therewith he left us, and we devoured rather than read everything connected with these two gigantic events. In half an hour the marshal returned, and, as he seemed to wish to know what we thought of the terrible news, and no one else was in a hurry to reply, I spoke as follows:

> One cannot give an opinion upon accomplished facts over which one has no power. As for Louis XVIII, let us hope the best of his wisdom. As for Napoleon, if we had escaped the disaster which, owing to him, is now come upon us, we should have undergone it next year; or, if we had escaped it next year, we should have undergone it the year after. Since the disaster was bound to come sooner or later, better today than tomorrow—the abyss is not so deep.

A kind of "agreed" was expressed in the faces and the gestures of the majority of the bystanders.

We did not break up till six in the morning. It was decided to send an address from the generals to the king, and I was commissioned to prepare it. At nine we met again, and I read my draft. "That will do," said the marshal, and the rest agreed. The duty of conveying it to Paris was entrusted to General Delcambre.

On May 11 General Foucher of the artillery arrived at Hamburg, with the title of Royal Commissioner to the 13th Corps. He brought the news that the Prince of Eckmühl was succeeded in the command of it by Lieutenant-General Count Gerard. His supersession, as well as the choice of General Fouchér for the mission, astonished and distressed us. Fouchér had no services nor merit of any kind, and his selection could only be the result of an intrigue. The supersession of the marshal, too, seemed quite uncalled for. He might have at least been allowed time to declare himself. This insult to a man before he had been put to the test was an offence to the whole army, and seemed to us all the more serious that it gave evidence of a contempt for all good manners, a hostile disposition towards the army, and a precipitation betokening more passion than wisdom. What guarantee remained to generals and subalterns alike when one of their chiefs of highest rank was condemned unheard?

The marshal gave us a dinner next day, and could not well avoid inviting Foucher. In the course of the meal this general by favour of the emperor carried his ostentatious royalism to the point of saying, "I should be prouder of being appointed lieutenant by Louis XVIII than I am of having been appointed lieutenant-general by Bonaparte!"

The words were received with cries of "Oh! oh!" and I noticed them by saying, "Anyone who makes a remark of that kind can have nothing to be proud of in any of his steps." Everyone looked at him, but his silence showed that the cap fitted. After dinner everyone avoided him, and he presently took his leave.

Before parting from the marshal, we decided, as a protest against the insult that had been offered him, to give him a dinner at Rainville's. At first we settled not to ask Foucher, but he heard of it, and persuaded Vichery, the only one of us who was on terms with him, to speak for him. Vichery succeeded in getting an invitation for Foucher, but this only saved His Majesty's Commissioner from one snub to inflict another upon him; such an one, indeed, as no other would have borne. He was placed a long way from the marshal and hardly noticed.

After dinner, on our return from Altona, we betook ourselves to the theatre. I was in my box with my *aides-de-camp* when General Cesar de Laville came in. "Would you believe it?" said he, unable to refrain from laughing—"after all that has passed, General Foucher carried his familiarity so far as to go to the prince's box. But he will not have anything to boast of, for hardly had he entered when the prince got up, went to him, and said, 'General, you can only have come here to bore me or to insult me. If it is to insult me, I am a lieutenant-general like yourself; if it is to bore me, I declare to you that, as I am here to amuse myself, if you do not go at once I will kick you out!' And he went without a word. He did right, for the marshal was about to take him by the shoulders and turn him out."

In order to prolong the joke, I made my way at once to the marshal's box, going in as though I were looking for General Foucher, with the remark that I thought I had seen him enter. No more was wanted to smooth everyone's brow, except the marshal's, which was not to be smoothed so easily.

General Gérard arrived on the 24th, and the marshal departed on the 26th, marching with the first column, which I also accompanied to the Rhine. After the gratuitous outrage that had been done to him, and from the day when his supersession was announced, though I had never before appeared in his house except when sent for or invited, I went every morning to pay my respects to him, and I continued to do so till we reached Düsseldorf on June 10. Next morning I took my final leave of him, and I never again set foot in his house as long as he lived. Leaving him to march on, I went to Paris by post.

The Rhine, our natural frontier, lately ours by conquest, was Prussian; Prussians were still guarding French fortresses, and it was with a shudder that I saw them at home where we had lately been. When I reached Valenciennes and found myself again in France, it seemed to me that I was in a land bestowed on us by charity or left as a loan at high interest. If I saw French soldiers again, their noble standards had disappeared with our military renown, and the white flag, the white cockades, for me so far from spotless, appeared to me only as stained with defeat and disgrace.

Chapter 20

The End of our Greatness

Twenty-three years of terrible wars, begun with so much heroism, carried on so unflinchingly and gloriously, ended by blunders so great and disasters so appalling, had produced fatigue, exhaustion, disgust, anger. There had been an unanimous wish for peace, and peace had been obtained, but in the calm of repose the sentiment of honour resumed its rights. Having come to ourselves, we could fathom the depth of the abyss into which we had been hurled, and measure the distance from the giant whom we had lost to the man who took his place. Great errors, doubtless, had marked and had brought about the end of his mighty reign, but with him there had been great hopes and a future in view, while those who figured in his place offered neither security nor hope. No one could venture to expect anything from a family in which the only man was a woman, and which was driven astray by the rage for vengeance. Then what forebodings did we not reach when our thoughts stayed on the heir to the crown of Louis XVI, and on those who seemed certain to be his successors; the first of these a prince who, in his youth, had scandalized the world by his profligacy and extravagance, whose conduct during the war had made his own partisans proclaim his cowardice.

The opinion to this effect, which was manifest in 1814, was, as is well known, justified by the future. No one remained more strange to France and her affairs than Charles X. His reply to a man who pointed out to him that the encroachments of the priests were opposed to all the interests of France is well known: "*It is a question of my salvation and not of France.*" As for his sons, or those who were called so,[1]—one an

---

1. It is well known that the father of the Duke of Berri was supposed to be the son of the postmaster at Agen, a sturdy fellow employed as a counterjumper at Bordeaux. Certainly there was nothing of the Bourbon about (continued next page),

imbecile, the other a boor—they played their parts in such a way as to afford means to judge alike both of their dangerous dispositions and of their profound incapacity to do anything except become unpopular in France.

The man who had contributed most to their restoration, and who made the most efforts to keep them within proper limits, so that he might be able to keep them on the throne, in the hope of reigning in their name, was M. de Talleyrand. Having lost the emperor's favour, and offended by being kept out of public affairs, he hoped to find in the Restoration a means of appeasing his vengeance and playing a great part. The story told with reference to his disgrace is that his treachery having been proved by authentic documents, which the emperor had under his hand, the emperor sent for him with a view to his confusion and utter ruin; but having begun by overwhelming him with reproaches and insults, and having shouted loud enough to be heard, he deemed him sufficiently punished, or perhaps thought it as well, with such a man, to leave some opening for reconciliation, and so sent him away without touching on the real reason of his wrath. This crafty personage, perceiving from the inquiring and spiteful looks of those before whom he had to pass on his way out that they were searching in his face for traces of the tempest which he had passed through, said, "What a pity that so great a man should be so ill-bred!"—and the laugh was again on his side.

Of a truth, the good advice and the pretty wit of M. de Talleyrand could not save princes who, as Napoleon said, had in five-and-twenty years of deserved misfortune learnt nothing and forgotten nothing. They insulted the army, they dismissed all the respectable officials, they snatched away all that could be snatched from a nation that had already been despoiled. Less than this would have been the ruin of Napoleon at the height of his power and renown. Discontent became general, and everyone became the mouthpiece of it. One day an *émigré*, entering the Tuileries, stopped in front of the sentry and said, "Well, you're satisfied now—you get your advances to the day, whereas under Bonaparte everything was in arrear, even to your pay."

"And suppose we liked to give him credit?" retorted the soldier drily, as he turned his back.

General Lamarque's phrase to a Bourbonist who was boasting about the repose which he enjoyed, "This repose is only a halt in the

---

the Duke of Berri; he was strong and thick-set, heavy-shouldered, short-necked, with neither dignity, grace, nor elegance, wit or good manners.

mud," is not less expressive, and forms a terrible pendant to the remark made by an Englishman to M. de la Roserie: "You would not have got the Bourbons if we had had anything worse to give you."

However reserved one might wish to be in taking part in the new political events, it was necessary either to give up everything and cease to live at Paris, or to follow all the generals and marshals who went to the palace, and begin by seeing the Minister for War, on whom we were dependent. That ministry was occupied by General Dupont. Personally, he had always shown me kindness, nor did I suppose that he would have any reason for ceasing to do so; but when I heard of his appointment I had not been able to escape the disagreeable impression which it had made on our army.

The post had been offered to Count O'Connell, but he refused it because, as he said, it ought not to be held save by a general with an honourable record in the wars of the Revolution and of the Empire, a condition which General Dupont had ceased to fulfil at Baylen. It was, accordingly, with a painful feeling of antipathy that I called upon him, and the consciousness that I was ill at ease deprived the general himself of the ease which, in fact, he could only have in the presence of men who had no feeling for the honour of their country. The audience, therefore, was short and unimportant.

My presentations to the king and the other members of the royal family offer nothing worth recording. I need only say that *Monsieur* [2] received us with inconceivable grace, as one might receive amnestied criminals; and that *Madame* displayed all the harshness appropriate towards rebels whom one still hopes to see punished. One prince succeeded, amid all the posturings and meannesses of the court, in preserving his dignity and commanding esteem. While Louis XVIII, the Count of Artois, the Duke of Berri, even the Prince of Condé, by the aid of foreign swords, had been doing all they knew to find ways of carrying out their plans for the destruction of liberty, which they had not been able earlier to realise, the Duke of Orleans formed an exception which public opinion gratefully recognised, and his past conduct was imputed to him as so much in his favour.

The story of his wanderings and travels is well known. He returned with a great stock of observations and recollections, which formed fresh stores for his incredible memory. No man ever gained so much accomplishment from misfortune. It would be difficult to express what I felt on first meeting him again. All our old relations

---

2. [That is, the Count of Artois, afterwards king as Charles X.]

and the wonderful vicissitudes of the intervening period came before me in a rapid vision, and the kindness with which he received me, surpassing all I could have hoped, added to the impression. After referring to the events at Tournai (but not to his unfortunate note, of which I on my side said nothing), and expressing his regrets for the death of my father, he questioned me as to my intention of seeking further employment.

Again my stupid awkwardness, as on all other occasions when I was questioned about myself, showed itself, and, instead of telling him what was no less simple than easy to say—that the possibility of entering his service would exceed any hopes that I could frame—I merely answered that I had not yet made up my mind. I learnt afterwards from M. Pieyre that not only might I easily have become *aide-de-camp* to the duke, but that he had even thought of suggesting it, and the only obstacle was the way in which I had held aloof.

Meanwhile, Napoleon was watching from Elba the course of events and calculating the progress of the general exasperation. In order to take action, he was waiting only for the dissolution of the Congress of Vienna and the dispersion of the sovereigns there assembled. But an incident, disastrous in the highest degree, compelled his premature departure from Elba. I refer to the rebellion of the Count of Erlon and the march of that general on Paris.[3] On March 7, 1815, I had gone to bed at half-past one, after executing the deed of conveyance of a property which I had just bought at Richelieu, in the department of Indre-et-Loire.

On waking seven hours later I heard that Napoleon had landed. My consternation may be imagined. I did not, certainly, reckon myself among the partisans of the Bourbons, being too much of a Frenchman to attach myself to people who were not Frenchmen at all. At the same time, though I had deeply lamented the emperor's fate, I had not sufficient confidence in him to rejoice at his return. Even granting that he succeeded, could I believe that the result would be anything else than that one man would have his revenge, not that there would be any return of good fortune in the interest of the country? Lastly, as concerned myself, I had no reason to expect from him any

---

3. [As the result of an intrigue set on foot by Fouché in the interest of the old revolutionary party, Generals d'Erlon, Lefebvre-Desnoettes, and the brothers Lallemand were to bring troops from the north-east of France, where they were in command, to Paris. D'Erlon, as a matter of fact, did not leave Lille, except to escape prosecution, but the others got as far as Compiègne a few days after Napoleon landed.]

more advantages than I had obtained in the days of his greatness and prosperity, when favours and rewards were so freely distributed. The Bourbons caused me no regret; Napoleon offered me no hope. Devoid alike of ambition and of desire for revenge, solitary in my feelings as in my thoughts, I remained outside of the delirium that possessed France, no less than of the terror which reigned at court.

Under the pretence of taking part, in an emergency, in the defence of the capital, independently of a few troops, bands of assassins were fetched to Paris from the south and from La Vendée. It was a fresh edition of those wretches from Marseilles who, in 1792, had brought about the 10th of August, and massacred the poor creatures with whom the prisons of Paris were crowded. It was a justification by the Bourbons themselves of the most hideous deeds of the Revolution. There was, indeed, no difference, except one of words, between the crimes for which under Charles IX the pretext was Catholicism, under the Convention patriotism, under Louis XVIII the destruction of the Liberals and the Bonapartists.

Just as at the very worst epochs lists of victims were made out by districts, so, in addition to a few men like the Duke of Bassano, who were important enough to make their removal desirable as soon as possible, and for whose benefit special attempts at assassination were devised or made, the generals, with a few exceptions, were placed on the lists in a body. I was warned that I had not been forgotten. But crimes of this kind, when intended to take effect too widely, usually end in a muddle, so that in the present case two or three nights of danger seemed the worst that I had to expect. Thanks to my friend Rivierre de l'Isle, I had a hiding-place in the office of the king's household, and could be almost sure of being warned of the day when I had better sleep away from home. After all, this general execution came to nothing, because it could not do otherwise. Schemes of this kind, when once got wind of, never end in anything but general contempt.

Events progressed with gigantic steps. Reaching Grenoble with his weak escort, in a moment, owing to the spontaneous impulse of La Bédoyère and his regiment, Napoleon got possession of that place, with all the troops there, and of all the population of Dauphine. Proceeding to Lyons, he found a fresh army there, and there, regarding his colossal undertaking as accomplished, he resumed the sovereign authority, and issued those two famous decrees, dissolving the chambers, summoning the meeting of the *Champ de Mai*, and all the rest. Everything rallied to his call. With the swoop of an eagle he traversed the space which divided him from Paris, and took possession of the capital, whence, as well as from the rest of the kingdom, the friends of the Cossacks had fled before him.

The king had appointed Marshal Macdonald commander-in-chief of what he was pleased to call his army, with Belliard as his chief of staff. It was not a fortunate selection. His courage was not of the catching kind, and he himself would have chilled the most enthusiastic. When I called upon him, on his return from Lyons, I could not get a serious word out of him. He greeted me with a peal of laughter and with the words, "Well, here we are in a pretty mess. Deuce take me if I know how we shall get out of it!"—and other witticisms of the same kind.

March 19 was a Sunday, and I thought it was my duty to go to the palace. I went there accordingly with the feeling which takes one to the bedside of a dying man. I even took part in the cheers with which Louis XVIII was greeted at the moment of his leaving the chapel. Thinking that I had done all that etiquette demanded, I was about to leave the palace and go home when Marshal Macdonald informed me that I was to take the command of all the troops who were about to be sent towards Charenton. I was specially ordered to have a bridge constructed with all speed, below the junction of the Seine and the Marne, to serve as a means of communication and of retreat for the troops encamped at Villejuif, where the headquarters were to be placed. I was to defend this bridge, and, if necessary, to blow it up as well as Charenton. Like the man in the *Fourberies de Scapin*, I constantly repeated to myself, "What business have I in this accursed galley?" However, I said nothing, and went to Belliard immediately to get his orders.

At about eight in the evening I got off with my old *aide-de-camp*, Major Vallier, and reached Charenton, where I took up my headquarters in the least ill-looking house that I could see. I found that such troops as were there, amounting to 5,000 or 6,000 men, were totally untrained, clothed in rags, shod with slippers, and had for head-covering anything that could answer the purpose, including some red nightcaps. Such were the troops with which I had the king's orders to fight and vanquish Napoleon. At length the mayor appeared. His devotion to the cause lacked nothing except results. He had been asked for a thousand rations—not one had been delivered. He was to have supplied one hundred workmen for the construction of the bridge; more than seventy were wanting, and my threats of military execution did not succeed in producing another score. I demanded four vehicles to go to Vincennes for provisions and cartridges, and it was past nine on the 20th before I got one. Towards eleven in the evening, the night being dark and rainy, I was at the place where the bridge was being thrown, not so much over the river as into it.

However, by encouraging the engineer officer in charge of the work and his men, I was presently able to feel sure that the bridge would be finished by ten the next morning, and had just drawn up and sent off my first report to Marshal Macdonald, when General Rouget de Lisle, brother of the author of the *Marseillaise*, one of the two major-generals who were to join me, arrived with Colonel Allouis, who was to act as chief of the staff in my division. At half-past two came Colonel Boilleau of the artillery, with orders to stop the work on the bridge at once, to destroy what had been done, and to send away the workmen. All this without any written order and without a word for me. With anyone else than Boilleau, I should have taken no notice of the order, but I knew him well and had confidence in him; so that I merely made him write out and sign in the name of the commander-in-chief a statement of the order which he had brought.

Just at eight o'clock I received a note from my friend Rivierre, who had promised to keep me informed of anything that might affect my conduct; it was in the following words:

The King and the Royal Family went off at midnight. Great agitation prevails in Paris. I think all is lost.

This news I kept a dead secret. I had my orders, and I thought my duty was to carry them out. I therefore continued my preparations for defending the bridge of Charenton. A fresh letter came from Paris. This was from my second major-general, saying that he thought it of no use to join me. Then my chief of staff asked leave to go home to see how his wife was. I gave him permission, and two hours afterwards I received a letter from him saying that, if I waited at Charenton for orders from those who had sent me, I should have to wait a long time. He was not coming back, and he advised me to return promptly. I showed this letter to General Rouget, who laughed over it with me, but thought no more than myself that his task was accomplished. We stayed because we thought that the disappearance of the sovereign is the disappearance only of a man, and not of the authority which he represents, and that, if this authority has not been transferred by a legal surrender of power, it cannot be disregarded by soldiers who are careful of their honour and their duty. We remained therefore, but by no means pleased with Marshal Macdonald, who had returned no reply to three reports which I had sent him.

About 1 p.m. the 7th Cuirassiers crossed the bridge of Charenton and drew up in line in rear of that village, with its right on the road to Paris, in a silence unbroken at the shouts of "Long live the King!" which the royal officers and volunteers had raised at sight of it. The colonel made his men dismount and came to me. He did not know what was going on at Villejuif, only he told me that all the troops who had been collected at that point were recrossing the Seine and the Marne, and that those who were expected had been countermanded. He added in a tone of annoyance, "I received by word of mouth the order that I have just executed. I was, indeed, told that I should receive fresh orders here; but I cannot recognise any that do not come from Paris, and, if in an hour's time I have not received any, I shall go myself to look for them." To which outburst of temper I made no reply.

Hearing about half-past three that a fresh regiment of *cuirassiers*—the 4th—was coming, I went to meet it. As it entered Charenton some volunteer officers renewed their shouts, which were taken up energetically by the colonel of the 4th, and more or less vigorously by seven or eight officers and as many troopers. Passing through the place, the 4th drew up in line in front of the 7th, but no man of either corps left the ranks, and the colonel remained in front of his regiment. After this had lasted an hour, Lieutenant-General Girardin arrived. We conversed; there was no doubt that the left banks of the Seine and the Marne were abandoned. Girardin had orders to collect his division at Saint-Denis. One brigade had gone there direct, and he was to proceed thither with the second, consisting of these two regiments of *cuirassiers*. He summoned, therefore, the commanders of those two corps and informed them of the movement they were to make. The colonel of the 4th said he was ready, but the lieutenant-colonel of the 7th said that his colonel was in Paris, and he himself was forbidden to stir till he returned. "By whose orders did your colonel go to Paris?" asked General Girardin.

"I do not know."

"The only commander," said the general, "is the one who is present. That your colonel is to blame will be no excuse for you. His absence is a dereliction of duty; it puts him out of the command and leaves you in charge. Thus, as your regiment forms part of my division, you will sound to horse and follow the 4th."

"Very sorry, general, but when my colonel went off to get news he required my word of honour that the regiment should not budge till he came back. I may regret that I gave my word; but he received it, and I cannot go back from it."

"Then you refuse to obey my orders?"

"I have no choice."

"General," cried the colonel of the 4th, "an officer who allows himself to give such an answer ought to be put under arrest on the spot!"

The lieutenant-colonel looked at the new speaker and smiled. The smile, which struck me, meant that the 7th would no more allow such an arrest than the 4th would execute it; and General Girardin was too sharp to misunderstand it. He merely added, "In circumstances where each man is the arbiter of his own conduct, each man must take his own share of responsibility. As for me, I have done my duty." Thereupon he ordered the 4th and 7th to mount. The 4th obeyed, and at the word "March!" followed General Girardin, all trumpets sounding. The colonel once more cried, "Long live the King!" which only three or four voices, not including Girardin's, took up, showing that the regiment would not go very far. The 7th remained dismounted, motionless and in dead silence.

This scene was a final proof of the perplexity of my position. I was now the only person holding out for the king either around or in Paris; but, in spite of my own feelings, in the midst of the general collapse I was determined to behave as I should have done in my own cause, and as if I still retained some assurance of success—that is, without posturing, without hesitation or weakness. Then I paid a last visit to my advanced posts, shifting their positions and encouraging them. How often have I said to myself since, that if by any chance Napoleon had taken that road and come up to the bridge of Charenton I should have opened fire and blown up the bridge! It would have made no difference; but in the cruel position into which fate had brought France a soldier's most sacred duty was a strict observance of his orders. A phrase of my wife's expresses exactly what I then felt.

I was talking once of my position on that 20th of March, and some general had exclaimed at the necessity to which I had been reduced of giving orders to fire upon Napoleon and his escort if they should appear by the road which I was bidden to defend. Zozotte said, "You forget, general, that honour must come before opinion." Such was indeed the problem set to my conscience as a soldier. I was doomed to carry out against a giant, against one whom I had so much admired, the orders given me by pygmies whom I disdained; but, to quote Zozotte again, "What is the use of being on bad terms with one's conscience when one has always to live with it?"

So I would have fired on Napoleon—in which case nothing would have remained but to run after Louis XVIII. A momentary exile would have placed me, like others, in the Chamber of Peers; all my tribulations under both Bourbon reigns would have been laid to rest and my misfortunes avoided. Yet I should have felt a regret, perhaps a remorse, which fate has happily spared me.

At six o'clock orders came to return to Paris, and I set out at once. In the Rue de la Grande Pinte I was taken for Marshal Ney, and cheered; two hundred paces further my white cockade got me hooted. I did not, however, like to take it off till I was at home, and so made my way by unfrequented streets to the Rue Caumartin, where I lived. That same evening I took my report to Marshal Macdonald's house. They had no news of him, and advised me to send my packet to Lille. I do not know if he ever received it.

When I left Marshal Macdonald's, with the feeling of having settled my last account with the Bourbons, I became the plaything of an irresistible force dragging me towards the Tuileries. It was a quarter-past nine. Napoleon had just arrived, and at least 20,000 persons were crowding the approaches to the Pavilion of Flora, the staircase, and the apartments, which last I thought I should never reach. When I did get there the shouting had ceased, but everyone was talking at once, till you could not make yourself heard. For some hours the people formed the only court of the chief whom France had once more raised on her shield. Suddenly Napoleon reappeared. There was an instantaneous and irresistible outburst.

At sight of him the transports rose to such a pitch that you would have thought the ceilings were coming down; then, as after a thunderclap, every man came to himself, quivering with ecstasy and stammering like a man intoxicated. Catching sight of me in the middle of the throng, the emperor uttered my name with a nod and a kindly smile. He could read my emotion in my face, and yet it was hardly three hours since I had been a soldier of the Bourbons, with my guns turned against him. Now, however, I seemed to have become a Frenchman once more, and nothing could equal the transports and the shouts with which I tried to show the part I was taking in the homage rendered to him.

Never did Napoleon exercise a greater moral influence than at that moment. If the return from Waterloo was to complete the melancholy work of the return from Moscow, the impression made by this return from Elba was worthy of that produced by the return from Egypt. Unhappily, the weaker he grew, the more he fell a prey to his vanity; and, just as by negotiating at Moscow he had allowed time for the army from Turkey to fall on his rear, or as by negotiating at Dresden he had allowed time for the Russians and Prussians to double their forces and bring them to the front, so by waiting at Paris to write a letter to the kings of Europe, which none of them would receive, to make a Constitution which deprived him of 200,000 men, to make a display at the *Champ de Mai* and play at memories when present realities were crying aloud, he gave the coalised forces time to attack him with 600,000 troops.

The boundless enthusiasm which marked the opening of the Hundred Days resulted in a general disposition to merriment, and at first people gave way to it with all the less restraint that it seemed to be a guarantee of the happiness of which it was really the result. But the laughter and exultation came to an end. People became grave because bad news kept coming in; discontented because they foresaw that Napoleon would not realise the hopes which he had given to France; uneasy because everything pointed to a new and terrible war. In this situation, where all impressions were strongly felt, three events produced a profound sensation, and were regarded as presages of misfortune.

The first was the death of the Prince of Neuchâtel. The story told at first was that he had been flung from a window in the palace of Bamberg—whither, not daring to appear before Napoleon after being captain of the King's Guard, he had retired—by the officers of a regiment passing through the town, in revenge for the death of a young man who had been tried and shot by his orders at Schönbrunn in 1809. My own belief, after all possible inquiries, is that Berthier had gone to the top of the palace to see these troops pass, had got on to the outer sill of an attic window, and there had been struck by apoplexy, a common malady in his family, and fallen down.

The second event which shook public security was the news that Napoleon's letters to the sovereigns of Europe had not been received, showing that the allied sovereigns did not deign to notice him, but left him to the Congress. The third was the defeat and deposition of Murat, and the counter-revolution at Naples; a misfortune for Napoleon and a subject of sad presentiment for France.

Meanwhile preparations went on for the ceremony of the *Champ de Mai*. On May 31 a great platform had been constructed in front of the École Militaire; the Champ de Mars was filled with troops, and the sun, flashing on 60,000 bayonets, seemed to make the vast space sparkle. It was a superb scene, and I can still see Hortense sketching that imposing picture. Beside her were her two young sons, not less noticeable for their beauty than for the elegance of the hussar uniforms they wore. These children, for whom, considering the situation of the King of Rome, it seemed possible that a vast future might be in store, were condemned by inexorable fate, the one to a premature death, the other to an even more terrible end, had not Louis Philippe saved him from the penalty to which his outrage at Strasburg rendered him liable.[4]

A *daïs* for the throne had been constructed projecting towards the Champ de Mars, on which Napoleon took his place, followed by his brothers Joseph, Lucien, and Jerome. Throwing back his mantle with a dignity and grace which recalled the lessons of Talma, he delivered a discourse which, in spite of some extremely happy and adroit phrases, was imperial rather than French. From that day Paris presented the twofold appearance of a camp about to be struck, and a vessel with its decks clearing for action. Not long ago hundreds of leagues divided Paris from the front of our lines; now the guns were about to thunder only sixty leagues from the Seine.

The time necessary for the troops, which had been present at the *Champ de Mai*, to arrive at their destination expired on June 10, and everything proclaimed the immediate departure of Napoleon. The following day was Sunday, and I attended the last Mass which he heard at the Tuileries and the last audience which he was to give there. I never took my eyes from Napoleon, and the more I studied him the less could I succeed in seeing him as he had been in the days of his strength and his greatness.

Never has the impression which the sight of him made upon me at the moment when destiny was about to pronounce between the world and him, ceased to be present to me; his look, once so formidable and piercing, had lost its strength and even its steadiness; his face, which I had often seen, now beaming with kindness, now moulded in bronze, had lost all expression and all its forcible character; his mouth,

---

4. [General Thiébault did not foresee the *coup d'état*, still less Sedan, or the final clause might have been omitted.]

compressed, contained none of its ancient witchery; his very head no longer had the pose which used to characterise the conqueror of the world; and his gait was as perplexed as his demeanour and gestures were undecided. Everything about him seemed to have lost its nature and to be broken up; the ordinary pallor of his skin was replaced by a strongly-pronounced greenish tinge which struck me. A prey to the darkest forebodings, I left the palace where I was never to see him again, and returned to my house full of wishes which I did not believe.

My division was to be collected and encamped near Montrouge, where my headquarters were established, together with those of the Count of Valence. As the troops were not to begin arriving before the 20th, I had continued to sleep at my own house, merely going to Montrouge two or three times with the count to make sure that everything required by the troops would be ready. On the morning of the 20th I was making my arrangements to go and settle myself there, when I heard some one striding through my dining-room and drawing-room, of which the doors were open, and beheld Captain Viennet coming to the threshold of my bedroom; with perturbed countenance he halted at sight of me, threw up his arms, and cried in a voice of terror, "All is lost!" walking about the while like a man whose reason is overthrown. It was thus that I heard of the disaster at Waterloo and the return of Napoleon to Paris.

In moments of misfortune it is always that which is most to be dreaded that seems most probable, and, in spite of myself, my anxiety turned upon the line which the Chamber of Deputies would take. I went, therefore, to the lobby of the House. Everything was in a state of tumult and buzz, men going in and out, disappearing and reappearing, talking to people of all kinds, who, like the deputies themselves, looked as if they had been bitten by tarantulas. At that moment all disunion, any change of authority, might be fatal, and yet when I left the Chamber I could no longer doubt that this was the melancholy spectacle which the majority meant to give us. From, the Chamber I went to the Ministry of War to find out what was to become of the first corps of the reserve. I learnt that the troops which were to compose it were receiving fresh orders, that our appointments were regarded as null and void, and that so far our part was over before it had begun. I hastened to inform the Count of Valence of this.

Next morning at nine o'clock I was at the Elysée. The thought that the foreigner was advancing on the heels of our soldiers to defile

France a second time with his presence kindled me with a sort of patriotic frenzy, and took me back almost involuntarily towards the man in whom, to my eyes, the sole hope of safety was embodied. On entering the palace, I was struck by the solitude which prevailed; the gallery was deserted; not more than a dozen or fifteen persons were in the room to which it led. I had scarcely entered when a door opened close to the place where I was; Napoleon appeared. I made two steps towards him, and, bowing more deeply than usual, I said, "Allow me, sir, to lay at your feet the expression of a devotion no less profound than respectful."

"It is France of which we must think at this moment," he replied.

"More than ever," I returned, "it is in your person that one must show pity for her."

He looked hard at me, turned his eyes away, and passed on to someone else. I withdrew, and these were the last words that I was to exchange with that extraordinary man.

One secret, painful to recall, impossible to omit, belongs to the last period of the Hundred Days. I owe my knowledge of it to my old intimacy with Cadet Gassicourt. I have kept it religiously; and if I now cease to consider it as a secret, it is because the only two men who had a personal interest in it have long ceased to exist, and it has passed into the domain of history.

All those who knew Gassicourt are aware that to a face at once handsome, kindly, and far more noble than that of his royal father,[5] he united perfect style and manners. He had found it necessary to separate from his wife, but, as this involved the sacrifice of an income of 30,000 *francs*, he decided to recoup himself by starting a druggist's business under the name of Cadet, well known in the profession, since his reputed father had been in that capacity *primus inter pares*. The name of Cadet was a guarantee of success to start with; Gassicourt's own superiority did the rest, and the result justified his hopes. The emperor had occasion for a druggist attached to his person; Gassicourt was selected, and at once had rooms assigned to him in the Tuileries and in each of Napoleon's residences. He made the campaign of Wagram with the imperial headquarters, and after it he was decorated and appointed Knight of the Empire, which made him the first druggist who had ever been invested with a feudal title. Lastly, on the return from Elba he hastened to resume his service with Napoleon.

Such was his position when, in the first days of June, he was sent

---

5. There can hardly be any doubt that Gassicourt was a son of Louis XV.

for to Napoleon's study. After a few words as to the serious position of things, and the chances of a reverse which must not be survived, or a captivity which could not be endured, he received, under the injunction of the strictest secrecy, orders to prepare with his own hands a dose of infallible poison, put into the smallest possible compass. In order that it might be perfectly concealed and constantly within reach, he was to place it in a locket that could not be opened except by some one who knew the trick of it. In consternation at such an order, Gassicourt implored Napoleon to allow him a few words. They were uttered with all the marks of violent emotion, were listened to kindly, but remained without effect.

The order therefore was executed, and shortly before Napoleon's departure for Waterloo Gassicourt placed the locket containing the terrible dose in Napoleon's own hands. In the night of the 21st of June a fresh order summoned him in all haste to the Elysée. Napoleon had just swallowed the poison, but, new ideas having changed his determination, he called upon Gassicourt to prevent its action. Terrified as he was, his hair standing on end, in a cold sweat, Gassicourt nevertheless did all that was humanly possible. Vomiting was at once induced, and sustained by means of copious draughts, and he was able to hope that the assimilation of the poison had been prevented.

Yet, when relating these facts to me three years after Napoleon had gone to St. Helena, he could not avoid the dread lest the poisoning might have consequences. When there was talk of Napoleon's sufferings, he shuddered at the idea that they might be the result of it; and when Napoleon was dead, and it was known that his death resulted from a lesion to the stomach, he said to me ten times if he said it once:

> Some particles of the poison cannot have been extracted, and thenceforward sooner or later death was inevitable.

On July 4 our unfortunate army abandoned the capital and retired behind the Loire. On the 7th the enemy's troops polluted Paris for the second time, and on that day of shame and grief I held no communication with anyone. On August 8 Napoleon left France. After his momentary resurrection it was like a second death, in which, in spite of the harm which he had done us, we felt that we shared. Five years later he was to die for good and all, leaving the world widowed of the highest greatness it had known; the dead giant left a void which the future will not fill. A mighty meteor, setting on fire all that he met on his scintillating track, he still lights up the world which he has quitted. If he was the splendour of his age, he is, above all, the glory and honour of the human race, the pride of creation. Like the sun, he had his spots, but to him alone can be applied, without appearance of unseemliness, the motto of Louis XIV "*Nec pluribus impar.*"

ALSO FROM LEONAUR
AVAILABLE IN SOFTCOVER OR HARDCOVER WITH DUST JACKET

THE FALL OF THE MOGHUL EMPIRE OF HINDUSTAN *by H. G. Keene*—By the beginning of the nineteenth century, as British and Indian armies under Lake and Wellesley dominated the scene, a little over half a century of conflict brought the Moghul Empire to its knees.

LADY SALE'S AFGHANISTAN *by Florentia Sale*—An Indomitable Victorian Lady's Account of the Retreat from Kabul During the First Afghan War.

THE CAMPAIGN OF MAGENTA AND SOLFERINO 1859 *by Harold Carmichael Wylly*—The Decisive Conflict for the Unification of Italy.

FRENCH'S CAVALRY CAMPAIGN *by J. G. Maydon*—A Special Correspondent's View of British Army Mounted Troops During the Boer War.

CAVALRY AT WATERLOO *by Sir Evelyn Wood*—British Mounted Troops During the Campaign of 1815.

THE SUBALTERN *by George Robert Gleig*—The Experiences of an Officer of the 85th Light Infantry During the Peninsular War.

NAPOLEON AT BAY, 1814 *by F. Loraine Petre*—The Campaigns to the Fall of the First Empire.

NAPOLEON AND THE CAMPAIGN OF 1806 *by Colonel Vachée*—The Napoleonic Method of Organisation and Command to the Battles of Jena & Auerstädt.

THE COMPLETE ADVENTURES IN THE CONNAUGHT RANGERS *by William Grattan*—The 88th Regiment during the Napoleonic Wars by a Serving Officer.

BUGLER AND OFFICER OF THE RIFLES *by William Green & Harry Smith*—With the 95th (Rifles) during the Peninsular & Waterloo Campaigns of the Napoleonic Wars.

NAPOLEONIC WAR STORIES *by Sir Arthur Quiller-Couch*—Tales of soldiers, spies, battles & sieges from the Peninsular & Waterloo campaingns.

CAPTAIN OF THE 95TH (RIFLES) *by Jonathan Leach*—An officer of Wellington's sharpshooters during the Peninsular, South of France and Waterloo campaigns of the Napoleonic wars.

RIFLEMAN COSTELLO *by Edward Costello*—The adventures of a soldier of the 95th (Rifles) in the Peninsular & Waterloo Campaigns of the Napoleonic wars.

AVAILABLE ONLINE AT **www.leonaur.com**
AND FROM ALL GOOD BOOK STORES

www.ingramcontent.com/pod-product-compliance
Lightning Source LLC
Chambersburg PA
CBHW021958160426
43197CB00007B/179